Soundings of Things Done

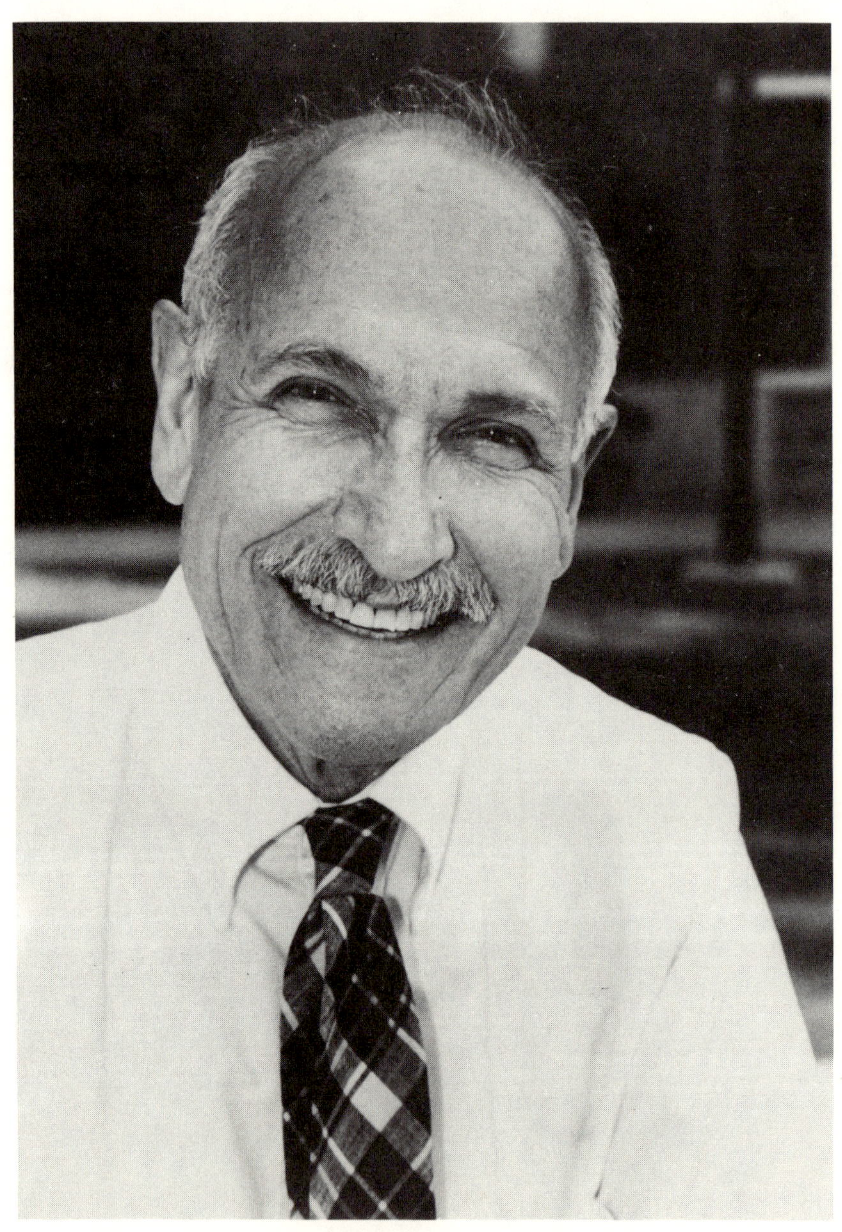

S. K. Heninger Jr.

Soundings of Things Done

Essays in Early Modern Literature in Honor of S. K. Heninger Jr.

Edited by
Peter E. Medine
and Joseph Wittreich

Newark: University of Delaware Press
London: Associated University Presses

Associated University Presses
440 Forsgate Drive
Cranbury, NJ 08512

Associated University Presses
16 Barter Street
London WC1A 2AH, England

Associated University Presses
P.O. Box 338, Port Credit
Mississauga, Ontario
Canada L5G 4L8

The paper used in this publication meets the requiremts
of the American National Standard for Permanence of Paper
for Printed Library Materials Z39.48-1984.

Library of Congress Cataloging-in-Publication Data

Soundings of things done : essays in early modern literature in honor of S. K. Heninger, Jr. / edited by Peter E. Medine and Joseph Wittreich.
p. cm.
Includes bibliographical references and index.
ISBN 0-87413-606-7 (alk. paper)
1. English literature—Early modern, 1500–1700—History and criticism. I. Medine, Peter E. II. Wittreich, Joseph Anthony. III. Heninger, S. K.
PR423.S68 1997
820.9'003—dc20 96-1363
CIP

PRINTED IN THE UNITED STATES OF AMERICA

Contents

Foreword

STUART CURRAN

Tim Heninger is a man of parts—many parts. You can tell it from the lengthy entries of the card catalog in the library or from the citation in *Who's Who*. I prefer the medium of postcards. This spring one arrived from an area of Turkey somewhere to the south of the storied plain of Ilium. Last fall there was one from Samarkand. Since it came from the outer reaches of Scythia, it naturally took more than three months to reach its destination. That card bore the stamp, with familiarly thrusting heroics, of a country that had not existed for several years. Probably in Samarkand, notwithstanding its three-quarters of a century of imperial hegemony, it had never really existed at all. On the Silk Road time is relative: the past overlays the present the way carpets are piled in a bazaar.

Tim told me that in Bokhara, as he began his passage through a stack of camel bags, squinting at colors, thumbing the textures, he attracted the attention of a crowd of merchants who, having supervised his inspection, went to their tents and returned with prize wares. There, on that age-old axis of antiquity and art, without a common linguistic ground, two cultures conversed at the crossroads. Tim's journey along the Silk Road began in the deserts of western China and ended, many weeks later, in the Hermitage Museum of St. Petersburg. Transportation was often uncertain and unsafe; by American standards the food was barely edible; the accommodations were primitive; sand blew everywhere and penetrated everything; the days were blistering; at night it froze.

Now that Tim Heninger is retired the postcards come at all times of the year and from all corners of the globe. He is a man of many parts, a man for all seasons.

Of course Tim doesn't just travel. Whatever the season there is always the garden.

The amaryllis were a wedding gift to his parents. Then there was one, valentine-red, an icon of enduring love. Now doubled and redoubled and redoubled again, there are many: in summer bulblets proliferate, come out of the ground in the fall, are returned in the spring, a cycle bonding the natural and human. They have bloomed through Tim's entire life, a vernal assurance exfoliating across time, multiple, generous in excess.

On the other hand, the succulents. Some of these flower with amaryllis-like abandon. Others patiently settle in. Some look like pebbles, dented wafers from faraway deserts: austere botanical intensities, they do not seem so much to grow as to abide. Tim has more of these than I have ever seen. They too last a long time—given patience and proper care.

Tim knows their names, their histories, their idiosyncrasies, their needs. He will introduce you to them all—if you have the time. He has always had the time.

Of course, he lives in a glass house. The sun streams in as if it were Samarkand. The plants thrive. The venerable weavings scintillate in the glancing of light. The light, too, redoubles, as pieces of fine glass, essence of sand, catch the rays, refracting them upon the panes they penetrate. Now the process is subtle, a mere satisfaction to the seasoned onlooker. Once it was like the garden: a profusion of prisms, an efflorescence of color garbing the naked eye. Nowhere and nothing to hide.

The collection of glass finally got too big. Last year, before the journey along the Silk Road, it was moved to a museum as a foundation for future accession. It was begun long enough ago that the great names in late-nineteenth-century art glass could still be pursued by someone of modest means. Tim came to know the principal specialist dealers and slowly accrued an archivist's dream of major examples. But it wasn't just history. When Tim spent his seasons at the Huntington Library outside Los Angeles and his children were living near Seattle, he became acquainted with all the glassblowers in between. They were way stations on his road, and his car filled up with boxes as he returned along it. These were not the stars of art nouveau, just people who knew their craft, dependent on a small number who loved it.

Tulips, jacks-in-the pulpit, calla lilies, calyxes of crystal, tropical stems of magenta and blue, tubular exotics from fiery hothouses, Matisse-like violences of clashing color. Cosmographical. You never use a fine vase for flowers, Tim told me: the water will eventually etch the glass.

There were also etchings, drawings, prints. I remember a large portfolio of them in a frame distending from the wall. Somewhere in there was just the thing, he told Joe Wittreich, who was then elaborating his research on Blake's uses of Milton. Just the thing were six of the nine illustrations of Blake's second set for *Paradise Lost*, the originals of which are in the Boston Museum of Fine Arts. They were reproduced only once, in the copies Tim owned. "Take them," he said. (Today prints of the second set are nowhere to be found, not for love or money.) Not for money, just love.

And books. Endless riches, or so it seemed to a new assistant professor, each book with a history, an idiosyncrasy, a time, a place, a human destiny. He could tell you much about them—if you had time. In Europe after the Second World War books were a luxury to those without food. Tim went to Oxford to study and came home with a library. His copy of the first edition of Coleridge's *Biographia Literaria* cost £1 6s. But Coleridge was hardly Tim's passion; not even Spenser was. It was Renaissance science. Tim learned to talk about the weather while he was in England and returned home to write about it. It wasn't the actual weather he wrote about (but, then, it isn't in those social rituals either); it was the weather of four centuries past, and not even that. It was the very idea of the weather—then or now—which has nothing exactly to do with actual weather.

Fittingly, for a person who has been to Troy and Samarkand and Oxford, Tim knows more about the cosmos than anyone I ever met. You don't really have to ask him to tell you about it: he has been writing about it for a good (some would say an excellent) half-century. Even when he was annotating Spenser he was telling us about the cosmos. It is a very interesting topic and has been extensively illustrated. A profusion of etchings, a cosmographical glass, to be sure.

The winters of Madison, Wisconsin, are just plain bleak. It is useful to have a just sense of the cosmos. Forced bulbs help. The wan light refracted through flowery glass pretends to vernal warmth. Spring could be bleak there too. The savage war of far-off jungles spilled over into the streets. Napalm for the jungle; tear gas for the campus. Tim, chair of the department—no job description required him to interpose himself between the learning he revered and the empire of "Chaos and ancient Night." He stands at the door of the faculty club, colleagues behind him, unfailingly courteous: "Officer, may I please see your badge number." Pepper gas straight in the face. So much for cosmic order.

Young scholars might well wonder what was enduring in this pained immediacy. Tim invited all the assistant professors to his home, not once, but again and again. Ham and redeye gravy and books: good talk beginning early and lasting far into the night; the past overlaying the present like so many carpets in a bazaar. So much, so very much for cosmic order. When in turn I became chair, I never forgot this. The word for it was, of course, noble.

Heninger's Law: The symmetry that effects universal correspondences between the microcosm and macrocosm requires puns for its proof, particularly bad puns. At these Tim, beaming with pleasure, outshines his adolescent son—morning, noon, and, for symmetry, night.

The seminar room of the Huntington Library. John Steadman introduces Lawrence Ryan of Stanford, editor of *Neo-Latin News*—in Latin: a feat we duly appreciate. The audience bears a uniformly purposeful and pious face: if togas had been for rent, we would have been the Roman senate. In the pristine stillness a laugh, not a mere laugh, a guffaw, impropriety itself. A generous laugh of cosmic proportions. Steadman shyly smiles at his success. It is easy to forget how learned Tim is—or how funny.

I realize that I have never seen him unsmiling.

Of course, it all connects: a man of parts, a man for all seasons, a Renaissance man. Prismatic. And that's not all.

Acknowledgments

Peter E. Medine thanks the Folger Shakespeare Library and the Huntington Library for permission to reproduce the figures that illuminate his own essay. Joseph Wittreich thanks the PSC-CUNY Research Foundation for the time and resources that allowed him to complete his essay, as well as to edit this volume. Indeed, the editors are enormously grateful to their respective institutions, the University of Arizona and the Graduate School of the City University of New York, for their many courtesies.

With kind permission, Judith H. Anderson's essay is reprinted from *Words That Matter: Linguistic Perception in Renaissance England* (forthcoming). Permission comes from the publishers, Stanford University Press. No portion of this essay can be reproduced without the written permission of Stanford University Press.

Illustrations accompanying Arthur F. Kinney's essay that are not from his own collection are from:

(1) *Sidney and Spenser: The Poet as Maker* by S. K. Heninger Jr. (University Park: Pennsylvania State University Press, 1989), 21. Copyright © 1989 by Pennsylvania State Univesrity. Reproduced by permission of the publisher.

(2) *Mythologies* by Roland Barthes, translated by Annette Lavers. Translation copyright © 1972 by Jonathan Cape, Ltd. Reprinted by permission of Hill and Wang, a division of Farrar, Straus & Giroux, Inc.

The figures accompanying the essay by Anne Lake Prescott are reproduced by permission of The Avery Architectural and Fine Arts Library, Columbia University in the City of New York and The Beinecke Rare Book and Manuscript Library, Yale University. Illustrative matter accompanying the essay by Jean R. Brink is by permission of The Huntington Library, San Marino, California; The British Library; The Public Record Office of Surrey, England; and The Warden and Fellows of All Souls College, Oxford.

The figures accompanying the essay by Don Wayne are reproduced by permission of the National Trust Photographic Library, The Country Life Picture Library, and the Victoria and Albert Museum.

Introduction

PETER E. MEDINE

Sidney begins his *Apology for Poetry* by asserting the primacy of poetry among the learned disciplines. In a comparison that goes back to Aristotle and was favored by his humanist contemporaries, he points out that philosophers and historians frequently employ the methods of poetry, especially rhetoric and fiction: "[E]uen Plato . . . though the inside and strength were philosophy, the skinne as it were and beautie depended most of Poetrie. . . . And euen Historiographers (although theyr lippes sounde of things doone . . .) haue been glad to borrow both fashion and perchance weight of Poets."[1] Besides furnishing other disciplines with methods and authority, poetry claims for its province universal knowledge and learning. Every discipline has the "workes of Nature for [its] . . . obiect"; the astronomer studies the heavens, the mathematician "diuerse sorts of quantities," and the historian "what men haue done" (155–56). Only the poet, Sidney continues, "disdayning to be tied to any such subiection . . . dooth growe in effect another nature, . . . not inclosed within the narrow warrant of her guifts, but freely ranging onely within the Zodiack of his owne wit" (156). Ultimately poetry excels all other disciplines because it comprehends all of their subjects, combining and recombining them in variations limited only by the poet's powers of invention.

The expansiveness of this vision of imaginative literature rests on the assumption that a poem—however elusive its ontology—is as much a "thing done" as the records of history or the precepts of philosophy. The assumption is evident not only in the assertions of theorists like Sidney but also in the exegesis of the learned commentators, who in order to elucidate literary texts include information that is textual, grammatical, rhetorical, musical, historical, biographical, and even scientific. In short, a literary work—the "thing done"—reaches beyond itself to virtually all subjects and sets forth a world of surpassing meaning and interest, a world Sidney describes as "golden."

The following twelve essays assume these two perspectives on English literature of the early modern period. Six of the essays focus primarily on literary texts; the others focus primarily on broader topics or contexts that bear on the imaginative literature of the period.

The first two essays offer fresh readings of works by Roger Ascham and Edmund Spenser, beginning with examinations of the authors' respective relationships to their patrons. Peter E. Medine's essay "The Art and Wit of Roger Ascham's Bid for Royal Patronage: *Toxophilus* (1545)" recounts the author's calculated attempts to gain support from men of position for various literary endeavors before securing the king's patronage for his vernacular dialogue on archery. Medine sees the work as an early example of *Kunstprosa* that aims to demonstrate the resources of English, develop the venerable themes of art and learning, and acquire royal patronage. In "Eulogies to Elegies: Poetic Distance in the April Eclogue," Richard C. McCoy analyzes "April" of *The Shepherds Calendar*. McCoy takes up the tantalizing question of Spenser's connections with the so-called Areopagus, the circle of writers more or less resident at Leicester House at the end of the 1570s. Reading "April" in light of contemporary politics, McCoy traces within the eclogue Spenser's concern over the "place" of poetry in the court of Elizabeth during the middle years of her reign. In the hybrid encomium of "April," he argues, Spenser carefully distances himself from his patrons, including the queen herself.

Judith H. Anderson's essay "Weighing Words with Spenser's Giant" centers on Book V of *The Faerie Queene*, the Legend of Justice, and studies the titular theme in an examination of the dynamic between idealism and materialism informing the narrative. Anderson suggests that in Book V justice concerns not an inner world of private virtues and beliefs but the material world of history. She develops her argument from a detailed discussion of Spenser's ambivalent treatment of language in the Legend of Justice and of Artegall's halting progress within the narrative as a whole.

The next two essays consider the question of literary authority. In "Appropriating the Author of *The Faerie Queene*: The Attribution of the *View of the Present State of Ireland* and *A Brief Note of Ireland* to Edmund Spenser," Jean R. Brink reopens the question of Spenser's authorship of the Irish tracts. Brink reviews the history of their printing—the *View* first printed in 1633 and the *Note* in 1884—and presents new evidence for skepticism about the textual authority of these works in the Spenserian canon. In "Imitation and Authority in Donne's 'Anatomy' and Lanyer's 'Salve Deus,'" Susanne Woods analyzes two poetic works published almost simultaneously—one by a man and another by a woman—and considers the poets' self-authorization to undertake their particular works. Woods examines the subject and the occasion of each poem and observes that Donne, placing himself in an explicitly patriarchal tradition stemming from Moses, distances himself from his subject, whereas Lanyer, placing herself in a comparatively feminist tradition of reading the

Passion of Christ, tends to identify herself with hers. Authorizing themselves in these different ways, the poets engender their texts.

In "The Renaissance Dramatic Heritage of *Samson Agonistes*," Richard S. Ide reconsiders the interpretive crux of Samson as bloody revenger and agonizing Christ figure. Proceeding from the trope of Samson's pulling down of the temple as theatrical spectacle, Ide invokes the tradition of Elizabethan Christian tragedy to see Samson's torment as both fitting punishment and necessary cure. Whereas in his earlier career Samson serves as God's "reprobate scourge," he ultimately emerges as God's "inspired minister," acting virtuously and in accord with God's providential purpose.

In the second half of the collection, the focus shifts to comparatively broader topical considerations that in various ways contextualize the literary works and issues of the period. The first two of these essays are descriptive and illustrative, exploring the political implications of various cultural artifacts, including literary texts. In "Imaging England: The Chorographical Glass," Arthur F. Kinney discusses the rise of chorography during the reigns of Elizabeth and James. Chorographical depictions not only map the realm in the strict sense but also include a variety of information about the geography, agriculture, demography, and history of the areas. Kinney sees such representations as conscious assertions of a unified Britain with imperial aspirations, which Elizabeth and James urged with ever stronger voices. Anne Lake Prescott, in "Housing Chessmen and Bagging Bishops: Space and Desire in Colonna, 'Rabelais', and Middleton's *Game at Chess*," analyzes how authors in fifteenth-century Italy, sixteenth-century France, and early-seventeenth-century England use the trope of chess. She demonstrates how exploitation of the trope reveals the sexual, ecclesiastical, and national politics of these widely disparate works, remote from one another in form, language, and time.

The next two essays are corrective, if not revisionist, and concern topics contemporaneous and contemporary. In "Donne's Recreative Misogyny: The Critic as Spoilsport," Stanley Stewart analyzes recent Donne criticism by "radical feminists" and "cultural materialists." He inquires into the epistemological assumptions underlying readings of Donne's elegies as "misogynist" and as reflective of "patriarchal anxieties." Employing Wittgensteinian critiques of philosophical investigation, Stewart proposes that the evidence for Donne's poetry being "misandrist" is at least as great as that for its being misogynist. The argument concludes with a call for a reconsideration of Donne's amatory poetry in light of the period in which it was written.

In "The First Individual," Edward W. Tayler examines the concept of individuality—the notion that each person constitutes a unique personality—during the early modern period. Since at least the time of Burkhart, the concept has been regarded as one of the distinctive features of the "Renaissance."

Tayler shows how relatively late in England this concept emerged, dating it specifically during the 1640s in the early career of the Cambridge Platonist Henry Moore. Tayler suggests that before Moore, the evidence is overwhelming that the age—and indeed the preceding medieval period—possessed no philosophical vocabulary or model of thought that permitted persons to refer to themselves as "individuals" in the modern sense of the word.

The last two essays treat basically literary topics within the broad sweep of seventeenth-century economic and political history. In "'A More Safe Survey': Social-Property Relations, Hegemony, and the Rhetoric of Country Life," Don E. Wayne examines the topographical poem from roughly 1600 to 1650. Using Gramsci's notion of "hegemony" as a highly fluid process of adjusting social and economic relations, Wayne traces a growing institutional separation between "state apparatus" and "civil society" that accompanied the emergence of agrarian capitalism in early modern England. Wayne sees the topographical poem as particularly suited to such economic development, providing an apt form for the celebration of prudent management, domesticity, and conjugality—virtues increasingly prized in a national culture identified with property in land.

In "'Under the Seal of Silence': Repressions, Receptions, and the Politics of *Paradise Lost*," Joseph Wittreich reconsiders the evidence for the early reception of Milton's poem. He argues that critics from the eighteenth century on have dated too late the commencement of Milton's reputation as a poet and that *Paradise Lost* acquired stature as a grand and powerful poem soon after its publication in 1667. The persistent misreading of literary history results mainly from a failure to perceive—or to acknowledge—the extent to which Milton's careers as poet and polemicist were intertwined in the seventeenth and early eighteenth centuries. Milton's reputation as a vengeful rebel, a heretic, and a defender of regicide created a highly problematical "horizon of expectation" for *Paradise Lost*. One response was the so-called aestheticization of the poem, whereby it was seen as a modern rival of the great classical epics. Another was to politicize it, to see it as an essentially prophetic work in a strongly politicized scriptural tradition.

As the above discussion suggests, all twelve of the essays historicize their subjects, whether particular literary works or broader literary topics, and thus exhibit the methodology followed by the man they honor, S. K. Heninger Jr. If the historical methodology is a constant, the specific strategies of the essays vary widely, including textual criticism, paleography, codicology, stylistics, interpretive analysis, metacriticism, history of ideas, reception theory, and cultural criticism. In this way, the breadth and scope of the volume reflect Heninger's richly productive career and the distinctive brand of his complexly layered historicism, his philosophical bent, his diverse intellectual interests and writing as editor, critic, aesthetician, theorist, and historian of ideas and culture.

The paths pursued in these essays are often ones that Heninger himself opened. Remaining true to his habit of working at the leading edge of Renaissance studies, the essays closely scrutinize and often challenge the suppositions behind existing orthodoxies and readings, some of which are Heninger's own. Perhaps the best way of paying homage to Heninger's achievement is to strive for such scope and diversity within the early modern period, conceiving of the period broadly and in full knowledge of the perils of periodizing. The range provides for a pluralism that encourages competing perspectives as well as clashing attitudes—a confirmation of the Blakean adage that the eye altering alters all.

Notes

1. G. Gregory Smith, ed., *Elizabethan Critical Essays,* 2 vols. (Oxford: Oxford University Press, 1904), 1:152–53.

Soundings of Things Done

Part I

The Art and Wit of Roger Ascham's Bid for Royal Patronage: *Toxophilus* (1545)

PETER E. MEDINE

I

IN *The Advancement of Learning*, Francis Bacon writes that Roger Ascham suffers from the first distemper of learning and that his work exemplifies that Ciceronian "excess" of "copie" which results from hunting "more after words than matter; and more after the choiceness of the phrase, and the round and clean composition of the sentence . . . than after . . . worth of subject, soundness of argument . . . or depth of judgment."[1] Bacon's criticism has set the terms, if not the limits, of nearly all subsequent discussion of Ascham's *Toxophilus*. George Krapp, George Williamson, Alvin Voss, and Janel Mueller concentrate on Ascham's style (his "words"); others, notably Lawrence V. Ryan, Thomas Greene, and K. J. Wilson, while not ignoring style, tend to concentrate on Ascham's subject or theme (his "matter").[2] During the last thirty years, virtually all commentators on *Toxophilus* defend Ascham against the charge of stylistic decadence. The defense has been vigorous and frequently instructive. But it nearly always reflects a measure of uneasiness about Ascham's perceived lack of high seriousness, about what one sympathetic commentator calls Ascham's ingeniousness at manipulating his material and style.[3]

In this essay I shall revisit Bacon's charge that Ascham was excessively preoccupied with "words" and reconsider *Toxophilus* as the product of a highly self-conscious artistry calculated to achieve financial as well as literary aims. It will be helpful first to reconstruct the context of *Toxophilus* and trace Ascham's efforts to secure patronage outside the university. I shall then consider some of the general principles of prose composition that Ascham seems to have followed in his treatise. Finally, in an effort to analyze the ways in which *Toxophilus* realizes its author's aims, I shall turn to the work itself, to its makeup as a physical artifact as well as to its content and form.

II

Ascham's letters furnish a fairly detailed record of attempts to secure support from various literary patrons during the period 1540 through 1545, when *Toxophilus* appeared in print and was formally presented to Henry VIII, the dedicatee.[4] The record reveals Ascham as a man above all anxious to improve his financial and professional standing. He begins in 1541 with an appeal to Robert Holgate, bishop of Llandoff and president of the Council of the North.[5] Ascham had fallen seriously ill some six months earlier and had remained convalescing with his parents in his native Yorkshire; he was now apparently without means even to return to Cambridge. Ascham's highly mannered letter of compliment and petition offers an explicit statement of the conventional transaction between client and patron. Having sketched his background and current predicament, Ascham comes to the point: "[I]f your Lordship would deign in some measure to supplement my means, thus broken and weakened, on behalf of literary studies . . . I will publicize to all learned men that my studies were sustained and preserved by your aid and munificence" (*Whole Works,* 1:21). The publicizing of Holgate's generosity would appear in a dedication of a literary work, and, judging from the reference to "all learned men," probably a scholarly work on a theological topic. Since no later reference to Holgate appears in Ascham's correspondence, it seems most likely that the bishop ignored the bid and negotiations never went forward.

Later the same year Ascham wrote to Edward Lee, archbishop of York, this time specifying the work he might undertake. "There are on all the . . . canonical epistles of Paul *scholia*, which are called *Graecia*, gleaned from most prudent and ancient fathers, which I know remain unknown to those who have only Latin [and no Greek]" (*Whole Works,* 1:19). These scholia are excerpts that the tenth-century Thessalian bishop Oecumenius was thought to have assembled from Greek patristic writers including Chrysostom, Basil, and Theophylactus. The editio princeps of Oecumenius appeared in Verona in 1532, and it is likely that Ascham worked from this edition. Encouraged by Lee, Ascham pressed ahead over the next year on a Latin translation of the commentary on Paul's Epistle to Titus. In 1543 he traveled to the archbishop's residence in London to make a personal presentation of a manuscript copy of his translation.

The results were mixed. Lee granted Ascham a sum of cash and a commitment for a semiannual pension of twenty shillings. Subsequent references to Lee suggest that Ascham regarded the bishop as his principal if not sole patron (*Whole Works,* 1:42–46). At the same time, the highly conservative Lee took offense at one passage in the commentary on Titus.[6] The bishop returned the dedicated book to Ascham with directions that he reexamine the passage and reconsider whether he ought to busy himself with such weighty subjects as theology. Ascham hastened to apologize and implored friends to intercede. His efforts do not seem to have been very effective, and Ascham soon found payment of his pension periodically delayed. Lee died in September 1544, and Ascham wrote to his Cambridge friend John Seton that it was "now necessary [for him] . . . to seek another patron" and asked him to support his offer of service to Stephen Gardiner, bishop of Winchester and influential adviser to the king (*Whole Works,* 1:60–61). Gardiner himself never assumed the role of literary patron, but as we shall see he served Ascham well in advancing his interests.

Meanwhile Ascham was busy on other fronts. John Cheke had left Cambridge in 1543 to supervise the education of Prince Edward. It was thought that the Regius Professorship of Greek that he held would fall vacant, and by early summer 1544 when Ascham arrived at court to promote his own candidacy, there were at least two other applicants. He evidently received encouragement from Sir William Paget, a principal secretary, and Ascham shortly wrote a formal request for Paget's support (*Whole Works,* 1:50–53). In the event Cheke did not resign the professorship until 1547 when Nicholas Carr was chosen. Perhaps emboldened by his first experience at court, Ascham wrote two poems of commendation in the autumn, one in honor of the birthday of the Prince of Wales and another to the king (*Whole Works,* 3:277–81). There is no evidence that either of these poems resulted in immediate reward, though it is plain that Ascham now had an entrée into court circles.

A striking feature of Ascham's efforts during this period is his moving from secular to sacred subjects and then back again. In his first two attempts to gain support, he stressed that he had devoted his principal efforts to secular studies ("sojourning in the land of Egypt," as he puts it) but that now he intended to seek the promised land of sacred studies (*Whole Works,* 1:17–21). In fact, he would labor over his project on the Pauline epistles for several years. When he ran afoul of Lee, however, Ascham quickly assented to his judgment that he should confine himself to subjects of "lesser weight or lesser danger" and announced that he had taken up a translation of Sophocles' *Philoctetes.* "This," he continued, "will be published in your [Lee's] name unless your Lordship is plainly averse to this proposition" (*Whole Works,* 1:31–33). But the next year Ascham revealed that he was working again on his favorite Greek father, Chrysostom (*Whole Works,* 1:47–49). A few months later he immersed himself in a project of a very different order, the vernacular treatise on archery, which he was still revising in early 1545 to the neglect even of his beloved Herodotus (*Whole Works,* 1:73–75).

Shifting of attention from subjects of one sort to another is not necessarily indicative of cynical opportunism. Central to the well-established humanist enterprise is the belief in the value and relevance of Greek and Latin literature to scriptural and theological studies. Ascham writes in the wake of his unintentional offense of Lee that he will spend his scholarly life on the "study of God's word, attended by the reading of Plato, Aristotle, and Cicero, which is, as it were, its attendant and handmaid" (*Whole Works*, 1:45). Notwithstanding such assertions, he admits that "when [he] was translating the book [the commentary on the Epistle to Titus], [he] was thinking about what was unsound and unorthodox about as much as [he] was thinking about what was happening at the same moment in Utopia" (*Whole Works*, 1:44). The evident frustration and irritation at Lee's taking offense indicate Ascham's relative indifference to theological issues per se. Clearly these issues did not fire his scholarly interest as they did Colet's or Erasmus's.

What did matter very much to Ascham was the aesthetics of the work he was treating. In his initial letter to Lee, he explains that the commentaries on Paul constitute a "work . . . in which someone could try his style with as much enjoyment as profit for the public" (*Whole Works*, 1:19). In other words, the stylistic felicities of a well-translated version of the text would delight as much as its content would benefit the audience. The very elegance of Ascham's prose, whether Latin or English, argues a high degree of care and stylistic self-consciousness. As we shall see, in 1545 he would express his low opinion of contemporary English prose and offer specific criticisms (*Whole Works*, 1:79–81). On another occasion, he would suggest the pains he took with very fine points of style. In his letter to Seton concerning the translation of Oecumenius, he explains that in using the Erasmus translation of the Epistle to Philemon, he emended the text: "I have followed Erasmus in everything, except that I translate *deprecor* for *rogo*, having the great M. T. Cicero for my authority [in such contexts]" (*Whole Works*, 1:24). Similar concern with style and form appears in Ascham's projected translation of Sophocles, in which he planned to render the Greek tragedy in the fashion of Seneca "with the same iambic lines and nearly all the choric meters that Sophocles used" (*Whole Works*, 1:32). Nothing further is heard of the translation, and it was probably never finished. But again, the preoccupation with matters of style, form, and technique is manifest.

The preoccupation extended to the artifice and presentation of the text. Ascham had cultivated a fine italic hand, which he employed not only in his capacity as secretary to the university for official documents but also in tutoring Edward and later his prize student, the princess Elizabeth.[7] He prepared his own fair copies of the translations of the commentaries on Titus and Philemon. These volumes consist of the text of the commentary itself prefaced with an epistle of dedication and personal presentation. Two of them—the texts of the prefatory epistles and commentaries on Philemon and Titus—survive and are remarkable examples of informal publication of the highest quality.[8] Their excellence is hardly accidental, and in the preface to the commentary on Philemon dedicated to Seton, Ascham remarks that the gift he has prepared is one "from which you may take not a common pleasure but a pleasure that is substantial, *not simply pleasing the eyes* for a time but also pleasing very much the mind for a long time" (my emphasis).[9] This particular manuscript book is so perfectly executed and has so "pleased the eye" that some have mistaken it for a printed book.[10]

From all of the efforts that we have been discussing, the trajectory of Ascham's career during the early 1540s emerges quite clearly. Beginning in 1541 with unsolicited letters to provincial bishops from his native North, Ascham had progressed in 1544–45 to personal, frequently seconded petitions to members of the highest court circles, including royalty. These efforts bore fruit. The forty-shilling annuity from Lee increased his annual income to roughly seventeen pounds, just under 50 percent of the forty-pound annuity attached to the Regius professorships. Perhaps more important, Ascham had established contacts beyond the university: in 1544 he received a handsome offer from Lord Mountjoy to serve as tutor to his son, which he declined; in 1545 he was in a position to solicit Gardiner and the king himself for preferment as secretary to a nobleman in Henry's service abroad (*Whole Works,* 1:35–37, 79–81).

Ascham's efforts to secure the support of those in power rested entirely on his abilities and promise as a scholar and conformed to the patron-client conventions of the period. Thomas More, Thomas Elyot, John Cheke, John Leland, and Thomas Wilson all dedicated serious, even grave books to their king. In fact most of the sixty-odd books dedicated to Henry deal with religious, political, or educational subjects.[11] So in appealing to potential patrons through the dedication of celebratory verses and translations of authors like Oecumenius and Sophocles, Ascham stood squarely in the tradition of the Christian humanists of the first half of the sixteenth century.

When Ascham made his major bid for royal patronage, however, he chose not a work of traditional humanist scholarship but a vernacular treatise on archery, hardly a subject the sixteenth century regarded as serious or grave. What led Ascham to such a choice in the most important undertaking of his early career? Why did he not proceed with a Latin, or for that matter a vernacular, translation of a classical or theological work, the sort of project he had been working on? As we explore this question, we need to remember that one aim remained unchanged: to secure patronage, this time royal patronage, which would mean not only financial reward but also professional advancement and prestige.

III

The subject of archery enables Ascham to do several things. He can appeal to the king's own enthusiasm for the activity; he can promote an activity he believes conducive to the national welfare; he can make various political comments that would undoubtedly please the king; and he can fashion a statement that recoups and celebrates England's cultural heritage. Perhaps most important, in undertaking such a project, Ascham can demonstrate his learning in a highly innovative, ironic way. Ascham is explicit about this point and stresses it repeatedly.

In listing an early version of *Toxophilus* among his credentials for the Regius Professorship of Greek, Ascham writes that once the work appears in print it will "not be an insignificant sign of my insignificant learning" (*Whole Works,* 1:52). He expresses the same hope in the epistle dedicatory of the printed version, concluding that he trusts that *Toxophilus* will be "some signe of my minde, towardes . . . learninge."[12] Then in the spring of 1545 Ascham elaborates, explaining that he wants

> certain distinguished men who thought that I was distracted from graver subjects by the excessive pursuit of archery to know . . . that I have not, as Aristophanes says, τῷ τοξεύειν ἐκτετοξεῦσθαι [shot away] all my time. (*Whole Works,* 1:81)

The "distinguished men" are obviously not Ascham's new supporters at court, such as Paget, Gardiner, and the king; nor are they sympathetic colleagues like Seton and Cheke. Presumably they are academics at Cambridge who view scholarly activity from a narrowly conservative perspective.[13] Ascham is now addressing himself to a different audience. It is secular, political, and nationalistic; and while nonacademic, this audience is intellectually sophisticated in a liberal, humanistic sense. Punning on the classical Greek text from which he coins his title,[14] Ascham expresses his intention to vindicate himself as a scholar. In addition, while reflecting traditional humanist scholarship, the pun indicates the irony of *Toxophilus*, in which the author undertakes to demonstrate his learning in a vernacular treatise on archery.

Ascham comments specifically on his decision to write in the vernacular, and his comments provide an instructive approach to the ironic structure of *Toxophilus*, bearing not only on its prose style but also on its subject matter and method of argumentation. Ascham's self-consciousness about his art is nowhere more evident than in his observation that his recourse to English violates convention and entails personal sacrifice. "[To] haue written this boke either in latin or Greke," he points out in the epistle prefatory, "had bene more easier & fit for mi trade in study" (x). He explains his choice on various grounds. The first is the standard humanistic concern to reach readers who had no Latin or Greek, to enhance the "pleasure or commoditie [benefit], of the gentlemen and yeomen of Englande" (xiv). He continues with the opinion that "as for the Latin or greke tonge, euery thyng is so excellently done in them, that none can do better." This line of reasoning implies a need for new forms of expression in the vernacular for a relatively broad English audience,[15] a point Ascham underlines in the following: "In the Englysh tonge . . . euery thinge [is done] in a maner so meanly, bothe for the matter and handelynge, that no man can do worse." Further on in this passage, and earlier in a letter to Gardiner concerning *Toxophilus* (*Whole Works,* 1:79–81), Ascham specifies what he sees as wrong with contemporary vernacular prose and indicates the principles guiding his own prose.

In emphasizing that he has departed from "nearly every writer of English," Ascham says that he has done so not because he finds English in itself deficient

> but because men very unlearned and presumptuous pursue this kind of study [i.e., vernacular writing]. They take up worthless subjects that are unsuited to their abilities, in which they flee proper and plain words and do not know how to fashion truly expressive metaphors. (*Whole Works,* 1:79–80)

Essential to word choice and figurative language is clarity, the quality of expression that renders the statement meaningful. Much of the difficulty with contemporary prose comes from the misappropriation of loan words, the use of "straunge wordes as latin, french and Italian, [which] make all thinges darke and harde" (xiv). The same criterion applies to syntax, though like most sixteenth-century commentators Ascham has little to say about syntax apart from diction, as in the opening of *The Scholemaster:*

> [I]n learninge farther hys Syntaxis . . . [the student] shall not vse the common order . . . wherby, [he] commonlie learneth, first, an euill choice of wordes, (and right choice of wordes, saith *Caesar,* is the foundation of eloquence) than, a wrong placing of wordes: and lastlie, an ill framing of the sentence, with a peruerse iudgement, both of wordes and sentences. (182)

To put the criticism another way, the injudicious choice and misplacement of words and poorly constructed periods violate the principle of decorum, of finding the appropriate word to express one's exact meaning. Violation of decorum results in not only meaningless but frequently ridiculous and uncomely prose.

Ascham's program is complex. He is by no means calling for a simplistic nativism; he requires highly traditional discipline. For instance, he attributes the ineptitude of contemporary authors to their having "not even tasted dialectic and rhetoric . . . and so they seek to cast the vernacular statements not in language that is indigenous and proper but foreign and strange" (*Whole Works,* 1:80). Good English prose depends on training in Latin grammar, composition, and literature, which in practice were loosely subsumed under the discipline of rhetoric, and in the dialectic that still consisted of Aristotelian logic and the academic debate. In this respect Ascham's program remains conservative and neoclassical, though never rigid or narrowly authoritarian. Ascham's ideal is a mode of writing that comprehends a wide range of expression. Although taken from the unfinished *Report and Discourse Written of the Affaires and State of Germany* written a decade later than *Toxophilus*, the following passage aptly summarizes the principles that govern Ascham's criticism and writing of prose throughout his career, and certainly in *Toxophilus*: clarity of diction, strength of syntactical construction, decorous adjustment of expression to subject, and awareness of appropriate classical models.

> The stile must be alwayes playne and open: yet sometime higher and lower as matters do ryse and fall: for if proper and naturall wordes, in well ioyned sentences do lyuely expresse the matter, be it troublesome, quyet, angry or pleasant, A man shal thincke not to be readyng but present in doying of the same. And herein *Liuie* of all other in any toung, by myne opinion carieth away the prayse. (126)

In all of his self-conscious discussion of his writing, whether of the Latin translations of Greek commentaries or the vernacular *Toxophilus,* Ascham addresses himself primarily to style, chiefly word choice and figurative language. Although he seldom refers to substance, it is evident that he regards it as important. In one passage discussed above, he points out that unlike contemporary authors he has "pursued a topic to which [he is] not unequal on account of [his] skill [in archery]" (*Whole Works,* 1:81). That is, he has firsthand, expert knowledge of what he is writing about. In the same passage Ascham points to the necessity of casting that knowledge in a logically compelling statement, as he indicates the great importance of *dialectic[a] ad ratiocinationem* (logic for purposes of developing an argument).[16] On at least one occasion he reveals a deep awareness of the connection between style and substance. In his remarks on the commentary on the Epistle to Philemon, he pays careful attention to the text of Erasmus's translation and substitutes of *deprecor* for *rogo*. The emendation, Ascham explains, rests on no less authority than Cicero, "who says that when we *deprecamur* we do not deny our deed, but ask forgiveness for our transgression, which this whole letter to Philemon concerns" (*Whole Works,* 1:24). Here word choice is decidedly substantive, for the particular meaning of the preferred word bears directly on the overarching theme of the epistle.

Ascham's expressions of interest in substance, argumentation, and the connection between style and substance are few; but they reflect concern, if not insight. The question therefore arises of why Ascham spends an apparently disproportionate amount of time in worrying the question of style, even—in C. S. Lewis's words—style narrowly conceived.[17]

The fact is that style presented problems that substance did not for the scrupulous midcentury writer. As Ascham himself explains repeatedly, there was little in the way of a usable native literary tradition that would provide a rich lexicon or larger models of form and structure.[18] Like many others during the century, Ascham focuses on the special problem of diction. Ascham greatly admires Chaucer and calls him "oure Englyshe Homer" (25), but Chaucer's language was remote and imperfectly understood. He singles out Chaucer for the *moralitas* of his work and quotes him in translation (25, 27, 29). Ascham also refers to the popular native romance, which presumably included Malory, but finds such writing wanting in every respect: "In our fathers tyme nothing was red, but bookes of fayned cheualrie, wherin a man by redinge, shuld be led to none other ende, but onely to manslaughter and baudrye" (xiv–xv).

Given that there were no suitable models in English and that his formal education and intellectual heritage consisted largely of the classics, it is only natural that Ascham would rely heavily on ancient Greek and Latin. As we have seen, the decision to write in English complicates his classicism. He points out that it would have been easier and more befitting his academic calling to have written in Latin or Greek. Instead he eschews the classicized Latin of his fellow humanists and undertakes to embody the high ideals of the Ciceronian aesthetic in good English prose. This undertaking may have stemmed from his professed humanist desire to reach a broad English audience, from his desire to strike out and write something in English worthy of his nation, or from his desire to please a new court audience. But in addition, the choice of the vernacular deepens the irony of the overall strategy. While the vernacular may seem at first the most unlikely vehicle for Ascham to demonstrate his learning with, it actually is a very decorous choice, given the ostensibly unsophisticated nature of the subject. We shall see that Ascham brings to bear on this subject enormous erudition and scholarship. We shall also see that—as Ascham pointedly anticipates in his prefatory statements—he takes pains to forge in his native English a style that meets the considerable challenge of emulating the classics.

Let us turn now to the work itself and consider some of the features of its argument, style, and format.

IV

Ascham divides *Toxophilus* into two books cast in the form of a dialogue between Philologus (Lover of Learning) and Toxophilus (Lover of the Bow). Book A defends archery as a pastime beneficial to the individual and to the nation; Book B describes the equipment and technique. The dialogue begins with Philologus's challenging of the proposition that archery possesses serious value. Toxophilus responds by recounting how throughout history all great nations have prized archery for its benefits in both peace and war. It is of particular value to the scholar who tends to lead a sedentary life. By the conclusion of Book A, these arguments have convinced Philologus, and he asks

Toxophilus to discuss the technical aspects of the art of archery so that he himself might become proficient. Book B treats the equipment of archery in detail and then the technique of shooting properly. Interwoven throughout are digressions on education, morals, politics, and particular contemporary figures and events.[19]

The structure of *Toxophilus* is at once firm and functional. Book A focuses sharply on the question of the value of archery and falls into two large sections, the first on the importance of archery during peace (7–32) and the second on its importance during war (39–55). The question is joined, and Philologus opens the discussion and indicates the general content of the entire treatise:

> Than Toxophile, if it be so as you do saye, let vs go forwarde and examin howe plentifullie this is done that you speke, and firste of the inuention of it, than what honestie & profit is in the vse of it, bothe for warre & peace, more than in other pastimes, laste of all howe it ought to be learned amonges men for the increase of it. (6)

Accordingly the dialogue treats the "inuention" of archery (6–7), its value in peace (7–32) and in war (39–56), the nature and aim of learned arts (56–68), and how archery may be learned (Book B). Within this overall organization of the materials, a clearly articulated infrastructure orders the development of the argument in each book.

In Book A, the more dialectical of the two books, the infrastructure consists of a series of clearly indicated steps in the process of persuasion, as Toxophilus answers Philologus's objections to archery. Besides marking Philologus's gradual movement from adversary to partisan of archery, Philologus's concessions at eleven distinct points advance and shape the argument on a fundamental level.[20] Each concession reformulates the question to be decided and anticipates the next topic. For example, soon after the discussion begins, Philologus concedes that princes have historically held archery in high regard but points out to Toxophilus that he has scarcely proved "why shotinge ought so of it selfe to be regarded" (9), which argument Toxophilus then takes up. At a later stage, Philologus adduces several prooftexts against archery, which Toxophilus readily puts to his own use. Philologus acknowledges that Toxophilus has "turned [all these texts] to the hygh prayse of shotinge" and continues: "[L]et me heare I praye you nowe, those examples whiche you haue marked of shotyng yourselfe: whereby you are, and thinke to persuade other, that shoting is so good in warre" (39). Toxophilus then obliges. In roughly half of these instances, Ascham casts Philologus's concessions in a conditional sentence, which not only points to the next set of topics but also looks forward to Philologus's ultimate embracing of Toxophilus's argument, as in the following: "If you can proue this thing so playnly, as you speake it ernestly, then wil I, not only thinke as you do, but become a shooter and do as you" (12). Finally, regretting his lack of natural ability, Philologus remarks: "And surely yf I knew that I were apte, and that you woulde teache me howe to shoote, I would become an archer, and the rather, bycause of the good communication, the whiche I haue had with you this dayes, of shooting" (58). Here Toxophilus has made the case for archery and has convinced Philologus. Philologus's concession nevertheless anticipates the general question of learning an art and the particular question of learning archery, the subject of the rest of the treatise.

Structuring the dialogue of Book A in this way, Ascham presents a thoroughly integrated argument. Moreover, the regularly marked concessions enliven the exchanges between Toxophilus and Philologus and provide the distinctive drama of Platonic dialogue: the exchanges raise expectations and create interesting displays of argumentation and frequently of wit.

Since there is no adversarial relationship in Book B, there is little comparable drama. Philologus is now an eager learner and collaborator, and the method is topical and expository rather than dialectical. The opening exchange of Book B between Philologus and Toxophilus encapsulates the book's contents in great detail and illustrates the technique:

> PH. What is the cheyfe poynte in shotynge, that euerye manne laboureth to come to? TOX. To hyt the marke. PHI. Howe manye thynges are required to make a man euer more hyt the marke? TOX. Twoo. PHI. Whiche twoo? TOX. Shotinge strayght and kepynge of a lengthe. . . . (69)

The passage continues in this vein for some thirty lines touching on every topic and on the order and rationale of their treatment in Book B. The passage concludes:

> PHI. You speake nowe Toxophile, euen as I wold haue you to speake: But lette vs returne agayne vnto our matter, and those thynges whyche you haue packed vp, in so shorte a roume, we wyll lowse them forthe, and take euery pyece as it were in our hande and looke more narowlye vpon it. (70)

The method of the dialogue is not that of the late Platonic dialogues or even Cicero's *De oratore*, both of which stand behind Book A and receive specific notice. The dialogue of Book B recalls Cicero's *De partitione oratoria*, a manual of rhetoric in which the master (Cicero) answers questions about the art from an eager pupil (Cicero's son).[21] The argument is highly discursive as the two interlocutors present the topics schematically and then proceed through them.[22]

No less than Book A, Book B rests on a carefully contrived structure. Instead of a series of concessions on Philologus's part, Book B consists of five sections of material, each schematically organized, presented, and concluded. The five sections cover: (1) equipment (70–96); (2) use of the equipment

(97–106); (3) wind and weather (106–16); (4) shooting straight (116–18); and (5) self-control (118–19). Ascham frequently subdivides these sections, especially the first two, on the "gear" of archery and on its use. For example, in the discussion of arrows ("shafts"), Ascham breaks this, the fifth subdivision of the first topic (97–106), into three ("A shaft hath three principall partes" (83), each of which parts he subdivides twice again. The feather alone receives five full pages of discussion (87–92).

Such schematization renders the presentation lucid and orderly, which is consistent with the book's expository mode. The strategy also creates the impression of completeness and thoroughness of treatment. Philologus frequently strengthens the impression by remarking on the surprising amount of detail the subject entails. "I woulde neuer haue thought," he comments midway through Toxophilus's discussion of the arrow, "you could haue sayd halfe so muche of a stele [shaft of the arrow], and I thynke as concernyng the litle fether and the playne head, there is but lytle to saye" (87). As it turns out, the feather alone requires 25 percent more discussion than the "stele."

Besides advancing the argumentation and exposition, the adaptation of the dialogue form in *Toxophilus* enables Ascham to take up a wide variety of materials and topics. These, in turn, serve his professed concerns to exhibit his learning and fashion a statement celebratory of English culture as worthy as the encomia of antiquity. Perhaps most conspicuous is Ascham's use of classical, biblical, and historical authorities. These loom large in Book A, in which Toxophilus argues for the virtue of archery as a pastime during peace (7–32) and—most prominently—in the argument for archery as essential to national defense (39–55). Having just conceded the seventh point and now virtually convinced, Philologus asks to hear about "those examples whiche you haue marked of shotyng your selfe: whereby you are, and thinke to persuade other, that shoting is so good in warre" (39). Toxophilus responds with a magisterial chronology of the uses of archery for military purposes from biblical times through the sixteenth century. The greatest part of the survey—fourteen of the sixteen pages—presents Hebrew, Greek, Roman, and early medieval examples. The richly illustrated review implicitly prepares for the distinguished history of English archery, which Toxophilus compasses in a comparatively spare rehearsal (53–54). As Toxophilus points out by way of introduction: "But now . . . concerning many examples for the prayse of English archers in warre, surley I wil not be long in a matter that no man doubteth in, & those few that I wil name, shal either be proued by the histories of our enemies, or els done by men that now liue" (53). Seven brief paragraphs of restrained prose recount English archery from Edward III and the Battle of Crécy to Sir William Walgrave's and Sir George Somerset's recent victory over the French. The statement requires neither length nor rhetorical flourish, since it indicates a historical reality that has shaped England's past and present and reveals England's destiny as heir to the civilizations of Israel, Greece, and Rome.

Toxophilus's strategy in these sections is scholarly and academic, proceeding historically and appealing to authority. In addition, Ascham takes pains to suggest the breadth of Toxophilus's learning. He is no mere "ancient," relying solely on classical authors. He includes medieval authors like Paul, deacon of Monte Cassino (720–800); Leo VI, called the Wise, Byzantine emperor from 886 to 911; and Nicholas de Lyra (c. 1265–1349); and moderns like Robert Gaguin (1425–1501), Jean Tixier, seigneur de Ravisy (d. 1524), Hector Boece (1465–1536), John Major (1469–1550), Peter Nannius (1500–1557), and Philip Melanchthon (1497–1560). He also refers to English contemporaries Sir Thomas Elyot (1490–1546) and John Cheke (1514–57). Besides adducing the authorities in the text proper, Ascham reinforces the scholarly form by means of marginal side notes to the writers and the works, frequently with specific references.[23]

In the course of demonstrating his learning, Ascham does more than assemble a vast array of sources on the behalf of one of his speakers. He demonstrates many of the rhetorical and dialectical skills that he disparages contemporary prose writers for lacking. One strategy appears early on when Toxophilus begins his case for archery by recounting its invention, a standard topic recommended in the rhetorical textbooks for introducing and providing the foundations for an argument.[24] In presenting the genesis of archery, Toxophilus refers within a third of a page to Pliny's *Natural History*, Plato's *Symposium*, the *Hymn to Apollo*, Genesis, Nicholas de Lyra, and Galen—all provided with citations in the margins. He concludes:

> So this great continuance of shoting doth not a lytle praise shotinge: nor that neither doth not a litle set it oute, that it is referred to thinuention of Apollo, for the which poynt shoting is highlye praised of Galene: where he sayth, that mean craftes be first found out by men or beastes, as weauing by a spider, and suche other: but high and commendable sciences by goddes, as shotinge and musicke by Apollo. (6–7)

Besides marshaling an impressive list of authorities within a short space, Toxophilus displays a deftness and lightness of touch in manipulating them. The skill and the grace result from the shrewd identification of the origins of archery and the highest of art forms. The association with Apollo aggrandizes and dignifies archery, anticipating a major theme of Ascham's defense later in the treatise, that of the sheer aesthetic beauty of form properly executed.

On another occasion, Ascham reverses the situation and puts Toxophilus in the position of defending his assertions against Philologus's appeal to authority. The question concerns the kind of feather to be preferred, that of the eagle or the goose. Philologus invokes the authority of Hesiod's account of Hercules' favoring eagle and not goose feathers for arrows. Toxophilus's first tactic is to dismiss Hercules' view as extreme and then to shift the focus from the mythological to the everyday, asserting that "as for Hercules, seynge nether water nor lande, heauen nor hell, coulde scarse contente hym to abyde in, it was no meruell thoughe a sely poore gouse fether could not plese him" (89). He then continues with a brief encomium of the goose:

> Yet welfare the gentle gouse which bringeth to a man euen to hys doore so manye excedynge commodities. For the gouse is mans comforte in war & in peace slepynge and wakynge. What prayse so euer is gyuen to shootynge the gouse may chalenge the beste parte in it. How well dothe she make a man fare at his table? Howe easelye dothe she make a man lye in hys bed? How fit euen as her fethers be onelye for shootynge, so be her quylles fytte onelye for wrytyng. (89)

The argument is less dialectical than rhetorical, as Toxophilus exploits the metonymic potential of the homely goose, specifying the domestic items the goose is the source of: feather beds and food as well as the feathers of arrows and the quills of pens. The concluding three sentences of this miniature encomium confirm the point and reflect Toxophilus's complete control of his material. The isocolon (similarity of length) and isoparion (similarity of syntactical and grammatical structure) gains particular emphasis from the identical rhythmic figures of the beginning of the sentences—all iambs: "How well," "Howe ease" (lye), and "How fit."

Ascham pursues a far more dialectical vein in the conclusion to Book A, where Philologus advances the position that disciplines ought to be pursued in order to achieve "excellencie" or "perfitnesse." Toxophilus argues that such pursuit is folly since fully realizing perfection is impossible and that one should seek only what is possible. Philologus proceeds with a series of pithy questions reminiscent of Plato's Socrates at his most incisive and reduces Toxophilus's position to an absurdity:[25]

> PHIL. Than by likely to hit the pricke alwayes, is vnpossible. For that is called vnpossible whych is in no man his power to do. TOX. Vnpossible in dede. PHIL. But to shoote wyde and far of the marke is a thynge possyble. TOX. No man wyll denie that. PHIL. But yet to hit the marke alwayse were an excellent thyng. TOX. Excellent surelie. PHIL. Than I am sure those be wiser men, which couete to shoote wyde than those whiche couete to hit the prycke. TOX. Why so I pray you. PHIL. Because to shote wyde is a thynge possyble, and therfore as you saye youre selfe, of euery wyse man to be followed. (65–66)

The point that Philologus clinches with irrefutable logic is that one necessarily seeks what is impossible in all arts and disciplines, whatever they may be. "[In] good sadnesse [seriousness] Toxophile," he says in a friendlier tone, "thus you se that a man might go throghe all craftes and sciences, and proue that anye man in his science coueteth that which he shal neuer gette" (66). The conclusion prepares the way for Book B and Toxophilus's undertaking to illustrate and teach the art of archery.

The above illustrations from the argument of *Toxophilus* reveal the scholarly skills of the author: his command of learned materials, his breadth of learning, and his mastery of various modes of dialectical argumentation. In the following section, we consider Ascham's achievement as a prose stylist.

V

In keeping with the strategy of bringing to bear enormous learning on the subject of archery, Ascham likewise lavishes great care on the style of *Toxophilus*. As we have seen, prose style is a matter he concerns himself with generally and discusses specifically in the prefatory epistles to *Toxophilus*. His remarks there point to a sophisticated combination of nativism and classicism, a program he clearly follows in the body of his treatise. His vocabulary eschews both the Latinate neologizing occasionally evident in Elyot and the extreme Saxonist tendency found in Seton and Cheke. The diction measures up to the standard Ascham ascribes to Aristotle: that prose should reflect the speech of common people and the thought of the wise (xiv).

The syntax is even more of a hybrid of the classical and native. It is largely paratactic. That is, the rhetorical periods typically depend on grammatical coordination effected by coordinating conjunctions *(and, or, but,* or *yet),* or by connective adverbs *(for, therefore, thus, moreover),* or simply by clausal juxtaposition marked by a colon.[26] The following sentence is illustrative:

> *And* surely the bowmen of Athens did wonderful feates in many battels, *but* specially when Demosthenes the valiant captayne slue and toke prisoners all the Lacedomonians besyde the citie of Pylos, where Nestor somtyme was lord: the shaftes went so thicke that daye (sayth Thucydides) that no man could se theyr enemies. (43)

Critics have long pointed out that heavy parataxis was a salient feature of English prose until well into the early modern period. In the words of a recent critic, "conjoined clauses [i.e., parataxis of all kinds] had been a staple resource of native prose composition for well over a century and a half before [1550]" (Mueller, *Native Tongue and the Word,* 287). The majority of the rhetorical periods in *Toxophilus* exhibit the paratactic structure of native English prose.[27]

Into this matrix of traditional syntax Ascham introduces periods embellished by the so-called Gorgian figures, most frequently associated with the Athenian orator Isocrates (fourth century B.C.). These figures include: isocolon (corresponding members of similar grammatical structure), antithesis, and paromoion (corresponding members of similar sound). The following schematization of one of Ascham's periods is illustrative:

> Princes beinge children oughte to be brought vp in shoting:
> both bycause it is an exercise moost holsom,
> and also a pastyme moost honest:
> wherin labour prepareth the body to hardnesse,
> the minde to couragiousnesse,
> sufferyng neither the one to be marde with tendernesse,
> nor yet the other to be hurte with ydlenesse:
> as we reade how Sardanapalus and suche other were,
> bycause they were not brought vp with outwarde honest
> payneful pastymes to be men:
> but cockerde vp with inwarde noughtie ydle wantonnesse to
> be women.
>
> (9)

Within this period Ascham embeds a series of parallel clauses, each successive pair of which is longer than the preceding pair and builds to the extended antithesis of the final one. The art of such prose drew the notice of contemporaries. In arguing for Ascham's superiority over the likes of Thomas Nashe, Gabriel Harvey remarks that "[i]t is for . . . Ascham to stand levelling of Colons, or squaring of Periods, by measure and number."[28] By "levelling and squaring" Harvey means the balancing and equalizing typical of the Isocratean period rather than of the grammatical subordination and rhetorical gradation of the rounded, cumulative Ciceronian.[29]

But Ascham's practice in *Toxophilus* conforms to larger Ciceronian principles. Cicero stresses the importance of commanding the full breadth of stylistic expression. In the *Orator*, he concludes that this capability distinguishes true eloquence: "Is erit igitur eloquens, ut idem illud iteremus, qui poterit parva summisse, modica temperate, magna graviter dicere" (101). This passage stands squarely behind the one quoted on page 30 as a summary of Ascham's stylistic ideal, according to which prose must be plain and accessible and at the same time reach "sometime higher and lower as matters do ryse and fall." Both passages imply the supreme classical doctrine of decorum: fitting the language to the matter. Both passages further imply the importance of each work being in itself stylistically varied. The author of the pseudo-Ciceronian *Rhetorica ad herennium* is explicit: "Sed figuram in dicendo commutare oportet, ut gravem mediocris, mediocrem excipiat adtenuata, deinde identidem commutent, ut facile satietas varietate vitatur" (4.12–16).[30] As we have seen, Ascham undertakes *Toxophilus* to exploit the resources of his native language and to demonstrate his own literary proficiency. It follows that within the distinctive stylistic mode of *Toxophilus*, he would seek to display a wide range of English expression. The range includes: (1) the colloquial; (2) the technical and analytic; and (3) the ornately learned and on occasion loftily poetic. These categories are fairly comprehensive; certainly they are representative and illustrative of Ascham's practice in *Toxophilus*.[31]

Perhaps the most vivid instance of Ascham's colloquial style occurs in the section on gambling:

> What false dise vse they? as dise stopped with quicksiluer and heares, dise of a vauntage, flattes, gourdes to chop and chaunge whan they lyste, to lette the trew dise fall vnder the table, & so take vp the false, and if they be true dise, what shyfte wil they make to set the one of them with slyding, with cogging, with foysting, with coytinge as they call it. (25)

The vividness of the passage arises principally from the diction, which Ascham takes from the contemporary patois of gamblers: "dise of a vauntage," "flattes," "gourdes," "cogging," "foysting," and "coyting." He calls attention to his source with the phrase "as they call it." The pattern of repetition heightens the effect. In fact the entire section on gambling intensifies as it unfolds. Ascham proceeds to a virtually dramatic scene on page 26 in which professional sharks seduce an unwary party to join their game of craps. The scene concludes with the sensational passage on blasphemy. Toxophilus cites the apposite text from the Pardoner's Tale (lines 651–57) and relates what he claims to be personal experience of "two men . . . whose sayinges be far more grisely" than Chaucer's verses:

> One, whan he had lost all his moneye sware me God, from top to toe with one breath, that he had lost al his mony for lack of sweringe: The other . . . sware me by the flesshe of God, that yf swerynge would helpe him but one ace, he would not leue one pece of god vnsworne, neyther wythin nor without. (27)

Here the sensationalism arises from outrageous profanities, swearing by the "flesh of God" and "peces of god." Toxophilus calls it "grisely" because, as Chaucer's Pardoner explains, oath-swearers *almost literally* tear God apart, limb from limb. The section on gambling has prompted one commentator to see it anticipating the cony-catching pamphlets by nearly fifty years.[32]

Another instance of Ascham's colloquial style occurs in the digression on the Turkish threat to European Christendom. In this case the effect is not sensational but one of indignation, even sarcasm. Toxophilus focuses on the failure of will of the Christian states:

> But Christendome now I may tell you Philologe is much lyke a man that hath an ytch on him, and lyeth dronke also in his bed, and though a thefe come to the

> dore, and heaueth at it, to come in, and sleye hym, yet he lyeth in his bed, hauinge more pleasure to lye in a slumber and scratche him selfe wher it ytcheth even to the harde bone, than he hath redynes to ryse vp lustely. (49)

The force of this passage comes from the extended simile in which the "body of Christ"—the Church and by extension Christendom—appears in the trope of an all too fleshly person surrendering to self-indulgence. The coarseness of the image, vividly expressed in purely Germanic vocabulary—"ly[ing] drunke," "scratch[ing] him selfe wher it ytcheth"—is most appropriate to the thrust of Toxophilus's criticism.

The emotional tenor of the second stylistic category, Ascham's technical or analytical style, is naturally more restrained. Its conspicuous plainness and fluency, however, depend heavily on the manipulation of grammatical and rhetorical forms, as when Toxophilus is explaining why no account of archery survives from ancient Rome:

> In the commune wealthe of Rome . . . litle mention is made of shoting, not bycause it was litle vsed amonges them, but rather bycause it was bothe so necessarye and commune, that it was thought a thing not necessary or requyred of anye man to be spoken vpon, as if a man shoulde describe a great feaste he woulde not ones name bread. . . . but surely yf a feaste . . . lacked bread . . . than woulde men talke of the commodity of bread . . . that would not ones name it afore, whan they had it: And even so dyd the Romaynes as concernynge shootynge. (44)

This is Toxophilus at his most reasonable and genial in advancing his argument on the basis of negative evidence. A large part of the effect comes from the essential simplicity of the sentence structure and its preponderant conformity to the received English word order of subject, verb, and complement. Ascham extends the sentence in several ways: by the parallel subordinate clauses ("not bycause . . ." and "but rather because . . ."), which receive point through antithesis; by the correlative structure of the clause "so necessary . . . that"; and by the elaborated analogy to the homely example of bread and a feast. These measures generate a sentence of some length, whose members unfold in an easy and apparently loose sequence but rest in a firmly coherent frame. The sentence concludes in the almost conversational independent clause, "And even so dyd the Romaynes as concernyng shootyng," which perfects the rhetorical and logical structure of the whole.

Within this same stylistic register, Ascham can achieve very different effects, as for example the concision and curtness of the opening of the second Book:

> PHILOL. What is the cheyfe poynte in shootynge, that euerye manne laboureth to come to? TOX. To hyt the marke. PHI. Howe manye thynges are required to make a man euer more hyt the marke? TOX. Twoo. PHI. Whiche twoo? TOX. Shotinge streyght and kepynge of a lengthe. PHIL. Howe shoulde a manne shoote

> strayght, & howe shulde a man kepe a length? TOX. In knowynge and hauynge thinges, belongynge to shootyng: and whan they be knowen and had, in well handlynge of them: whereof some belong to shotyng strayght, some to keping of a length, some commonly to them bothe, as shall be tolde seuerally of them, in place conuenient. (69)

The speed and impact of the passage are a result of the brevity of the question-and-answer form of the exchange. Ascham accelerates the exchange through the grammatical and rhetorical integrity of each question and answer. The answer is a dependent clause and thereby firmly integrated with the question. In addition, the coordination, isocolon, and parison render the statement virtually schematic in its precision and clarity.

Two further examples of the technical and analytical style illustrate the detailed focus Ascham is capable of. The first comes from the long section dealing with the bow in Book II, pages 74–82:

> Euerye bowe is made eyther of a boughe, of a plante or of the boole of the tree. The boughe commonlye is very knotty, and full of pinnes, weake, of small pithe, and sone wyll folowe the stringe, and seldome werith to anye fayre couloure. . . . The plante proueth many times wel, yf it be of a good and clene growth. . . . The boole of the tree is clenest without knot or pin, hauinge a faste and harde woode by reasonne of hys full groweth, stronge and myghtye of cast, and best for a bow, yf the staues be euen clouen. (76–77)

Here Toxophilus is at his most expository, as he describes physical materials (types of wood) and analyzes their properties (appearance and performance). His method is to combine generalization with detail, so that each sentence begins with a comprehensive assertion and proceeds to a series of phrases or clauses of specific substantives. The passage receives its particular clarity from the straightforward word order of the simple declarative sentence.

The second passage dealing with the bow is equally focused, but in this case Ascham brings out a warm engagement on Toxophilus's part. He is discussing the importance of providing a new bow with a proper finish:

> Whan you haue broughte youre bowe to suche a poynte, as I spake of, than you must haue an herden or wullen cloth waxed, wherewith euery day you must rubbe and chafe your bowe, tyll it shyne and glytter withall. Whyche thynge shall cause it both to be cleane, well fauored, goodlye of coloure, and shall also bryng as it were a cruste, ouer it, that is to say, shall make it euery where on the outsyde, so slypperye and harde, that neyther anye weete or wether can enter to hurte it, nor yet any freat or pynche, be able to byte vpon it: but that you shal do it great wrong before you break it. (79)

As the concluding dependent clauses emphasize through their Gorgian figuration, the purpose of the described procedure is of great practical importance:

protecting the bow. The description of the procedure itself highlights its sensuousness, bringing out the tactile and visual qualities in the carefully paired doublets. Notwithstanding the homely English diction—"herden," "wullen," "rub," and so on—the passage transforms the bow into a quasi-aesthetic object, or at least suggests the pleasing sensuousness of the procedure.

In contrast to the manifestly colloquial and studiously plain styles examined so far, the third stylistic category includes prose that is frequently learned and occasionally poetic. Two examples will illustrate. The first comes from the argument for the importance of archery in times of war, in which Toxophilus comments on military training and history:

> But chefely I woulde wisshe and (if I were of authoritie) I wolde counsel al the yong gentilmen of this realme, neuer to lay out of theyr handes .ii. authors Xenephon in Greke, and Cesar in Latyn, wher in they shulde folowe noble Scipio Africanus, as Tullie doeth saye: In which .ii. authors, besydes eloquence a thing most necessary of all other, for a captayne, they shuld become the hole course of warre, which those .ii. noble menne dyd not more wyselye wryte for other men to learne, than they dyd manfully exercise in the fyelde, for other men to followe. (33)

Here Toxophilus argues from authority, invoking the names that the world of learning endorsed as the supreme authors of military history, Xenophon and Caesar. In addition, following Cicero Toxophilus invokes Scipio Africanus, the heroic military commander of the early Roman Republic, as an embodiment of the recommended ideal. The ideal includes the ability to speak as well as to act and reaches back in antiquity at least as far as Homer, who in the *Iliad* depicts the greatest of the heroes, Odysseus and Achilles, as men of great speech and great deeds. In this way the learned allusions broaden the argument so as to embrace all of antiquity, thus strengthening its force and authority. Characteristically, the passage concludes with two Gorgian parallelisms—"not more wyselye wryte . . . dyd manfully exercise . . ."—that express the composite ideal of verbal and military excellence.

The second example of the relatively lofty style is Toxophilus's relation of his experience of once seeing the wind. The passage does not have the densely learned texture of the previous example but possesses instead a rhythmic fluency. Toxophilus has made the point that one of the greatest challenges of the art of archery is judgment of the weather, particularly the wind, since it is invisible. To illustrate, he narrates the following:

> To se the wynde, with a man his eyes, it is vnpossible, the nature of it is so fyne, and subtile, yet this experience of the wynde had I ones my selfe, and that was in the great snowe that fell .iiii. yeares agoo: I rode in the hye waye betwixt Topcliffe vpon Swale, and Borowe bridge, the waye beyng sumwhat trodden afore, by waye fayrynge men. The feeldes on bothe sides were playne and laye almost yearde

> depe with snowe, the nyght afore had ben a litle froste, so that the snowe was hard and crusted aboue. That morning the sun shone bright and clere, the winde was whistelinge a lofte, and sharpe accordynge to the tyme of the yeare. The snowe in the hye waye laye lowse and troden wyth horse feete: so as the wynde blewe, it toke the lose snow with it, and made it so slide vpon the snowe in the felde whyche was harde and crusted by reason of the frost ouer nyght, that therby I myght se verye wel, the hole nature of the wynde as it blewe that daye. And I had a great delyte & pleasure to marke it, whyche maketh me now far better to remember it. Sometyme the wynd would be not past .ii. yeardes brode, and so it would carie the snowe as far as I could se. An other tyme the snow woulde blowe ouer halfe the felde at ones. Sometyme the snowe woulde tomble softly, by and by it would flye wonderfull fast. And thys I perceyued also that the wind goeth by streames & not hole togither. For I should se one streame wyth in a Score on me, than the space of .ii. score no snow would stirre, but after so muche quantitie of grounde, an other streame of snow at the same very tyme should be caryed lykewyse, but not equally. For the one would stande styll when the other flew a pace, and so contynewe sometime swiftlyer sometime slowlyer, sometime broder, sometime narrower, as far as I could se. Nor it flewe not streight, but sometyme it crooked thys waye sometyme that waye, and somtyme it ran round aboute in a compase. And somtyme the snowe wold be lyft clene from the ground vp in to the ayre, and by & by it would be al clapt to the grounde as though there had bene no winde at all, streightway it woulde rise and flye.
>
> And that whych was the moost maruayle of al, at one tyme .ii. driftes of snowe flewe, the one out of the West into the East, the other out of the North in to the East: And I saw .ii. windes by reason of the snow the one crosse ouer the other, as it had bene two hye wayes. And agayne I should here the wynd blow in the ayre, when nothing was stirred at the ground. And when all was still where I rode, not verye far fro me the snow should be lifted wonderfully. This experience made me more meruaile at the nature of the wynd, than it made me conning in the knowlege of the wynd: but yet therby I learned perfitly that it is no meruayle at al thoughe men in a wynde lease theyr length in shooting, seying so many wayes the wynde is so variable in blowynge. (112–13)

The subject of seeing what is invisible requires not argumentation but narration and description. Ascham therefore has Toxophilus begin by locating the experience in space and time and detailing the circumstances. The locale and details of such ordinary phenomena as the crusted and loose snow, the clarity of the winter's day, and the blowing wind prepare for the most extraordinary event of virtually seeing the wind. The account moves gradually from the ordinary to the extraordinary in four distinct stages: (1) the wind blowing in various directions at various speeds; (2) the wind blowing irregularly and sporadically; (3) the wind blowing vertically as well as horizontally; and (4) the wind blowing in streams that intersect, the "moost meruayle of all."

Enhancing the movement of the account is the pervasive parataxis; sixteen of the seventeen sentences display conjunctive coordination and nine begin with a coordinating conjunction. In addition Ascham employs other figures of repetition that are characteristic of native prose. There are the doublets, which are frequently embellished with assonance—for example, the "nature of it is so fyne and subtile." There are alliteration and assonance, as in "the wind was whisteling a lofte" and "[the] snow would tumble softly." There is rhythmical anaphora—"For the one [i.e., airstream] would stand styll . . . and so contynew sometime swiftlyer, some time slowlyer, sometime broder, sometime narrower." The repetitive patterns of syntax and sound reinforce the literary description of the wind and suggest its very undulation.

Besides suggesting the blowing wind, the distinctive eloquence of the passage evokes its wonder and elusiveness. As a natural phenomenon, wind is a manifestly powerful force that can be heard and felt and whose effects can be observed. Yet it can never itself be seen, and its nature remains ultimately inscrutable. The inscrutability—the mystery—is what the passage expresses so effectively. While the prose consists largely of description and narration, it also includes the response of Toxophilus. He speaks, for example, of the "great delyte and pleasure [he took] to marke it [the wind]." The response comes from his seeing what he had never before seen but had only imperfectly sensed. Like any learning experience, this one pleases. It does so *not* because Toxophilus now perfectly understands the wind but because he appreciates its mystery. Ascham has Toxophilus summarize the conclusion in a neatly pointed isocolon figured antithetically. "This experience made me more meruaile at the nature of the wynd, than it made me connyng in the knowledge of the wynd." Toxophilus marvels at what he recognizes he can never fully comprehend or accurately predict; as the passage shows, he has acquired humility. In the process Toxophilus illustrates his earlier claim that the "greatest enemy of shooting is the wynde" and indicates the need for disciplined art that will enable the shooter at least to approach the "perfitnesse" of consistently hitting the mark. In acquiring humility, Toxophilus also reveals the need to respond to the wind imaginatively. Ascham's casting the prose of the passage in so distinctly imaginative a mode is fully consistent with this point.

The foregoing examination of the prose style of *Toxophilus* reveals the broad range of expression that mid-sixteenth-century English was capable of in the hands of a skilled craftsmen. For purposes of discussion, I have categorized the examples discussed into three groups, traditionally described as "low," "middle," and "high." But whatever categories one devises, the rich variety of the style of *Toxophilus* emerges clearly. It is all the more remarkable for Ascham's having achieved such variety within a distinctive stylistic mode, one which combines elements from both the native English tradition and elements from the traditions of ancient Greece and Rome. Whatever else, the achievement reflects a high degree of self-consciousness and painstaking work on the part of the author. These qualities, moreover, receive concrete testimony from the record of the composition, printing, and format of *Toxophilus*.

VI

Ascham evidently went about *Toxophilus* with the same care and deliberation that we observed in his other literary efforts discussed above in section 2. Ascham first mentions his treatise in early summer 1544 in his application to Paget for the Regius professorship (*Whole Works,* 1:52). He explains that this work *de re sagittaria* is in press *(sub praelo)* and that he hopes it will be in print in time for presentation to the king as he departs on his military expedition to France. Henry set out on 14 July, sooner than expected and some time before the printer had finished. Ascham seems to have welcomed the opportunity to withdraw the manuscript in order to revise it. Shortly before Lent the next year, he remarks that he has been totally absorbed *in meo Toxophilo*, which was finally printed by Edward Whytechurch, printer to the king, in late spring or early summer (*Whole Works,* 1:75). On the basis of the comment in the epistle dedicatory that the treatise was in some stage of completion before spring of 1544, it appears that Ascham spent over a year revising it.

Ascham also took great care with the physical production of *Toxophilus*. The printing seems to have been scrupulously checked. A complete collation of the located nineteen copies reveals over fifty instances of stop-press correction. That is an unusually high number of corrections for a quarto of 190 pages, and many of them are sufficiently substantive to suggest the author's own hand. Most unusually, the book bears no title page but has instead a lavish engraving of the Tudor royal arms modified to emblemize particular features of the royal dedication. (See illustration.) The image of the book with the word *VERITAS*—the Bible—and the image of the bow and arrow with the word *VINCIT* suggest active militancy. The visual and grammatical collocation—"Truth" (of the Bible) "Conquers" (with the aid of the English longbow)—encapsulates the Protestantism and nationalism that the English humanists characteristically embrace. The elegiac couplets in the scrolls elaborate and specify the two political motifs. One celebrates the ecclesiastical victory of Henry's secession from Rome; the other, his recent military victories over the Scots and the French. The cartouche contains English verse, appropriately in a stanza of rime royal.

The formality and ceremony of the frontispiece and the epistle dedicatory to the king received further expression in the book's presentation to its dedicatee. Very shortly after *Toxophilus* was printed, Gardiner and perhaps Paget arranged for Ascham to have a royal audience at Greenwich. The royal presentation copy is unlocated, but, as one may judge from other presentation copies that survive, Ascham must have had prepared a specially bound copy inscribed in his own elegant hand.[33] This copy Ascham then carried to Henry and Catherine as they received other petitions and gifts while presiding over the

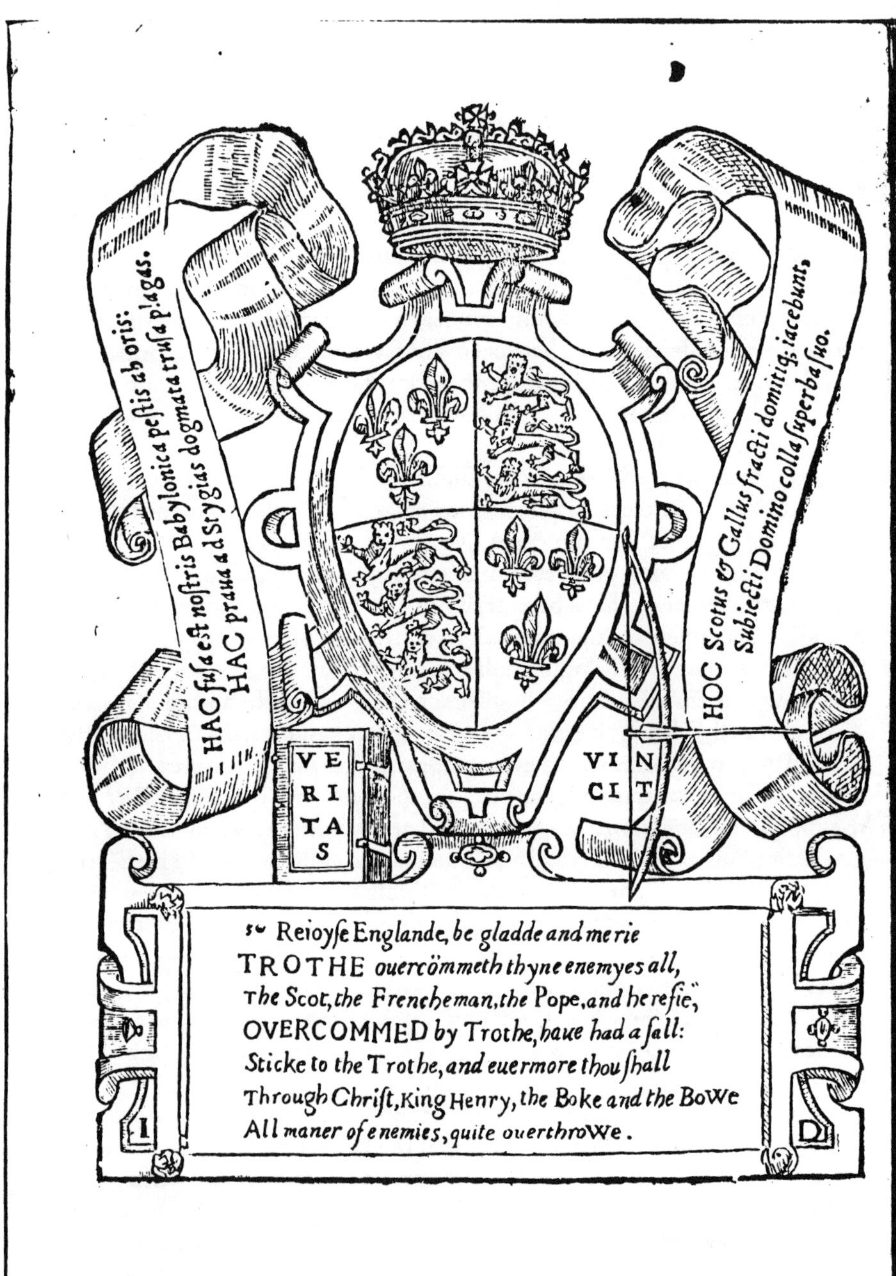

Frontispiece from Roger Ascham, *Toxophilus* (1545). By permission of The Huntington Library, San Marino, California.

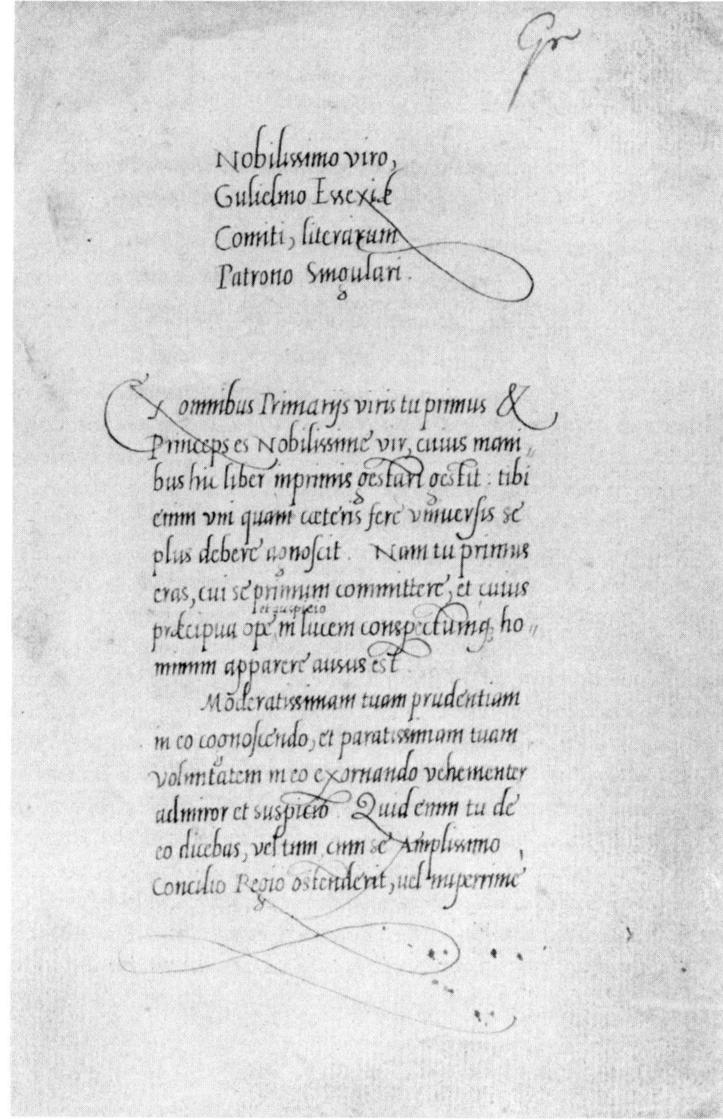

Gr

Nobilissimo viro,
Gulielmo Essexiae
Comiti, literarum
Patrono singulari.

Ex omnibus Primarijs viris tu primus &
Princeps es Nobilissime vir, cuius mani
bus hic liber imprimis gestari gestit: tibi
enim uni quam caeteris fere universis se
plus debere agnoscit. Nam tu primus
eras, cui se primum committere, et cuius
praecipuam opem in lucem conspectumque ho
minum apparere ausus est.
Moderatissimam tuam prudentiam
in eo cognoscendo, et paratissimam tuam
voluntatem in eo exornando vehementer
admiror et suspicio. Quid enim tu de
eo diebus, vel tum cum se Amplissimo
Concilio Regio ostenderit, vel nuperrime

Ascham's Dedication to William Parr, Earl of Essex, from leaves prefatory to *Toxophilus.* By permission of The Folger Shakespeare Library, Washington, D.C.

court at Greenwich. We have a glimpse of the scene in a passage from Ascham's letter of thanks to William Parr, earl of Essex and brother to the queen. Ascham expresses his gratitude to Parr for his support in getting *Toxophilus* approved by the council for publication and then praising it to Catherine and Henry:

> I shall cherish forever in my memory what you declared about it when it was presented to the most honorable King's Council and most recently when it was carried very modestly and fearfully to His Royal Majesty. For I still seem to see, as though gazing with admiration, how you extolled this book to her Majesty Queen Catherine when she asked by chance what book it was, and how you commended it with an agreeable countenance, indicating your divine pleasure in it and prophesying extraordinary fame for it. (*Whole Works,* 1:77–78)

We may infer that the queen called her husband's attention to the book and that it attracted his interest. As we have seen, *Toxophilus* was among other things a celebration of the Christian militancy of the realm that Henry was at the very moment preparing for further territorial expansion across the Channel. It was as well a studied exhibition of Ascham's own learning and wit, qualities that Henry himself had aspired to, if not cultivated, throughout his life.

It is therefore scarcely surprising that Henry rewarded Ascham with an annuity of ten pounds (*Whole Works,* 1:412). This was a sum that Gardiner felt should have been greater. Nearly ten years later Ascham recalls with gratitude Gardiner's support, writing, "[W]hen King Henry first gave it [the annuity] at Greenwich, your lordship in the gallery [was] there asking me what the king had given me, and knowing the truth, your lordship said it was too little, and most gently offered to speak to the king for me" (*Whole Works,* 1:412). The fact is that the annuity was quite handsome—a full 25 percent of the annuity accompanying a Regius professorship—and that it marked the beginning of Ascham's royal preferment as tutor to Elizabeth, as secretary to the ambassador to Charles V, and as Latin secretary under both Mary and Elizabeth. Clearly Ascham's efforts in *Toxophilus*—his self-consciousness, his art, and his irony—brought him financial reward and professional advancement. He did indeed hit the mark.

Notes

1. *The Works of Francis Bacon,* ed. James Spedding, R. L. Ellis, and D. D. Heath, 7 vols. (London: Longmans, 1859), 3:283–84.

2. George Krapp, *The Rise of English Literary Prose* (Oxford: Oxford University Press, 1915), 292–99; George Williamson, *The Senecan Amble: A Study in Prose Form from Bacon to Collier* (Chicago: University of Chicago Press, 1951), 74–75; Alvin Vos, "The Formation of Roger Ascham's Prose Style," *Studies in Philology* 71 (Fall 1974): 344–70; "Form and Function in Roger Ascham's Prose," *Philological Quarterly* 55 (July

1976): 5–18; Janel Mueller, *The Native Tongue and the Word: Developments in English Prose Style* (Chicago: University of Chicago Press, 1984), 322–46; Lawrence V. Ryan, *Roger Ascham* (Stanford, Calif.: Stanford University Press, 1963), 49–81; Thomas Greene, "Roger Ascham: The Perfect End of Shooting," *English Literary History* 36 (December 1969): 609–25; and K. J. Wilson, "Ascham's *Toxophilus* and the Rules of Art," *Renaissance Quarterly* 29 (Winter 1976): 30–51.

3. Ryan, *Roger Ascham,* 71. Vos remarks that nearly "all modern students of Renaissance prose have been of a divided mind concerning Roger Ascham's style" ("Form and Function," 305).

4. Ascham's letters appear in *The Whole Works of Roger Ascham,* ed. J. A. Giles, 3 vols. in 4 (London: John Russell Smith, 1864–65); hereafter cited as *Whole Works*. The publication of *Toxophilus* and its presentation to Henry are discussed below in section VI.

5. *Whole Works,* 1:20–21.

6. The offending passage concerns Paul's direction to Titus that he select as elder or bishop a suitable man who was among other things the "husband of one wife" (Titus 1:6). Reference to the fact of married clergy in the early Church and observation of opposition to marriage as heretical struck one as conservative as Lee as controversial (*Whole Works,* 1:43–45).

7. See Ryan, *Roger Ascham,* 26, 82–83, and Alfred Fairbank and Bruce Dickens, *The Italic Hand in Tudor Cambridge* (Cambridge: Cambridge University Press, 1962), 7–8, 11–12. Tradition holds that Ascham was especially admired for his penmanship by his humanist brethren; see illustration (page 47). In his *Life of Sir John Cheke* (London, 1705), John Strype writes of Cheke's excellence in this regard: "Add this . . . that he brought in fair and graceful Writing by the Pen, as he wrote an excellent accurate hand himself. And all the best Scholars in those times practised to write well. So did Smith and Cecyl, and especially Ascham; who, by his exquisite Hand, was the Person appointed to teach the Lady Elizabeth to Write. So that fair Writing and good Learning seemed to commence together" (45).

8. Oxford, Bodleian Library, MS Rawlinson D.1317 and Cambridge, St. John's College, MS L.3.

9. Cambridge, St. John's College, MS L.3 fol. x.

10. See James Bass Mullinger, *The University of Cambridge from the Earliest Times to the Royal Injunctions of 1535,* 2 vols. (Cambridge: Cambridge University Press, 1873), 2:43 n. 3. Compare Ryan, *Roger Ascham,* 301.

11. See Franklin Williams, *Index of Dedications and Commendatory Verses in English Books Before 1641* (London: Bibliographical Society, 1962), 92–93.

12. Roger Ascham, *English Works: Toxophilus, [The] Report of the Affaires and State of Germany, The Scholemaster,* ed. William Aldis Wright (Cambridge: Cambridge University Press, 1904), x. All quotations of these works come from this edition and are noted parenthetically.

13. Ryan sees Ascham's concern to justify himself to his Cambridge colleagues as the prime reason for writing *Toxophilus* (*Roger Ascham,* 52–53).

14. The name *Toxophilus* comes from τόξον (bow) and φίλος (lover). The Greek phrase Ascham incorporates in the letter quoted above, τῷ τοξεύειν ἐκτετοξεῦσθαι (by shooting wasted), is adapted from a parenthetical, participial phrase in Aristophanes' *Plutus:* τὸ ἐμὸν μὲν αὐτοῦ τοῦ ταλαιπώρου σχεδὸν / ἤδη νομίζων ἐκτετοξεῦσθαι βίον (thinking not for myself, having already had the quiver of life shot away) (34–35).

15. Ascham points to the inclusive English audience he is aiming at by the prefatory epistles: the first addressed to the "most graciouse . . . Kyng Henrie the viii," the

second to "ALL GENTLE MEN AND YOMEN OF ENGLAND." The same inclusiveness receives visual expression in the frontispiece (see illustration on page 46 and discussion on page 45).

16. Ascham's German colleague, Johannes Sturm, insisted on the study of rhetoric, on practice in style and imitation, and in training in dialectic. He regarded dialectic and rhetoric as inseparable in the matter of *inventio,* the devising of an argument appropriate to the subject at hand. See *De Amissa Dicendi Ratione* (Strasbourg, 1543), fols. 17, 33v. Compare Ryan, *Roger Ascham,* 60–61.

17. C. S. Lewis, *English Literature in the Sixteenth Century Excluding Drama* (1953; reprint, Oxford: Oxford University Press, 1963), 281.

18. See R. F. Jones, *The Triumph of the English Language: A Survey of Opinions Concerning the Vernacular from the Introduction of Printing to the Restoration* (Stanford, Calif.: Stanford University Press, 1953), 3–31, 68–142.

19. Book A has five major digressions: on music training in the schools, 12–16; on gambling, 21–29; on John Cheke, 45–46; on the Turkish threat to Christian Europe, 48–50; and on an appeal for union of Scotland and England, 51–53. Book B has two rather shorter digressions: on Sir Humphrey Wingfield, 97; and on poor judgment of parents in sending their sons to university, 109–11. These parts of the treatise may be read as developments of various points apposite to the overall argument, of course, and not as digressions in the strict sense of the word. See Ryan, *Roger Ascham,* 51–52, for one such reading.

20. Pages 9, 10, 12, 19, 21, 31–32, 39, 55, 56, 58, and 62.

21. Ryan points out that the student-teacher dialogue appeared widely in the Middle Ages and the Renaissance for instruction of mechanical as well as liberal arts. See *Roger Ascham,* 76 nn. 64, 65.

22. In fact the second part of the table of contents, "A Table conteyning the seconde booke" (xx) is presented as a scheme containing the topics outlined in the first paragraph on 69–70.

23. The suggestion of scholarly apparatus appears in other ways. Passages from Chaucer are quoted and then single lines and half lines are quoted again for particular comment, much in the fashion of learned commentaries ordinarily appearing in discussions of classical texts and Scripture (25–27). Similarly, at one stage (35–39), Philologus cites a series of five texts from classical authors against Toxophilus. This is very much in the vein of the formal disquisition in which prooftexts are adduced by one controversialist and responded to by his opponent.

24. See Thomas Wilson, *The Art of Rhetoric (1560),* ed. Peter E. Medine (University Park: Pennsylvania State University Press, 1994), 55 and notes.

25. Most often Toxophilus prevails in his arguments against Philologus and seems to represent something like a normative voice, though plainly not at this point. The treatise is a dialogue, and we should not expect a perfectly consistent identification of the persona Toxophilus with Ascham. In the nostalgic recollections of Sir Humphrey Wingfield and John Cheke, however, the connection between Toxophilus and Ascham is inescapable.

A remarkably explicit statement of Ascham's understanding of the use of personae and fiction occurs on page 28, where the author has Toxophilus answer Philologus's suspicion that he must have gambled a good deal himself in order to know so much about the vice. Toxophilus says: "Thynges be knowen dyuerse wayes. . . . And then shulde Homer haue bene the best capitayne, moost cowarde, hardye, hasty, wyse and woode, sage and simple." Nevertheless in *The Scholemaster* Ascham refers to a "book of the Cockpit" that he is writing or going to write (217). Camden reports that "since he [Ascham] was overly given to dice and cockfighting, he lived and died in poverty" (*Annales Rerum Anglicarum, et Hibernicarum, Regnante Elizabetha* [London, 1615], 150).

26. Parataxis is contrasted with syntaxis or hypotaxis, syntactical structuring that depends on subordination. Classic studies of English syntax that take into account this distinction include Leon Kellner, *Historical Outlines of English Syntax* (London and New York: Macmillan, 1892), secs. 97–99 and George O. Curme, *Syntax* (Boston: D. C. Heath, 1931), 28–30, 89, 176. A recent reevaluation of this approach appears in Mueller, *Native Tongue*, 1–40.

27. Of the sentences in *Toxophilus*, 54.1 percent exhibit parataxis. I count those sentences as paratactic which: (1) begin with *and, but, yet, or, for,* or *therefore;* and/or (2) display internal coordination.

28. G. Gregory Smith, ed., *Elizabethan Critical Essays*, 2 vols. (Oxford: Oxford University Press, 1904), 2:277.

29. See Vos, "Formation of Roger Ascham's Prose Style," for a thorough review of the question of Ascham's style as Isocratean or Ciceronian.

30. See also *De or.* 3.177 and cf. 3.210–11. Frequently commentators would assert a rigidly—and distinctly un-Ciceronian—principle of decorum whereby a work would exhibit one and only one style. See Wilson, *Art of Rhetoric*, 195/9–12 and accompanying note.

31. Categories or "levels" of style are always problematic. These groupings resemble the three levels posited in the Ciceronian tradition, from the *Rhetorica ad Herennium* to Quintilian: low, middle, and high. Sensitive rhetoricians—like Cicero himself—recognize the arbitrariness and artificiality of the scheme; it nevertheless served to organize discussions of style for over a millennium and a half. See Wilson, *Art of Rhetoric*, 195/3–4 and accompanying note.

32. Ryan, *Roger Ascham*, 59.

33. Surviving letters record that Ascham sent inscribed presentation copies of *Toxophilus* to the Prince of Wales; William Parr, brother to Queen Catherine and the earl of Essex; Thomas Wriothesley, the lord chancellor; Sir Anthony Denny; Bishops Day, Gardiner, and Nicholas Heath; and probably Cranmer, Paget, and Barnaby Fitzpatrick, Prince Edward's young companion (*Whole Works*, 1:77–83, 84–85). Edward's copy, with the prince's own signature and in the original binding, is now in the Pierpont Morgan Library (PM 20522); Parr's, along with Ascham's autograph dedication, is in the Folger Shakespeare Library (STC 837 c2)—see illustration on page 47; Wriothesley's with two leaves of Ascham's autograph dedication is in the Cambridge University Library (Pet.A.2.37).

Eulogies to Elegies: Poetic Distance in the April Eclogue

RICHARD C. McCOY

I.

S. K. HENINGER Jr. begins his massive study of Sir Philip Sidney and Edmund Spenser in "Leicester House, 1579-80," which refers to the London home of Sidney's powerful uncle, Robert Dudley.[1] Firmly grounded in this specific space and time, Heninger speculates with characteristic caution about the site and significance of the "Areopagus" conjured up in the correspondence of Spenser and his friend, Gabriel Harvey. Heninger concludes that the "Areopagus" was probably neither a real place nor group but rather "a product of Spenser's and Harvey's high-spirited joking, most likely a pipedream of the over-confident Harvey." He also casts doubt on a close connection between Spenser and Sidney even while arguing for the latter's powerful intellectual and poetic influence.[2]

Heninger's informed restraint is exemplary, but the mysteries surrounding the beginning of Spenser's career continue to tantalize. Questions persist about Spenser's relationship with his peers and patrons, and the larger question of the place of poetry and the poet remains. If neither Spenser nor his verse found a home in Leicester House and if the Areopagus is a fantasy, then how does the poet answer the question posed in *The Shepheardes Calender*'s October eclogue: "O pierlesse Poesye, where is then thy place?" His inaugural work provides some of the answers, but they are typically enigmatic. Sobered by Heninger's skepticism, I wish to reconsider the enigmas of Spenser's early work and career, returning to some basic questions about the place of poetry in Spenser's time.[3]

The tone of the correspondence between these "two universitie men" on the make is notoriously unclear: intimate and inscrutable, apprehensive and presumptuous, jocular and rhapsodic.[4] Spenser first describes the Areopagus as the creation of Sidney and Dyer; it is a poetic regime from which "balde

Rymers" are banished and in which a revival of quantitative metrics is imposed by fiat. He admits with all due modesty to "some use of familiarity" with these two illustrious men and declares himself "drawen more to their faction."[5] Harvey responds by proclaiming that "your new-founded *Areion pagon* I honoure more, than you will or can suppose: and make greater accompte of the twoo worthy Gentlemenne, than of two hundreth *Dionisii Areopagitae*, or the verye notablest Senatours, that euer *Athens* dydde affourde of that number" (*Poetical Works*, 639). While acknowledging that "no one has known quite what to make of the Areopagus," Richard Helgerson reminds us how seriously experiments in quantitative verse were taken by a large number of contemporary poets.[6] Moreover, he discerns in Spenser's desire to "have the kingdom of our own language" an ambitious attempt to reshape English culture and "the forms of nationhood."[7] From this perspective, the Areopagus takes on the contours of a quasi-autonomous poetic domain, in which, in the words of Harvey's extravagant "Encomium Lauri," a "Poet of right stampe, ouerawith th'Emperour himselfe" (*Poetical Works*, 625).[8]

Nevertheless, the letters express considerable skepticism toward poetry's more grandiose aspirations. Harvey questions the wisdom of letting "our Pen and Inke, and Time, and Wit, and all runneth away in this goodly yonkerly [i.e., youthful] veine" (629). Indeed, in the last of the "Three Proper and Wittie Familiar Letters," Harvey contrasts Spenser's lofty ideas with his own more practical plans, declaring his determination to pursue "those studies and practyzes, that carrie as they saye, meate in their mouth" (628). He teases Spenser by citing two stanzas of that "perfecte paterne of a Poete," Cuddie, "*alias* you know who," as Cuddie complains about the "little good . . . and much lesse gayne" that poetry has brought him (628). At the same time, Harvey archly professes admiration for another one of *The Shepheardes Calender*'s authorial surrogates by declaring that "Master *Collin Cloute* is not euery body" (628). Harvey acknowledges his friend's singularity and distinction from his peers while implying that his devotion to "Mistress Poetrie" and hopes for the rewards she will bestow on him are a bit foolish if not mad: "[H]e peraduenture, by the meanes of hir speciall fauour, and some personall priviledge, may happely liue by *dying Pellicanes*, and purchase great landes, and Lordeshippes, with the money, which his *Calender* and *Dreames* haue, and will affourde him" (628). Harvey continues "*extra iocum*" to concede that he "like[s] "your *Dreames* passingly well" for their inventive and "*Hyperbolicall Amplifications*," but he still maintains that there can be no "semblaunce of Comparison . . . betweene the incomprehensible Wisedome of God, and the sensible Wit of Man" (628). To deflate Spenser's visionary aspirations, Harvey here deploys Sidney's distinction between genuinely "vatic" or inspired verse and that which is man-made. Threatening to say "I told you so," he invidiously contrasts Spenser's favorite undertaking with a properly classical "lost" work: "If so be the *Faerye*

Queene be fairer in your eie than the *Nine Muses*, and *Hobgoblin* runne away with the Garland from *Apollo*: Marke what I say, and yet I will not say that I thought, but there an End for this once, and fare you well, till God or some good Aungell putte you in a better minde" (628). In Harvey's view, Mistress Poetry becomes as fantastic a figure as the Faerie Queene. Those who pin their hopes on either one may end up looking as credulous as Dapper in Ben Jonson's *Alchemist,* who is tricked into believing that his fairy aunt will "leave him three or four hundred chests of treasure,/ And some twelve thousand acres of Faery land."[9]

Harvey's own determined efforts to restrict himself to "practyzes, that carrie as they saye, meate in their mouth" prompted him to dance attendance on the real queen and her most powerful courtiers; no fantasies of Mistress Poetry or the Faerie Queene for him. In 1578, he composed a collection of Latin verses in honor of Elizabeth's visit to Audley End, entitled the *Gratulationes Valdinenses*, and he presented it to her in person. It included praise for several prominent figures, including Dudley, Oxford, Hatton, and Sidney. Unfortunately, he also used the work to proclaim the eligibility of his patron, the earl of Leicester, for marriage to the queen, and his publication of these verses subsequently embarrassed him when the earl's secret marriage to Lettice Knollys came to light the next year.[10] His poetic efforts came to grief, and his performance during the royal progress made him the object of Thomas Nashe's ridicule many years later.[11] Harvey's embarrassment was one of the occupational hazards, as I have suggested elsewhere, of those who applied their creative efforts to courtly spectacle and intrigue.[12]

Spenser initially seemed ready to risk these hazards as he sought the patronage of these same powerful figures. Throughout their correspondence, the younger poet abjectly acknowledges Harvey as his superior in age and wisdom. Spenser professes his own determination to emulate as far as possible the works of his mentor while admitting his own limited capacity to do so, signing these letters with the same nom de plume employed in *The Shepheardes Calender*: "Immerito." In a postscript to one, Spenser describes one of his most intriguing "lost" works: "Of my *Stemmata Dudleiana*, and especially of the sundry Apostrophes therein, addressed you knowe to whome, must more aduisement be had, than so lightly to sende them abroade: howbeit, trust me (though I doe neuer very well,) yet in my owne fancie, I never dyd better: *Veruntamen te sequor solum: numquam vero assequar*" [Nevertheless, I shall follow only you, but I shall never overtake you] (*PoeticalWorks*, 612). As its title indicates, the *Stemmata Dudleiana* was probably a genealogical encomium of the earl of Leicester, modeled, by his own account, on Harvey's *Gratulationes Valdinenses*. Spenser is worried about even naming the recipient, much less publishing it, but Harvey urges him to get on with it. In his response, Harvey makes his own preference for such works and their practical value clear, saying that the *Nine Muses* and the *Stemmata Dudleiana* "shal go for my money when all is done: especiallye if you would but bestow one seuennights pollishing and trimming vppon eyther. Whiche I praye thee hartily doe, for my pleasure, if not for their sake, nor thine owne profite" (*Poetical Works*, 620).

Despite his declared resolve to emulate Harvey and Harvey's own encouragement of this course, Spenser never published the *Stemmata Dudleiana*. The tone of his description has led some scholars to conclude that the work was never printed because he was finally too nervous about the consequences. Josephine Waters Bennett says in her gloss of this passage that "pedigrees setting forth claims to royal blood, however remote, were always dangerous in the Tudor period. Leicester was already under a cloud for having married the Queen's second cousin. . . . We know that in 1580 Leicester was interested in his ancestry, perhaps because he hoped for an heir, but he would certainly object to the publication of a genealogy of the Dudleys because it would be certain to arouse jealousy and resentment."[13] Yet Leicester subsidized a small army of heralds and poets to tone up his pedigree, and his protégés obliged him with some fantastic creations. Robert Cooke, the Clarenceux herald, traced Dudley back to the legendary Guy of Warwick, and George Ferrers, a lawyer at Lincoln's Inn and one of the authors of the *Mirror for Magistrates*, traced him back to King Arthur.[14] For a writer seeking Leicester's patronage, this was one of the main roads to favor and advancement, and Spenser's fascination with Arthurian genealogy could have readily lent itself to such an enterprise.[15] The other route was courtly entertainment staged on the earl's behalf, and that was the means embraced by many members of the Areopagus, including Harvey, Dyer, and the esteemed Sir Philip Sidney. Dyer composed his "Song of the Oak" for Sir Henry Lee's Woodstock entertainment in 1575, and the earl's noble nephew devised the *Lady of May* as an entertainment for the queen at his uncle's Wanstead estate in 1578.[16] During his own brief residence at Leicester House from 1579 to 1580, Spenser declined to take either route, allowing the *Stemmata Dudleiana* to vanish without a trace while contributing nothing to courtly pageantry sponsored by the earl.

Instead he published *The Shepheardes Calender*, dedicating it, after some hesitation, to Sir Philip Sidney rather than Leicester. With this work as well, the same anxieties about patronage intrude on the correspondence. Indeed, Spenser advertises his ambivalence about both the work and its audience in another letter to Harvey. He says that he "was minded for a while to haue intermitted the vttering [i.e., publication] of my writings: leaste by ouer-much cloying their noble eares, I should gather a contempt of my self, or else seeme rather for gaine and commoditie to doe it, for some sweetnesse that I haue already tasted. Then also me seemeth the work too base for his excellent Lordship"

(*Poetical Works*, 635). Spenser solicits his friend's advice by asking him "to call [his] wits, and senses togither, (which are alwaies at call) when occasion is so fairely offered of Estimation and Preferment. For, whiles the yron is hote, it is good striking, and minds of Nobles varie, as their Estates" (635). Even as he praises Harvey's sharp eye for the main chance, he recognizes that the favor of the great is no less precarious than their fortunes. And, once again, despite his deference to his friend's alacrity in grasping an occasion, Spenser finally declines to follow in Harvey's footsteps. Harvey was later mocked by Nashe for his tendency to "thrust himselfe into the thickest rankes of the Noblemen and Gallants, and whatsoever they were arguing of, he would not misse to catch hold of."[17] Spenser, by contrast, seems more inclined to draw back from such encounters, "leaste by ouer-much cloying their noble eares, I should gather a contempt of my self."

Spenser's skittish withdrawal from the ranks of the nobility and their ceremonial occasions offering "Estimation and Preferment" is perhaps his most telling gesture. The contrast with another poet who aspired to laureate status is striking. Ben Jonson was handsomely rewarded for composing masques for courtly entertainment, but he still insisted that, "though their voice be taught to sound to present occasions, their sense or doth or should always lay hold on more removed mysteries."[18] Spenser detaches his own verses from "present occasions" more resolutely and completely than Ben Jonson ever did. Indeed, he clearly defines detachment as his general poetic strategy in his "Letter to Ralegh" when he declares his determination to place *The Faerie Queene* "furthest from the daunger of enuy, and suspition of present time" (*Poetical Works*, 407).

II

Spenser's April eclogue is especially fascinating because the pressures of "present occasion" manifestly encroach upon it. Several critics have noted its general resemblance to court pageantry in its flattery of the queen; as the Argument explicitly indicates, "this Aeglogue is purposely intended to the honor and prayse of our most gracious souereigne" (*Poetical Works*, 431).[19] However, the poem involves much more than simple compliment. In a series of influential articles, Louis Adrian Montrose has explored the complex political maneuvers at work in the April eclogue. As he explains, the "rhetoric of royal encomium provides . . . a purified medium for the pursuit of socio-economic advancement. The Elizabeth cult can serve the personal aesthetic and material ends of her worshippers."[20] He develops this argument further in "The Elizabethan Subject and the Spenserian Text," contending that by publishing *The Shepheardes Calender* "as a *book*," Spenser attains a degree of authorial autonomy allowing "an interplay between submission and resistance to the project of royal celebration which ostensibly defines it."[21]

At the same time, the April eclogue may be inspired by motives more provocative than self-promotion, since it bears the marks of topical controversy and factional intrigue. Spenser may have been working on his patrons' behalf as well as his own. In *Pastoral and Ideology*, Annabel Patterson places the publication of *The Shepheardes Calender* amid the fierce conflict over the marriage negotiations with Alençon, Elizabeth's French suitor. John Stubbs lost his hand and Sir Philip Sidney lost the favor of the queen for writing against the match, but, as Patterson points out, *The Shepheardes Calender* was printed by Hugh Singleton, printer of Stubbs's tract, and was dedicated to Sidney, suggesting an alignment with the opposition. Nevertheless, Spenser's own opposition was particularly subtle, oscillating "between the poetics of accommodation and the poetics of dissent."[22] David Norbrook shows how the April eclogue's innovative celebration of the queen's virginity subtly advanced the altered agenda of Leicester and Sidney, now that Leicester was no longer a candidate for marriage.[23] Up to 1579, courtly entertainments such as George Gascoigne's masque of Zabeta, Sidney's *Lady of May*, and Harvey's *Gratulationes Valdinenses* urged the queen to settle the succession by marriage, preferably to Leicester. After that date, with Leicester out of the running and a hated French heretic as a prospective consort, her courtiers found royal chastity increasingly praiseworthy, and this became the keynote for her annual Accession Day tilts and other spectacles during the remainder of her days. As Susan Frye has shown in her study of Elizabeth, the "queen's virginity" was indeed "'a powerful political weapon' . . . [but] it was a weapon not always in Elizabeth's hands."[24] Moreover, as Frye shows, representations of the queen served the competing interests of Elizabeth and her subjects, and Spenser was particularly adroit at defining chastity on his own terms.[25]

In the April eclogue, Spenser not only touches on the complex sexual politics of the cult of Elizabeth, but he also evokes the courtly "practyzes" pursued with so little success by his mentor, Gabriel Harvey—specifically, genealogical encomium and poetic prestation. Colin Clout's "laye / Of fayre Eliza" (*Aprill*, lines 33–34) begins with a kind of mythopoetic Tudor *stemma*, praising Elizabeth's illustrious ancestors, and, after orchestrating a gathering of muses and graces, nymphs and maidens reminiscent of courtly pageantry, it concludes with an exchange of gifts and gratitude: "Let dame Eliza thanke you for her song" (*Aprill*, line 150). Harvey's own personal presentation of his *Gratulationes Valdinenses* to the queen during her "progresse at Audley in Essex" is recalled in the gloss of "September" which also explicitly identifies him as the shepherd, Hobbinoll (*Poetical Works*, 455).

Nevertheless, Spenser persists in a pattern of evasion and withdrawal throughout the eclogues. In the April eclogue, Colin is jilted by Rosalind and abandons his friend Hobbinol, complaining of his "great misaduenture in Loue, whereby his mynd was alienate and with drawen not onely from him, who moste loued him, but also from all former delightes and studies, . . . and other his laudable exercises" (431). Colin's role as courtly celebrant is renounced but taken over by Hobbinol, who declares, "[T]hen will I sing his laye / Of fayre *Eliza*, Queene of shepheardes all" (*Aprill*, lines 33–34). Elsewhere, E.K.'s notoriously cryptic commentary hedges on the identity of Colin Clout by refusing to name names, but he shows no such reluctance in the case of his friend: "Nowe I thinke no man doubteth but by Colin is euer meante the Author selfe. Whose especiall good freend Hobbinoll sayth he is, or more rightly Mayster Gabriel Haruey" (*Poetical Works*, 455). Hobbinol/Harvey is further "outed" in the gloss of "Januarye," which imputes to him the "sauour of disorderly loue, which the learned call paederastice" (422–23). Richard Rambuss suggests that "Spenser seems to be disowning Harvey by opening up the secret of Hobbinol" on several fronts while slyly displacing both his "career (and erotic?) ambitions" onto his "especiall good freend."[26] As Rambuss demonstrates, Spenser uses the manipulation of secrets both as a "strategy of self-promotion" and a means of keeping "his distance from aristocratic and royal power."[27]

Spenser is playing a very complicated game in *The Shepheardes Calender*, one which allows him an advantage over those more directly engaged in courtly entertainment and intrigue. He carefully detaches his praise from historical circumstance and from actual performance, thus avoiding the risks associated with both. Colin's "laye / Of fayre Elisa, Queen of shepheardes all" is an imaginary apostrophe for an encounter that never happens. It is composed by a fictional persona who is no longer there, and then it is sung by another in his absence. Eliza is said to be "in place" (line 131), but the poem is a virtuoso exercise in elegiac displacement. Despite its elaborate praise for the queen, the April eclogue embraces a strategy prescribed with a certain bitter urgency in *The Tears of the Muses*. That much darker poem attacks those "mightie Peeres" who

> onely striue themselues to raise
> Through pompous pride, and foolish vanitie;
> In th'eyes of people they put all their praise,
> And onely boast of Armes and Auncestrie.
> (*The Tears of the Muses,* lines 91–94)

As I have noted elsewhere, these are the same complaints made in the October eclogue, but there they are aimed explicitly at the stars of the cult of Elizabeth.[28] When Cuddie is encouraged to praise both the queen and Leicester, "the worthy whome shee loueth best" (*October*, line 46), he refuses, insisting that "Mecaenas is yclad in claye" (line 61) and "mighty manhode brought a bedde of ease" (line 68). In both passages, the feelings of anger as well as fear lurking behind Spenser's apprehensions about patronage are manifest. He contends that the "mightie Peeres" of his own day provide neither support nor inspiration sufficient to sustain heroic poetry. Later in *The Tears of the Muses*, Erato, the muse of erotic poetry, prescribes a generic solution for dealing with such disappointments, urging lovers to "change [their] praises into piteous cries, / And Eulogies turne into Elegies (*The Tears of the Muses,* lines 371–72).

In the April eclogue, a similar strategy is employed. Disappointed in love, Colin becomes "alienate and with drawen" from all his formerly "laudable exercises"; in Spenser's time, the adjective meant laudatory as well as praiseworthy. His former praises of Eliza are recorded by Hobbinol, but the idealizing direct address of courtly eulogy becomes an elegiac recollection of lost harmony. Praise is now framed and replaced by "piteous cries" for Rosalind. Indeed, "Eulogies turne into Elegies" throughout *The Shepheardes Calender* as Colin continues his complaints. Jeffrey Knapp traces this same tendency in the move from the April eclogue to the November eclogue. The latter eclogue's lament for Dido suggests "Colin's new preference for elegy . . . [and] the passing of his interest in paeans to Elisa," but, in fact, that preference was already manifest in the April eclogue as well, where "not only Colin's abandonment of the song but also Hobbinol's elegiac rendition of it break the fullness of relation, the perfect fit, that once obtained among poet, queen and countryside."[29] Colin delivers the same message as Erato, urging others to cease their songs of love and turn their elegies to eulogies:

> Sing now ye shepheards daughters, sing no moe
> The songs that Colin made in her prayse,
> But into weeping turn your wanton layes.
> (*November*, lines 77–79)

This particular poetic recourse has been described by Peter Sacks as the "elegiac strategy."[30] He sees it as a literary defense against rage, disappointment, and loss. The beloved object is necessarily relinquished to the past, even to death, but then recovered in a sublimated and symbolic form. In the April eclogue, rather than addressing the queen directly and appealing immediately for her support, Spenser places both her person and his verse at a great spatial and temporal distance, and the tactics establishing this distance are discernible in each section of the poem.

Before the eclogue even begins, it betrays anxieties about even naming, much less addressing, the queen. The fears resemble those expressed in Spenser's letters about other "sundry Apostrophes therein, addressed you knowe to whome" (*Poetical Works*, 612). The Argument admits that Colin's lay was "sometime made in honor of her Maiestie, whom abruptely he termeth Elysa" (431). By abbreviating Elizabeth to Elysa, the poet "abruptely" nicks off a portion of her name. The presumptuous familiarity of such a nick-name arouses additional anxieties in E.K.'s gloss of this eclogue: "In all this songe is not to be respected, what the worthinesse of her Maiestie deserueth, nor what to the highnes of a prince is agreeable, but what is moste comely for the meanesse of a shepheards witte, or to conceiue, or to utter. And therefor he calleth her Elysa, as through rudenesse, tripping in her name: and a shepheards daughter, it being very vnfitt, that a shepheards boy brought vp in the shepefold, should know, or euer seme to haue heard of a Queenes roialty" (433). What Angus Fletcher has termed the "taboo of the ruler" entails some of the same strictures as taboos of the Deity: thou shalt not take the name of the queen in vain.[31] This skittishness about naming the queen is typical of Spenser and part of a larger pattern pervading all his work, most notably *The Faerie Queene*. Elizabeth Bellamy traces "the poet's unsuccessful effort to nominate Elizabeth," and she attributes the failure to Spenser's predilection for allegory, a genre whose remoteness from literal reality ensures "the absence of Elizabeth-as-presence."[32] However, rather than seeing his reluctance to name the queen as a failure, I see it as the secret of his success. Allegory, like elegy, is embraced because it has the advantage of being "furthest from . . . present time" (*Poetical Works*, 407), and its fragmentary reflections avoid the perils of a direct encounter.

The royal *stemma* near the start of Colin's lay persists in this pattern of evasion, literally glossing over the more embarrassing aspects of Elizabeth's family history. In actuality, the queen's origins were a source of scandal and peril. Her mother's fall from favor threatened the infant Elizabeth with the stain of illegitimacy and the loss of the throne, but in Spenser's account, Anne Boleyn is effaced by allusion to the myth of Pan and Syrinx. The latter union was, of course, unconsummated, as several commentators have remarked, and this makes Elizabeth the offspring of an immaculate conception.[33]

For shee is Syrinx daughter without spotte
Which Pan the shepheards God of her begot
    So sprong her grace
Of heavenly race,
No mortall blemishe may her blotte.

(*Aprill*, lines 50–54)

As Peter Sacks points out, the tale of Pan and Syrinx stands as the etiological myth at the heart of the "elegiac strategy." Pan loves and pursues Syrinx, but the maiden eludes his grasp by changing into river reeds. In Ovid's account, Pan plucks the reeds and makes them into panpipes through which his sighs resonate, "and charmed by the sweet tones, the god exclaimed: 'This union at least, shall I have with thee.'"[34] The tale is an exemplum of successful mourning and creative sublimation, the primal instance of turning eulogies to elegies. Moreover, Spenser adapts the myth, as Louis Montrose has shown, to make Elizabeth into his subject in both senses of the term: begot of the shepherd's pipe, she is transformed into poetry and the poem itself.[35] In the process, she becomes the indulgent "Mistress Poetrie" described in Harvey's mocking letter whose "speciall fauour" will allow him to prosper and "purchase great landes, and Lordeshippes."

As for the historical details of Elizabeth's genealogy, these are neatly skirted by this mythopoetic metamorphosis. Palgrave remarks on the potential bad taste of a "genealogy which speaks of Henry VIII as Pan, [and] of Anne Boleyn as Syrinx," but the commentary calls attention to "the most famous and victorious King, her highnesse Father, late of worthy memorye K. Henry the eyght" (*Poetical Works*, 434) while delicately avoiding any reference to her mother.[36] The poem's Petrarchan mixture of the "Redde rose medled with the White yfere, / In either cheeke" is duly glossed as a tribute to "the vniting of the two principall houses of Lancaster and of Yorke: by whose longe discord and deadly debate, this realm many yeares was sore traueiled, and almost cleane decayed. Til the famous Henry the seuenth, of the line of Lancaster, taking to wife the most vertuous Princesse Elisabeth, daughter to the fourth Edward of the house of Yorke, begat the most royal Henry the eyght aforesayde, in whom was the firste vnion of the Whyte Rose and the redde" (434). Scandal is evaded in the poetry by an account that remains at the level of the mythopoetic and symbolic. The factual details and conspicuous omissions unavoidable in a real genealogy are restricted to the commentary.

Spenser deploys the conventions of court pageantry in a similarly detached fashion. Several details recall the circumstances of Leicester's elaborate Kenilworth entertainment while avoiding the tensions surrounding them. The Muses play and sing to Eliza and the Graces dance around her, transforming her into "a grace, / To fyll the fourth place / And reigne with the rest in heaven" (*Aprill*, lines 115–17) in a carefully choreographed and hierarchical assembly of mythic and pastoral figures. The nymphs who follow are described as "Ladyes of the lake . . . / That unto her goe" (lines 120–21). The choreography descends from the lofty heights of classical myth to the more homely terrain of Arthurian legend, provoking E.K.'s outburst against "certain fine fablers and lowd lyers such as were the authors of King Arthur" (*Poetical Works*, 434). This descent also brings the poem closer to English earth in another sense, since the Lady of the Lake recalls the company who greeted the queen upon her arrival at Kenilworth castle. There too, according to "Robert Langham's *Letter*,"

> the Lady of the Lake (famous in King Arthurz book) with too Nymphes wayting upon her, arrayed all in sylks, attending her highnes comming . . . met her Maiesty with a wel penned meter and matter after this sorte: First of the auncientee of the

> Castl, whoo had been ownerz of the same, een till this day, most allweyz in the handes of the Earls of Leyceter, hoow she had kept this Lake syns king Arthurz dayz, and noow understanding of her highnes hither cumming, thought it both offis and duety in humbl wyse too discoover her and her estate: offring up the same, her Lake and poour thearin, with promis of repair unto the Coourt.[37]

The queen's tart response to this grand display of magnanimity on Dudley's part deflated these effusions, according to Langham's comical account: "[W]e had thought indeed the Lake had been oours, and doo you call it yourz noow? Well we wyll heerin common more with yoo hereafter."[38] She thus reminded everyone listening that her host was her dependent and his "gift" was already hers. In this instance, the magnanimous gestures of ritual gift-giving or prestation failed to finesse tensions over property and parity.[39]

The humble "shepheards daughters," the last and lowliest to assemble in response to Colin's song, echo another of Kenilworth's varied entertainments, but here concerns about propriety rather than property intrude. Colin orders around these lowly country lasses more forcefully than any of the others, and he is particularly insistent on maintaining sexual as well social decorum:

> Let none come there, but that Virgins bene,
> To adorne her grace.
> And when you come, whereas shee is in place,
> See, that your rudenesse does not you disgrace:
> Binde your fillets faste,
> And gird in your waste,
> For more finesse, with a tawdrie lace.
>
> (lines 129–35)

The stanza reveals some of the same sexual and social tensions as Shakespeare's comic encounters between court and country, but they remain more muted here. In *The Winter's Tale*, the merriment of the shepherds' festival with its promise of "tawdry lace" and other trifles is shattered by a ruler who asserts the incompatibility of humble pleasures and sovereignty. "Tawdry lace" is an artifact symbolic of these tensions between high and humble. It was sold at fairs on the feast of St. Audrey or Ethelrida, an Anglo-Saxon princess whose throat tumor prompted her to repent of her own bejeweled ostentation. The cheaper, cloth necklaces named for the dead saint and favored by country lasses were a way of simultaneously warding off and defying such a punishment because they were humbler yet showy. The word's etymological development indicates this ambiguity as it came to mean gaudy, cheap, and meretricious in the course of the seventeenth century.

As the "shepheards daughters" gather around their queen, bearing their floral tributes, Colin seems to worry that their gifts may prove tawdry in the later sense, and he fears that their "rudeness" may bring "disgrace." Such offerings as the "Sops in wine, / worne of Paramours" (lines 138–39) recall the toasting and drinking, as the *Variorum* notes, of a traditional wedding feast.[40] At Kenilworth, Elizabeth was also entertained by a rustic "Brydale," and Langham's *Letter* emphasizes the coarse comedy of this particular show. The wedding procession is led by "three prety puzels [i.e., maids]" bearing cakes before the bride, but "the woorshipful Bride" is described as "a stale stallion [courtesan] and a well spreed [i.e., well-bedecked] (hot as the weather waz) God wot and an ill smellyng waz she: a xxxv. yeer old, of cooler brounbay, not very beautifull indeed but ugly fooul ill favord: yet marveloous fayn of the offis, bycauz she hard say she shoold dauns before the queen, in which feat she thought she woold foote it as finely az the best."[41] Noting that this ridiculous figure is actually younger than Elizabeth, Susan Frye reads this as yet another insulting travesty of the marriage question of the sort that Leicester periodically dared to stage; an earlier pageant "on the question of marriage" prompted Elizabeth to complain that "this is all against me."[42] Again, the tensions implicit in the "brydale" at Kenilworth resemble those suffusing Shakespeare's comedies. The queen is thrust into the midst of a crowd of "country copulatives" led by a bride resembling *As You Like It*'s Audrey, "a poor virgin, sir, an ill-favored thing, sir, but mine own."[43] Spenser's more poetic "shepheards daughters" are removed from the "ill smelling" atmosphere and cruder energies of both the Elizabethan pageant and stage.

In Spenser's verse, these imaginary encounters are purged of the dramatic conflicts suffusing courtly entertainments. As a consequence, he gains considerable control over the production. At Kenilworth, in her response to the Lady of the Lake or George Gascoigne's "Savage Man," no matter how eloquent or ingenious the tribute, the queen had the last word, and, as Robert Langham says of the latter exchange, her words were generally judged "the best part of the play."[44] In the April eclogue, Spenser deals with the problem of prestation through a self-contained orchestration of gift-giving and gratitude. He does all the talking while declaring that the gift is hers, not his, to give: "Let dame Eliza thanke you for her song" (line 150). Similarly, Spenser preserves social and sexual decorum and maintains a balance between high and low by keeping them at a distance from one another and making their encounter wholly imaginary.

Nevertheless, the eclogue's ending raises the basic question of how effectively Spenser's elegiac strategy works. Despite the confidence of Colin's final notes, the skeptical responses of its immediate audience and the commentator are withering. When Colin ends with a last promise to the ladies that, "When Damsines I gether, I will part them all you among" (lines 152–53), E.K.'s gloss is contemptuous, dismissing the plums as a "a base reward of a clownish giver" (*Poetical Works*, 435). Colin's fellow shepherds are no less derisive. Thenot calls him a "foolish boy" (line 155) and Hobbinol agrees: "Sicker I hold him, for a greater fon, / That loues the thing, he cannot purchase" (line 159).

Hobbinol's rebuke repeats the key term of Harvey's mockery of "Master Collin Cloute" in the correspondence. There too Colin is ridiculed for his expectation that he can live by writing poetry and "purchase great landes, and Lordshippes, with the money which his *Calendar* and *Dreames* haue, and will affourde him" (628).

By ending the April eclogue with this odd emphasis on the problem of purchase, Spenser implicitly turns the tables on those who mock him and answers doubts about the effectiveness of his approach. At the most banal and obvious level, Hobbinol's scorn for a man who "loues the thing, he cannot purchase" seems manifestly obtuse in its confusion of two incompatible values; love can never be purchased, or, in the still plausible sentiments of popular song, "Money can't buy me love." At a deeper poetic level, the word's origins in *pour chacier* indicate links to the hunt as well as to commerce, but the beloved cannot be grasped in either fashion, as Hobbinol seems to assume. Indeed, Pan, in pursuing Syrinx, "loves the thing, he cannot purchase," because even the god chases a woman he cannot catch. But Harvey's original critique is more trenchant, showing that patronage rather than love is the real issue and exposing fantasies of "speciall fauour" bestowed by "*Mistresse Poetrie*" or Dame Eliza as mere illusions. His letter reverses the mystifications, probed so shrewdly by Louis Montrose, in which the pastoral poet "puts public relationships of power into intimate relationships of love."[45] Nevertheless, Spenser still has the advantage, since he recognizes that Harvey's seemingly practical resort to "those studies and practizes, that carrie as they saye, meate in their mouth" allows him no greater "purchase" on patronage than Colin attains. Spenser instead prefers a more oblique approach.

Spenser's recognition of the futility of courtly "purchase" is the root of what Jeffrey Knapp has defined as Spenser's radical but strategic unworldliness.[46] A key factor in Spenser's approach is his rejection of the courtly obsession with access and proximity. As Knapp explains in his analysis of *Colin Clouts Come Home Again*, "[N]earness is itself the problem: courtly lust is not so much a dereliction from as an ardency for Elizabeth's 'blessed presence.'" In that poem, the Shepherd of the Ocean or Walter Ralegh is saved from further ruin by banishment, but Colin wisely chooses to leave, and his detached, "otherworldly meditation" on Elizabeth allows him a more "measured" relation to the queen and her court.[47] This detachment has obtained from the beginning of Spenser's career, since the April eclogue "presents Colin as already alienated from Eliza."[48] Spenser consistently prefers withdrawal to access, fictive *re*presentation to courtly presentation, elegy to eulogy, because all these moves allow him a greater degree of autonomy. In Knapp's account, Spenser leaves behind the insular constraints of Elizabethan court politics for a utopian Fairyland that "to the literal-minded, seems groundless" but frees him to move between England, Ireland, and the New Jerusalem.[49]

This utopian unworldliness suffuses the April eclogue, and it acquires an epic as well as elegiac resonance at its conclusion in the emblems that stand as the last word. Thenot and Hobbinol quote key passages from Aeneas's plaintive address to Venus, his mother. The gloss identifies the source, explaining each emblem as a celestial compliment to Elizabeth by providing a "similitude of diuinitie" (*Poetical Works*, 435). But this is only part of the story; it ignores the characteristic Virgilian undertone of pathos and renunciation. After landing near Carthage, Aeneas encounters his mother disguised as a youthful huntress, and he mistakes Venus for a virginal nymph of Diana or perhaps the goddess herself ("O dea certe").[50] After asking how to address her, he pleads with her to relieve his labor by telling him where he is. She recounts Dido's story of tragic loss and flight and tells him to seek his lost comrades at Dido's palace. Having given him these dubious directions, leading him to the woman who almost diverts him from the course of empire, Venus departs, at which point Aeneas recognizes and reproaches her: "Why do you mock your son . . . with these lying apparitions [falsis ludis imaginibus]? Why can't I ever join you, hand to hand, to hear, to answer you with honest words?"[51] She remains impervious to his complaints, soaring off to Paphos and wrapping him in a mist. For Aeneas, the moment of illumination is a moment of loss and disorientation. Eulogistic compliment ("O dea certe") proves true, since the nymph is indeed a goddess, but it turns into an elegiac lament as she abandons him. As Pan's experience shows, the desired object always eludes our grasp at the moment we have it in hand.

"Quam te memorem virgo?" The poem ends with the same question with which it began: how should the poet finally address the queen "whom abruptely he termeth Elysa." The gloss soars beyond the Argument's initial embarrassment about the indecorum of pastoral nicknames to conclude that "Elisa is no whit inferiour to the Maiestie of her, of whome that Poete so boldly pronounced, O dea certe" (435). However, as the emblem's verb *(memorem)* indicates, such an address is inevitably commemorative and elegiac, and the connection can only be sustained from a distance. The emblems' message is muted, concealing the bitter pathos and anger of Aeneas's reproaches behind courtly compliment. These emotions surface in Erato's admonition in *The Tears of the Muses*. In prescribing the elegiac strategy, she urges "gentle Spirits" bred, as Aeneas was, "in Venus siluer bowre" to resist idealizing those whom they love and need:

> Now change the tenor of your ioyous layes,
> With which ye vse your loues to deifie,
> And blazon foorth an earthlie beauties praise,
> Aboue the compasse of the arched skie:
> Now change your praises into piteous cries,
> And Eulogies turne into Elegies.
>
> (*The Tears of the Muses*, lines 361–72)

From this perspective, the last words of the April eclogue, "O dea certe," take on a subliminally harsh irony, since, in its commitment to the elegiac strategy, the April eclogue still resists the impulse to "deifie" the queen even as it evokes the encomiastic aura of the cult of Elizabeth.

Spenser thus draws back from the obsequious effusions embraced by Harvey and other colleagues and contemporaries who pursued influence and reward. Spenser was, of course, just as eager to secure patronage as his friend, and, despite the Harvey's misgivings, his writings did eventually secure a royal pension. Nevertheless, in his account of Spenser's career, Richard Rambuss concludes that the poet finally considered the reward too little and too late, and he discerns evidence of further estrangement from the court in Spenser's later works.[52] I would argue that this estrangement prevailed from the beginning in subtle and qualified forms, transforming courtly eulogy to pastoral elegy in the earliest work. This modicum of poetic detachment gave *The Shepheardes Calender*, even at its most celebratory, a degree of prophetic unworldliness that could subsequently support the fiercest attacks on coarse careerism and mercenary self-promotion. Milton's attack on the "blind mouths" of his own day would thus vindicate Spenser's reluctance to resort directly to those "practizes, that carrie as they saye, meate in their mouth" so enthusiastically recommended by his friend and mentor, Gabriel Harvey.

Notes

1. S. K. Heninger Jr., *Sidney and Spenser: The Poet as Maker* (University Park: Pennsylvania State University Press, 1989), 1–17.

2. Ibid., 10–14.

3. For an earlier discussion of some of these issues, see my chapter "Edmund Spenser: Furthest from . . . Present Time," in *The Rites of Knighthood: The Literature and Politics of Elizabethan Chivalry* (Berkeley: University of California Press, 1989), 127–55.

4. Harvey claimed that he never intended these letters for publication, but most readers see this as a wholly conventional protest against the stigma of print; see Virginia Stern, *Gabriel Harvey: His Life, Marginalia, and Library* (Oxford: Clarendon Press, 1979), pp. 59–61.

5. *The Poetical Works of Edmund Spenser,* ed. J. C. Smith and E. De Selincourt (London: Oxford University Press, 1912), 635. Hereafter cited in the text as *Poetical Works.*

6. Richard Helgerson, *Forms of Nationhood: The Elizabethan Writing of England* (Chicago: University of Chicago Press, 1992), 25–30.

7. See his "Introduction: The Kingdom of our Own Language," in ibid., 1–18.

8. Virginia Stern reads this poem as mock-encomium marked by the humorous hyperbole found throughout the correspondence; see her *Gabriel Harvey,* 64.

9. Ben Jonson, *The Alchemist* 5.4.54–55. Jonson and Harvey share a humanist contempt for folk belief in the Fairy Queen. Shakespeare also makes this into comic

material, showing how Falstaff is duped by superstitious fears in *The Merry Wives of Windsor,* but Bottom's case in *A Midsummer Night's Dream* is, of course, more complicated.

10. Stern, *Gabriel Harvey,* 43.

11. *Have with You to Saffron-Walden,* in *The Works of Thomas Nashe,* ed. Ronald McKerrow (1903; reprint, Oxford: Blackwell, 1958), 3:70–79.

12. McCoy, *Rites of Knighthood,* 130.

13. *The Works of Edmund Spenser, A Variorum Edition* (Baltimore: Johns Hopkins University Press, 1949), 10:268. Henceforth referred to as the *Variorum.*

14. Marie Axton, *The Queen's Two Bodies: Drama and the Elizabethan Succession* (London: Royal Historical Society, 1977), 62. For a discussion of Dudley's strenuous interest in his own genealogy, see McCoy, *Rites of Knighthood,* 32–42 and Susan Frye, *Elizabeth I: The Competition for Representation* (Oxford: Oxford University Press, 1993), 68.

15. Various scholars think that the *Stemmata Dudleiana* did resurface in *The Ruines of Time* and *The Faerie Queene,* 2.10 and 3.3, but any explicit connection to Dudley has been erased; see the *Variorum,* 10:268.

16. For a discussion of Dyer's service to Leicester and his role in the Woodstock Revels, see Ralph M. Sargent, *The Life and Lyrics of Sir Edward Dyer* (1955; reprint, Oxford: Clarendon Press, 1968), 18, 30–34.

17. Nashe, *Works,* 3:75.

18. Ben Jonson, preface to *Hymenaei,* in *The Complete Masques,* ed. Stephen Orgel (New Haven: Yale University Press, 1969), 76.

19. See Thomas Cain, "The Strategy of Praise in Spenser's 'Aprill,'" *SEL* 8 (winter 1968): 45–68.

20. Louis Adrian Montrose, "'The perfect paterne of a Poete': The Poetics of Courtship in *The Shepheardes Calender,*" *Texas Studies in Literature and Language* 21 (winter 1979): 40. For a comparably shrewd discussion of the mixed interests at work in courtly pageantry, see his "Celebration and Insinuation: Sir Philip Sidney and the Motives of Elizabethan Courtship," *Renaissance Drama,* n.s., 8 (1977): 3–55.

21. Louis Adrian Montrose, "The Elizabethan Subject and the Spenserian Text," in *Literary Theory/Renaissance Texts,* ed. Patricia Parker and David Quint (Baltimore: Johns Hopkins University Press, 1986), 319–23.

22. Annabel Patterson, *Pastoral and Ideology* (Berkeley: University of California Press, 1987), 119–23.

23. David Norbrook, *Poetry and Politics in the English Renaissance* (London: Routledge & Kegan Paul, 1984), 84. Norbrook sees Spenser's work as the "fullest embodiment of the political ideals of Sidney and his circle" (109).

24. Frye, *Elizabeth I,* 10.

25. Ibid., 114–35.

26. Richard Rambuss, *Spenser's Secret Career* (Cambridge: Cambridge University Press, 1993), 59. Rambuss says that, despite his apparent betrayal of Hobbinol/Harvey, Spenser still completely shares his mentor's careerist ambitions at this point, a position I would qualify. For another discussion of secrecy in *The Shepheardes Calender,* see Patterson, *Pastoral and Ideology,* 127–29 and her *Reading Between the Lines* (Madison: University of Wisconsin Press, 1993), 47. For a discussion of its homosocial subtext, see Jonathan Goldberg's *Sodometries: Renaissance Texts, Modern Sexualities* (Stanford, Calif.: Stanford University Press, 1992), 74–81.

27. Rambuss, *Spenser's Secret Career,* 4.

28. McCoy, *Rites of Knighthood,* 132.

29. Jeffrey Knapp, *An Empire Nowhere: England, America, and Literature from "Utopia" to "The Tempest"* (Berkeley: University of California Press, 1992), 90, 92.

30. Peter M. Sacks, *The English Elegy: Studies in the Genre from Spenser to Yeats* (Baltimore: Johns Hopkins University Press, 1985), 5.

31. Angus Fletcher, *Allegory: The Theory of a Symbolic Mode* (1964; reprint, Ithaca: Cornell University Press, 1982), 272.

32. Elizabeth J. Bellamy, "The Vocative and the Vocational: The Unreadability of Elizabeth in *The Faerie Queene,*" *ELH* 54 (spring 1987): 4–6.

33. Thomas Cain, *Praise in "The Faerie Queene"* (Lincoln: University of Nebraska Press, 1978), 14–24.

34. Ovid, *Metamorphoses,* trans. Frank Justus Miller, Loeb Classical Library (London: Heinemann, 1916), 12.

35. Montrose, "Elizabethan Subject and the Spenserian Text," 321–23.

36. Spenser, *Variorum,* 7:274–75.

37. Robert Langham, *A Letter* (1575), ed. R. J. P. Kuin (Leiden: E. J. Brill, 1983), 40–41. For a discussion of this incident, see my *Rites of Knighthood,* 43 and Frye, *Elizabeth I,* 68–69.

38. Langham, *A Letter,* 40–41.

39. The classic study of prestation or ceremonial gift-giving as a form of "struggle among nobles to determine their position in the hierarchy" is Marcel Mauss, *The Gift: Forms and Functions of Exchange in Archaic Societies,* trans. Ian Cunnison (1925; reprint, New York: Norton, 1967), 4.

40. Spenser, *Variorum,* 7:287.

41. Langham, *A Letter,* 50. Kuin notes that the bride's age has been altered upwards from thirty to thirty-five in both editions of the text.

42. *Calendar of State Papers, Spanish, Elizabeth (1558–1567),* ed. Martin A. S. Hume (London: Her Majesty's Stationery Office, 1892), 1:404. For a discussion of Leicester's potentially insulting entertainments, see Frye, *Elizabeth I,* 62, 170 n. 6 and McCoy, *Rites of Knighthood,* 42.

43. *As You Like It* 5.4.55–58.

44. Langham, *A Letter,* 46.

45. Louis Adrian Montrose, "'Eliza, Queen of shepheardes,' and the Pastoral of Power," *English Literary Renaissance* 10 (spring 1980): 157.

46. "Elisa as a necessarily desirable and necessarily unobtainable object makes the pastoral ideal she embodies seem itself unpurchasable," while "Rosalind's unpurchasability . . . [helps] to clarify and then liberate the otherworldliness inscribed at the heart of the worldly pastoral Colin used to celebrate, the pastoral of the virgin Elisa" (Knapp, *An Empire Nowhere,* 93–94).

47. Ibid., 184.

48. Ibid., 316.

49. Ibid., 105, 185.

50. See the discussion of Spenser's use of the Virgilian Venus-Virgo figure in Barbara Bono, *Literary Transvaluation: From Vergilian Epic to Shakespearean Tragicomedy* (Berkeley: University of California Press, 1984), 61–79; and Anthony di Matteo, "Spenser's Venus-Virgo: The Poetics and Interpretive History of a Dissembling Figure," *Spenser Studies* 10 (1992): 37–70. I find di Matteo's emphasis on the figure's irreconcilable ambiguities (38) more persuasive than Bono's view of Spenser's determination to

"embrace" the Venus-Virgo (65) in a "syncretic accommodation" of her inconsistencies (p. 79).

51. Virgil, *The Aeneid* 1.407–9.

52. Rambuss, *Spenser's Secret Career*, 80.

Weighing Words with Spenser's Giant

JUDITH H. ANDERSON

CHARACTERISTICALLY, *The Faerie Queene* contains perceived threats to its own assumptions and conditions of meaning; that is, it includes and, often with pronounced ambivalence, attempts to control them. This is especially true of questions concerning the fictionality or illusionism of art, such as those associated with the evil magicians of the poem, with the idealization of Elizabeth I, and with the substantiality of Fairyland itself.[1] It pertains as well to Spenser's most outspoken treatment of language—"words"—which occurs in the episode of the leveling Giant that caps and comments on Artegall's initial exploits in Book V.

This episode opposes the materialism embodied in the Giant to the immaterial conceptions, ultimately founded on idealism or faith, that Artegall voices. It is hardly surprising that Artegall is allowed to win his debate with the Giant, but perhaps more so that his literally conclusive triumph should be figured in the material elimination of his opponent, who is summarily pushed from a cliff to destruction in the sea below. If this is justice, it operates in the Giant's own terms. The materialism of these terms recalls, yet graphically exceeds and politicizes, the "sinews in tropes" and "muscles and tendons in figures" found repeatedly in early modern treatments of rhetoric.[2] Artegall's rhetorical triumph, as its figuration suggests, is so enmeshed in ironic or otherwise disturbing nuances as to render it more problematical than first meets the eye. It is typical of Book V in this respect.

Artegall's debate with the Giant does not introduce the first signs of strain in this book between metaphorical and material dimensions of meaning, between concept and history, or between words and things, but it focuses them more sharply. This debate initiates conceptualization of the problem of embodying justice—of fleshing it out in a real world. That such strains and problems exist self-reflexively in Book V has long been an established critical position, which Annabel Patterson has recently brought to bear on the relation of the fifth book to Spenser's *View of the Present State of Ireland*.[3] My present concern is with their more specific relation to language and to a question the Giant's challenge to Artegall poses: "How and how much do words weigh?" Verbal weight carries both a metaphorical and a material value in this question, and embodying justice encounters head-on the implication of graphic and rhetorical characteristics in ideological, psychological, and historical ones. Moreover, they all revolve, at times dizzily, around the multivalence of *res*—the things of this world, higher things, and the things of rhetoric.

Artegall encounters the Giant just after having overseen the severing of Lady Munera's hands and feet and their display—"on high, that all might them behold"—as conspicuously material tokens for moral and political edification. From the outset, the Giant whom Artegall beholds is an emblematized and highly visible figure, standing "Vpon a rocke, and holding forth on hie / An huge great paire of ballance in his hand."[4] Despite the intervention of two stanzas to account for other matters—the drowning of the remainder of Lady Munera and the razing of her castle—the narrator's line of vision, along with Artegall's and our own, moves essentially from the dismembered tokens of Munera, hung on high, to the elevated Giant. It thus moves suggestively but ambivalently from the visual display of severed members to a gigantic embodiment of materialism. But what is being questioned in this ironic movement? The efficiency of Artegall's "great iustice"? The materialism of its means? Or the persistence of materialism itself? Like the Cave of Mammon, at whose core lies an inclusive and a corrosive materialism, the Giant is a sight whose significance threatens containment, and the debate in which Artegall engages him is a profoundly disturbing locus of meaning in the poem. The appearance of the Giant questions the very province of symbolism and specifically that of the symbolism of justice, in which the resistance of matter (e.g., a woman's severed hands and feet) to higher meanings is peculiarly marked.

Consistently, the episodes preceding the sight of the Giant underline such resistance. In the first of these, Artegall adjudicates between the conflicting stories of Sanglier and the Squire on the basis of the Judgment of Solomon, but his decision, while correct, has two conspicuous loose ends that the biblical model noticeably lacks, namely, a decapitated woman and her murderer. Sanglier's largely symbolic punishment, to bear the dead woman's head for a year as a mark of "shame," ill fits the actual crime or the subsequent "ador[ation]" of Artegall's justice by the effusive squire (i.28, 30). Here, the seam between literal and symbolic meanings or between material and generically romantic ones appears designed to exhibit severe signs of strain.

In the second episode, the defeat of Pollente and the execution of Munera, Artegall again establishes justice, but at a cost to his own ideality. His victory over Pollente is punctuated by a reductive emphasis on the mundane and material that approaches mock-epic. It includes attention to Artegall's prowess as a swimmer that is parodically digressive in length and focus ("But *Artegall* was better breath'd beside") and descriptions of combat whose imagery and rhythm similarly disappoint heroic and generic expectation: "They snuf, they snort, they bounce, they rage, they rore," thus enacting the sounds of mortal conflict between a dolphin and a seal.[5] Details of description are likewise designed to embarrass the justice of Lady Munera's execution. It is utterly unclear, for example, whether Lady Munera's hands and feet are literally or symbolically gold and silver: her "hands of gold" could either be gold-dispensing or her fingers richly adorned—"fretted *with* gold wyr"—like those of her prototype Lady Meed, and her feet could similarly be furnished with jewelry or network slippers of "choice" (Spenser's "trye") silver.[6] The notion of "choice" silver itself suggests an aesthetic or symbolic meaning. The distressing fact that Lady Munera is "holding vp her suppliant hands on hye" and "kneeling . . . submissiuely" when her extremities are summarily "Chopt off, and nayld on high," makes still harder the task of the apologist who—unlike even Artegall—would ignore "her seemelesse plight." At once unseemly and seamless—perhaps unseeming, or real, as well—her plight is a whole not separable into abstract and human segments (indeed, into concept and body) and to it Artegall proves conspicuously unable adequately to respond (V.ii.26–27).[7]

When, on the heels of Munera's dismemberment, the "mighty Gyant" enters the second canto, he is a looming physical presence whose figure focuses and mocks the cumulative incongruities between higher and lower meanings in the early episodes (30). Besides being an imposing sight, the Giant is a notably vocal figure—a talker, indeed, a boaster, and, with unwitting irony, in large part his own exegesis. Since he is physically a giant, it is ironic that in principle he is also an egalitarian, one who would balance heaven with hell and "reduce vnto equality" all earthly things (32). To reinstate a presumed original justice, he would reorder the components of the natural world, and from his reordering that of the social world would naturally follow:

> Therefore I will throw downe these mountaines hie,
> And make them leuell with the lowly plaine:
> These towring rocks, which reach vnto the skie,
> I will thrust downe into the deepest maine,
> And as they were, them equalize againe.
> Tyrants that make men subiect to their law,
> I will suppresse, that they no more may raine;
> And Lordings curbe, that commons ouer-aw;
> And all the wealth of rich men to the poore will draw.
>
> (V.ii.38)

Throughout, the Giant's argument is materialistic in the literal sense, since it is based on an injustice determined by quantity, appearance, and sight: "Seest not, how badly all things present bee," he demands, before continuing, "The sea it selfe doest thou not plainely see / Encroch vppon the land there vnder thee?" (37). Obviously, seeing is believing in these lines. But in them, insistent punning (see/sea), which is only nominally and inadvertently the Giant's, is also unusually obvious, and like the Giant's desire to reduce the high and mighty to the "lowly plaine," it anticipates—indeed, participates in—the leveling of the Giant himself, who is literally to be "thrust downe into the deepest maine" and "in the sea . . . dround" with narrative irony so blatant as to be vindictive (49).[8] Earlier, the Giant has been described as "mighty," in this context a word carrying the memory of its medieval force, which is not simply "powerful" in a brute sense but "capable of enacting"; for the medieval writers whom Spenser manifestly read, it is God who is (al)mighty.[9] Within the context of the present canto, the narrator's designation of the Giant's might is at once skeptical and frightened, ironic and anxious, a point to which I shall return.[10]

In striking contrast to the pessimistic speaker of the proem to Book V, Artegall counters the Giant's perception of a fundamental injustice in the arrangement of the world and his desire to rectify it by asserting an underlying principle of Ptolemaic order—"The earth was in the middle centre pight"—and by affirming his own belief that this principle has been immutably established in accordance with "heauenly iustice" (35–36). In this connection, he both denies the possibility that significant change has ever occurred, for "mongst them al no change hath yet beene found," and categorically rejects its desirability: "All change is perillous, and all chaunce vnsound." His negative efforts anticipate Jove's absolute denial of presence and power to Mutability in the Cantos bearing her name, and they also recall such earlier moments as when Guyon and the Palmer fettered Occasion, implicitly and vainly trying to stop time and its inevitable concomitant, the forward movement of narrative and hence of the quest.[11]

More urgently and immediately, Artegall's premises oppose the historically grounded anxieties voiced conspicuously (paradox intended) by the speaker of the fifth proem:

Me seemes the world is runne quite out of square,
From the first point of his appointed sourse,
And being once amisse growes daily wourse and wourse.
. . . .
Right now is wrong, and wrong that was is right,
As all things else in time are chaunged quight.
Ne wonder; for the heauens reuolution
Is wandred farre from, where it first was pight.

(V.pro.1, 4)

The reemergence of this pessimistic view in the Giant's words and the extension of it to the social order further enforce its claim on our attention and impart a measure of authority to it within the narrative. Its reemergence also attests to the pressure of its historically material existence, which is well documented for the late sixteenth century and includes relevant causes ranging from new stars, prophecies, and seemingly irregular planetary movements to crop failures, inflation, enclosures, poverty, and vagrants in England, to worries about the importation of Anabaptist communism from the Continent and recurrent Irish uprisings somewhat closer to home.[12] In light of this persistently troubled view in both the historical *and* the Faerie contexts—that is, in the world and the poem—Artegall's unqualified absolutism is *made* to look suspect. In this, it resembles the hyperbolic praise lavished on him in his early exploits, whose actual conduct and outcomes we have seen to be conceptually strained and recurrently touched by whiffs of parody.[13]

When the Giant is confronted with Artegall's categorical assertions, he, too, is stubborn, and he insists all the more on the evidence of his senses. Interestingly enough, his insistence causes Artegall to shift—to change—from an argument dependent on an immutable cosmos to a nearer and considerably more dynamic one based on a natural cycle of loss and recovery, flourishing and fading, birth and death:

> How euer gay their blossome or their blade
> Doe flourish now, they into dust shall vade.
> What wrong then is it, if that when they die,
> They turne to that, whereof they first were made?
>
> (V.ii.40)

While this shift in the argument accommodates to a greater extent the Giant's position regarding "things in sight" and could be construed as a generous or politic effort to reach him, it also represents a more complex and immediate engagement with matter. Insofar as it is merely a development of Artegall's original position, however, it exposes the underlying allegiance of his cyclical view to stasis: change might exist, but it makes no real difference; nothing *really* changes.

And even as the increased engagement with matter comes, as if to offset it, Artegall more emphatically employs an argument based on faith. He slips easily from flowers and the biblical resonance of their fading into "dust" to the more human context of death and to a rhetoric exceeding the fate of flowers: now he depends on "the voice of the most hie," the "great Maker," to have ordained "What euer thing is done" (40–42). The authority of this voice is higher than the towering Giant, and the stanzas describing its action are, in Thomas Roche's apt words, "a tissue of Biblical paraphrase."[14] They are, in fact, so much such a tissue that they yield the poem's meaning to another context:

> They liue, they die, like as he doth ordaine,
> Ne euer any asketh reason why.

The hils doe not the lowly dales disdaine;
The dales doe not the lofty hils enuy.
He maketh Kings to sit in souerainty;
He maketh subiects to their powre obay;
He pulleth downe, he setteth vp on hy;
He giues to this, from that he takes away.
. . . .
Ne any may his mighty will withstand;
Ne any may his soueraine power shonne,
Ne loose that he hath bound with stedfast band.

(V.ii.41–42)

If not wholly unprecedented, these lines do not represent the ordinary syntax and rhythm of Spenser's writing. They contrast noticeably, for example, with the conversational quality of Artegall's words to Sanglier and the squire in the preceding canto (e.g., i.25) and with his exchanges with the Giant earlier in the present debate:

Thou that presum'st to weigh the world anew,
And all things to an equall to restore,
In stead of right me seemes great wrong doth shew,
And far aboue thy forces pitch to sore.
. . . .
Thou foolishe Elfe (said then the Gyant wroth)
Seest not, how badly all things present bee,
And each estate quite out of order goth?

(V.ii.34, 37)

Unlike Artegall's biblical paraphrase, lines such as these are touched by the rhythm and diction of everyday living, and they actually participate in propositional debate.

In contrast, the ritualized rhythms of Artegall's paraphrase participate less in the development of dialogue than they testify to the importation of meaning—literally, to its portability and imposition. What is "heard" in the passage is less truly a "voice" than a text, a rhythmically and allusively defined block of biblical writing, visibly and audibly a "set piece" that occupies the narrative and differs markedly from the immediate and larger contexts surrounding it in the poem. Such a text is broadly comparable to the "prefabricated unit of meaning" of which Nigel Barley has written in characterizing proverbial utterances and to the "sing-song effect" Maurice Bloch calls intoning—a ritualized "repeating [of] what had been said before." Bloch's analysis is further relevant: he characterizes words in ritual as having little explanatory (or propositional) power and sees them performing "less as parts of a language and more as *things*, in the same way as material symbols." They are "frozen" statements, whose "repetition reminds us that we are not dealing with an argument, since an argument is a basis for another argument." Most tellingly in regard to Artegall's style of debating, Bloch interprets the frozen statement as "the use of form for power"—a politically potent substance.[15]

Effective as Artegall's biblically set piece is in its own right, its admissions sound also at times like an argument based merely on necessity or on fortune: "He pulleth downe, he setteth vp on hy; / He giues to this, from that he takes away." While other echoes of the rhetoric of Despair in Artegall's assertions—"When houre of death is come, let none aske whence, nor why"—might summarily be dismissed on the ground that the Knight of Justice argues for faith, not self-homicide, dismissal begs the question. If there is one thing that the Book of Justice makes abundantly and explicitly clear, it is that in a real world faith is not identical with justice, the impersonal cardinal virtue that, by virtually any traditional definition—Aristotle's, Cicero's, Aquinas's, or Hooker's—concerns not an inner world of private virtues and beliefs but the material world of history.[16] Certainly from the point of view of the Giant and "the people" whom he represents, the self-abnegation of Artegall's faith must itself be a form of self-destruction: "What wrong then is it, if that when they die, / They turne to that, whereof they first were made"—dust into dust without any real sense of loss, let alone indignation. Faith is not an answer to the Giant's arguments to the same extent or in the same sense that a Ptolemaic position and a total denial of change would have been, had these proved credibly demonstrable. Artegall's shift from such "scientific" or relatively verifiable positions to an argument based wholly on faith is revealing, for in making it he discards the visual or perceptual criteria commonly used to theorize appearances into a "real" system that organizes matter from dense to rare.[17] Again his shift suggests the threatening historical reality of what the Giant so visibly and audibly—so materially—embodies.

Artegall's set piece in this debate has a natural association with other frozen pieces in the poem to which it is formally and thematically analogous, and these cast a proleptic or retrospective light upon it. The temptation of Despair in Book I, in which Redcrosse is counseled, "in true ballance . . . weigh thy state," affords a pertinent example (I.ix.45). As this episode shows, Despair can use and misuse Scripture, together with all the other sententious resources available in the period for moral guidance. Despair's temptation, like Artegall's invocation of faith, is itself a pastiche of traditional echoes—classical and proverbial, as well as scriptural—and even today, their familiarity conveys something of their cultural power:

> . . . all ends that was begonne.
> Their times in his eternall booke of fate
> Are written sure, and haue their certaine date.
> Who then can striue with strong necessitie,

That holds the world in his still chaunging state,
Or shunne the death ordaynd by destinie?

(I.ix.42)

Similarly drawing on the formulaic content and rhythm of traditional sources, the next stanza begins, "The lenger life, I wote the greater sin, / The greater sin, the greater punishment," and it subsequently explains that "life must life, and bloud must bloud repay / . . . For he, that once hath missed the right way, / The further he doth goe, the further he doth stray." The lines cited from these two stanzas recall eight proverbial sources and two scriptural ones, all of which strike me as being still available to cultural memory: for example, "Whatever has a beginning has an end"; "Blood will have blood"; "Death keeps no calendar"; "The time of death is certain"; "All men must die"; "The farther you go, the farther behind"; "The longer the life, the greater the misery"; and "The force of necessity is irresistible."[18] Essentially, Despair's lines thus consist not merely of "vaine words," as Una characterizes them in her last-ditch effort to cancel their force, but of sentiments that carry considerable ideological "weight," the cultural and therefore unavoidably psychological weight of frozen matter (I.ix.53). In view of this fact, it makes sense that some critical doubt should have arisen as to whether Despair or Redcrosse speaks in a number of these lines.[19] Of course such ambiguity is symbolically appropriate in them, since Despair, the ghastly figure whose description mirrors that of the Knight rescued from Orgoglio's dungeon, now bids to become one with him. While the doubt that Despair's lines generate has meaning within the quest of Redcrosse, however, it also suggests the extent to which lines that recall the content and cadences of traditional sources can take on a life of their own, the poet's awareness of this fact, and his skill in utilizing it.[20] This poet knows how to use frozen words; his use, moreover, is not an innocent one.

Within the fifth book itself, a near example of such use occurs in an exchange between Artegall and Burbon, the knight who seeks to defend his possession of the lady Flourdelis and whose name alludes conspicuously to "Bourbon" (Henri de Navarre and subsequently Henri IV of France). When Burbon is challenged by a "rude rout" and throws away his battered shield in order to defend his lady more effectively, Artegall considers this act Burbon's dishonorable betrayal of his "honours stile," or knightly identity, and advises him to "Dye rather, then doe ought, that mote dishonour yield" (V.xi.44, 55). But Burbon answers Artegall's proverbial wisdom with some of his own, since he thinks that he can in time "resume" his former shield: he argues that "To temporize is not from truth to swerue, / Ne for aduantage terme to entertaine, / When as necessitie doth it constraine." Artegall, hardly to be outdone in this vein, replies by doubling the proverbial context: "Fie on such forgerie (said *Artegall*) / Vnder one hood to shadow faces twaine. / Knights ought be true, and truth is one in all" (56).[21] Again the weighted lines in which traditional wisdom is concentrated are problematical, and as Artegall's subsequent decision to assist Burbon suggests, neither view is without force and reason. Burbon's view favors temporal and material considerations, Artegall's ideal and absolute ones. It seems no accident that Artegall's words closely echo those he speaks earlier to the leveling Giant: "For truth is one, and right is euer one" (ii.48); nor is it accidental that his words to Burbon are followed almost immediately by his seemingly contradictory decision to assist the apostate knight, even though his doing so compromises his already belated quest through yet further delay. The claim of unity, a single truth, is more and more entangled in irony, or doubleness, duplicity, in the fifth book, a situation that extends into the sixth book and finally to the Mutability Cantos. Within this entanglement, the claims of material existence—bodies in history—are increasingly real and persistently relevant to language and conspicuously so when language is frozen into a thing, a material symbol or *res*.

While the biblical origin of the most formulaic portion of Artegall's words to the Giant may argue for immunizing them from the problems surrounding other invocations of traditional wisdom like those I have cited, the fact that the sentiments introducing the Giant's proposal to curb aristocratic power and to redistribute wealth—"Therefore I will throw downe these mountaines hie, / And make them leuell with the lowly plaine"—also come from the Bible further complicates this argument.[22] The earlier gap between Artegall's own invocation of the Judgment of Solomon and the actual situation in canto 1 adds yet another wrinkle (or Derridean fold) to it. The larger context of Book V, and specifically the strains between material and ideal values everywhere evident in it, argues still more strongly against such reductive immunization.

Accentuated and isolated by its form as well as its content, Artegall's frozen speech exists within a worldly frame that oddly both heightens and questions its difference from the material concerns and events of this world. This is a crucial fact in a book of Justice, which, unlike the books treating personal virtues, must deal with a world that is external and historical. When, in debating the Giant, Artegall shifts his focus from an utterly unchanging cosmos to the cyclical changes of the natural world, including the cycle of mortality, his belated admission of evident change, though ever so carefully balanced by a profession of personal faith, acknowledges the weight of material concerns and, indeed, the persistent reality of matter. Once again, this episode anticipates the Mutability Cantos, yet in the penultimate stanza of Mutability, unlike the Artegallian debate, a sense of loss will outweigh the consolation of a recurring cycle:

> Which makes me loath this state of life so tickle
> And loue of things so vaine to cast away;

Whose flowring pride, so fading and so fickle,
Short *Time* shall soon cut down with his consuming sickle.[23]

In comparison to these lines, Artegall's guarded acknowledgment of materiality sounds detached ("How euer gay their blossome or their blade / Doe flourish now, they into dust shall vade") and defensive ("What wrong then is it, if that when they die, / They turne to that, whereof they first were made?"). In this context, his biblical paraphrase looks even more like a power play, a material assertion of form meant to compensate for the material vacuum his otherworldly beliefs have created.

As if uncomfortably aware of the likelihood of further debate once the ritual of biblical paraphrase recedes, Artegall takes the offensive and challenges the Giant of materialism directly. Brooking no response, he abruptly shifts the argument—in fact, the balance—once again from ponderable things to those imponderable:

For take thy ballaunce, if thou be so wise,
And weigh the winde, that vnder heauen doth blow;
Or weigh the light, that in the East doth rise;
Or weigh the thought, that from mans mind doth flow.
But if the weight of these thou canst not show,
Weigh but one word which from thy lips doth fall.
For how canst thou those greater secrets know,
That doest not know the least thing of them all?
Ill can he rule the great, that cannot reach the small.[24]

Presumably, a word is "the least thing of them all." It is the ultimatum that is clearly on a continuum with greater things, and the Giant's response indicates that he is specifically disconcerted ("abashed") at the prospect of weighing one, conceivably because this prospect hovers uncertainly between metaphorical and material meanings—between "weigh" in the sense of evaluate, consider, and "weigh" in the literal sense of relative poundage.[25] The Giant's abashment implicitly acknowledges something—verbal *res*, a meaning—not strictly material. To this extent, like Artegall, he shows some movement toward a healthier balance between material and immaterial concerns.

But only momentarily. He overcomes his abashment to extend his materialism uncompromisingly to language, insisting that "the least word that euer could be layd / Within his ballaunce, he could way aright" (44). Challenged by Artegall to determine whether "right or wrong, the false or else the trew" is heavier, he flings these into the balance, "But streight the winged words out of his ballaunce flew." Like the traditionally winged words of Homer, these participate in a reality that does not abide material measurement, but, like a good Baconian, the Giant dismisses their evidence against him on grounds of the inherent—and, despite himself, the figurative—lightness of words and tries instead, without success, to weigh truth, essential truth, against falsehood. But all his balance discovers is that "the false will [not] with the truth be wayd" (45). Falsehood, apparently incommensurable with truth, just slides off the scale, in effect enacting itself as mere absence and denial, whether of truth, goodness, or positive being.

Surprisingly at this juncture, Artegall tells the enraged Giant that the scales prove nothing, at best serving only to "betoken" right or wrong. His immediate point is that the scales are mechanically faultless, despite their finding against the Giant's view, yet his statement implies that the Giant's earlier weighing of the material world, which found for the Giant, is meaningless as well. The word *betoken* is slippery, however, and all the more so because Artegall's employment of it is unique in *The Faerie Queene*. Presumably, by it he means "signify," "denote," "indicate," "be a token of," but there is a basic ambiguity in the meaning of the substantive *token* that carries over into its verbal cognate: *token* means both "something that serves to indicate a fact" and "something serving as proof of a fact or statement; an evidence"—on the one hand, something that merely points to a thing and, on the other, something that has demonstrative validity in itself.[26] The latter meaning would grant a degree of autonomous authority to the evidence of the scales, as, indeed, to other quantitative measurements, such as those by which phenomena that were irrational in a Ptolemaic order could be more clearly tracked and questioned. It would therefore grant some measure of definitive reality to the material realm. With an elusive, layered irony, the ambivalence of Artegall's word *betoken* thus weighs to an extent against him and the validity of his position. If the Giant's scales betoken that he cannot weigh words, they have earlier betokened that inequality exists.[27]

In invoking the word *betoken*, Artegall evidently *means* to argue that, while the Giant's scales can indicate relative weight—more exactly, weight relative to a fundamental principle—they are unable to determine the validity of the principles themselves according to which judgment must be rendered and material considerations weighed.[28] For

> in the mind the doome of right must bee;
> And so likewise of words, the which be spoken,
> The eare must be the ballance, to decree
> And iudge, whether with truth or falshood they agree.
>
> (V.ii.47)

Like *vox*, "voice," the ear is here another material supplement of the mind; put otherwise, it listens like the ear of a Renaissance jurist, to subjective intention, in which "both *mens [legislatoris]* and *ratio [legis]*" are conflated and found to be "not only beneath and behind the words of the law" but "also prior to the words" that express it.[29] Artegall's explanation is less about ears versus eyes, speech versus writing, than it is about mind versus mere matter—about "the doome" within the mind to which "words, the which be spoken," must be referred if they are to bear any true meaning or verbal *res*. In terms of the broader basics being debated, Artegall's words—materially tripping him up, perhaps—indicate not simply the truism that human beings have minds as well as senses but a far stronger privileging of the "inward mind," repeatedly in this poem a phrase that implies the recesses of memory in Neoplatonic and Augustinian senses.[30] Artegall opts both for an subjective conception of truth, as against an external and a quantifiable one, and for an interiorly valorized conception of language, as against one that is material. His choice distinctly favors the Platonic end of the philosophic spectrum. Considered from this vantage point, his inward ear actually listens, like Augustine's, essentially to intuition.[31]

Within a context of idealism such as that attributed to Plato or Augustine, even to speak the inner word of truth, let alone to write it, is to subject it to a compromising degree of materialization. In Letter VII, a Platonic document sometimes attributed to Plato himself, the epistler expresses his distrust of language most emphatically: "[N]o intelligent man will ever be so bold as to put into language those things which his reason has contemplated." When he adds that this is particularly the case with written language, he does not erase the impression that *any* form of externalized expression obscures or distorts truth: for a Platonist, the "knowledge and understanding of real objects is not found in sounds nor in shapes but *in minds*; names, descriptions, bodily forms, and concepts do as much to illustrate the particular quality of any object as they do to illustrate its essential reality" (my emphasis). The Platonic epistler, anticipating his Neoplatonic successors, describes true knowledge as a "flash of understanding" in which the mind is "flooded with light."[32] Augustine similarly describes an understanding that floods the spirit in a rapid flash ("intellectus quasi rapida coruscatione perfundit animum"), and he repeatedly remarks how much actual speech, "the sound of our mouth," differs from it ("quantum distet sonus oris nostri ab illo ictu intelligentiae").[33] In his epistemology, true understanding is preverbal (with reference to ordinary human language), and the relation of the truth that shines within to the words we speak remains at best obscure.[34] Committed to time and space through syntax and figurality, any human language is for Augustine inherently flawed.[35]

In the context of debate with the Giant, Artegall's views, which are neither those of the proem to Book V nor necessarily coextensive with Spenser's, are touched by the antilinguistic extremism of Platonism and by what I would imagine to be the projected anxieties of the poet. As we have seen, however, Artegall's voice is neither unqualified by material considerations at this point nor unchallenged by other passages in the poem. While the Giant's fatal errors have first been to let Artegall radically shift the ground of argument from things seen to things unseen and then to suppose that words, concepts, and principles can be weighed in purely material terms, the Giant's failure has not affected visible, palpable inequalities in any way except to shift them from sight. Moreover, in doing so, it has raised the classic specter of the failure of words to refer in some intrinsic way to things, or at least to material things.

Although Artegall invokes the mind and the ear and the Giant's arguments have been blatantly associated with matter and sight ("Seest not, how badly all things present bee, / . . . The sea it selfe doest thou not plainely see / Encroch vppon the land there vnder thee"?), these alignments are offset by other material considerations: by Artegall's earlier recourse to display—Pollente's head or Lady Munera's hands and feet, for example; by the assertions of his own weighted words, meant to suggest "the voice of the most hie," perhaps, but more evidently composing a portable piece of frozen rhetoric; and most dramatically by Talus's shouldering the Giant "from off the higher ground" of argument to the sea below:

Like as a ship, whom cruell tempest driues
  Vpon a rocke with horrible dismay,
  Her shattered ribs in thousand peeces riues,
  And spoyling all her geares and goodly ray,
  Does make her selfe misfortunes piteous pray.
  So downe the cliffe the wretched Gyant tumbled;
  His battred ballances in peeces lay,
  His timbered bones all broken rudely rumbled,
So was the high aspyring with huge ruine humbled.

(V.ii.50)

This stanza comes after Artegall wins his argument with the hapless Giant and serves as the materially conceived, conclusive expression of his victory. The terms of its conception contrast sharply with the knight's high-minded sentiment that "in the mind the doome of right must bee." Although at two nominal removes from Artegall—one through the intervention of a simile and another through that of Talus—the narrator's use of the adjective "cruell" in describing the Giant's fate participates in the recurrent association of Artegall with cruelty prior to his fall at Radigund's hands and his subsequent rescue by Britomart.[36] According to traditional ethical theory, cruelty is the vice that specifically opposes justice, the wrong that negatively balances or—in view of the incommensurability of right and wrong Artegall urges to the Giant—perhaps fails to balance its right. Crucially and repeatedly in Book V, the narrative returns to this troubling question of balance, and as we have seen, it already implicates the matter of words, hence the poem itself, in its outcome.

How and how much *do* words weigh? From the first episode of Book V, when Artegall adjudicates the conflicting testimonies of Sanglier and the squire, through the last—the onslaught of Envy, Detraction, and the Blatant Beast—the relation of words to truth is at issue. In the early episodes, words in themselves do not fare especially well; they are ineffectual, their testimony invariably superseded by more material considerations or by actions, as when the Giant is shouldered off the cliff. Artegall decides between Sanglier and the squire on the basis of "signes," not words as such; his words to the Giant are abruptly replaced by explosive force; when his own word conflicts with Braggadocchio's, he invokes "signes," and he requires "tokens"—material evidence—from Guyon to establish the latter's right to the stolen horse (i.24, ii.49, iii.21-22, 32). Correspondingly, the pleas of Lady Munera and the arguments of the Giant are brushed aside; the railings of Braggadocchio, that quintessential windbag, are rightly punished; and the mutual pledges of Amidas and Bracidas to their original loves are readily accommodated to fortune's redistribution of wealth through the action of the sea. In all these episodes, words prove themselves verily to be "the least thing of them all."

The later cantos of Book V are complexly and historically materialistic, rather than crudely so like the early cantos; yet in them, although words may acquire more weight, they gain little more positive value. For example, Radigund advises her handmaid Clarinda to add "art" to her temptation of Artegall, "euen womens witty trade, / The art of mightie words, that men may charme," and Artegall remains Radigund's prisoner largely because he has imprudently pledged his word to her (V.v.49). What ultimately redeems him is his keeping his loyalty to Britomart; we might regard this as his keeping his word, but the poem never refers specifically in this way to his loyalty. It mentions only his inner troth, his loyalty or integrity (V.vi.2, cf. v.56). Even tokens become deceptive when Dolon mistakes Britomart for Artegall, but words still fare no better, for those that Dolon's vengeful sons speak to Britomart are simply "strange"—alien—to her ear (V.vi.34, 38). The words of rationalized interpretation that the priest of Isis imposes on Britomart's dream are similarly dubious, ill sorting with the powerful imagery of its passion. Malengin is "smooth of tongue," and Malfont "a welhed / Of euill words, and wicked sclaunders" (V.ix.5, 26). Strikingly, like Munera's hands and feet, Malfont's tongue is nailed to a post: the punishment for his transgression is thus to fix, immobilize, and thoroughly materialize his speech. His speech is reduced to an organ of utterance, and Homer's "winged words" seem mocked and cynically monumentalized in his. Malfont's fate threatens both its opposites, whether unrestrained or immaterialized expression.[37] Like the Giant of materialism, Malfont embodies an amorphous but very real danger whose meaning is hard to contain, though clearly this danger touches free expression and, indeed, language itself to the quick.[38]

In a Lacanian essay that bears suggestively on Book V, Joan Copjec has described Vergil's *Fama* (rumor or report) as a paranoid image of the dismembered body that "appears at a point where the narration has reason to doubt its own omniscience, its own position as source of knowledge." It is at this point that "a cry [in the form of *Fama*] is torn from the throat of the narrative which [forcefully] reattaches it to the events of the world." Like *Fama* or like Malfont, the dismembered Giant who tumbles down the cliff can also be seen as "a hypostasized image of speech, an intrusion which is simultaneously the very *substance* of the narrative," its own self-reflexive commentary on its own mode of existence ("Anxiety of the Influence Machine," p. 44; my emphasis). For Copjec, the paranoia of such nightmarish images inheres in the ordering and alienating impulses of speech itself (pp. 55–56); that paranoia should particularly inform moments in the heightened order of allegorical fiction would seem to follow: witness *Fama*.

The rest of Spenser's fifth book only strengthens the indictment of language, perhaps inevitably after such specters as Malfont and the Giant. In the trial of Duessa, Zeal, a figure bent essentially on winning, is characterized as one "that well could charme his tongue, and time his speach / To all assayes" (ix.39). Recalling Clarinda's art (not to mention Despair's), Zeal's charmed tongue is not entirely reassuring, and it is less so in view of the ambivalent behavior of Mercilla that succeeds its triumph (ix.50–x.4).[39] As earlier remarked, Artegall's second debate concerning justice, this time with Burbon, issues in affirmation of a univocal truth that his action promptly belies. Yet all these precedent reservations in Book V regarding the role of language pale in the face of its final episode, the assault on Artegall by Envy, Detraction, and the Blatant Beast, whose hundred braying tongues are sharpened by the "cursed tongs" and "bitter wordes" of these two hags (xii.41–42). Unlike the falsehood that merely slides off the Giant's scale, these words have a very real impact, stinging and piercing, biting and wounding. As Artegall passes "afore" Envy, her "halfe-gnawen snake . . . Bit him behind, that long the marke was to be read," and her poison is just the prelude to the "bitter wordes" of Detraction and the Beast (xii.39–42). Like Artegall's shift from an outright denial of change to a recognition of material realities, however carefully hedged, this ugly episode acknowledges the biting reality of words, figurally, affectively, and also historically, since it blatantly alludes to the fate of Arthur, Lord Grey de Wilton; that is, it acknowledges the reality of words in terms that are fully material. Thus this episode, too, bitterly reattaches the narrative "to the events of the world." At the same time, however, the disfiguring end of Book V might also be seen to enable Book VI, in which words have real effects, whether physically, as when the Beast bites Timias and Serena, or ideally, as when the Graces materialize to dance on Mount Acidale. But if Acidale overshadows the end of Book VI, and if the range of verbal possibilities that Spenser's fables display is weighted finally toward idealism, these hedged conditions remain barely and painfully valid.

NOTES

1. See Susanne Lindgren Wofford, *The Choice of Achilles: The Ideology of Figure in the Epic* (Stanford, Calif.: Stanford University Press, 1992), 230–31, 236; James Nohrnberg, *The Analogy of "The Faerie Queene"* (Princeton: Princeton University Press, 1976), 758–59; and A. Leigh DeNeef, *Spenser and the Motives of Metaphor* (Durham, N.C.: Duke University Press, 1982), 95–97.

2. E.g., Gabriel Harvey's *Ciceronianus*, trans. Clarence A. Forbes, introduction and notes by Harold S. Wilson (Lincoln: University of Nebraska, 1945), 53, 77.

3. "The Egalitarian Giant: Representations of Justice in History/Literature," in *Reading between the Lines* (Madison: University of Wisconsin Press, 1993), 80–116. Patterson builds on the perception that Spenser examines "the contradiction between [the] principle and practice" of justice (89); for earlier argument of this view, see Judith H. Anderson, "'Nor Man It Is': The Knight of Justice in Book V of Spenser's *Faerie Queene*," 1970, reprinted in *Essential Articles for the Study of Edmund Spenser*, ed. A. C. Hamilton (Hamden, Conn.: Archon, 1972), 447–70; idem, *The Growth of a Personal Voice: "Piers Plowman" and "The Faerie Queene,"* (New Haven: Yale University Press, 1976), 154–55, 164–73, 184–86; and s.v. "Artegall," in *The Spenser Encyclopedia*, ed. A. C. Hamilton et al. (Toronto: University of Toronto Press, 1990), 62–64. Another relevant essay is Stephen Greenblatt's "Murdering Peasants: Status, Genre, and the Representation of Rebellion," in *Representing the English Renaissance* (Berkeley: University of California Press, 1988), 1–29, here 19–23; Greenblatt identifies Artegall's responses with "Spenser's" too unproblematically, however.

4. *The Faerie Queene*, V.ii, 26, 30, in *Works: A Variorum Edition*, ed. Edwin Greenlaw et al., 11 vols. (1938–57; reprint, Baltimore: Johns Hopkins University Press, 1966). Subsequent reference is to this edition *(Variorum)*; *The Faerie Queene* is cited as *FQ*.

5. The quotations come from *FQ*, V.ii.15, 17. For a description of Artegall's skill in swimming that is digressive in length, see stanza 16, especially lines 6–9:

> For *Artegall* in swimming skilfull was,
> And durst the depth of any water sownd.
> So ought each Knight, that vse of perill has,
> In swimming be expert through waters force to pas.

6. Langland's description of Lady Meed's fingers is taken from *Piers Plowman*, II.11: *Will's Visions of Piers Plowman, Do-Well, Do-Better, and Do-Best*, ed. George Kane and E. Talbot Donaldson (London: Athlone, 1975); this edition provides the relevant sixteenth-century variants. Like Munera, Meed is an ambivalent figure. The medieval adjective *try* ("trye") appears to have been rare at best by Spenser's time and its archaic coloring further suggests the intertextual influence of Langland's poem at this point.

7. Michel Foucault, *Discipline and Punish: The Birth of a Prison*, trans. Alan Sheridan (New York: Random House, 1977) is relevant: "the great spectacle of punishment ran the risk of being rejected by the very people to whom it was addressed" (63, also 59–69).

8. My use of the words *narrator*, *narrative*, and *poet* in these pages is deliberate. Their relation in *The Faerie Queene* is complex, but it is not an issue that I have space to examine here. For the most impressive recent treatments of it, see Harry Berger Jr., "Narrative as Rhetoric in *The Faerie Queene*," *English Literary Renaissance* 21 (Winter 1991): 3–48; and idem, "'Kidnapped Romance': Discourse in *The Faerie Queene*," in

Unfolded Tales: Essays on Renaissance Romance, ed. George M. Logan and Gordon Teskey (Ithaca: Cornell University Press, 1989), 208–56. Berger privileges narrative, equating the narrator with it. *Poet* becomes either an irrelevant term, similarly replaced by *narrative* (or *discourse*) or else the historical Spenser, upstaged and subverted by his poem. I am grateful to Harry Berger for reading this essay and giving me a number of very helpful suggestions.

9. *OED*, s.v. "Mighty": *adj.*, 1. "Possessing 'might' or power"; s.v. "Might," *sb.*: 1.a. "The quality of being able (to do what is desired); operative power"; 3. "Great or transcendent power or strength; mightiness."

10. Kurt Goldstein's description of the pathological anxiety triggered by perceived threats to the human sense of order and by actual disorder aligns itself suggestively with Artegall's response to the leveling Giant and at times, as here, with that of the narrative or narrator as well: *The Organism: A Holistic Approach to Biology Derived from Pathological Data in Man* (New York: American Book, 1939), 35-55, 291-306; *Human Nature in the Light of Psychopathology* (Cambridge: Harvard University Press, 1940), 85–119. Goldstein's data remain relevant, although their cultural implications would likely be interpreted in more repressive terms today. For a Lacanian interpretation of the paranoid confusion of Real and Symbolic inherent in an anxious or overbearing sense of order, see Joan Copjec, "The Anxiety of the Influencing Machine," *October* 23 (Winter 1982): 43–59, esp. 52–56.

11. Strikingly, when Occasion is bound in II.iv, the characters just stand around talking to one another: action stops, and the incursion of Atin is needed to get it going again. I have treated this episode further in "The Knight and the Palmer in *The Faerie Queene*, Book II," *Modern Language Quarterly* 31 (June 1970): 160–78.

12. On stars and planets, see Francis R. Johnson, *Astronomical Thought in Renaissance England: A Study of the English Scientific Writings from 1500 to 1645* (1937; reprint, New York: Octagon, 1968), e.g. 214. Johnson observes that the physical foundations of the Aristotelian system were "disastrously shattered" by "the new star of 1572, the comet of 1577, and the other comets that appeared in the last two decades of the sixteenth century" (214). Cf. Stephen Toulmin and June Goodfield, *The Fabric of the Heavens: The Development of Astronomy and Dynamics* (New York: Harper & Row, 1961), 184–98. Garrett Mattingly, *The Defeat of the Spanish Armada* (1959; reprint, London, 1970), 159–68, offers an example of the readiness of Europeans to respond to prophecy as the fin de siècle approached. On the agricultural and more generally economic difficulties experienced by the English in the 1590s, see John Guy, *Tudor England* (Oxford: Oxford University Press, 1988), 456; Buchanan Sharp, *In Contempt of All Authority: Rural Artisans and Riot in the West of England, 1586–1660* (Berkeley: University of California Press, 1980), 10–11, 13, 36–40; and Steve Rappaport, *Worlds within Worlds: Structures of Life in Sixteenth-Century London* (Cambridge: Cambridge University Press, 1989), 13–15, 136–37, 148–50. Although Rappaport is anxious to emphasize the stability of Tudor society and to deemphasize the impoverishment of its members, he acknowledges that the 1590s were "a decade of exceptional hardship," indeed, the only one in which London's problems conceivably threatened public order (378). With respect to Ireland, even a glance at Spenser's *View* is enough to indicate the imminent turmoil that surrounded the poet there. Aside from pressures in England and Ireland, the episode of the Giant has also been associated with the perceived threat of the Anabaptist movement: *Variorum,* 5:175–76. The growing number of impoverished vagrants in England, the dispossessed and famished inhabitants of the Irish countryside, and the Anabaptists all seemed near at hand to embody the cosmic disturbances.

13. See Anderson, *Growth of a Personal Voice*, 184–86, for my assumptions regarding the historical grounding of the speaker's view in the fifth proem and idem, "Nor Man It Is," 450–54, for those regarding the parodic elements of Artegall's early exploits.

14. *The Faerie Queene*, ed. Thomas P. Roche Jr. (1978; reprint, New Haven: Yale University Press, 1981), 1193. See also the biblical citations in *The Faerie Queene,* ed. A. C. Hamilton (London: Longman, 1977), 541. In addition to the biblical references given by Roche and Hamilton, I would invoke the cadence of Ecclesiastes, e.g., 3.1–8.

15. "Symbols, Song, Dance and Features of Articulation," *European Journal of Sociology* 15, no. 1 (1974): 55–81, here 69, 75–76, 79. The preceding quotation from Nigel Barley is in "A Structural Approach to the Proverb and Maxim," *Proverbium: Bulletin d'Information sur les Recherches parémiologiques* 22 (1972): 737–50, here 740.

16. Anderson, "Nor Man It Is," 447–70, esp. 461–66.

17. Alexandre Koyré describes the implications of the "scientific and philosophical revolution" of the early modern period in terms that illuminate what underlies Artegall's argument with the Giant, namely, "the disappearance, from philosophically and scientifically valid concepts, of the conception of the world as a finite, closed, and hierarchically ordered whole [a cosmos] . . . and its replacement by an indefinite and even infinite universe" whose components inhabit a single level of being. Such a universe "implies the discarding by scientific thought of all considerations based upon value-concepts" and "the utter devalorization of being, the divorce of the world of value and the world of facts." *From the Closed World to the Infinite Universe* (Baltimore: Johns Hopkins University Press, 1957), 2.

18. See Charles G. Smith, *Spenser's Proverb Lore* (Cambridge: Harvard University Press, 1970), nos. 53, 68, 155, 160, 179, 240, 472, 570. For the scriptural references, see the annotations of Roche's and Hamilton's editions and Naseeb Shaheen, *Biblical References in The Faerie Queene* (Memphis, Tenn.: Memphis State University Press, 1976), 82.

19. Hamilton's edition of *FQ* and Paul J. Alpers, *The Poetry of "The Faerie Queene"* (Princeton: Princeton University Press, 1967), 354–55.

20. Cf. George T. Wright on the "sacralizing character" of verse: "An Almost Oral Art: Shakespeare's Language on Stage and Page," *Shakespeare Quarterly* 43 (Summer 1992): 159–69, e.g., 166–67.

21. See Smith, *Spenser's Proverb Lore,* nos. 157, 231, 791, 891.

22. See Luke 3.5, "Every valley shall be filled, and every mountain and hill shall be brought low," cited by Hamilton in his edition of *FQ*, 541. As Hamilton observes, the Giant's context is apocalyptic.

23. In the interest of the evident ambiguities of these lines, I have dropped the comma at the end of the first of them. For discussion, see Harry Berger Jr., "The *Mutabilitie Cantos*: Archaism and Evolution in Retrospect," in *Spenser: A Collection of Critical Essays,* ed. Harry Berger Jr. (Englewood Cliffs, N.J.: Prentice-Hall, 1968), 146-76, here 172, and Anderson, *Personal Voice*, 201.

24. *FQ* V.ii.43; my emphasis. This stanza recalls 2 Esdras 4.5, 10–11; unlike the impersonally intoned ritual dominant in the preceding stanzas, it is addressed directly and primarily to the Knight's opponent and exhibits other rhetorical characteristics of dialogic exchange. (In the Geneva Bible, the books of Esdras are considered apocryphal.)

25. S. K. Heninger Jr.'s discussion of the materiality of words in J. C. Scaliger's theory of poetry affords a useful historical context for this stage of Artegall's debate

with the Giant. See S. K. Heninger Jr., *Sidney and Spenser: The Poet as Maker* (University Park: Pennsylvania State University Press, 1989), 211–14.

26. *OED*, s.v. "Betoken," 1. *trans.*, 2, 3, 4; s.v. "Token," 1.a, 3.a. While *Betoken* occurs uniquely in Spenser's fifth book, the form *betokening* appears in *Amoretti* 62, verse 4, where it means "being a sign, or omen of," "giving promise of," "auguring" (*OED* 3): "with shew of morning mylde he [the new year] hath begun, / betokening peace and plenty to ensew." Interestingly, *token(s)* is a word that occurs with unusual frequency in Book V. Versions of this word, including *betoken*, occur ten times in V, out of a total of twenty times in the other books, including VII. The 1596 addition, plus the Mutability Cantos, accounts for sixteen of the twenty occurrences. The various ways of "betokening" clearly engaged Spenser's interests to a greater extent as the relation of Faerie to the everyday world became more problematical.

27. Patterson, *Reading*, 95, recognizes "clear narrative and iconic indications that the confrontation between Knight and Giant is not simply a case of right versus wrong."

28. I am unaware of an adequate gloss on the first five lines of stanza 47 and therefore offer my own. In recent years, Roche's edition affords the fullest gloss on the Giant's efforts to weigh truth and falsehood and specifically concerns stanzas 48–49, but his gloss merely cites *Variorum*, 5:180. Hamilton's edition invokes the Aristotelian doctrine of the mean as early as stanza 45. Cf. as well the narrator's disapproval of Avarice in Book I, who "right and wrong ylike in equall ballaunce waide" (iv.27). As Roche remarks, the weighing episode in Book V is strained and, I think, significantly so.

29. See Ian Maclean, *Interpretation and Meaning in the Renaissance: The Case of Law* (Cambridge: Cambridge University Press, 1992), 142–58, here 155, 157, on thementalism of Renaissance jurisprudence and its corollary, the supplemental role of words; similarly, 181, 183, 202; also Samuel E. Thorne, ed., *A Discourse upon the Exposicion and Understanding of Statutes, with Sir Thomas Egerton's Additions* (San Marino, Calif.: The Huntington Library, 1942), 57–62, 77.

30. *FQ* IV.viii.26. For further discussion of this point, see Anderson, "'Myn auctour': Spenser's Enabling Fiction and Eumnestes' 'immortall scrine,'" in *Unfolded Tales: Essays on Renaissance Romance,* ed. George M. Logan and Gordon Teskey (Ithaca: Cornell University Press, 1989), 16-31, esp. 27–28. Cf. also St. Augustine, *On Christian Doctrine*, trans. D. W. Robertson Jr. (1958; reprint, Indianapolis, Ind.: Bobbs-Merrill, 1984), 70–71 (Bk. II.xxxv). Wofford, *Choice of Achilles,* 346, characterizes the "inward turn" of the allegory at this point as an evasive effort "to transform the giant from political to moral allegory."

31. Margaret W. Ferguson, "Saint Augustine's Region of Unlikeness: The Crossing of Exile and Language," *Georgia Review* 29 (winter 1975): 842–64, here 861–62, on the inward ear; 847 and 853 are also particularly relevant.

32. See M[iriam] T[herese] Larkin, *Language in the Philosophy of Aristotle* (The Hague: Mouton, 1971), 17 (preceding quotation), and Letter VII, 342e–343a, 344b, in *The Collected Dialogues of Plato, Including the Letters,* ed. Edith Hamilton and Huntington Cairns (New York: Random House, 1961), 1590–91. Plato's letters are often characterized as "doubtfully genuine." Among them, Letter VII has been given the most credence: see R. G. Bury, trans., *Plato* (London: Heinemann, 1929), 391–92, 472; and Glenn R. Morrow, trans., *Plato's Epistles*, rev. ed. (Indianapolis, Ind.: Bobbs-Merrill, 1962), 5, 9, 14, esp. 16. Morrow suggests that the letters "were written, if not by Plato himself, at least by some well-informed member of the Platonic circle, at a date very shortly after the death of Plato" (13). Ludwig Edelstein rejects Plato's authorship of Letter VII but describes this letter as an "important interpretation of Plato's life and

doctrine which must go back to the first decades after his death" (*Plato's Seventh Letter* [Leiden: E. J. Brill, 1966], 4, 76–85). The letters have long been a part of the Platonic tradition: e.g., early Hellenistic catalogs of Plato's writings include a collection of letters; Timaeus, an early historian, makes use of them; and Cicero quotes and refers to Letter VII as Plato's (Morrow, *Plato,* 13; Edelstein, *Plato's Seventh Letter,* 1). Harry Berger Jr.,'s recent essays on Plato's dialogues have interpreted them as proto-Derridean inscriptions, deeply distrustful of logocentrism: e.g., "Levels of Discourse in Plato's Dialogues," in *Literature and the Question of Theory,* ed. Anthony J. Cascardi (Baltimore: Johns Hopkins University Press, 1987), 75–100; and "*Phaedrus* and the Politics of Inscription," in *Plato and Postmodernism,* ed. Steven Shankman (Glenside, Pa.: Aldine Press, 1994). For all these reasons, I have emphasized a tradition of Platonic interpretation in the present paragraph—a tradition of which Augustine is a notably influential exemplar (and Calvin after him).

33. "De catechizandis rudibus," in *Patrologia Latina,* ed. J. P. Migne (Paris: Garnier, 1887), 40:311–12.

34. See R. A. Markus, "St. Augustine on Signs," *Phronesis* 2, no. 1 (1957): 60–83, esp. 77. While these views are debated in the secondary literature on Augustine, I do not see how any reading of his actual works can avoid them. For a classic statement of Augustine's position, see *The Trinity,* trans. Stephen McKenna, in *The Fathers of the Church* (Washington, D.C.: Catholic University of America Press, 1963), 45:475, 477–78, 487 (Bk. XV.x.19, xi.20, xiv.24): e.g., the "word cannot be uttered in sound nor thought in the likeness of sound, such as must be done with the word of any language; it precedes all the signs by which it is signified" (478:xi.20). In a stimulating essay, Linda Gregerson assumes the relevance of Augustine to Spenser's first book but does not acknowledge the ambivalence at best of Augustine's attitude to any kind of human language and not merely to its written forms: "Protestant Erotics: Idolatry and Interpretation in Spenser's *Faerie Queene,*" *ELH* 58 (Spring 1991): 1–34.

35. See Ferguson, "Saint Augustine's Region of Unlikeness," 847, 853: Augustine acknowledges "that his own language traps him" because "there is something in the nature of language which necessitates a spatial understanding of a difference—an unlikeness—that is not spatial . . . at all."

36. E.g., *FQ* V.ii.15, 18, iii.22; v.13, vii.22. After Radegone, the remarkably few instances in which cruelty touches Artegall are qualified by circumstances and explicable in the terms I have argued in *Growth of a Personal Voice*, 168–73.

37. Among other meanings, the figure of Malfont glances parodically at an early modern orthoepy that sought a physical basis in the functioning of the mouth and throat for the sounds of letters: see, for example, John Hart's *Orthographie* (1569; reprint, Menston, U.K.: Scolar, 1969). Hart aims for a spelling that is "natural" rather than conventional. I discuss Hart and his relation to frozen language (and to Spenser) in *Words that Matter: Linguistic Perception in Renaissance English*, forthcoming from Stanford University Press.

38. For recent commentary on Malfont, see Elizabeth Bieman, *Plato Baptized: Towards the Interpretation of Spenser's Mimetic Fictions* (Toronto: University of Toronto Press, 1988), 182–85; Mihoko Suzuki, *Metamorphoses of Helen: Authority, Difference, and the Epic* (Ithaca: Cornell University Press, 1989), 193–95; and Theresa M. Krier, *Gazing on Secret Sights: Spenser, Classical Imitation, and the Decorums of Vision* (Ithaca: Cornell University Press, 1990), 214–15. Lately, the number of commentators who do *not* treat Malfont in a significant way is surprising: for a tantalizing three-liner, however, see Richard A. McCabe, *The Pillars of Eternity: Time and Providence in "The Faerie*

Queene" (Kill Lane, Blackrock, County Dublin, Ireland: Irish Academic Press, 1989), 78.

39. Michael O'Connell's discussion of Mercilla's behavior is useful: *Mirror and Veil: The Historical Dimension of Spenser's "Faerie Queene"* (Chapel Hill: University of North Carolina Press, 1977), 150–54.

Works Cited

Alpers, Paul J. *The Poetry of "The Faerie Queene."* Princeton: Princeton University Press, 1967.

Anderson, Judith H. "Artegall." In *The Spenser Encyclopedia*, edited by A. C. Hamilton, Donald Cheney, and W. F. Blissett, 62–64. Toronto: University of Toronto Press, 1990.

———. *The Growth of a Personal Voice: "Piers Plowman" and "The Faerie Queene."* New Haven: Yale University Press, 1976.

———. "The Knight and the Palmer in *The Faerie Queene*, Book II." *Modern Language Quarterly* 31 (June 1970): 160–78.

———. "'Myn auctour': Spenser's Enabling Fiction and Eumnestes' 'immortall scrine.'" In *Unfolded Tales: Essays on Renaissance Romance*, edited by George M. Logan and Gordon Teskey, 16–31. Ithaca: Cornell University Press, 1989.

———. "'Nor Man It Is': The Knight of Justice in Book V of Spenser's *Faerie Queene.*" 1970. Reprinted in *Essential Articles for the Study of Edmund Spenser*, edited by A. C. Hamilton, 447–70. Hamden, Conn.: Archon, 1972.

———. *Words that Matter: Linguistic Perception in Renaissance English.* Stanford, Calif.: Stanford University Press, forthcoming.

Augustine, Saint. "De catechizandis rudibus." In *Patrologia Latina*, edited by J. P. Migne, 50:311–12. Paris: Garnier, 1887.

———. *On Christian Doctrine.* Translated by D. W. Robertson Jr. 1958. Reprint, Indianapolis, Ind.: Bobbs-Merrill, 1984.

———. *The Trinity.* Translated by Stephen McKenna. In *The Fathers of the Church.* Washington, D.C.: The Catholic University of America Press, 1963.

Barley, Nigel. "A Structural Approach to the Proverb and Maxim." *Proverbium: Bulletin d'Information sur les Recherches parémiologiques* 22 (1972): 737–50.

Berger, Harry, Jr. "'Kidnapped Romance': Discourse in *The Faerie Queene.*" In *Unfolded Tales: Essays on Renaissance Romance*, edited by George M. Logan and Gordon Teskey, 208–56. Ithaca: Cornell University Press, 1989.

———. "Levels of Discourse in Plato's Dialogues." In *Literature and the Question of Theory*, edited by Anthony J. Cascardi, 75–100. Baltimore: The Johns Hopkins University Press, 1987.

———. "The *Mutability Cantos*: Archaism and Evolution in Retrospect." In *Spenser: A Collection of Critical Essays*, edited by Harry Berger Jr., 146–76. Englewood Cliffs, N. J.: Prentice-Hall, 1968.

———. "Narrative as Rhetoric in *The Faerie Queene.*" *English Literary Renaissance* 21 (winter 1991): 3–48.

———. "*Phaedrus* and the Politics of Inscription." In *Plato and Postmodernism*, edited by Steven Shankman. Glenside, Pa.: Aldine Press, 1994.

Bieman, Elizabeth. *Plato Baptized: Towards the Interpretation of Spenser's Mimetic Fictions*. Toronto: University of Toronto Press, 1988.

Bloch, Maurice. "Symbols, Song, Dance and Features of Articulation." *European Journal of Sociology* 15, no. 1 (1974): 55–81.

Bury, R. G., trans. *Plato*. London: Heinemann, 1929.

Copjec, Joan. "The Anxiety of the Influencing Machine." *October* 23 (winter 1982): 43–59.

DeNeef, A. Leigh. *Spenser and the Motives of Metaphor*. Durham, N.C.: Duke University Press, 1982.

Edelstein, Ludwig. *Plato's Seventh Letter*. Leiden: E. J. Brill, 1966.

Ferguson, Margaret W. "Saint Augustine's Region of Unlikeness: The Crossing of Exile and Language." *Georgia Review* 29 (winter 1975): 842–64.

Foucault, Michel. *Discipline and Punish: The Birth of a Prison*. Translated by Alan Sheridan. New York: Random House, 1977.

Goldstein, Kurt. *Human Nature in the Light of Psychotherapy*. Cambridge: Harvard University Press, 1940.

———. *The Organism: A Holistic Approach to Biology Derived from Pathological Data in Man*. New York: American Book, 1939.

Greenblatt, Stephen. "Murdering Peasants: Status, Genre, and the Representation of Rebellion." 1983. Reprinted in *Representing the Renaissance*, edited by Stephen Greenblatt, 1–29. Berkeley: University of California Press, 1988.

Gregerson, Linda. "Protestant Ethics: Idolatry and Interpretation in Spenser's *Faerie Queene*." *ELH* 58 (Spring 1991): 1–34.

Guy, John. *Tudor England*. Oxford: Oxford University Press, 1988.

Hart, John. *Orthographie*. 1569. Reprint, Menston, U.K.: Scolar, 1969.

Harvey, Gabriel. *Ciceronianus*. Translated by Clarence A. Forbes. Introduction and notes by Harold S. Wilson. Lincoln: University of Nebraska Press, 1945.

Heninger, S. K., Jr. *Sidney and Spenser: The Poet as Maker*. University Park: The Pennsylvania State University Press, 1989.

Johnson, Francis R. *Astronomical Thought in Renaissance England: A Study of the English Scientific Writings from 1500 to1645*. 1937. Reprint, New York: Octagon, 1968.

Koyré, Alexandre. *From the Closed World to the Infinite Universe*. Baltimore: The Johns Hopkins University Press, 1957.

Krier, Theresa M. *Gazing on Secret Sights: Spenser, Classical Imitation, and the Decorums of Vision*. Ithaca: Cornell University Press, 1990.

Langland, William. *Will's Visions of Piers Plowman, Do-Well, Do-Better, and Do-Best*. Edited by George Kane and E. Talbot Donaldson. London: Athlone Press, 1975.

Larkin, M[iriam] T[herese]. *Language in the Philosophy of Aristotle*. The Hague: Mouton, 1971.

Maclean, Ian. *Interpretation and Meaning in the Renaissance: The Case of Law*. Cambridge: Cambridge University Press, 1992.

Markus, R. A. "St. Augustine on Signs." *Phronesis* 2, no. 1 (1957): 60–83.

Mattingly, Garrett. *The Defeat of the Spanish Armada*. 1959. Reprint, London: Jonathan Cape, 1970.

McCabe, Richard A. *The Pillars of Eternity: Time and Providence in "The Faerie Queene."* Kill Lane, Blackrock, County Dublin, Ireland: Irish Academic Press, 1989.

Morrow, Glen R., trans. *Plato*. Rev. ed. Indianapolis, Ind.: Bobbs-Merrill, 1962.

Nohrnberg, James. *The Analogy of "The Faerie Queene."* Princeton: Princeton University Press, 1976.

O'Connell, Michael. *Mirror and Veil: The Historical Dimension of Spenser's "Faerie Queene."* Chapel Hill: University of North Carolina Press, 1977.

Patterson, Annabel. *Reading between the Lines*. Madison: University of Wisconsin Press, 1993.

Plato. *The Collected Dialogues of Plato*. Edited by Edith Hamilton and Huntington Cairns. New York: Random House, 1961.

Rappaport, Steve. *Worlds within Worlds: Structures of Life in Sixteenth-Century London*. Cambridge: Cambridge University Press, 1989.

Shaheen, Naseeb. *Biblical References in The Faerie Queene*. Memphis, Tenn.: Memphis State University Press, 1976.

Sharp, Buchanan. *In Contempt of All Authority: Rural Artisans and Riot in the West of England, 1586–1660*. Berkeley: University of California Press, 1980.

Smith, Charles G. *Spenser's Proverb Lore*. Cambridge: Harvard University Press, 1970.

Spenser, Edmund. *The Faerie Queene*. Edited by A. C. Hamilton. London: Longman, 1977.

———. *The Faerie Queene*. Edited by Thomas P. Roche Jr. 1978. Reprint, New Haven: Yale University Press, 1981.

———. *Works: A Variorum Edition*. Edited by Edwin Greenlaw, Charles Grosvenor Osgood, and Frederick Morgan Padelford. 11 vols. 1932–57. Reprint, Baltimore: The Johns Hopkins University Press, 1966.

Suzuki, Mihoko. *Metamorphoses of Helen: Authority, Difference, and the Epic*. Ithaca: Cornell University Press, 1989.

Throne, Samuel E., ed. *A Discourse upon the Exposicion and Understanding of Statutes, with Sir Thomas Egerton's Additions*. San Marino, Calif.: The Huntington Library, 1942.

Toulmin, Stephen, and June Goodfield. *The Fabric of the Heavens: The Development of Astronomy and Dynamics*. New York: Harper & Row, 1961.

Wofford, Susanne Lindgren. *The Choice of Achilles: The Ideology of Figure in the Epic*. Stanford, Calif.: Stanford University Press, 1992.

Wright, George T. "An Almost Oral Art: Shakespeare's Language on Stage and Page." *Shakespeare Quarterly* 43 (summer 1992): 159–69.

Appropriating the Author of *The Faerie Queene:* The Attribution of the *View of the Present State of Ireland* and *A Brief Note of Ireland* to Edmund Spenser

JEAN R. BRINK

I. Posthumous Attributions to the Spenser Canon

IN an article examining Spenser's patronage connections with Sir Philip Sidney and Robert Dudley, earl of Leicester, S. K. Heninger Jr. has called into question the legends suggesting that Spenser "played a significant role in the power brokerage of Elizabethan England as one of Leicester's agents."[1] Heninger's skepticism concerning Spenser's career has resulted in a long overdue reassessment of his literary biography, but the poet's centrality to the politics of Elizabethan Ireland remains largely unquestioned.[2] Two texts are responsible for this perception of Spenser: the *View of the Present State of Ireland* and *A Brief Note of Ireland*. Relying on postcolonialist interpretations of these prose tracts, critics see Spenser as a key figure in the development and administration of England's colonial policies in Ireland.[3] Even though there is no contemporary evidence for attributing either the *View* or *A Brief Note of Ireland* to Spenser, these texts are used both to gloss his literary work and reconstruct his career.

The *View* was not attributed to Spenser until 1633, when it was printed by James Ware.[4] It did not appear in Spenser's collected works until the 1679 folio, an edition that included at least one other work now regarded as spurious.[5] *A Brief Note of Ireland* consists of three comparatively short tracts on Ireland, entitled respectively "A breife note of Ireland," "To the Queene," and "Certaine pointes to be considered of in the recovery of the Realme of Ireland." They were first attributed to Spenser by Alexander Grosart in 1894, well over three hundred years after Spenser's death. Following Grosart, Rudolf Gottfried included these tracts in the *Spenser Variorum* in 1949.[6]

The confusion surrounding Spenser's biography and canon is by no means unique. Anecdotes are so intertwined with fact in the biographies of many literary and political figures that it becomes difficult to distinguish facts from inferences that have gained credibility through repetition. The difficulties are compounded when we attempt to sort out the attribution of works to major literary figures. Printers and booksellers have always been eager to increase the canon of major figures since they stand to make higher profits by selling copies of their works. Numerous seventeenth-century political manuscripts were attributed to Sir Walter Ralegh that we now recognize as part of a bogus canon that began to develop during his lifetime and burgeoned after his death.[7] Defining the canon of a Chaucer or a Shakespeare most frequently involves the rejection of works spuriously attributed to him on the basis of subject matter or initials.

Nineteenth-century editors frequently complicated the canon because they preferred to claim new works for an author rather than to sift the evidence for attribution. Alexander Grosart, for example, after concluding that works signed J. D. or I. D. had to be either by John Donne or Sir John Davies, attributed sonnets in *A Poetical Rhapsody* to Davies on the grounds that they could not have been written by Donne. Because he also decided that Davies had repented of his wild youth when he wrote *Nosce Teipsum* (1599) and went to Ireland in 1603, Grosart arbitrarily attributed all poems signed J. D. that were written after 1603 to John Davies of Hereford, whom he also edited.[8] Consequently, we find *A Scourge for Paper-Persecutors or Papers Complaint* by J. D. (1624) attributed to John Davies of Hereford without commentary, even though the writing master had died six years earlier.

Once an edition of a major work is received as standard and regarded as authoritative, and the careers of critics and commentators become vested in particular attributions, it requires considerable objectivity to reconsider the evidence—even when attributions were made posthumously with little justification.

The attribution to Spenser of tracts on Ireland illustrates these problems. It is conceivable that Spenser wrote a tract—or even tracts—on Ireland, but no contemporary reference or manuscript witness identifies Spenser as the author of such a tract prior to James Ware's 1633 edition of the *View*. A prudent editor would be as hesitant to endorse this attribution to Spenser as that of *Axiochus*.[9] In the case of the three unrelated manuscripts, *A Brief Note of Ireland*, I will put the point more forcefully: These tracts should never have been attributed to Edmund Spenser. If he had not been the author of the *Faerie Queene*, and reputed to be the author of the *View*, no one would ever have attributed them to Spenser.

When attribution is uncertain, two kinds of evidence, internal and external, are usually considered. Internal evidence consists of ideas, stylistic features, and verbal echoes characteristic of other works known to have been written by a particular author. Following the publication of Samuel Schoenbaum's *Internal Evidence and Elizabethan Dramatic Authorship* in 1966, critics have become increasingly cautious about relying on stylistic evidence in cases of authorial attribution.[10] External evidence includes facts about how a particular text was produced, ranging from scribal identification to contemporary references concerning authorship and even to contemporary allusions to the text itself. More weight now attaches to external evidence and to the circumstances of physical production and distribution of texts than to stylistic analysis.[11]

Critics, however, continue to assume that modern editions of sixteenth-century works represent authoritative texts and that they need not be subjected to bibliographical analysis. Under the auspices of D. F. McKenzie and others, a new term, the sociology of texts, has been coined to suggest the importance of regarding texts as products of social and institutional processes of transmission as well as approaching them as physical artifacts.[12] New historicists and cultural materialists have also redirected attention to the cultural contexts in which literary works were produced, while at the same time reminding us that current concerns may shape our reconstruction of the past. Somewhat ironically, the New Schools—whether labeled New Criticism or New Historicism—have sustained the widespread belief that twentieth-century standard editions, even those prepared before the work of R. B. McKerrow and W. W. Greg was fully absorbed, are reliable.[13]

II. Authorship of the *View of the Present State of Ireland*

To illustrate the kinds of problems that beset the uncritical attribution of the *View* to Spenser, it is only necessary to recount the basic facts concerning its entry into the Stationers' Register and its posthumous publication. In 1598 the publisher Matthew Lownes attempted to obtain a license to print a manuscript of the *View*. Lownes's manuscript may have been Bodleian, MS Rawlinson B. 478, which contains a copy of a complete text of the *View* and the note: "Mr. Collinges I pray enter this Copie for mathew Lownes to be prynted when he do bringe other authorytie. Thomas Man."[14] Although this note appears to be in a late-sixteenth- or early-seventeenth-century hand, its presence in Rawlinson B. 478 is anomalous. I am unaware of any other instance in which a note regarding entry into the Stationers' Register was written in the manuscript itself. Neither this note nor the entry in the Stationers' Register mentions Spenser. The scribal text of MS Rawlinson B. 478 concludes with the initials E. S. but does not mention Spenser by name. The name was later added to the title page in a different ink and hand. The binding has also been tampered with and papers have been inserted into the front of the manuscript containing an attribution to Spenser. Since none of this material is in the hand of the scribe who copied the manuscript, it carries little or no weight in terms of attribution.

Lownes evidently abandoned the project of printing the *View* in 1598; nothing suggests that it was suppressed, although that assumption pervades recent secondary scholarship.[15] Lownes seems to have taken a serious interest in the works of Edmund Spenser. In 1609 he obtained a manuscript copy of the "Mutabilitie Cantos," which he added to the Spenser canon by printing these stanzas at the end of his edition of the *Faerie Queene*. After producing the 1609 folio of the *Faerie Queene*, Lownes brought out folio editions of the complete works. The format of the folios—most works are separately paginated—suggests that Lownes printed and reprinted the works individually as they ran out, frequently with individual title pages, and then gathered them under more general title pages. Thus, a 1617 folio may contain works that were actually printed in 1611 or 1613.[16] While Lownes probably assembled the works in this manner to save money, his methods made it very easy to add a new work. The popularity of mixed genres, such as Sidney's *Arcadia*, makes it unlikely that Lownes would have hesitated to print prose with poetry. Ben Jonson's 1616 folio included a mixture of genres, and, even if Lownes had qualms concerning mixing genres, he could certainly have printed a separate edition of the *View*.

It is bibliographically significant that Lownes, who had a manuscript of the *View* in 1598, never attributed this work to Edmund Spenser. Two explanations suggest themselves: By 1611 Lownes had lost or disposed of his manuscript of the *View* and could not obtain another copy. But since no manuscript of the "Mutabilitie Cantos" has survived—in contrast to at least twenty-one manuscripts of the *View*—it seems likely that the enterprising Lownes could have secured a copy. Alternatively, Lownes may not have associated the E. S. who wrote the *View of the Present State of Ireland* with Edmund Spenser.

Spenser's editors have not addressed the early bibliographic history of the *View*. In 1949 when Rudolf Gottfried prepared the text for the *Spenser Variorum*, he made no attempt to supply a physical description of the fifteen manuscripts then known (9:506–7). Because no such description was even attempted, serious questions, such as when Edmund Spenser's name was added to a particular title page or when, or if, a leaf containing an attribution was inserted, were simply ignored. Watermarks facilitate the dating of the earliest possible circulation of a particular manuscript, but this kind of physical evidence for dating the *View* has never been considered. In 1980 Peter Beal identified four additional manuscripts of the *View*, and two others have since come to light.[17] These new manuscripts have neither been described nor collated with the *Spenser Variorum*, which continues to be received as authoritative. In spite of questions about authorship, dating, and textual authority, critical commentary on Spenser and Ireland, based on his assumed authorship of the *View*, continues to proliferate. A critical bibliography of the extant Spenser manuscripts remains to be prepared; only this kind of bibliography can resolve issues ranging from authorial attribution to textual authority.

My preliminary work on such a bibliography of Spenserian manuscripts has revealed some interesting and potentially quite significant facts. For example, I have conclusively identified the same watermark in at least three extant manuscripts of the *View*. These versions were copied on the same paper, possibly at the same time: Huntington Library, Ellesmere MS 7041; Cambridge, Gonville and Caius MS 188.221; and British Library, Sloane MS 1695. A cockatrice watermark on the paper dates these manuscripts at the earliest from 1611 to 1621.[18] These particular manuscripts, demonstrably copied after Spenser's death, have been crucial to the construction of the standard editions of the *View*.

Gottfried transcribed Huntington Library, Ellesmere MS 7041 and used it as his copy-text, claiming that he had exactly "reproduced" it with no alterations other than the following: "all abbreviations, except in the case of numbers, of proper names, and of words abbreviated in modern usage, are spelled out; and all marginalia, as well as many of the deleted words are omitted" (9:39). He adds that he fully collated this text with only two of the extant fifteen manuscripts: Cambridge, Gonville and Caius College, MS 188.221 and Bodleian Library, MS Rawlinson B. 478, but offers no substantive argument for ignoring the twelve other manuscripts. He does not explain why he decided to collate only three manuscripts, two of which were those previously used by W. L. Renwick. It is indicative of the state of textual scholarship on Spenser that Gottfried used a seventeenth-century manuscript as the copy-text for the *Spenser Variorum*. Gonville and Caius MS 188.221, which both Renwick and Gottfried used to correct their copy-texts, dates from the seventeenth century and was copied on the same paper as Ellesmere MS 7041. In light of physical evidence that key manuscripts of the *View* date from the seventeenth-century, Ware's assertion that the E. S. who wrote the *View of the Present State of Ireland* was Edmund Spenser seems even more questionable.[19]

The manuscript source(s) for Ware's edition have never been satisfactorily identified. Gottfried's oft-repeated judgment that James Ware edited the text of the *View*, softening anti-Irish statements, is based on unacceptable bibliographical practice. Gottfried collated Ware's edition against his own copy-text without considering the possibility that Ware is likely to have used a different manuscript as his copy-text. Ellesmere MS 7041 is located among the Ellesmere papers at the Huntington Library and contains an annotated index

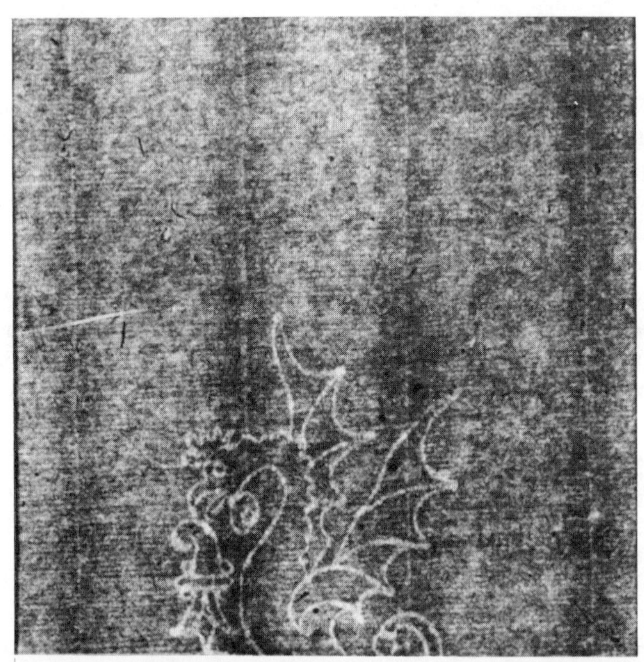

Cockatrice Watermark (Heawood, No. 842) from HEH Ellsmere MS. 7041. By permission of the Huntington Library, San Marino, California.

prepared by Sir Thomas Egerton, who died in 1617; nothing connects this manuscript with Ware.[20]

In his preface to the *View,* Ware says that he is reprinting a manuscript *Ex Bibliotheca Remi in Christo patris D. Jacobi Vsserij Archip. Armachani*, but his statement is troubling in two ways: First, it is puzzling that he cites a specific provenance for the manuscript of the *View,* but not for the Campion and Hanmer histories of Ireland, both of which survived only in manuscript and were printed for the first time in 1633. Second, and even more problematical, no copy of the *View* is in Ussher's library at Trinity College. In the *Spenser Variorum* Gottfried handles this problem ambiguously by describing Trinity College, Dublin, MS E.3.26 (now Trinity MS 589) as T (9:39), but later acknowledges that "no copy of the *View* can be traced in the seventeenth-century lists of the manuscripts, among them Ussher's, at Trinity" (9:517).[21] The handwritten catalog prepared by John Lyons, *Catalogus Codicum Manuscriptorum Bibliotheca Coll: Trin: & Universitatis Dublin* (1745?) states on f. 89V [p. 176] "N.B.> Numbers E.23, E.25, E.26, E.27 were claimed about 50 years ago as belonging to the Auditor General's Office and were accordingly delivered up . . . in their place were put some volumes purchased from Mr. Mercier in 1807." The manuscripts purchased from Mercier were placed in the book presses or shelf space freed by this delivery. Trinity E.3.25, for example, contains a collection of pieces chiefly relating to Ireland, including a letter from "Sr P: Sidney to Q. Elizabeth" on her marriage. Thus, the copy of the *View* at Trinity College (formerly E.3.26 and now Trinity 589) was unquestionably a late acquisition.[22]

Further, the *View* is not mentioned in any of the extant lists or catalogs of either Ussher or James Ware's library.[23] A catalog of James Ware's manuscripts was prepared by Robert Hughes in 1648, and Trinity College has a typescript of Hughes's catalog. It contains references to works on Ireland including a folio volume of letters and government papers collected by Geoffrey Fenton, B. 3 (p. 9); "Annales Hiberniae a primis incolis, usq. ad annum Dom. 1600," C1 (p. 13); "Rerum Hibernicarum Annales, ab anno Dom. 1579. usq; ad annum 1590. Hibernice," C2 (p. 15), and the much-copied tract by Patrick Finglas dating from the reign of Henry VIII on proposals for resolving conflict in Ireland (C2), p. 15. Hughes's catalog, however, contains no references to Edmund Spenser or to any work with a title resembling that of the *View.* Several commonplace books belonging either to Ussher or to Ware detail the acquisition of various manuscripts or books; for example, Trinity E.4.13 mentions Richard Beacon (f. 24), Edmund Campion (f. 51), R. Stanyhurst (f. 156), E. S., *De rebus gestis Britanniae* (f. 58). Both Stanyhurst and Hanmer are quoted in another commonplace book of Ware's: British Library, Add. MS 4821, 144 and 130. Penciled into the Trinity College copy of the catalog of Edward Bernard, *Catalogi Librorum Manuscriptorum Angliae et Hiberniae* (1697), is a note to the effect that some of the manuscripts belonging to Clarendon "passed to the Chandos Collection and thence to the Rawlinson." That may have been the case with item 60.60, "Edm[und] Spencer's present State of Ireland, 4to."[24] Bernard has another interesting reference to Spenser in the catalog of manuscripts belonging to Peter le Neve. There he lists "Edmund Spenser's View of the Present State of Ireland, AD 1584."[25]

In summary, while we can be sure that Trinity 589 was not part of Ussher's library, it is unclear which, if any, extant manuscripts of the *View* may have served as the copy-text(s) for Ware's edition. Further, there appears to be no supporting bibliographical evidence, from book lists or commonplace books, that either Bishop Ussher or James Ware owned a manuscript of the *View*.

III. A History of the Attribution of *A Brief Note of Ireland* to Spenser

The attribution of *A Brief Note of Ireland* to Spenser, deriving from his supposed authorship of the *View*, first occurred in a series of unwarranted inferences in an anonymous article on Edmund Spenser that appeared in *Dublin University Magazine* (1861):

> Our next trace of the poet is as the writer, soon after his arrival in London, of two treatises on the insurrection for the instruction of the Secretary of State. These able documents, besides disclosing intimate knowledge of the causes which incited Tyrone, gave masterly advice as to the best mode of suppressing revolt. . . . The two manuscript State Papers written by Spenser immediately before his death are still unpublished. One is lengthy and adds to the proofs his printed treatise gives of his consummate abilities.[26]

The author of this article knew of Ware's printed edition of the *View*, but since he describes one of the two state papers as lengthy, he is probably referring to P.R.O., SP63/202, Pt. 4/58, a manuscript of the *View* in the Public Record Office, and P.R.O., SP63/202, Pt. 4/59, the much shorter "To the Queene," which discusses the reasons for Tyrone's rebellion.

While preparing the biography of Spenser for his full-scale edition of Spenser's works, Alexander Grosart pursued the tantalizing suggestion that there were unpublished works by Spenser in the Public Record Office and decided that three documents wrapped in a bundle with the *View* and numerous other works on Ireland were "Spenser's own State-Papers." He congratulated himself on being the first to attribute them to Spenser:

> It is incomprehensible that neither Collier, nor Professor Hales, nor Dean Church, nor any one should have taken the pains to get at these vital Spenser documents. All the more rare is my good fortune to be the first to print and use them.[27]

Grosart printed the three anonymous manuscripts in appendix 5 of his biography under the rubric *A Brief Note of Ireland*, even though this title is actually the title of only the first document. When the printed calendars were prepared, Ernest Atkinson described them in entries immediately following his description of the *View*.[28] The three documents have no substantive relationship to each other and may not have been written by the same person. They have no title page, but are grouped arbitrarily as P.R.O., SP63/202, Pt. 4/59. No provenance is known except that when Grosart printed them in 1884, he stated that they derived from Bundle 188, No. 18.[29]

In short, there is no evidence supporting the attribution of these texts to Spenser. Essentially, Grosart used the three works making up *A Brief Note of Ireland* to elaborate a picture of Spenser as a heroic figure, calm in the face of adversity. The passage requires quotation in full:

> [B]etween the 9th and 24th of December, 1598, Spenser and his wife and family arrived in London. That he arrived in no panic-terror or as having lost his head, is proved by a State-Paper addressed by him to the Queen direct, and not one line of which ever has been printed. . . . It was delivered doubtless by Spenser himself in London to the Secretary of State, along with the "Dispatch" of Norreys of 9th December. This all-important Paper, and the others accompanying, are in the well-known handwriting of Sir Dudley Carleton, and all are carefully noted by him as written by Spenser (spelled "Spencer"). There comes first "A briefe note of Ireland"—most noticeable for its very commonplace of topographical information. The pulse of the man who wrote it was not fevered. Next a Letter or rather State-Paper "To the Queene." Finally, "Certaine Pointes to be considered of in the recovery of the Realme of Ireland." . . . The "Certaine Pointes" are very much a condensation of the *Veue of Ireland*, and tell us that whatever of sorrow and disappointment had come upon its writer, he was lion-hearted still, and bated no jot of hope or resolution. (230)

Grosart's attribution of *A Brief Note of Ireland* to Spenser is based on two claims: (1) that "all [the manuscripts] are carefully noted . . . as written by Spenser," and (2) that "this all-important Paper and the others accompanying, are in the well-known handwriting of Sir Dudley Carleton."

A Brief Note of Ireland actually consists of three folio manuscripts, the first of which is entitled "A Breife Note of Ireland" (f. 195R).[30] The second manuscript is entitled "To the Queene" (ff. 196R–199R) and the third, "Certaine pointes to be considered of in the recouery of the Realme of Ireland" (ff. 199R–200R). The manuscripts are not attributed to Spenser; no author is cited either in the title or at the conclusion of these texts (reproduced below as appendix A). Grosart's claim that they are "carefully noted as being by Spenser" is based on an inscription written on the back of the last folio of the third document. The inscription reads: "A briefe discourse of Ireland by Spencer" (appendix B). The texts of the three documents are written in a seventeenth-century secretary hand, whereas the inscription is in an italic hand of a much later date. It is also interesting that the word "breife" appearing in the first document is here spelled "briefe" and that Spenser's name is spelled Spencer. An inscription added later to the back of one of three anonymous documents is scant evidence for authorial attribution. Following this logic, any note in any manuscript could serve as a basis for attribution.

Grosart's assertion that the documents are in the "well-known hand of Dudley Carleton" is equally untenable.[31] The three component texts of *A Brief Note of Ireland* are written in a secretary hand; italic is used to highlight the titles, marginal gloss, and opening portions and transitions within the documents. The secretary graphs are quite distinctive—for example, the long *h*, horned *a*, *d* with a back extending back to the left, and crossed *g*. Not one of these secretary graphs is characteristic of the hand of Dudley Carleton. In 1598/9 Dudley Carleton was part of a diplomatic party in Ostend. A letter of his dated 9 January 1598/9 to John Chamberlain is reproduced as appendix C. Even a cursory inspection shows that Carleton consistently uses an italic *h, a, d, c,* and *g*. Further, it is highly unlikely that Carleton, who served primarily on the continent during the late sixteenth century, would have been employed to copy documents collected in the State Papers, Ireland. The paleographic evidence that Spenser's contemporary Dudley Carleton was not the copyist of these documents is so strong that the case need not be argued on any other grounds. Thus, the two ostensibly factual claims upon which Grosart founded his attribution of these documents to Spenser do not withstand scrutiny.

W. L. Renwick, Spenser's first twentieth-century editor, questioned Spenser's authorship of *A Brief Note of Ireland*, particularly of "To the Queene," on the grounds of its inflated style.[32] Rudolf Gottfried also based his editorial judgments on style, but remained convinced that Spenser was the "chief, if not sole author" of *A Brief Note of Ireland* and so attributed all three documents to him in the *Spenser Variorum* (9:536). In 1937 Violet Hulbert accepted all of Grosart's claims concerning the manuscript evidence,[33] though she raised problems of consistency between the *View* and *A Brief Note of Ireland,* for example, discrepancies between the military strategies advocated by the authors of the two tracts. It is not clear why Ciaran Brady dismisses Hulbert's arguments in his article on *A Brief Note of Ireland* in the influential *Spenser Encyclopedia* (1990). Brady doubts Spenser's authorship of "A Breife Note" and "To the Queene," but insists that he wrote "Certaine pointes," because it is "closest in emphasis and argument" to the *View*:

> Here, shorn of pleasant antiquarian digressions, inconsistent qualifications, and a subtle evasion of logical consequences, is the essence of the brutal argument of the *Vewe*. As such, though modest in itself, "Certaine pointes" is an invaluable tool in a critical analysis of the complexities and internal contradictions of *Vewe*; and it is understandable that some scholars unwilling to confront the fundamentally ruthless thrust of the *Vewe* have chosen to ignore this piece also. (112)

Brady wants to accept Spenser's authorship of part of *A Brief Note of Ireland* in order to bolster his interpretation of the *View*. The manuscript evidence makes this awkward. The copyist begins "Certaine pointes" in the middle of the folio page on which "To the Queene" ends, making it difficult to conclude that Spenser's authorship of "To the Queene" is doubtful but that "Certaine pointes" is definitely by Spenser. The note on the back of the last folio page of "Certaine pointes" could refer to any one of the three manuscripts or to all of them. The important point is that the attribution is in a different and later hand than that of the copyist. Whoever wrote the note attributing one or more of these works to Spenser was not the copyist.

IV. Description of the Extant Manuscripts of *A Brief Note of Ireland*

The three manuscripts entitled *A Brief Note of Ireland* appear together only in the State Papers, Ireland in the British Public Record Office. Since the State Papers, Ireland were not calendared until after Grosart had printed *A Brief Note of Ireland* in his 1884 edition, his influence may account for these three unrelated documents being treated as one item in the calendar. The first manuscript, "A Breife Note of Ireland," is copied separately on f. 195R, while "To the Queene" and "Certaine pointes" are copied together as a continuous unit (ff. 196–200). Nevertheless, the paper of the manuscripts of "A Breife Note of Ireland" and "To the Queene" bear recognizably the same watermark. "Certaine pointes" does not reveal a watermark, but is copied continuously with "To the Queene." The watermarks on the paper of "A Breife Note of Ireland" and "To the Queene" do not assist in dating the manuscripts.

When Ernest Atkinson edited the Irish state papers in 1895, he listed *A Brief Note of Ireland* immediately after the *View* and attributed both to Spenser even though neither manuscript is signed. He gathered a miscellaneous series of memoranda, tracts, and manuscript histories relating to Ireland at the conclusion of volume 202, part 4, of *Calendar of State Papers, Ireland*. These materials, numbered as items 55–85, appear under the bracketed date 1598 because none of them could be dated precisely. For example, Number 57 is described as "Memorandum concerning the affairs of Munster [a portion of some manuscript history]"; Number 58 as "A Vewe of the present state of Irelande, discoursed by waye of a diologue betweene Eudoxus and Irenius"; 59 as "A briefe note of Irelande"; 60 as "A declaration of the present state of the English Pale of Ireland, and of many the causes which hath brought the same to ruin"; 61 as "A summary discourse of this Realm of Ireland, whereby may partly the means be seen whereby it is brought out of square." In addition there are other undated memoranda, documents, and notes on finances. Several long tracts are calendared: 75, "A Discourse to show 'that planting of colonies, and that to be begun only by the Dutch, will give best entrance to the reformation of Ulster'"; 76, another copy of the preceding; 81, "Paper on the condition of Ireland, endorsed by Sir Robert Cecil, 'Observations'"; 82, "Rough memoranda about Ireland; Edward VI. to Elizabeth"; and 83, "Tractate entitled 'Ulster's Unity' by Francis Jobson," a treatise formally dedicated to Queen Elizabeth.

These tracts, memoranda, and histories are unrelated to each other; neither their dates nor authorship can be confirmed. In fact, though some commentators think that the *View* and "Certaine pointes" offer uniquely Spenserian solutions to the conquest of Ireland, their arguments are commonplace in tracts purporting to instruct the English government on solutions to the Irish problem.[34] Francis Jobson's plans, for example, are remarkably similar to those advanced by the author of the *View*. He recommends that an army of eleven thousand chosen men be used to subdue Ulster and specifies locations for military fortifications. He concludes that famine will end the rebellion: "The incursions of the rebels will be hindered, famine in short time will join in fight with them," and "in one year, or little more, make an end of all those miserable toils and troubles, and of the great charge of Her Highness."[35] *A Brief Note of Ireland*, or any of its component parts, could have been written by any one of the authors of these anonymous tracts on Ireland.

Both Grosart and Brady speculate that the manuscripts referred to as *A Brief Note of Ireland* were dispatches carried by Spenser from Norris to Cecil in England.[36] Enclosures and accompanying materials, however, are carefully indicated in the *Calendars*; for example, the letter written by Norris to the Privy Council on 9 December from Cork is calendared as item 15; its enclosure, a list of Munster noblemen committed to rebellion, is calendared as 15.I and printed in italics immediately following the dispatch.

Examination of the present physical state of the three manuscripts of *A Brief Note of Ireland* confirms Atkinson's judgment in treating Norris's dispatches separately from these and other tracts on the Irish problem.[37] These manuscripts were never folded. If these manuscripts figured as part of a dispatch carried by Spenser in December 1598, then we would have to imagine him threading his way through enemy rebels while carrying unfolded folio leaves to England. The surviving manuscripts may also be copies of missing original documents. In that case, the seventeenth-century copyist's failure to identify Spenser as the author renders suspect all later attributions. In short, there is no evidence for supposing that these documents were ever part of an official dispatch carried by Spenser or anyone else; they are tentatively dated 1598 and appropriately bound and calendared with other anonymous works on Ireland, including the *View*.

Since the attribution of tracts on Ireland to Spenser usually rests on internal evidence, we should now review the substantive grounds for connecting *A Brief Note of Ireland* to the *View.*

"A breife note of Ireland"

The first of the three manuscripts making up *A Brief Note* bears no substantive relation to the text of the *View* that precedes it or to "To the Queene" that follows it. This manuscript (see appendix A) is a memorandum setting forth evidence that the English kings "haue lands of inheritance as Lords of Ireland in good substance beside the title of the Crowne." It argues that the English royal family could claim Irish territory on the basis of inheritance as well as conquest and is conspicuously unrelated to the Munster Rebellion, the topic of greatest concern to the English in 1598. The Munster colonists had either abandoned or lost their homes and had fled to Cork; their situation was hopeless unless the English government sent in more supplies and troops. A document concerned with royal property rights was irrelevant to their present concerns. The colonists urgent need was to persuade the Privy Council that a major military intervention, such as Essex was to attempt in 1599, was essential.

"To the Queene"

Rudolf Gottfried says that *A Brief Note of Ireland* "must date from the last three months of 1598, when the condition of the Munster undertakers was most hopeless" (9:536). Only the second document (see appendix A), an unsigned, undated letter addressed "To the Queene," refers unmistakably to the Munster Rebellion and so is likely to have been written prior to December 1598. It must be reiterated that the only basis for connecting this anonymous letter with Spenser is the inscription on the back of the last folio of "Certaine pointes," the third manuscript of *A Brief Note of Ireland* (f. 200V). No initials appear in the heading or at the conclusion of the manuscript. Thus, assumptions of Spenser's authorship depend entirely on internal evidence, principally upon verbal parallels between this document and the *View.* Since we cannot be completely certain that the *View* was written by Spenser, only the verbal parallels with works definitely by Spenser merit attention. The kinds of parallels that Gottfried cites between "To the Queene" and Spenser's *Faerie Queene* are illustrated by the following: "vouchsafe moste mightie Empresse our Dred soveraigne to receive" is listed as a parallel to *Faerie Queene* I.pr.4.9: "vouchsafe, O dearest dred"; numerous other instances in which Spenser uses "vouchsafe" in the initial position are also cited. Other parallels range from the unconvincing "miserable wretches" and "wretched miseries" in *Faerie Queene* II.x.62.3

to the relatively more persuasive "plunged in this Sea of sorrowes" and "plung'd in sea of sorrowes" in *Faerie Queene* I.vii.39.2 (9:430–40). None of the verbal parallels between "To the Queene" and Spenser's poems, however, involves sufficiently distinct or rare words to be conclusive. Moreover, Spenser's *Faerie Queene* was probably in print when the *View* was composed, and so even verbal echoes prove little.

If the telling question is asked, Did the author of the *View* also write "To the Queene"?, the answer has to be no. The dissimilarity in political views is far too great; if Spenser wrote one tract, he can scarcely have written the other. The author of the *View* has Irenius describe the earl of Tyrone as a cunning villain: "And now he playeth like the frozen Snake, whoe being for Compassion releived bẏ the husbandman, sone after he was warme, began to hisse, and threaten daunger even to him and his" (168). After Irenius says that O'Neale has no right of seignory in the North, Eudoxus exclaims that he is "glade" to have objections to use against those who "slaunderouslye . . . barke at the Courses which are helde againste that Trayterous Earle and his Adherentes" (9:170). In contrast, the author of the letter addressed "To the Queene" attributes the first cause of Tyrone's rebellion to "the indirect desire of one persons privat gaine to whom your Maiestie Comitted this vnfortunat gouernment" (9:236). The author blames Lord Deputy Fitzwilliams for committing injustices that made Tyrone "dislike of such bad dealing" and "finde greuance at the government (as in deede vnder correction me seemes some cause he had)" (9:237). It is difficult to imagine that Edmund Spenser would have adopted this sympathetic stance toward Tyrone after the sack of Kilcoman in October 1598.

The author of "To the Queene" was also antagonistic toward Sir John and Sir Thomas Norris, two of Spenser's patrons. In December 1598 Sir Thomas Norris, lord president of Munster, sent a "Mr. Spenser" with dispatches to the Privy Council; there is no reason to doubt that this Mr. Spenser was the poet who died in London on 13 January 1599. On 21 December, alluding to his previous correspondence, Norris wrote to the Privy Council reminding them that he had used a "Mr. Spenser" as a messenger: "It may please your honourable Lordships. Since my last of the 9th of this month, sent by Mr. Spenser, wherein I manifested the misery of this country. . . ."[38] Sir Thomas wrote to the Privy Council on 9 December from Cork, and on 13 December he wrote to Sir Robert Cecil; both of these letters arrived at Whitehall on Christmas Eve, 24 December 1598, making it likely that the two letters, dated respectively 9 and 13 December, made up one dispatch carried by Spenser.

It is most unlikely that "To the Queene" was written by anyone in Norris's confidence. It would have been obvious to Norris and his close acquaintances that December 1598 was not the time to engage in special pleading. Elizabeth was displeased by Norris's handling of the forces in Munster; on 29 November she angrily wrote to him that she held him responsible for not taking more severe and immediate action when the rebellion first broke out:

> [Y]ou are not freed by all reporters from this information; that, in the beginning, when the traitor grew to head with a ragged number of rogues and boys you might have better resisted than you did, especially considering the many defensible houses and castles possessed by the undertakers, who, for aught we can hear, were no way comforted nor supported by you, but either for lack of comfort from you, or out of mere cowardice, fled away from the rebels upon the first alarm.[39]

Elizabeth's principal authority for the unfavorable reports concerning Norris and the Munster undertakers was her kinsman the earl of Ormond.

The author of "To the Queen," like the earl of Ormond and his supporters, attacks the Norris family. He charges that dissension among the English leaders encouraged the earl of Tyrone to rebel and singles out Sir John Norris, Thomas's recently deceased older brother, for particular criticism:

> the devision of the gouernment here betwixt Sr willm Russell and Sr Iohn Norris. Of which the one being sharplie bent to prosecute him the other thought by good treaties rather wynn him to make fair warrs But by some it was thought that the onely purpose of Sr Iohn Norris in handling thinges after that sorte was to obtaine the absolute gouernment to him selfe. (9:237–38)

No one in the service of Sir Thomas Norris had anything to gain from repeating gossip unfavorable to Sir John.

Spenser's authorship of "To the Queene" would mean that he had insinuated a private letter into official dispatches, a letter, moreover, that repeated slander against the brother of the man who employed him as a messenger. Spenser addressed a dedicatory sonnet to Sir John Norris in *Faerie Queene* (1590), and Sir Thomas was his closest neighbor. Moyallo, or Mallow as it is called today, was the estate of Sir Thomas Norris and was located less than five miles from Spenser's Kilcolman. These patronage relationships make Spenser's authorship of "To the Queene" most improbable.

"Certaine pointes to be considered of in the recovery of the Realme of Ireland"

The third document in *A Brief Note*, "Certaine pointes," appears in three manuscript versions: P.R.O., SP63/202, Pt. 4/59; British Library, Harleian MS 3787, f. 184, where it is entitled "Certen poinctes to be considered in the recovering of Ireland"; and Oxford, All Souls MS 155, f. 58, where it is entitled "Certaine notes to be considered of in the recoveringe of the Realme of Ireland."[40] While "Certaine pointes," like "To the Queene," bears some superficial resemblance to the *View*, it also differs significantly. The author of "Certaine pointes" recommends an open pardon for the rebels and wants that pardon to be in force for ten to twelve days. The author of the *View*, who may have better understood the logistics of offering a pardon to a scattered rural population, advocates that the pardon be offered for twenty days. The author of "Certaine pointes" favors a general conquest followed by the construction of garrisons; in contrast, the author of the *View* wants to establish garrisons from the outset. The author of "Certaine pointes" believes that ten thousand men can subdue Ireland in six months; the author of the *View* estimates that it will take ten thousand foot and one thousand horse at least eighteen months to achieve a conquest. The author of "Certaine pointes," then, is considerably more optimistic than the author of the *View*. If we suppose that Spenser wrote both the *View* and "Certaine pointes," then we have to envisage him becoming more optimistic about conquering Ireland after the Tyrone Rebellion and the sack of Kilcolman, a very unlikely scenario.

In addition to the text appearing as the third part of *A Brief Note of Ireland* in the P.R.O., there are two additional known manuscripts of "Certaine pointes." Ray Heffner first pointed out that British Library, Harleian MS 3787, f. 184, "Certen poinctes" is attributed to Spenser.[41] Manuscript endorsements of this kind should be approached critically because they may merely illustrate the penchant that manuscript collectors have had for endorsing tracts on Ireland as the work of Edmund Spenser.[42] Nevertheless, both Rudolf Gottfried and Ciaran Brady find this second attribution of "Certen poinctes" to Spenser persuasive. As is clear from the reproduction in appendix D, the hand making the attribution differs markedly from that of the copyist. In this folio manuscript the title and text are in a neat secretary hand; the endorsement, "Spensers discourse breifly of Ireland," appears in different ink and in a late italic hand. Gottfried accepts this suspect endorsement as authenticating Spenser's authorship of all three manuscripts in *A Brief Note of Ireland*.

Rather than confirming Spenser's authorship of "Certaine pointes," the conclusion of Harleian MS 3787, f. 184—especially the last six lines—renders Spenser's involvement in preparing this syllogistic exercise dubious:

> But if the reformacon shall nevertheless be intended then theise proposicions are therin to be weighed and considered.
> That there can be no conformitie of gouernment, where there is noe conformitie of religion/.
> That there can be no sounde agreament betwene twoe equall contraries viz: the Inglish and the Irish./
> That there can be no assurance of peace where the worser sorte are the stronger
> And that all which may be the head of anie faction, is to be remoued, or weakend
>
> Marke Irishe when this doth fall
> Tirone and tire all

A Peere out of Ingland shall come
The Irishe shall tire all and some
    Sir Patrick to St George a horseboye shalbe sene
And all this shall happen in ninetye nyne.[43]

One hopes that the collector or bookseller who attributed this document to Spenser did not do so because of the concluding poem. In fact, the presence of this doggerel in the manuscript could be used as internal evidence against Spenser's authorship.

The third manuscript, "Certaine notes," Oxford, All Souls MS 155 (appendix E) is closer in content and format to P.R.O., SP63/202, Pt. 4/59 than to British Library, Harleian 3787, f. 184. All Souls MS 155 contains a number of seventeenth-century political speeches, letters, and poems. This text of "Certaine notes" is neither attributed to Edmund Spenser nor to an unidentified E. S.

To summarize the manuscript evidence for Spenser's authorship of the third part of *A Brief Note of Ireland*: No manuscript of "Certaine pointes" identifies Edmund Spenser as the author in the hand of the scribe in which the text of the manuscript is written. The attributions to Spenser of "Certaine pointes" in P.R.O. and Harleian MS 3787 were added later—probably long after the *View* had been attributed to the author of the *Faerie Queene*. Once Spenser's authorship of the *View* was accepted, then those who wanted to add to the canon of the author of the *Faerie Queene* attributed anonymous tracts and notes on Ireland to Edmund Spenser—even in instances in which little or no actual evidence supported these attributions.

V. Ware and the *View*

It is possible to show conclusively that Dudley Carleton did not copy *A Brief Note of Ireland* and that no substantive evidence supports the identification of Edmund Spenser as the author of the three seventeenth-century manuscripts comprising P.R.O., SP63/202, Pt. 4/59. While it can be demonstrated that *A Brief Note of Ireland* should not have been attributed to Spenser, the attribution of the *View* to the author of the *Faerie Queene* is a far more vexed problem. An immense amount of physical evidence remains to be analyzed; at least twenty-one manuscripts are known to have survived. Principles of comparative analysis cannot be developed until a preliminary physical description exists for all of the known manuscripts. It may finally prove to be wiser to identify versions of the *View* rather than to attempt to construct a single text.

Until much more is known about the surviving text(s) of the *View*, I prefer to accept the negative witness of Spenser's contemporaries on the issue of Spenser's authorship. In 1610 Barnaby Rich failed to mention Spenser in an attack on contemporary historians of Ireland:

> But these three, Giraldus Cambrensis, Edmund Campion, and Richard Stanyhurst, are the only authors that have patched and pieced together the history of Ireland. . . . For the rest that hath been attempted by Holinshed and Hooker, they have referred the whole matter of what they have writ concerning Ireland to those men's authority: Holinshed to what had been collected by Campion and Stanyhurst; and Hooker, to no more than he had translated out of Giraldus Cambrensis.[44]

Even though Rich inveighs mightily against those who borrowed from earlier sources, many histories were compilations. It is possible that a manuscript "View of Ireland" was drafted by Edmund Campion, revised by Richard Stanyhurst, and even revised again by E. C. S., who was familiar with the records surviving from the deputyship of Sir John Perrot. Rich affords only one of a number of instances in which we would expect to find reference to Spenser's authorship of the *View* but do not. Sir John Davies, who pays tribute to Spenser's *Faerie Queene* in *Orchestra*, fails to mention the *View of the Present State of Ireland* in *A Discovery of the True Causes Why Ireland was Never Entirely Subdued* (1612). Davies had access to a manuscript of the *View* that belonged to Sir Arthur Chichester (British Library, Add. MS 22022).

To conclude: We should keep in mind that when James Ware prepared the first printed edition of the *View of the Present State of Ireland* and attributed it to Edmund Spenser, he was not publishing an edition of Spenser's works. He was making available histories "collected by M. Hanmer, Ed. Campion, and E. Spenser" (1633). In his biographical notes on Spenser attached to the *View*, he says that a servant lost the last part of the *Faerie Queene*, but he removes that anecdote when he returns to Spenser's biography in *De scriptoribus Hiberniae. Libri duo* (Dublin: Ex Typog. Soc. Bibliopolarum, 1639). In this later work, Ware omits the anecdote about the loss of the conclusion to the *Faerie Queene* and repeats Spenser's biography almost verbatim from Camden. Nothing in Ware's handling of Spenser's biography suggests that he knew the poet well enough to be sure that he was the author of the *View*.

Furthermore, though in his preface to the *View* (1633) Ware pays tribute to the "good effects that 30. yeares peace have produced," the Anglican establishment was not as sanguine as this dedicatory flourish might suggest. In April 1627, six years before Ware attributed the *View* to Edmund Spenser, Bishop Ussher in a speech to the General Assembly at Dublin Castle outlined the policies that were later to be implemented by Cromwell:

> We have not used that policie in our Plantations that wise States have used in former times. They, when they settled new Colonies in any place, did commonly translate the Ancient Inhabitants to other dwellings. We have brought new Planters into the Land, and haue left the old Inhabitants to shift for themselves; . . . and seeing themselves deprived of their means and maintenance, which they and their *Ancestors* have formerly injoyed, will undoubtedly be ready when any occasion is offered, to disturb our quiet.[45]

Ware's purpose in printing the *View*—and the histories of Campion and Hanmer—in 1633 was to provide historical support for the increasingly hostile attitudes of the Anglican administration toward the Irish. He seems to have appropriated the name of the author of the *Faerie Queene* to advance his political agenda; his attribution should be considered doubtful unless confirmed by independent support.

NOTES

1. S. K. Heninger Jr., "Spenser and Sidney at Leicester House," in *Spenser Studies: A Renaissance Poetry Annual*, ed. Patrick Cullen and Thomas P. Roche Jr., 8 vols. (New York: AMS Press, 1990), 8:239–49.

2. In 1990 and 1991 entire sessions of Spenser at Kalamazoo were devoted to Spenser's biography. Recent biographies include: Patrick Cheney, *Spenser's Famous Flight: A Renaissance Idea of a Literary Career* (Toronto: University of Toronto Press, 1993); Richard Rambuss, *Spenser's Secret Career* (Cambridge: Cambridge University Press, 1993); and Gary Waller, *Edmund Spenser: A Literary Life* (New York: St. Martin's Press, 1994). In addition, Judith Anderson and David Richardson are editing a collection of essays on Spenser's life forthcoming from the University of Massachusetts Press.

3. Summarizing recent studies, Julia Lupton states that "Spenser's antiquarian approach, like Giraldus' before him, is racial in focus and racist in intent." See "Mapping mutability: or, Spenser's Irish Plot," in *Representing Ireland: Literature and the Origins of Conflict, 1534–1660,* ed. Brendan Bradshaw, Andrew Hadfield, and Willy Maley (Cambridge: Cambridge University Press, 1993), 96. Several essays in this collection use readings of the *View* to interpret the *Faerie Queene*. See also Richard F. Hardin, *Civil Idolatry: Desacralizing and Monarchy in Spenser, Shakespeare, and Milton* (Newark: University of Delaware Press, 1992), 91–123, esp. 119–23 where both the *View* and *A Brief Note* are used to gloss the *Faerie Queene*.

4. My references will be to the Huntington copy entitled *A View of the State of Ireland, Written dialogue-wise betweene Eudoxus and Irenaeus, By Edmund Spenser Esq. in the yeare 1596. Whereunto is added the History of Ireland, By Edmund Campion, sometime fellow of St. Iohn's Colledge in Oxford. Published by Sir Iames Ware Knight.* (Dublin: Society of Stationers, 1633). The *View* has survived as a single text, but is usually bound with histories of Ireland written by Edmund Campion and Meredith Hanmer. Each history is printed with separate signatures, but they are linked together by comprehensive title pages. For a complete bibliographical discussion of the various states, see Francis Johnson, *A Critical Bibliography of the Works of Edmund Spenser Printed before 1700* (Baltimore: Johns Hopkins University Press, 1933), 48–53.

5. This folio also saw the introduction into the canon of *Britains Ida*, a poem first attributed to Spenser in 1628 by Thomas Walkley, who confided in a preface to his readers that "the ablest and most knowing men" had assured him that the poem was by Spenser, "of whom it were pitty that anything should be lost" (*Britains Ida: Written by that Renowned Poet, Edmond Spencer* [London: Thomas Walkley, 1628]). *Britains Ida* was printed with Spenser's works until 1923, when Ethel Seaton established it as the work of Phineas Fletcher ("Phineas Fletcher—A New MS," *Times Literary Supplement,* 22 March 1923, 199 and reply by F. S. Boas, *TLS,* 29 March 1923, 216).

6. *Prose Works*, in *The Works of Edmund Spenser: A Variorum Edition*, edited by Edwin Greenlaw et al., 11 vols. (1938–57; reprint, Baltimore: Johns Hopkins University Press, 1949), 9:235–45. All references will be to this edition of the *Works;* volume and page numbers will be cited parenthetically.

7. Stephen May, *Sir Walter Ralegh* (Boston: G. K. Hall, 1989), 124.

8. See my "The Dating of *Nosce Teipsum*," *Huntington Library Quarterly* 37 (November 1973): 19–32.

9. For Gottfried's rationale in accepting the attribution to Spenser of *Axiochus*, see *Works*, 9:487–96.

10. Samuel Schoenbaum, *Internal Evidence and Elizabethan Dramatic Authorship* (Evanston, Ill.: Northwestern University Press, 1966), 107, 150. For an exemplary attribution study, see Donald W. Foster, *Elegy By W. S.: A Study in Attribution* (Newark: University of Delaware Press, 1989), 75–79.

11. David V. Erdman, "The Signature of Style," *Bulletin of the New York Public Library* 63 (1959): 45–46. See also Arthur Sherbo, "The Uses and Abuses of Internal Evidence," in *Evidence for Authorship: Essays on Problems of Attribution,* ed. David V. Erdman and Ephim G. Fogel (Ithaca: Cornell University Press, 1966), 7.

12. D. F. McKenzie, *Bibliography and the Sociology of Texts*, The Panizzi Lectures 1985 (London: British Library, 1986), 1–20.

13. For a critique of the standard editions of the *View*, see my "Constructing the *View of the Present State of Ireland*," in *Spenser Studies: A Renaissance Poetry Annual*, ed. Patrick Cullen and Thomas P. Roche Jr. (New York: AMS Press, 1994), 11:203–28.

14. I wish to thank the Bodleian Library for permission to quote from manuscripts in the collection relating to the *View* and to Spenser. The note appears at the very end of the manuscript and is printed in *A Transcript of the Registers of the Company of Stationers of London,1554-1640*, ed. Edward Arber, 5 vols. (1875–94; reprint, Gloucester, Mass.: Peter Smith, 1967), 3:111 and in Edmund Spenser, *A View of the Present State of Ireland*, ed. W. L. Renwick, 2d ed. (Oxford: Clarendon Press, 1970), iv.

15. See Andrew Hadfield, "Was Spenser's *View of the Present State of Ireland* Censored? A Review of the Evidence," *Notes and Queries* 248 (December 1994): 459–63. See also Brink, "Constructing the *View*," 204–9. For the unsupported claim that Ware's 1633 edition of the *View* was also censored by the government, see Rambuss, *Spenser's Secret Career*, 112. No commentator explains why, if Spenser wrote the *View* and the Privy Council prevented its publication in 1598, the Privy Council would shortly afterwards recommend appointing him the sheriff of Cork (*Acts of the Privy Council of England,* n.s., ed. J. R. Dasent et al. [London: Her Majesty's Stationery Office, 1890], 29:204–5).

16. Francis Johnson, *A Critical Bibliography*, 47–48.

17. Peter Beal, *Index of English Literary Manuscripts* (London and New York: Bowker, 1980), 523–31. Dr. Christopher Ridgeway, librarian, Castle Howard, recovered the fifth manuscript. The sixth is described in Bernard Quaritch LTD., Sale Catalogue: Early Books and Manuscripts (Summer 1996), 24.

18. I wish first to acknowledge the American Philosophical Society for its support of my research on a critical bibliography of Spenser manuscripts. I also wish to thank the Huntington Library; Gonville and Caius College Library, Cambridge University; and the British Library for permission to describe the watermarks of manuscripts of the *View* in their collections. See Edward Heawood, *Watermarks, Mainly of the Seventeenth and Eighteenth Centuries*. Monumenta Chartae Papyraceae Historiam Illustrantia (Hilversum, Holland: Paper Publications Society, 1950), #842. I wish to correct my

error in "Constructing the *View*," 218, where I used provenance alone as grounds for accepting an early date for Ellesmere MS 7041.

19. Among the likely seventeenth-century candidates for authorship of the *View* is E. C. S., an intelligent and well-informed military man, who published an account of the deputyship of Sir John Perrot in 1626, under the title *The Government of Ireland under Sir John Perrot* (London: A. Mathewes, 1626).

20. I am indebted to Mary Robertson, keeper of manuscripts, Huntington Library, for confirming that these notes are in Egerton's hand. I would also like to thank the Huntington Library for granting me permission to describe manuscripts in the Ellesmere Collection and to reproduce the watermark from Ellesmere MS 7041.

21. Following Francis Johnson, *Critical Bibliography of the Works of Edmund Spenser Printed Before 1700*, 53, Peter Beal states that the Trinity College, Dublin MS 589 (formerly MS E.3.26) was owned by Archbishop James Ussher (1581–1656) and used as the copy-text for Ware's edition of 1633. However, in his review of Johnson, W. L. Renwick pointed out that the Trinity College copy of the View was not part of Ussher's library and "was not Ware's exemplar" (*Modern Language Review* 29 [October 1934]: 448). Even though Gottfried makes no attempt to identify Ware's copy-text, he concludes that Ware "deliberately softened or omitted passages which might be offensive to the Irish and, more particularly, Anglo-Irish feelings in his own time" (9:519).

22. I wish to acknowledge the assistance of Mr. Stuart O Seanóir, assistant keeper, Trinity College Library, Dublin, who determined that when Thomas Kingsmill Abbott compiled the modern printed catalog of Trinity manuscripts in 1900, he was not aware that the "Dialogue between Eudoxus and Irenius" was the same work as the "View of the Present State of Ireland." Abbott indexes the Trinity manuscript under "Dialogue" rather than under either "Spenser" or "View."

23. For secondary descriptions of Ussher's library, see the following: Bernard Meehan, "The Manuscript Collection of James Ussher," in *The Treasures of the Library, Trinity College Dublin*, ed. Peter Fox (Dublin: Trinity College and Royal Irish Academy, 1986), 95–110; William O'Sullivan, "Ussher as a Collector of Manuscripts," *Hermathena* 88 (1956): 34–58; and H. J. Lawlor, "Primate Ussher's Library before 1641," *Proceedings of the Royal Irish Academy*, 3d ser., 6 (1900): 216–64. In addition to examining printed sources, I also have consulted the handwritten book catalogs, book lists, and accessions and presentation lists for Trinity cataloged as MUN/LIB and sixteenth- and seventeenth-century book lists cataloged as Trinity MSS 1945, 2160, 2160A.

24. Edward Bernard, *Catalogi Librorum Manuscriptorum Angliae et Hiberniae* (Oxoniae: E theatro Sheldonian, 1697), 2:12.

25. Ibid., 2:390, #50. The date 1584 is earlier than any date given to *View of the Present State of Ireland.* The work alluded to may be Ric[hard] Stanyhurst, "De res Hibernicus," 1584 [O.2.7], which is described in Trinity Mun/Lib/1/14 (6) on f. 158V. In the secretary hand, it is easy to confuse capital letters and to mistake an *R* for an *E*. It possible that R. S. could be misread as E. S. Thus, this reference in Bernard may be a misreading of R[ichard] S[tanyhurst] as E[dmund] S[penser].

26. *Dublin University Magazine* 58 (1861): 143, 144.

27. Alexander Grosart, *The Complete Works in Verse and Prose of Edmund Spenser* (London and Aylesbury: Hazell, Watson, and Viney, Ltd., 1884), 1:231. Grosart knew of Ware's 1633 edition of the *View*, but rejected its authority and used Lambeth Palace, MS 510 as the copy-text for his edition of the *View*.

28. *Calendar of State Papers, Ireland, 1598, January-1599, March*, ed. Ernest George

Atkinson (1895; reprint, Nendeln, Liechtenstein: Kraus, 1974), 7:431. Hereafter cited as *CSPI*.

29. Grosart, *Complete Works*, 1:231, 537-55.

30. Public Record Office, State Papers 63, vol. 202, pt. 4, no. 59—hereafter PRO, SP 63/202/59.

To minimize confusion, I will use "A breife note of Ireland"—the actual spelling in the manuscript—to refer to the first of the three manuscripts printed as *A Brief Note of Ireland* in the *Spenser Variorum*. These documents have numbers stamped in the upper corner that do not correspond exactly to the foliation usually given at the bottom of the page. My references will be to the foliation, not to the stamped numbers.

31. Ciaran Brady's article on *A Brief Note of Ireland* in *The Spenser Encyclopedia*, ed. A. C. Hamilton (Toronto: University of Toronto Press, 1990), 111 reiterates that these manuscripts are in the hand of Dudley Carleton. Grosart's identification of the copyist is also repeated in the *Spenser Variorum*, 9:533 and Beal's *Index of English Literary Manuscripts*, 529.

32. *Spenser Variorum*, 9:535–36.

33. Violet B. Hulbert, "Spenser's Relation to Certain Documents on Ireland," *Modern Philology* 34 (May 1937): 345–53.

34. Nicholas Canny has made this point in articles such as "Edmund Spenser and the Development of an Anglo-Irish Identity," *Yearbook of English Studies* 13 (1983): 1–19 and "Identity Formation in Ireland: The Emergence of the Anglo-Irish," in *Colonial Identity in the Atlantic World*, ed. Nicholas Canny and Anthony Pagden (Princeton: Princeton University Press, 1987), 159–212. For an argument that the author of the *View* was uniquely inhumane in his arguments, see Ciaran Brady, "Spenser's Irish Crisis: Humanism and Experience in the 1590s," *Past and Present* 111 (May 1986): 17–49. See also Nicholas Canny and Ciaran Brady, "Debate: Spenser's Irish Crisis: Humanism and Experience in the 1590s," *Past and Present* 120 (August 1988): 201–15.

35. *CSPI*, 7:445–46.

36. Brady offers the following improbable conjecture: "It is possible that the group formed part of a larger collection of dispatches which Spenser brought from Munster to Whitehall in December 1598. Perhaps the spokesman for the Munster planters, he may have delivered their petition at court and seized the opportunity to present his own far more rigorous proposals which had been silenced through the suppression of *Vewe*" (112). However, if there were any physical evidence that these manuscripts were connected with Norris's official dispatches, the editor of the *Calendar* would have indicated that by printing them in italics immediately after Norris's letters.

37. For Norris's letters to the Privy Council and Sir Robert Cecil, see *CSPI*, 7:399–400, 404–5, 414–15. The *View* and *A Brief Note* are calendared at *CSPI*, 7:431–33.

38. P.R.O., SP 63/202 Part 4/36.

39. P.R.O., SP/63/202 Pt. 3/178 (29 November). A copy of this letter appears again in the State Papers, Ireland under the date of 3 December (P.R.O., SP/63/63/202 Pt. 4/4).

40. I wish to thank the Warden and Fellows of All Souls College, Oxford; the British Library; and the Public Record Office for permission to reproduce the manuscripts of *A Brief Note of Ireland* appearing as appendices to this article.

41. Ray Heffner, review of *A View of the Present State of Ireland*, by W. L. Renwick, *Modern Language Notes* 52 (January 1937): 58.

42. See, for example, Bodleian, MS Eng. Misc. f73, ff. 51–66. This manuscript is in a secretary hand and endorsed "Spensers discourse of Ireland termed Irelands good."

The author of this text sympathizes with Tyrone and disparages Sir John Norris, but outlines numerous points made by Irenius in the *View*.

43. Steven May, who is in the process of preparing a first-line index of all Elizabethan poetry, tells me that this may be the only instance in which this poem occurs.

44. Barnaby Rich, *A New Description of Ireland: wherein is described the Disposition of the Irish* (London: William Jaggard for T. Adams, 1610), C1R.

45. Nicholas Bernard, *The Life and Death of the Most Reverend and Learned Father of our Church, Dr. James Ussher, Late Archbishop of Armagh and Primate of all Ireland* (London: E. Tyler, 1656), 71.

Appendix A

Manuscripts Comprising *A Brief Note of Ireland*
(P.R.O. SP63/202, pt. 4/59):
— "Breife Note of Ireland" (f. 195R)
— "To the Queene" (ff. 196R–199R)
— "Certaine pointes to be considered of in the recouery of the Realme of Ireland" (ff. 199R–200R)

A breife note of Ireland

59.

The kinges of England have landes of inheritaunce as lordes of Ireland in good substaunce beside the title of the Crowne, as the

Erledome of Vlster

wholly lordes of Connought, Meth, of some parte of Leinster and some partes of Mounster.

Besides there are			
	in Ireland	5530	townes.
	in Leinster	930	
	in Connought	900	
	in Mounster	2100	
	in Vlster	2060	
	in Meth	540	

There is of arrable land in it 38640 plowlandes besides divers meadowes boggs and woods eache plowland conteineth 120 acres eache acre 4 perches in bredth and 40 in length eache perch 21 foote eache foote 12 inches. In Edward the 4 his tyme the Crowne had Ireland in his obedience it yelded the Crowne of England 14146li sterling taking but a noble for a plowland. And besides he received for Customes, fishings and other royalties 20000li yearlie paide to the Castell of Dublin as yet appeareth by [illegible]. And had above this the yearlie rent of Vlster, Connought, Meth, Leinster and Mounster, which was 22000li sterling, then this had they the ransomes of manie churches, wardes, mariages and gift of divers other good things

195

195

To the Queene

Out of the ashes of disolation and wastenes of this your wretched Realme of Ireland, vouchsafe most mightie Empresse our dred soveraigne to receive the voices of a fewe most unhappie ghostes, of whome is nothing but the ghost nowe left which lie buried in the bottome of oblivion farr from the light of your gratious sunshine which spreddeth it selfe on Countries most remote to the releeving of their destitute calamities and to the eternall advancement of your renowne and glorie yet upon this miserable land being your owne righte and [illegible] dominion letteth no one little beame of your large mercie to be shed either for unworthinesse of us wretches which no way deserve so great grace, or for that the miserie of our estate is not made knowne unto you but rather kept from your knowledge by such as by concealment thereof think to cover their blames concealed. Pardon therefore most gratious Soveraigne unto miserable wretches which without your knowledge and most against your will are plunged in this Sea of sorrowes to make their voices cast fordward unto you and to call for tymelie redresse unto you if yet at least any tyme be left that your majestie in your excellent wisdome may the better knowe how to redresse it, may the same vouchsafe to consider from what beginning the same first sprange and by what late evill meanes it is brought to this miserable condicion which we nowe complaine of.

The first cause of the rebellione

The first cause and roote thereof was the indirect desire of some persons private gaine, to whome your Majestie committed this unfortunate government, which whiles he sought the [illegible] with the [illegible] of enriching this your kingdome with a newe Countie, to witt the Countie of Monaghan, under that colour sought to enlarge his owne treasure and to [illegible] his frendes and kinsfolke in all the territories which might with better [illegible] have bene [illegible] in regarde the good should have therby redound unto you, had it not bene wrought by most unjust and dishonourable meanes. For after that he had receaved A.B. [illegible] [illegible] commission him to make him MacMahon for 10b. [illegible] afterwardes [illegible] other [illegible] [illegible] 3 [illegible] hanged him and in his stede invested the other [illegible] upon the land [illegible] of the Countrie [illegible] being terrified with the fare of so foule a treacherie, began eftsoones to withdrawe themselves and to [illegible] the Erle of Tirone unto them [illegible] which did not manifestlie [illegible] unto them nor [illegible] into open manifest rebellion but taking onlie dislike of suche bad dealing began to finde grevance at the government (as it [illegible] [illegible] conditions [illegible] some cause he had) for first he

The Erle of Tyrones entrance into treason and the causes thereof

might

might feare by that example lest he might be intrapped in the like
then was he by this new Countizing of the Countrie of Monaghan both
to loose that seignoritie which he claymed of that land and alsoe that
service which he claymed of Macmahon which by Comaundement of her Majestie
should be freed from his challenge. Besides he was by some his frends
made to beleeve (whether truelie or he knowes) that there was
a practise secretlie wrought by the Deputie either against his
life or libertie whereupon he kept himselfe aloofe and durst not
committ his safetie in to the hands of the [illegible] but offered still
if he might have leave to come into England freelie to iustifie
himselfe before her Majestie which whether he so truelie meant is uncertaine
but that leave would not have ben graunted him and if he had not performed it he might have bene in tyme disswaded before he had
growne unto that head that nowe he is. But as some of the
rest which then were about him felt him this wavering and doubtfull disposition they increased his offence with divers causes of dislike untill
such tyme as they might practise with her Majesties adversarie the King
of Spaine to drawe him to their partie and not with strong feares
and vaine hopes to feede his evill humor. Yet all this while
durst he not breake out into open disloialtie but so carried
himselfe as that he might make advantage of both parties
either to worke his owne cause of peace with her Majestie
by fearing her with his interdeale with the King of Spaine or
if he could not accomplishe this to use the same directly against
her. Yet all this while matters might have bene so managed
as that he might well enough have bene contained in reasonable
termes but that some were allwaies against it which wished
nothing more then to drive him from her Majesties obedience and to
Minister more matter of felonies still against him whereupon
he breaking at length openlie forthe yet was so [illegible] with
and so faintlie resisted as that meeting therewith some good
successes in first [illegible] greater harte thereby and having once
felt his owne strength and the faintnes of those which were sett
there to followe him grewe [illegible] insolent which he allso increased through occasion of the [illegible] of the government there
betwixt Sir William Russell and Sir John Norris. The
which the one being [illegible] him the other
thought by good treaties rather [illegible] to make faire warres
But by some it was thought that the onely purpose of
Sir John Norris in drawing thinges after that sorte was to
obtaine the absolute government to himselfe.

Dissention betwene Sir William Russell and Sir John Norris

Sir John Norris thought to get the government to him selfe

After which this change of government succeding the death of the noble
the 2 Barrones ensewing the sundrie alterations of counsells and
purposes following together with the division and [illegible] of
those themselves of her Majesties counsell here have since brought [illegible]
to [illegible]

Lord Burrowes

to that dangerous condition that now they stand in. / ffor from that head through collusion of the wardes conspiring together so sent a sparke into all partes of that realme and gathered in so short a space a contagion that nothing but a moste violent and dangerous remedie will serve to recover yt. ffor all the Irishe allmoste are confederated and have generallie agreed to shake of the yoke of their obedience to the Crowne of England. And now even the contagion is crept over hither into this province of Mounster which hath hitherto continued in reasonable good quietnes the which now so much the more it was later infected then the rest so much is it now worse then all the rest and become most lamentable miserable desolation like as a fire the longer it is kept under the more violentlie it burneth when it breaketh out /

Hither came over hither latelie of the rebells not past 2000 being sent by the said Traitor Earle of Tyrone presently upon whose arrivall all the Irishe rose up in Armes against the englishe which were latelie planted there so that in short tyme they became 5 or 6000 whereby manifestly appeareth that they were formerlie combined with them. / ffor as Captaine Tirrell one of the cheefe leaders of them said openlie he had before his coming up 80 of the best lords and gentlemens handes in writing, that him promising him to joyne with him here, which accordinglie they performed. And being straight upon the English as they dwelt dispersed before they could assemble themselves spoiled them all, their howses sacked and themselves forced to flie awaie for safetye, so many as they could catch they slewe and massacred miserablie the rest leaving all behinde them fled with their wives and children to such porte townes as were next them where they yet remaine like moste pittifull creatures naked and comfortles lying under the townes walles and begging aboute all the streetes daily expecting when the last extremitie shalbe laide upon them. Doubtles yo[r] Ma[tie] wold most rewfull yet see but some parte of the image of theis moste rufull & lamentable things would melt with remorse to see so many soules of yo[r] faithfull subjects brought hither to inhabit this yo[r] land of the which many were the last day men of good substance and habilitie to live, others of worth able to serve yo[r] Ma[tie], now suddenly become so wretched wights and miserable out castes of the worlde so that none of the Countrie people either vouchsafeth to commiserate, but rather to scorne and approbriouslie revile them as people abandoned of all helpe and hope and exposed to extreme miserie /

Tis surelie to think that a countrie so rich so well peopled so firmlie fenced and fortified with so manie stronge castells with manie faire walled townes and with sea hath walled it aboute should be so easilie wonne the inhabitants banished their goods spoiled their dwelling places desolated and all the land allmoste in a moment wonne without stroke striken without bloodshedd without

enemie

[illegible] or theire wicked [illegible], which [illegible] is almoste [illegible] they [illegible] become of man being such [illegible] and [illegible] example of the like [illegible] the English nation so mighte [illegible] of theire owne dominion lying [illegible] and barbarous people [illegible] of all goodnes and good pollicies be so suddenlie broken [illegible] and blowne away all with a blaste, they [illegible] not knowing the meanes [illegible]. Therefore it is not amisse to consider by what meanes and evill occasions all these mischeifes happened, the rather for the better redressing thereof and avoyding the like hereafter. Some think that the first plott by which the late undertakers of the [illegible] Lands there in Mounster were planted was not well instituted nor grounded upon sound advisement and knowledge of the countrie, for that more care was there taken for proffitt and [illegible] then for strength and safetie. For indeed what hope was there that a fewe of Englishmen [illegible] in peace placed abroade in sundrie places dispersed [illegible] shoulde be able to maintaine and defend themselves against a people newlie recovered out of the relikes of rebellion and yet practising armes and warlike exercises without anie provision therefore, which that first rebellious people shoulde have bene utterlie disarmed and [illegible] from the use of the like [illegible] and in stede thereof be compelled unto other more civill trades of life, which they shoulde have bene settled in by such sure establishment that they shoulde not have bene able to have swerved from the same.

The originall cause of all this mischeife happened at Mounster.

But the devisers thereof perhaps thought that the civill example of the English being sett before them and theire daylie conversing with them woulde have brought them by dislike of theire owne savage life to the liking and embracing of better civilitie. But it is farre otherwise, for in steede of following them they flie them and moste carefullie shunne them for 2 causes. First because they have ever bene brought upp licentiouslie and to live as they each one listeth, which they esteeme the [illegible] happines. So that to come to be brought into anie better order they accompte it to be restrained of theire libertie and extreame wretchednes. Secondlie because they naturallie hate the English, so that theire fashions they allso hate. The cause of this originall hate is for that they were conquered of the English, the memorie whereof is yet fresh among them and the desire both of revenge and allso of recoverie of theire lands and [illegible] yet revived and kindled amongst them by theire lords and [illegible] for which they both hate [illegible] and our lawes and customes. Therefore in the first institution there shoulde have bene provided for that [illegible] before [illegible] overturned [illegible] olde [illegible] shoulde have bene plucked downe. For to think to joyne and [illegible] them both together in an equallitie of state is impossible and will now be without danger of greate downefall such as nowe is happened.

Irish hate the English for two causes.

Howe they

haue they sence the same [illegible] ben quite robbed out. That were to bloudie a peace and yet theire continuall rebellions deserved some littell better measure than when they [illegible] planted there were [illegible] that they might haue ben framed and fashioned to anie thinge they shoulde haue [illegible] disarmed, stronge and stronge garrisons sett on them, wth they shoulde haue ben forced at theire owne charges to mantaine without anie charge to yor Matie. Sure theire disloyall dealinges were the cause thereof, which they would then haue ben moste glad to bere by wch meanes yor Matie might haue had even out of this province 3 or 4000 souldiers continuallie mantained unto you which you might at all tymes haue used to yor service wth continuall subiection and chaunge of state.

And this I undertake (under correction) upon all that I haue in the worlde, I shoulde haue bene assured you wth as litle greevance and burden of the countrie as nowe they beare allreadie. For the charge which nowe they promise beinge [illegible] of yor Ma^ts^ composition what of the present [illegible] the composition in that of sheriffes and [illegible] extortion and other dailie [illegible] occasions is no lesse then would maintaine you so great a garrison besides it is nowe [illegible] wth the peoples great discontentm^t^. That would be then yelded with their good will when they should be sure to knowe the uttermoste of theire charge.

That at the tyme of the late placing of inhabitants here, might haue easely bene established but the occasion was then let slipp when the countrey was weake and waste, yet sure the like is likely and must of necessitie insue againe after the subdueing of this present generall rebellion it is expedient to be minded before it be to be effected. But in the meane season we poore wretches wch nowe beare the burden of all our sighes powre out o^r^ moste humble and pitious plainte unto yor moste excellent Matie that it may please you to caste yor gratious eye unto the [illegible] regarde of o^r^ miseries wch being quite banished out of o^r^ inhabi-tance and the lands upon wch we haue spent all the small porcon of o^r^ abilities in building and erecting such houses of habitation [illegible] we haue [illegible] haue nowe nothing lefte but to [illegible] unto you for tymelie ayde, before wee be brought to utter distruction and o^r^ wretched lives [illegible] remaine unto us be made the pray of doggs and savage wilde beasts.

Whereas yor Matie as you haue hitherto made yor selfe throughe all the worlde a glorious example of pitie and clemencie and [illegible] unto these vile rebells (though moste unworthie thereof) so nowe by extendinge upon them the terror of yor wrath in su-pressing of theire continuall disloyaltie and disobedience you shall

shewe

spende the honorable tyme of yor [illegible] and [illegible] both yor
owne honor and all so the reputacon of yor people wth these base
rascalls through yor so longe sufferance and their so late exposed
supporte stayed and encouraged, with all moste all Christian princes
besides wch you shall settle a perpetuall establishment both of peace
(whereby yor charges shall be much decreased) and also of great strength
wch may from hence be drawne both to the better assurance of this
yor kingdome and also to the continuall service of that yor realme
of England. For wee well hope and that is some comforte
to us in all these o^r miseries that God hath put this [illegible]
minde so gentlie into all this rebellious nation the rather to
stirr upp yor Matie nowe after the experience of all their longe and
lewde & wicked pranckes and [illegible] universall reformacon of all
this realme wch nowe doth allmoste offer it selfe unto yor that
may worke a perpetuall establishm^t of peace and good
governm^t to yor Ma^ts great honor and no lesse profitt. So that
nowe at length you may have an end of wasting yor treasure
and people in this sorte as you have donne too longe and hindering
you from more honorable atcheivem^ts.

Pardon therefore moste gracious Soveraigne to [illegible] wretched wights
yor true faithfull subiects who too sharplie have tasted of these evills to pre=
sente unto yor Matie the feeling of their miseries, and to seke to imprinte
in yor princelie minde the true sense thereof whereby some dewe
redresse may be tymelie provided therefore before wee who feele and yor
Matie heare of that wch wee simple wretches [illegible] be quite undone.
But o^r feare is lest yor Ma^ts mercifull minde should
againe be wroughte to yor wonted mildnes counselled and perswaded by
some milder meanes either of pardons or protections, this rebellious
nation may be againe brought to some good conformation wch wee beseech
allmightie god to averte and to sett before yor gracious eyes the
iuste consideracon howe that impossible may be. For it is
not easie to thinke that they whoe have imbrewed themselves so
deeplie in o^r blood and inriched themselves wth o^r goods should endure
us to dwell againe amongste them: or that wee shoulde endure to
live amongst those peaceablie wthout takinge iuste revenge of
them for all o^r evills. Besides they having once thus shaken of
will evermore presume upon the pride of their owne strength wch they
have nowe proved through knowledge whereof they will be
emboldened ever hereafter upon the least dislike to revolte from
yor obedience. And the relapse of evills yor Matie well knowes
be moste perillous. Moreover howe great discourage it shall be to
protecte or pardon them wch not onelie have allreadie carried them
selves unnaturallie but nowe allso in their comon meetings and their

Preists

Which the petitioners do speake so lowdlie and dishonorable of yor most sacred Matie that it perceth [illegible] very loth to here it. But if yor highnesse will dispose yor selfe to be inclined to any such milder dealing wth them or to temporise any longer with hopes and exhortacions as hath bene done by yor gentlenes [illegible] then we humble beseech yor Matie to call us yor poore subiects alltogether awaye from hence that at least we may die in or countrie and not see the horrable calamities wch will therby come upon all this land and from hence perhapps further as it may well be thought. The wch the humblie beseeching allmightie god to put in yor gracious minde as may be moste for his glorie and yor owne kingdoms good we cease not dayly to pray unto allmightie god wch keepe and maintaine yor longe prosperous reigne over us in all happines

Finis

Certaine pointes to be considered of in the recovery of the Realme of Ireland.

Question — The question is whether be better and easier for her Matie to subdue Ireland thoroughly and bring it all under or to reforme it and to repaire her decayed ptes

Of these twoe that must needes be better and also easier which may be done with less { charge, perill, tyme

Reason — The assumpt then is that it will be lesse charge, lesse perill and lesse spending of tyme to subdue it alltogether then to go about to reforme it

Proofe of the reason — For if you seeke to reforme it then you must retaine and save the ptes that seme sounde and afterward recover the ptes that are [illegible].

To serve and retaine the obedience is verie harde and allmoste unpossible for that from them the partes unsounde with treasone both secrett and open procede.

Secret { by working underhand / treacherously

Open { by milde and gentle intreaty

To recover them must be { by warlike pursute / by milde and gentle intreaty.

By gentle treatie must be either by { offering peacable condicons / abiding till they seek for peace

To offer them is moste dishonorable and yet perhaps they will not accept yt being offered, which would be most dishonor.

To abide till they seke yt would be chargeable and lesse pillouse for they will not seke it till they be driven to it by force. Therefore they must nedes be driven to it by force.

But whether with great force or with smale force is nowe to be considered by comparing the { Charge / Perill / Tyme.

The lesse force semeth lesse charge but considering the long continuance that it will require and the perill thereby growinge both to Ireland and also to England it selfe in suffering so great a rebellion stand so longe on foote, it will in the end prove more chargeable and also much more dangerous and yet not so effectuall.

Resolucon

Besides in so longe continuance the countrie malady will consume all the forces.

The resolucon therefore approveth

That the greater force will finish that in one yere or 2 yeres which the lesse will not do in 4 or 5 yeres.

Lesse chargefull is the grosse accompte

Less perillous { To the forces themselves / To both the Realmes

the losse of tyme by meanes of the spedie finishing of the enterprise
Generall force must be the instrument but famine must be the meane for till
Ireland be famished it cannot be subdued.

But if the reformation shall neverthelesse be intended then these
propositions are thought to be considered and observed:

That there can be no conformitie of government where is no conformitie of
religion

That there can be no sound agreement betwene twoe equall contraries
viz. the English and Irish

That there can be no assurance of peace where the worst sorte are
the stronger

That all which make the head of anie faction is to be removed or weakened

This will be accomplished with 10000 men in
halfe a yere which will not be performed of 3000
in 2 yeres and the same 10000 wilbe there
[illegible] employed to the rest of the warr.

For the conveyance of the ports which are to be possessed stronglie as well
to let in our owne forces continuallie as to keepe out others and also for
the great releefe of townes there for the cause [illegible]

That the same is meetest to be begunne in Mounster and from thence
to proceede to the rest through Leix and Offalye.

That the laying of garrisons will make but a continuall warr unles
the Queene do first make her selfe mistris of the feild wherunto there
is necessarie a competent force of horse.

All that the garrisons can doe is but to take preyes, but if the
enemie were once broken he must be forced to scatter and then the
garrisons shall have good meanes of service upon the broken partes

If it shall seeme that the resolution to subdewe Ireland wholie with
stronge force is too bloodie and too cruell the same is thus to be
mitigated:

That before the great force goe forth a generall proclamation be
made that all which will come in tyme and submitt themselves absolutelie
within ten or twelve daies (the principall excepted) shall have
pardon of life onelie upon condition that theire bodies their lands
and theire goods shalbe at the disposition of her Majestie which if they
refuse what reason but afterwardes rigor should be extended to them
that will not receive mercie, and have utterlie renounced their obedience
to her Majestie.

Whereas manie of the lords of the countrie not longe before the
consideringe of this rebellion procured their freeholders to take their
landes of themselves by deed manie of which are since gone into rebellion

That provision may be made for the avoyding of such fraudulent
conveyances made onelie to defeat her Majestie of the benefitt of
theire attainder.

Appendix B

Attribution to Spenser on verso of, "Certaine pointes to be considered of in the recouery of the Realm of Ireland" (P.R.O. SP63/202, pt. 4/59. f. 200 V).
With permission of the Public Record Office, London.

A briefe discourse of Ireland

by Spencer

Appendix C

Letter from Dudley Carleton to John Chamberlain,
9 January 1598/9 (P.R.O. SP12/270/10).
With permission of the Public Record Office, London.

Mr: Chamberlain, heere are letters come from her
Ma:tie into these countries to draw away 2000 old
souldiers for the wars of Ireland. of wch number
shee hath ~~wrote~~ written for 600 to my Ld Governor
to be had owt of this garris.. I mervaile
owr state was no better understoode then
to send for 600 having but two companies
left. and those souldiers wch be of the be for
the most part dutches, and married men
exchanged wth the companies wch went away
for the service of the garrison. so as my Ld
will be hable to give small contentment to my
Ld of Essex, who besides his Mandate from
the Q: hath written wth all earnestnes to
~~my~~ him for the sufficiencie, and ready dispatch
of the men: theyr Rendez-vous is at
Vlushing the 20:th of this present. we are
heere putt in hope (by report but uppon no good
grownd) that my Ld Govern: shall be Govern:r of
Vlushing: I pray you as you heare any thing wch
concernes us in this, or any thing else lett me
heare fro you: I assure you the understandin
of matters wch I have by yr lres is my best
desert: and, though you may little think it,
you have credited me more wth my Ld Govern:
since my last comming over then all the frends
I have which recommended me to him. I pray you lett the Sandwich
post goe often betwixt us and for such newes
as we have you shall find I will be no
niggard. I can send you none now without
I should tell you that the Cardinal hath ever

danger of burning wth in the Citadell at Mylan all his goods were burnt, and he onely skaped in his shirt. one of his followers wrote the newes to a gentelman heereby, but sayth nothing of the manner whether it was done by treason or chaunce. but wisheth him=self at home because (as he sayth) they are all weary of keeping continuall watch about his person. They had a great tourney wherin the prince of Orenge carried away the best. Thus wth my very hartie comendations I comitt you to God.

Ostend. Januarie. 9th 1598.

Yrs most assuredly.

Dudley Carleton

I receaued no lres fro you since yr 20th of the last, but doe looke every day for owr London bote, wch I am sure will not come emptie he stayes so long.

Ytt this present is yor letter arriued of the 3d of Jan: wch makes me send you one wch hath lane long uppon my handes for want of carriage that you may see it is not my fault that you haue gott the start of me by so many letters

Appendix D

"Certen poinctes to be considered in the recovering of Ireland" (BL Harl. MS 3787, f. 184). With permission of the British Library, London.

Certen pointes to be considered in the recovery of Ireland.

The question is, whether it be better and easier for her Matie to subdue Ireland throughly, and bringe it wholy under, or to reforme it, and repaire her decayed partes.

Of these two, that must be better, and also easier, which maye be done, with lesse charge, lesse perill, and lesse tyme.

It is assumed then is, that it will be lesse charge, lesse daunger, and lesse spendinge of tyme, to subdue it alltogether, then to goe about to reforme it.

The reason is, if you seeke to reforme it, then you must first reteine it, and save the partes that stand sownde, and after recover the partes unsownde.

To save and reteine the partes sownde, is very hard, and almost impossible, for that from them, the partes unsownde, will receive both secret and open succour.

Secret, by workinge under hand treacherie, and open, by takinge it forcibly.

To recover them, must be either by warlike pursute or by gentle entreaty.

By entreaty, either offeringe them peaceable condicions, or abidinge till they sue for peace.

To offer them, is most dishonorable, and though they will not accept it, and then it will be more dishonorable.

To abide till they seeke it, would be chargeable, and also perilous, for they will not seeke it, till they be enforced.

Therfore they must needs be enforced.

Now whether with greate force or small, is it to be considered, and that by comparinge charge perill and tyme.

The lesse force semeth the lesse charge, but consideringe the longe continuance that it will require, and the perill therby growinge both to Ireland and England it selfe in sufferinge so great a rebellion, to stande so longe on foote it will in the ende prove more chargeable, and also more perilous: and yet not so effectuall, besides in so longe continuance the countrye malady, will consume all your forces.

The resolution therefore appeareth: That the greater force, which will finishe all in one or two yeares, where the lesse will not in fower or five yeares, is lesse chargeable in the grosse accompt, lesse perillous to the realme, and lesse losse of tyme, by meanes of the speedy finishinge of the enterprise.

Great force must be the instrument, but famine the meanes, for till Ireland be famished it can not be subdued.

But if the reformacion shall neverthelesse be intended then these questions are there to be weighed, and considered.

That there can be no conformitie of government, where there is not conformity of religion.

That there can be no sounde agreament, betweene two equall contraries viz the English and the Irish.

That there can be no assurance of peace, where the meaner side are the stronger.

And that all, which maye be the heade of any faction, is to be removed, or weakened.

Marke these when the okes fall
Frends and foes all
When out of England shall come
The Irish shall dye all and some:
The [illegible] to St George [illegible] shall stand
And all this shall happen in shorte tyme.

Certaine notes to be considered of in the reformacion of the Realme of Ireland

The question

whether it be better and easier for her Matie to subdue Ireland throughly and bringe it all under, or to reforme it, and repaire the decayed ptes therof, of which two, that is thought to be the better which may be done with least charge / least perill / least tyme

The proposicion is

That it wilbe least charges / least perill / least tyme to subdue it all togither then to reforme it

If you seke to reforme it you must first reteine and save those ptes that are sounde and then recover those ptes that are unsounde

To save and reteine the ptes sounde is verie harde and allmost impossible for that from them the ptes unsounde will receive both secret and open succour

Secret succour by working underhand treacherously
Open succor by taking it forciblie

To recover them must be either by offring them peaceable condicions or abyding untill they will seke peace

1\. To offer peace is dishonorable, and they [illegible] not anythinge it will be more dishonorable

2\. To abide untill they seke it wilbe chargeable and also perilous for they will not seke it till they be driven to it by force, and therefore they must be driven to it by force

But whether with a great force or smale force is more to be considered by comparacion — charge / perill / tyme

The lesse force semeth lesse charges but considering the longe continuance it will requier, and the perill thereby growinge both to Ireland and also to England it selfe

Appendix E

"Certain notes to be considered of in the recoveringe of the Realme of Irelande" (All Souls College MS 155, ff. 58R–58V). With permission of the Warden and Fellows of All Souls College, University of Oxford.

58v

in sufferinge soe great a rebellion to stande soe
a foote it will in the ende proue more charge[illegible]
dangerous, and yet not soe effectuall, besides
longe continuance, the countrie maladie [illegible]
consume the partes

The resolucion thereof appeareth	That the greater parte will finishe it in one or two yeares the lesser will not doe it in foure or five yeares —	is	lesse perill for the rest lives lesse chargeable greater triumph lesse losse of [illegible] meanes of the [illegible] finishinge the [illegible]
Wee as:	Great parte must be the instrument But famine must be the meane		for till force and famishe it cannot be

That if reformacion shall ensue the lesse be intended, these thinges propositions are therein to be considered and obserued.

That there can be no conformitie of gouernment where is no conformitie of religion

That there can be no sounde agreement betwene two equall countries

That there can be no assurance of peace where worse sort are the stronger

That all that maye make the head of any faction are to be remoued or weakned.

Imitation and Authority in Donne's "Anatomy" and Lanyer's "Salve Deus"

SUSANNE WOODS

> As a system, art as imitation solves many problems that plague contemporary theory before they become problematical. For example, since the work or art is imitating *something*, we can posit certainly that the something being imitated is an ultimate determinant of the artifact, so we prevent a number of questions about its mode of existence and final meaning. The ontological *situs* of the artifact resides in the object being imitated. Again, since *someone* has executed the imitation, there's a clear assumption that an active human intellect has been at work. Consequently, the imputing of authorial intention is no fallacy.
>
> —S. K. Heninger Jr.

AEMILIA Lanyer (1569–1645) and John Donne (1572–1631) were contemporaries in the generation after Sidney and Spenser. S. K. Heninger's important study of Renaissance poetics is of great value in looking at Lanyer and Donne together, which I have been doing as part of an ongoing inquiry into how Lanyer's interesting collection of poems, *Salve Deus Rex Judaeorum* (1611), helps us think more broadly about "authorship" in the early seventeenth century, the period when many critics believe the idea of "author" in the modern sense was just beginning to take root. [1] I am particularly interested in how poets in this period, especially women poets, claimed their authority, which was also an assertion of their own agency (as the Renaissance confusion of "author," "auctour," and "actor" suggests), a precursor of the modern self-defining subject. I want to be careful not to impose a modern view of agency on the writers of the Jacobean period, however, and (as Heninger insists) to respect the mimetic principles under which these poets wrote. But what could those be for Lanyer, in an age where Pauline precepts would seem to deprive women of the right to speak publicly? What does authority mean to Lanyer in her vocation as a public voice, and how does the idea of authority reflect and help to illuminate the more traditional male authoring strategies?[2]

Setting the "Salve Deus" against Donne's "Anatomy of the World" provides one case for examining these questions. The differences between the poems are of course substantial, and include genre, verse form, narrative strategy, and tone. Nonetheless these poems, both published in 1611 (although probably written about a year apart),[3] have some important common elements. While the "Anatomy" is a funeral elegy and "Salve Deus" is (or purports to be) a descriptive narrative of Christ's passion, both are long lyrics about "loss and the need for recovery," in Arthur Marotti's words describing Donne's *Anniversaries*.[4] Both poems seek patronage through expressing sympathy with a high-born family (in the "Anatomy" the sympathy is for the death of the Drury's fifteen-year-old daughter, Elizabeth; in Lanyer it is for the Countess of Cumberland's decline in status through the death of her husband and her daughter's loss of her expected patrimony). Both poems underscore the evil and injustice of the world, and both assert the authority of the poet, generically and specifically. I am interested in how a woman and a man, publishing in roughly the same year and with similar social goals, portray the world and claim authority for their portrayals.

The answers to these questions depend very much on how we read works written nearly four hundred years ago. As in Donne's time, our own "new philosophy calls all in doubt." While we cannot perfectly reconstruct the culture of 1611, neither (I believe) should we simply impose our own sociocultural constructs onto an alien time. I posit a way of reading that I call *diachronic*, a form of dialogic engagement with the Renaissance texts that seeks a dynamic interaction between the characteristic assumptions of the culture in which the text was produced and those of the reader's own culture. Heninger's work helps by reminding us that there were quite explicit assumptions about art in the Renaissance, and, while they were individually mediated or mediated by a class of writers, they were firmly based on Aristotelian and Christian Neoplatonic notions of mimesis, form, and the ultimate authority of God.[5]

While Heninger acknowledges that "art as imitation . . . is an outmoded aesthetic and that other systems based on other [non-representational] principles are also feasible," his own work has focused resolutely and magisterially on what Renaissance English authors knew and understood about the world and the arts, and how they sought to reflect the one by the other.[6] Nonetheless, much current theory would reject the skirting of ontological issues that Heninger implies in this essay's epigraph; the very object(s) imitated by Renaissance artists, the argument might go, are themselves sufficiently in flux to destabilize the artifact that seeks to imitate. For *verba* to follow *res*, for intellect to intend, there must be a reified something that the intellect seeks to represent. It is on this ground, I believe, that Heninger and much recent Renaissance criticism might contend. The contention, whether based on Barthes or Foucault, or Greenblatt or Montrose, would in some measure rest on the restlessness and indeterminability of Renaissance cultural history. If "the object being imitated" is ontologically uncertain, then the act of imitation necessarily shares that uncertainty. The act of imitation may seek to define or redefine the reality of what it presents, or fix or deny fixity to a culture in flux. If the author is a sociohistorical construct rather than an essentially independent agent, then we cannot even attribute so much intentionality to the act of imitation.[7] Art becomes a place where an indeterminate universe presents itself in sociohistorical fictions.

However, as Heninger has continued to point out, a poet such as Sidney "was not a postmodern man. Plato, not Saussure, was his point of reference in theorizing about language. With Cratylus, and the majority of writers in his day, Sidney believed that words do have inherent meanings fixed in the nature of things, and probably fixed by the deity as part of the providential scheme."[8] This simple assertion refers to a complex set of views, not always stable themselves, evident in Renaissance writings about the nature and role of art and the relation of humanity to the cosmos. No one knows more about these shifting topics than Heninger, and his portrait of the English Renaissance doctrine of imitation therefore becomes a reliable starting point for any discussion of Renaissance poetry and poetics.

Heninger's "model for the theory of art based upon imitation" is a variant of the familiar "coordinates of art criticism" posited by M. H. Abrams in the first chapter of his classic analysis of romantic expressivism, *The Mirror and the Lamp* (1953). In Heninger's terms, the "exhaustive and exclusive" list of elements for a mimetic criticism consists of "an artifact, the artificer who made the artifact, an object which the artificer imitated in making the artifact, and a percipient who observes the artifact." Although each component is separable, the dynamics of any mimetic theory derive from the interaction of these elements: "each element affects and is affected by every other element."[9]

And so to Lanyer and Donne. Heninger's model for theories of imitation, based as it is on dynamic relationships between fixed referents, is helpful for observing similarity and differences in Lanyer and Donne's claims of authority, and in defining a diachronic perspective on those claims—each coordinate (to use Abrams's term) has a different force and a different perceived relationship to the other coordinates depending on whether our larger context is felt to be primarily a function of Renaissance culture or primarily a function of our own. The very notion of author and authority, for example, differs radically between the early seventeenth and late twentieth centuries. In 1611 an author resided in a yet unfixed world between the interactive engagements of manuscript circulation and the comparatively fixed authority of print—between a social and individual conception of authorship.[10] In 1611 England, authority, even among the intellectual elite, depended ultimately and firmly on an authorizing God, while in late-twentieth-century Euro-American intellectual culture, which questions essentialism in any form, the source of authority is contingent and relative, and is explicitly construed in terms of political, military, or economic power.[11]

In the Renaissance authority resides ultimately with God, to whose voice "percipients" know they must listen, although it may be difficult to discern among the babble of disputing preachers and biblical interpreters. The relation of poet/artificer to his or her artifact and its object of imitation—to the poem and what it seeks to say—carries authority if it can be seen as a function of the poet's relation to God (the poet as *vates*, as Sidney derives it from Platonic and Biblical authority).[12] That function can be direct or indirect, since it can come from the poet's own relationship with God, or claim to speak for him, or it can come through the request of one through whom God's authority is dispensed—such as a social superior who may also be an actual or potential patron. Reading from the perspective of 1611, what we think of as the authoritative tone of a poem comes from the success by which the poet's artifact/poem conveys the poet's direct or indirect relationship with God. Authority can also come from a poem's subject, its object of imitation. Certainly Donne's "Anatomy" has what we might call an air of authority, achieved at least in part by its claim to represent a divine wisdom.

Renaissance readers seem to have valued and shared the poems they read primarily because of subject matter, Heninger's "object being imitated." While originality was no particular commendation, and, as E. K. reminds us, we are expected to value a clever style, "a prety epanorthosis,"[13] the first concern was that the object be worthy of imitation and the imitation intelligibly reveal the object. On this basis, Donne's portrayal of Elizabeth Drury, as representing an Astraean perfection whose abandonment of earth signals the world's decay, was controversial in its own time. William Drummond of Hawthornden reports that Ben Jonson "told Mr. Donne that if [the "Anatomy"] had been written of the Virgin Marie it had been something," an accusation apparently prompting Donne's reply "that he described the Idea of a Woman, not as she was."[14] The relation between the poet and the object imitated, therefore, is not a relation between John Donne and Elizabeth Drury (whom he never knew), but between the artificer and an idea of perfection.

Barbara Lewalski has located that idea securely within Donne's view of the Christian universe, noting that "Donne's sermons provide a precise, consistent, and clearly relevant gloss upon the term 'Idea' used in such a context." Specifically, "the Idea of Mankind," for Donne, as revealed in his sermons, is "the image of God"; even more particularly, as it applies to Donne's symbolic figuring of Elizabeth Drury in the "Anatomy," the "Idea" pertains to "the restoration of the image of God in man through grace."[15]

Joseph Hall's commendatory verses underscore Elizabeth Drury as the "subject" of Donne's verses, but a subject who evokes the "noble thought" the verses imitate:

> And thou the subject of this wel-borne thought,
> Thrise noble maid; couldst not have found nor sought
> A fitter time to yeeld to thy sad Fate
> Then whilst this spirit lives, that can relate
> Thy worth so well.[16]
>
> (lines 11–15)

Hall goes on to locate the authority of Donne's poem explicitly in the dynamic relationship between poet and subject matter:

> Admired match! where strives in mutual grace
> The cunning Pencill, and the comely face:
> A taske, which thy faire goodnes made too much
> For the bold pride of vulgar pens to touch.
>
> (lines 17–20)

A diachronic reading might first note the mimetic theory Hall invokes. Both the poet/painter analogy and the claim of authority through mutually reflected virtue are commonplaces of Renaissance interpretations of Aristotle, but with some important modifications that a late-twentieth-century perspective allows us to see. If the subject was primary in this period, Hall nonetheless invokes a struggle between the subject and the developing individual authority of the writer. Hall acknowledges what more recent critics, including Marotti, have assumed: that Donne takes over the poem to test his own move from coterie poet to public voice. The poem is not in any significant sense about the virtues of Elizabeth Drury, but it is about the world's disappointments and the authority of the writer to "grace" a subject with his eternizing power, even as he holds a mirror up to a decaying world and pronounces lastly on its deeds.[17]

As subject, Elizabeth Drury is a young woman who died unmarried, and much is made of her virginity. Hall calls her "happy maid" (line 33) and "Virgin soule" (line 45). In "A Funerall Elegie" Donne describes her "soone expir'd":

> Cloath'd in her Virgin white integrity
> For mariage, though it doe not staine, doth dye.
> To scape th'infirmaties which waite upone
> Woman, shee went away, before sh'was one.
>
> (lines 74–78)

At the outset of the "Anatomy" Donne implies her connection with the Virgin Mary: Elizabeth Drury is a "Queene" for whom heaven is as "her standing house" (lines 7–8); she is also a type of the co-redemptress, who would erase Eve's sin:

> She in whom vertue was so much refin'd,
> That for Allay unto so pure a minde
> She tooke the weaker Sex, she that could drive
> The poysonous tincture, and the stayne of *Eve*,
> Out of her thoughts, and deeds; and purifie
> All by a true religious Alchimy.
>
> (lines 177–82)

Donne's construction of her virgin purity and virtue excuses, even transforms, Elizabeth Drury's innate female weakness, which is alloy to her virtues and allows for an alchemical transformation of "all."

But what, given Heninger's model, is the relation between this object purportedly being imitated, Elizabeth Drury, this transforming alchemical force, and the artifact, the poem that imitates? She or "Shee" is a referent in the poem, but "shee, shee is dead," and her absence rather than her presence is the focus of the poem. The artifact that purports to celebrate this transforming virginal purity instead anatomizes the decay her absence signifies. In the final analysis, it is not "Elizabeth Drury" but poetry that mediates the space between that heavenly perfection and earthly decay, and it is verse that seeks to portray the relation between heavenly perfection (returned to heaven, as figured by the death of Elizabeth Drury) and the soul's aspiring hope of grace.

> . . . blessed maid,
> Of whom is meant what ever hath beene said,
> Or shall be spoken well by any tongue,
> Whose name refines course lines, and makes prose song,
> Accept this tribute. . . .
> . . . .
> And you her creatures, whom she workes upon
> And have your last, and best concoction
> From her example, and her vertue, if you
> In reverance to her, doe thinke it due,
> That no one should her prayses thus reherse,
> As matter fit for Chronicle, not verse,
> Vouchsafe to call to minde, that God did make
> A last, and lastingst peece, a song. He spake
> To *Moses*, to deliver unto all,
> That song: because he knew they would let fall,
> The Law, the Prophets, and the History,
> But keepe the song still in their memory.
> But such an opinion (in due measure) made
> Me this great Office boldly to invade.
> Nor could incomprehensiblenesse deterre

> Me, from thus trying to emprison her.
> Which when I saw that a strict grave could do,
> I saw not why verse might not doe so too.
> Verse hath a middle nature: heaven keepes soules,
> The grave keeps bodies, verse the fame enroules.
>
> (lines 443–47; 455–74)

Donne here asserts a mimetic theory of art, outlining the relationship among object of imitation, poem, poet, and what Heninger calls the percipient (and Abrams the "audience"). The effect of his statement is to efface the subject in favor of the poem, and displace its authority with that of the poet. The example of Moses allows the poet to "invade" and "emprison" his subject in the artifact of verse. What lasts is not the person but the song, not the object imitated but the mimesis itself, not the decaying physical presence but the mnemonic power of the record. Authority is in the word, not the act, and he who triumphs is he who imprisons his subject in his verse. Because "all" humankind "would let fall/ The Law, the Prophets, and the History," God has created the poet, whose voice will "keepe the song still in their memory." Yet Donne does not present himself as the blessed recipient of a divine vocation, but rather as a conquering intellect who sees where he may claim lasting power: "But such an opinion (in due measure) made / Me this great office to invade."

Donne situates his authority in the dynamic between the object being imitated and the poet's chaste sexual virility. According to Hall, Drury's "faire goodnes" cannot be touched by "vulgar pens,"

> Which had'st thou liv'd, had hid their fearefull head
> From th'angry checkings of thy modest red.
>
> (lines 22–23)

By contrast, Donne's "high songs" suggest no such violation of virgin purity in need of modesty's anger; instead, they "Serve but to sound thy makers praise, in thine" (lines 35, 36).

The diachronic dynamic makes it difficult to miss the danger a virgin may face from "vulgar pens." In Hall's terms, only Donne can authorize Elizabeth Drury to the world, for only he reflects the virtues he sets out to describe. This is, to be sure, the language of commendation, but it is also a fair reflection of Donne's portrayal of his virgin subject. Her purity is a tabula rasa that he can "invade," an untouched page on which he can write.

Donne achieves some of his authority from the accepted force of what he chooses to imitate: the decay of the world set against the pristine example of his "Idea of a Woman." These are acceptable topics for his time, but they do not adequately account for the tone of assurance in Donne's poem. Lewalski makes the point that "for Donne the Idea of a man, or of a woman, is—quite precisely—the image of God, since that is the pattern by which God created mankind, and Christ the true image of God is the pattern by which he restores mankind. . . . If, then, Donne declared his intention to praise Elizabeth Drury not as she was but rather as the Idea of a Woman, we may suppose that he undertook to praise the image of God created and restored in her."[18] This would situate the power of God, Donne's authority, exactly in his subject. But his subject is a deliberate cipher, and the poem is about decay and disappointment, not about transformed perfection. The image that God created and would restore is the soul of man, of this man, of the author, whose own virtue portrays a worldview authorized by the subject of God's image, the soul, this soul, this man, John Donne.

In the "Anatomy," Donne imitates the idea of the Christian soul, and, in the process, dominates his ostensible authorizing subject and becomes himself the authority for his vision of the world. He becomes God's image, redeemed through a new creation, his own. He becomes the voice of God. Elizabeth Drury has no independent existence outside the voice of the author. In more ways than the literal, Donne never met her, and neither do we.

This is not meant to devalue the power and interest of the "Anatomy," but to observe how this (male) poet engenders his subject and disengenders her as part of the process of asserting his own authority. The author represents the Author in the "Anatomy." There is a clear contrast with Lanyer's more complex approach to subject matter in the "Salve Deus."

Lanyer's ostensible subject in the "Salve Deus" is the passion of Christ and the empowering, redemptive virtue of that act and of Christ himself. The poem is dedicated to the countess of Cumberland:

> His Death and Passion I desire to write,
> And thee to reade, the blessed Soules delight.
>
> (lines 271–72)

While the poet conventionally receives her authority from the countess's patronage, the relationships among the patron, author, and divine subject of the poem are complex and tend to fuse the identity and authority of all three. While the godly authority that Donne ultimately claims for himself tends to distance him from his subject, to make him a transcendent divinity in relation to his poem, Lanyer's approach to authority merges her voice and presence with the creation of the poem (up to a point), making her much more of an eminent creative force within the territory of her creation.

Lanyer's invocation of her principal patron, the countess of Cumberland, is situated within the traditions of Jacobean patronage, and is the most immediate and visible way in which the poet claims the authority to write.[19] The stated purpose, as it was for Donne in the "Anatomy," Jonson, Spenser, and all poets who wrote epideictic verse, was to celebrate the patron and validate the patron's virtues.

The "Salve Deus" begins where Donne's "Anatomy" concludes: by claiming the eternizing role of verse. After acknowledging the departure of that great and perfect patron, Queen Elizabeth, who has already "ascended to that rest / Of endlesse joy and true Eternitie" (lines 1–2), Lanyer turns to the countess as next in line for the tribute of poet's praise:

> To thee great Countesse now I will applie
> My Pen, to write thy never dying fame;
> That when to heav'n thy blessed Soule shall flie,
> These lines on earth record thy reverend name.
>
> (lines 9–12)

Whereas in the "Anatomy" Donne's portrayal of the unknown Elizabeth Drury is hyperbolic and (Jonson at least believed) incidental, Lanyer's attention to the countess, her virtues and her sufferings, is grounded in the living reality of the countess's "sad soule, plunged in waves of woe" (line 34). One consequence is the sheer amount of attention paid directly to the countess; roughly 500 of the poem's 1840 lines address the countess directly, describe her situation (e.g., "Thou from the Court to the Countrie art retir'd, / Leaving the world, before the world leaves thee," lines 161–62), or praise her virtue and faithfulness. The central story of the poem's passion is framed by catalogs of women who failed to find the true good or sought it imperfectly, so that the countess's own devotion to Christ may be contrasted with, and yet gain force from, a historical community of suffering women.

What, then, is being imitated in this poem? Centrally, the traditional story of Christ's passion, which itself authorizes the artifact. As Donne's allusion to Moses suggests, there is no higher authority than the Bible. Yet Lanyer understands that, given the gender biases of her own culture, she is presenting that which "is seldome seene, / A Womans writing of divinest things."[20] Her strategy is to make the situation of women—of the countess, of the women with whom she is compared in the poem's frame, of the women who accompany Christ through the story as Lanyer tells it—inseparable from the passion itself. In trying to understand Lanyer's approach to authority as it is distinguishable from that of a male poet such as Donne, this conflation of women's stories with an imitation of the biblical passion is key. Heninger's categories of artist, thing imitated, and percipient are considerably less differentiated for Lanyer than they were for Donne.

Even Christ becomes a figure for female experience in Lanyer's poem. Since Barbara Lewalski's early article on Lanyer, it has become commonplace to note and marvel at the extent to which Lanyer infuses a female point of view into traditional materials.[21] Janel Mueller has taken these observations one step further by pointing out the extent to which the figure of Christ is feminized in the poem.[22] She argues that the male figures in the poem misconstrue Christ's authority and misunderstand his language, provoking his silence:

> They tell his words, though farre from his intent,
> And what his Speeches were, not what he meant.
>
> (lines 655–56)

A female identification with Christ, Mueller suggests, authorizes Lanyer to interpret Jesus' actions. Mueller cites "the pattern of fundamental misprision exhibited by all of the males in the story, friends and foes alike, while the female poet unfailingly understands what and who Jesus is. . . . [Lanyer's] Christ, like the ideal woman of the Puritan manuals, is silent except when induced to speak, and modest and taciturn when he does; he is gentle, mild, peaceable, and submissive to higher male authorities."

To take this further still, Lanyer's authority for her version of the biblical passion lies in her identification with, and ability to interpret, the passion of Christ. She who has the power to understand has the authority to speak, and that assumption runs throughout the "Salve Deus." The most famous example is of course the voice of Pilate's wife. From a small biblical text, but one that gives Pilate's wife the unquestioned right to speak (Matt. 27:19), Lanyer creates "Eve's apology" and an argument for female freedom and agency that (as far as we know) is without precedent. The wit and assurance of this section is a function of the assurance the speaker brings to her biblically defined right to interpret "divinest things."

Similarly, Lanyer eternizes the countess of Cumberland by identifying the countess's suffering with the suffering of Christ:

> He through afflictions, still thy Minde prepares,
> And all thy glorious Trialls will enroule:
> That when darke daies of terror shall appeare,
> Thou as the Sunne shalt shine; or much more cleare.
>
> (lines 53–56)

Like Elizabeth Drury, the countess is a model of virtue in opposition to the decay of the world in which she lives:

> . . . thou, the wonder of our wanton age
> Leav'st all delights to serve a heanv'nly King:
>
> (lines 169–70)

The countess is the representative Christian, the true bride of Christ who is the "Husband of [her] Soule" (line 253). Even more, Christ's passion and death have made the countess

. . . Dowager of all;
Nay more, Co-heire of that eternall blisse
That Angels lost, and We by *Adams* fall.

(lines 257–59)

Like Elizabeth Drury, the countess becomes "the Idea of a Woman." As "Co-heire" the countess becomes, in addition, the queen of heaven, a figure for the Virgin Mary or perhaps, given Protestant nervousness about the Mary's role, her displacement, the unmediated bridal soul. Lanyer has anticipated Jonson's objection to Donne's hyperbole by writing, to some degree, "of the Virgin Marie." But of course Lanyer also claims to represent her living patron "as she was."

What is being imitated, and where does authority reside? Lanyer imitates a biblical story central to the Christian faith. Authority resides with God and transfers to the poet by means of her patrons' perfect devotion and representative grace, and by an identity, elicited through the poem's mimetic choices, of Christ, patron, and poet. If, according to Donne, Elizabeth Drury "tooke the weaker sexe" to redeem Eve's sin ("Anatomy," line 179), by contrast Lanyer claims that her weakness is (like Paul's) an opportunity to demonstrate the power of Christ:

But yet the Weaker thou ["my deare Muse"]
 doest seeme to be
In Sexe, or Sence, the more his Glory shines,
That doth infuze such powerfull Grace in thee,
To shew thy Love in these few humble lines. . . .

(lines 289–92)

Her apparent weakness (note the use of "seeme") becomes an opportunity to underscore the divine grace that authorizes the poet's voice.

Toward the end of the poem, when Lanyer claims her call from God to eternize the countess's virtues, her vocation as a poet is no longer in spite of her gender, but because of it:

And knowe, when first into this world I came,
This charge was giv'n me by th'Eternall powres,
Th'everlasting Trophie of thy fame,
To build and decke it with the sweetest flowres
That virtue yields; Then Madame, doe not blame
Me, when I shew the World but what is yours,
 And decke you with that crowne which is your due,
 That of Heav'ns beauty Earth may take a view.

(lines 1457–64)

I suggested earlier that, as distinct from Donne's, Lanyer's creation evolves through her own participation in the world she creates. Thinking diachronically, a modern reader might take this point and pursue the implications for theories of gender and transgression. One might surmise that the seventeenth-century context required a submerged and apparently derivative authority for a woman, whereas a man was able to claim God's voice more directly. On the other hand, there is much that seems perfectly conventional and ungendered about Lanyer's approach to poetic authority. She praises the virtues of her patroness in order to "shew the World but what is yours," to eternize her fame and align it with the fame of heaven itself. In the process, since she is a woman, we can expect a certain amount of identification with the condition of women, and a self-effacement that includes gender as well as social degree

Yet this fusion of author with subject proceeds only up to a point. The creator never disappears entirely into her creation, and there is never a question about who is the maker of the poem—and the fame. As visionary and interpreter of Christ's passion, the poet is the giver and she offers the gift of Christ:

> Which I present (deare Lady) to your view,
> Upon the Crosse depriv'd of life or breath,
> To judge if ever Lover were so true,
> To yeeld himselfe unto such shamefull death.
>
> (lines 1265–68)

Lanyer's vocation is her authority. If she is not as fully the voice of God as Donne insinuates himself to be in the *Anatomy*, she is not as neat a contrast as might at first appear—indeed, as I have been arguing up until now. Her book's concluding envoy "To the doubtfull Reader" asserts a divine voice as explicitly as Herbert or Milton would later do:

> Gentle reader, if thou desire to be resolved, why I give this Title, Salve Deus Rex Judaeorum, know for certaine, that it was delivered unto me in sleepe many yeares before I had any intent to write in this maner, and was quite out of my memory, untill I had written the Passion of Christ, when immediately it came into my remembrance, what I had dreamed long before; and thinking it a significant token, that I was appointed to performe this Worke, I gave the very same words I received in sleepe as the fittest Title I could devise for this Booke.[23]

Much remains to be learned about how men and women approached the issue of authority, and even of mimesis. I do not mean to suggest that the similarities and differences I observe between Donne's "Anatomy" and Lanyer's "Salve Deus" are even necessarily typical of what further inquiry might produce, or that authority and mimesis are the only interesting areas for gender study in this period. What, for example, might we make of the differences between Isabella Whitney and the Elizabethan sonneteers in their approaches to courtly love? The differences between Elizabeth Cary and John Webster in their representations of female heroism or the idea of hubris? The differences between Lady Mary Wroth and her uncle, Sir Philip Sidney, in their presentations of the public and private realms of power?

Issues of authority and mimesis, both carefully theorized in the English Renaissance, are nonetheless good places to begin, and Heninger's work reminds us that the dynamic of a mimetic theory of art, though it may not be a viable theory for many in our time, was rich and complex in the sixteenth and seventeenth centuries. I have tried to give one example of how that traditional view provides a perspective on newly developing opportunities to look at gender differences among Renaissance poets. At the same time, we deceive ourselves if we think we can read those poets only through the lens of their own time. From the viewpoint of this century's Heraclitean flux, yet another dimension must be added to Heninger's artist-artifact-object-percipient: temporality itself. How time affects the art that stays and the eyes that read and recede through dying generations is another piece of the interpretive puzzle.

NOTES

1. See, e.g., Richard Helgerson, *Self-Crowned Laureate: Spenser, Jonson, Milton, and the Literary System* (Berkeley: University of California Press, 1983) and Wendy Wall, *The Imprint of Gender: Authorship and Publication in the English Renaissance* (Ithaca: Cornell University Press, 1993).

2. I use "authority" and "author" in the following senses described by the OED (second ed., 1989): Authority, "II. Power to influence action, opinion, belief. 5. Power over, or title to influence, the opinions of others; authoritative opinion; weight of judgment or opinion, intellectual influence. 6. Power to inspire belief, title to be believed; authoritative statement; weight of testimony." Author, "3. One who sets forth written statements. . . . 4. The person on whose authority a statement is made." These usages are found in the early seventeenth century and persist in the late twentieth, though refinements and connotations are inevitably different. It is worth noting, however, the spelling confusion in the fifteenth and sixteenth centuries between "auctour" and "auteur" that led by the end of the sixteenth century to "actor" and "author," connecting both with the idea of agency. It is not surprising that both "authorship" in the modern sense and the idea of individual agency developed more or less simultaneously over the course of the seventeenth century in England.

3. The "Salve Deus" was probably written after 1609, when Anne Cifford married Dorset, and was actually printed around October 1610, if we credit the date of 8 November 1610 in Alfonso Lanyer's presentation copy to Thomas Jones. See Susanne Woods, ed., *The Poems of Aemilia Lanyer: Salve Deus Rex Judaeorum* (New York: Oxford University Press, 1993), xlviii–xlix; this edition is based on the Huntington Library copy, HEH 62139, and will be the edition cited for this essay. "The Anatomy of the World" was certainly written after Elizabeth Drury's burial in December 1610, and probably after the success with her father of Donne's initial elegy, published along with the "Anatomy." In 1612 Donne published "The Anatomie of the World" as the subtitle of "The First Anniversarie" (i.e., of Elizabeth Drury's death), along with "Of the Progres

of the Soule," or "The Second Anniversarie." Commendatory verses by Joseph Hall precede each of these two poems, and "A Funerall Elegie" on Elizabeth Drury follows the "First Anniversarie." Two further editions of the combined work appeared in Donne's lifetime, in 1621 and 1625. Citations from "The Anatomy" are from Frank Manley, ed., *John Donne: The Anniversaries* (Baltimore: Johns Hopkins University Press, 1963), which I have compared with the Huntington Library copy of the 1611 edition (HEH 60189) to assure no significant differences with the first edition, since this is the edition that appears most closely to Lanyer's.

4. Arthur F. Marotti, *John Donne: Coterie Poet* (Madison: University of Wisconsin Press, 1986), 236.

5. S. K. Heninger Jr., *Sidney and Spenser: The Poet as Maker* (University Park: Pennsylvania State University Press, 1989), 59–69, 127–222 (chap. 4, "Critics on Imitation").

6. Ibid., 18.

7. Two relevant essays often cited in recent Renaissance criticism are Roland Barthes, "The Death of the Author," in *Image, Music, Text*, ed. Stephen Heath (New York: Hill and Wang, 1977), and Michel Foucault, "What Is An Author?" in *Textual Strategies: Perspectives in Post-Structuralist Criticism,* ed. Josue Harari (Ithaca: Cornell University Press, 1979). For recent works by scholars of the English Renaissance that dispute the post-Enlightenment notion of authorship, see, e.g., Jonathan Goldberg, "Textual Properties," *Shakespeare Quarterly* 37 (fall 1986): 213–17; and Arthur F. Marotti, "John Donne, Author," *Journal of Medieval and Renaissance Studies* 19 (1989): 69–82: "Thanks partly to poststructuralist criticism, we are able to see literary authorship as a cultural product rather than as a Platonic idea; we know that historically the 'author-function,' like literature itself, has changed, shaped by the social and material conditions of writing" (69).

8. Heninger, *Sidney and Spenser,* xii.

9. Ibid., 20–21.

10. Wall, *Imprint of Gender,* 8 and passim.

11. This is not to suggest that all modern critics are existentialists, agnostics, or atheists—I would characterize myself as a liberal Christian, for example—but that the hegemonic intellectual culture of late-twentieth-century Euro-America sees the universe in dynamic rather than static terms; we are the heirs of Heraclitus, not Parmenides. As the culture of 1611 was in many ways a compendium and interpretation of Plato, Aristotle, Pythagoras, Virgil, Ficino, and Calvin, ours is based on the dialectics of Hegel and Marx, the subjectivity of Rousseau and Freud, the contingencies of Saussure and Sartre, and the entropic determinism of modern physics. See, e.g., Wall: "I point to the importance of remembering the contingency, historicity, and instability of the very category of the 'author,' a concept that, in various permutations, goes on to become a critical and lasting literary convention" (ibid., 21).

12. Sir Philip Sidney, *An Apology for Poetry*, ed. Geoffrey Shepherd (London: Thomas Nelson and Sons, 1965), 98–99. See Shepherd's discussion of poetry as a skill used for sacred ends, 27–28.

13. Edmund Spenser, *Shepheards Calendar*, 1579, A2v.

14. "Conversations with Drummond of Hawthornden," in *Ben Jonson,* ed. C. H. Herford and Percy and Evelyn Simpson, 11 vols. (Oxford: Oxford University Press, 1925-52), 1:133.

15. Barbara Kiefer Lewalski, *Donne's* Anniversaries *and the Poetry of Praise: The Creation of a Symbolic Mode* (Princeton: Princeton University Press, 1973), 112–13.

16. Manley, *John Donne;* I have silently regularized the use of *i, j, u,* and *v.*

17. Marotti, *John Donne,* 236–42.

18. Lewalski, *Donne's* Anniversaries, 113.

19. Susanne Woods, "Aemilia Lanyer, Ben Jonson, and Authority through Patronage," *Ben Jonson Journal* 1 (1994): 15–30.

20. In the book's first poem, "To the Queenes most Excellent Majestie" (a dedication to Queen Anne), lines 3–4.

21. Barbara K. Lewalski, "Of God and Good Women: The Poems of Aemilia Lanyer," in *Silent but for the Word: Tudor Women as Patrons, Translators, and Writers of Religious Works*, ed. Margaret P. Hannay (Kent, Ohio: Kent State University Press, 1985), 203–24.

22. Janel Mueller, "The Feminist Poetics of Aemilia Lanyer's 'Salve Deus Rex Judaeorum,'" in *Feminist Measures: Soundings in Poetry and Theory*, ed. Lynn Keller and Cristianne Miller (Ann Arbor: University of Michigan Press, 1993).

23. Woods, *Poems of Aemilia Lanyer,* 139.

The Renaissance Dramatic Heritage of *Samson Agonistes*

RICHARD S. IDE

TO claim for Renaissance drama a substantial influence on *Samson Agonistes* is apparently to fly in the face of Milton's avowed authorities in tragic theory and practice. In *Of Education* Milton recommends "some choise comedies Greek, Latin, or *Italian*" and "[t]hose tragedies also that treate of houshold matters, as *Trachiniae*, *Alcestis*, and the like[,]" and for teaching the rules of Aristotelian decorum and literary genres, including "*Dramatic*," he also recommends Italian Renaissance theorists, "*Castelvetro*, *Tasso*, *Mazzoni*, and others" (2.397–98, 404).[1] In *The Reason of Church Government* Sophocles and Euripides are singled out as foremost among the writers of "Dramatick constitutions" (1.814). Moreover, in the prose preface to *Samson Agonistes*, entitled "Of That Sort of Dramatic Poem Which is Call'd Tragedy," those Greek tragedians are joined by Aeschylus as "the three Tragic Poets unequall'd yet by any, and the best rule to all who endeavor to write Tragedy." Dramatists also commended in the preface to *Samson* are the "Italians" for their traditional use of the chorus and their fidelity to classical dramatic form. Among others called on specifically to testify in defense of tragedy are Aristotle, of course, and Pareus, who reads the Book of Revelation "as a Tragedy."[2] Apparently indicted by their exclusion from this celebrated company are Shakespeare and other Renaissance tragedians.

Following the lead provided by Milton's preface, critics have evaluated *Samson Agonistes* in light of Greek tragedy,[3] of Italian Renaissance drama,[4] of Aristotle and Aristotelian theory in the Renaissance,[5] of Pareus and other commentators on the Book of Revelation,[6] of the Psalms and the Book of Amos, and of the exemplary heroism of Job and David.[7] Apparently daunted by the omission of references to Elizabethan drama in that same preface, critics who discern a relationship between *Samson* and earlier English drama have customarily limited themselves to drawing brief illustrative parallels to discrete plays, usually *Hamlet* and *Antony and Cleopatra*.[8]

Milton's apology for tragedy, however, like many apologies before it, does not have a definitive, prescriptive bearing on his actual dramatic practice,[9] and a substantial part of the Renaissance dramatic influence that he refuses publicly to entertain, presumably on formal and ethical grounds, enters *Samson Agonistes* through the back door, as it were, in order to provide an alternative perspective to that of his classical models. Milton's simultaneous acceptance and modification of his classical models may be focused instructively on the fourth great classical authority mentioned in the preface to *Samson Agonistes*, "*Seneca* the Philosopher . . . by some thought the Author of those Tragedies (at least the best of them) that go under that name" (Hughes, *John Milton*, 549). The Senecan tragic tradition had dominated Renaissance tragedy on the continent and had had a significant and—despite the convincing work of Joel B. Altman, Gordon Braden, Bruce Smith, and Robert Miola—still largely underestimated influence on Elizabethan drama in England.[10]

This essay will discuss two Renaissance generic legacies of the Senecan tradition in relation to *Samson Agonistes*—the revenge play and the conquror play—within the larger humanist framework of dramatized debate. The rhetorical "questions" and structural doubleness of French humanist tragedy, of Buchanan's biblical tragedies and Garnier's *Les Juifves* most notably, and of *Gorboduc* and other Inns of Court English Senecan tragedies have yet to be evaluated as a probable context for the familiar double perspective in Milton's play. As we know, where some critics see a Samson *furens* at the one extreme (the muscular, passionate, bloody revenger), others envision a Samson *oetaeus* (spiritually triumphant, a Christian type) at the other extreme. Perhaps this startling ambiguity might be better understood if *Samson Agonistes* were shown to be indebted to the Renaissance Senecan tradition.[11]

In his magisterial *The Tudor Play of Mind: Rhetorical Inquiry and the Development of Elizabethen Drama*, Joel B. Altman has recovered for students of English Renaissance drama a tradition of dramatized debate in which a *quaestio* or fictional realizations of *quaestiones* might be argued on both sides, *in utramque partem*. Of particular concern to this essay is Altman's chapter entitled "Seneca and the Declamatory Structure of Tragedy." As evident in *Medea*, *Tyestes*, *Troades* and elsewhere, Seneca's tendencies were to disengage the chorus from the plot and to unlink episodes so as to suggest that "tragedy is a loose collocation of sophistic forms, in which each section casts its distinctive light upon the subject at hand, and encourages only local judgments."[12]

Altman goes on to show how the Elizabethan Senecans in their Inns of Court tragedies, containing "two mutually exclusive readings," reflect precisely the cultural "pluralism" on which S. K. Heninger Jr. has centered his most recent book.[13] In *Gorboduc* a conventional reading in the tradition of the mirror for magistrates advanced by Eubolus and the chorus confronts Gorboduc's reading of the tragedy as deterministic, as a tragedy of dynastic curse. The "demonstrable tragedy of moral error" simply cannot be reconciled with "the tragedy of fate" that the hero perceives. An even more striking example of structural doubleness is that of Thomas Kyd's *Spanish Tragedy,* in which the frame—including the prologue, choric apparatus, and epilogue—points in one direction toward a "mysterious, mechanical world of a divinely sanctioned *lex talionis,*" while the dramatic action itself depicts a psychological and moral complexity that stands in ironic juxtaposition to the simple frame.[14]

Altman might have found additional support for his reading of Elizabethan Senecan tragedy had he followed another stream of the Senecan tradition flowing through continental humanist tragedy and the English closet dramatists in the countess of Pembroke's circle into the Elizabethan mainstream. The continental humanists frequently employed the technique of dramatized debate, as is especially evident in Robert Garnier's *Antigone* and *Cornelie* or La Taille's *Saul le furieux.*[15] Also noteworthy is the subgenre of topical Senecan tragedy. Plays such as Montcretien's *La Reine d'Ecosse*, which dramatizes both Elizabeth's position on the execution of Mary (Acts I–II) and that of the French Catholics (Acts III–V) "without making any effort to reconcile them";[16] or Daniel's *Philotas*, which dramatizes a soldier of heroic proportion (i.e., Essex) being victimized by base sycophants in Alexander's court (Acts I–IV), only to have reported later that, offstage and under torture, the hero apparently confessed his capital crimes (Act V)—these plays exemplify both structural doubleness and double perspectives. Even Chapman's *Conspiracy and Tragedy of Byron*, an ambivalent account of the contemporary French nobleman who reflected in so many obvious ways on Essex, exemplifies a characteristic double perspective. Of more direct interest to *Samson Agonistes,* however, are the continental biblical tragedies, three of which—George Buchanan's *Baptist* and *Jephtha* and Robert Garnier's masterpiece, *Les Juifves*—I will now briefly discuss.

Buchanan's *Baptist* is an especially interesting biblical tragedy in that in addition to the tyrant Herod and his manipulative queen, a second source of villainy, that of Malchus, representative of a repressive rabbinical regime, is also responsible for engineering John's demise. Buchanan's reformist, antipapal, anticlerical agenda is clear. Buchanan also makes a sharp distinction between the chorus as interlocutor—which in offering bad advice to John from a limited perspective serves as a foil to John's stoicism and belief in a Neoplatonic afterlife—and the chorus as privileged commentator that speaks from a carefully delimited Hebrew perspective, at once trusting in God's retributive justice and yet acknowledging as well the irreconcilable alternative vision of life as grimly deterministic, as a "lengthening chain of evils, knit together link by link" (V.162).[17] Interestingly, Buchanan's John is principally a reformer and satirist, not a harbinger of Christ; with historical fidelity, Buchanan depicts a benighted Hebrew perspective even as the dawn of the Christian era approaches. *The Baptist* does not articulate, much less advance, a Christian perspective on the action; that perspective must be brought to the play by Buchanan's Christian reader, if introduced at all.

Buchanan's *Jephtha* similarly eschews a Christian perspective, dramatizing instead two other visions of tragedy. The play shares the structural doubleness remarked above. First, the deliverer's victory over the Ammonites vindicates the Hebrew belief in God's abiding presence and active providence watching over and guiding his elect people (Acts I–II). However, when the wheel turns and Jephtha confronts the dilemma of sacrificing his daughter or breaking his vow to God, the Hebrew vision of tragedy gives way to a pagan, deterministic vision of human grief (Acts III–IV) as "links of [Fate's] interminable chain" (IV.84).[18] A final attempt to reconcile the determinism as well as caprice of the pagan perspective with that of the Hebrew perspective is as unsuccessful as it is desperate:

> So God, for woe or weal,
> The affaires of man doth onward wheel
> As nimble dust is driven
> By the swift-whirling wind of heaven.[19]

Critics readily acknowledge the influence of Greek tragedy on Buchanan's *Baptist* and *Jephtha*, but both plays are also steeped in the humanist Senecan rhetorical tradition of dramatized debate and double perspective.

The Senecan pedigree of Garnier's *Les Juifves* has never been in doubt. In *Les Juifves* Garnier constructs a biblical frame by which to judge the rebellious action of Sedecie and the tyrannical response of Nabuchodonosor. On the one hand, the Prophet, who begins and ends the play, and the chorus of Jewish women labor to vindicate God's punishment of the sinful Jews and—more successfully than in *Jephtha*—attempt to wrap the pagan notions of fortune and fate into the folds of divine purpose. At the end of the play, however, the Prophet's prediction of the future and of the coming of Christ establishes a Judeo-Christian hope that an inexorably just God is also a merciful one. The Christian perspective that Buchanan deliberately excluded from *The Baptist* Garnier deliberately introduces to *Les Juifves* to compete with the earlier pervasive "atmosphere of biblical doom."[20] Double perspectives were characteristic of the humanist Senecan tradition in general and these biblical tragedies in particular, but it should be noted that Milton received no definitive guidance on whether to introduce a Christian perspective into his Old Testament story.

Milton was keenly aware not only of Seneca's tragedies but also of continental and English Senecan traditions. Indeed, his jottings about possible biblical subjects for tragedies in the Trinity College manuscript, including those for a tragedy on "Paradise Lost" or "Adam Unparadiz'd," may have been significantly Senecan in conception. First, the humanist Senecan tradition provided Milton with the signal precedent for biblical tragedy. John Steadman's observation that "Milton had probably read humanistic dramas on biblical themes, some of them paralleling subjects on his own list" (*YP* 8.546) seems overly guarded. James Holly Hanford has discussed Milton's third and fourth dramatic sketches of the Fall in relationship to Andreini's *Adamo* and Grotius's *Adamus Exul* (*YP* 8:587–89), and it is highly unlikely that the biblical tragedies of the humanist reformers and, most particularly, those of John Buchanan, whom Milton greatly admired and whose religious and political agenda he shared, would be unknown to him. In sketching dramatic plans for a possible tragedy on "Baptistes" (*YP* 8:558), Milton must have known he would be entering into a dialogue with Buchanan's *Baptist.*

Second, the remark in Edward Phillips's biography of his uncle concerning the dramatic heritage of *Paradise Lost* is also telling:

> The subject was first designed a tragedy, and in the fourth book of the poem there are six verses, which several years before the poem was begun, were shown to me and some others, as designed for the very beginning of said tragedy. (Hughes, *John Milton,* 1034)

O. B. Hardison argues that Satan's anguished soliloquy at the beginning of Book IV, to which Phillips refers, is much closer to English Renaissance dramatic models than classical models, and points to the Elizabethan use of the "villain soliloquy" to introduce the motive (usually revenge) for the destruction and evil that follows (e.g., *Richard III* and *The Jew of Malta*).[21] But this structural device of the villain soliloquy is in fact a signature of Senecan tragedy and the Senecan tradition in general, whether one thinks of Juno's monologue in *Hercules Furens,* or Medea's in *Medea,* or Thyestes' in *Agamemnon,* or Megere's in Garnier's *Les Juifves,* or Videna's in *Gorboduc,* or Vindice's in *The Revenger's Tragedy,* or indeed Richard III's in *Richard III.* Additionally, the likely precedent for the appearance of three Senecan ghosts in Milton's sketches for British tragedies in the same Trinity College manuscript (see *YP* 8:546) are the ghosts that appear in the British tragedies of the universities and Inns of Court that were written in the Senecan tradition (e.g., *Locrine, The Misfortunes of Arthur*).

The evidence at hand would support, then, what this essay hopes to demonstrate: that Milton's knowledge of Senecan drama and of the continental and English Senecan traditions was extensive, and that his nurturing of a double perspective familiar to humanistic dramatic debate was not unexpected. Specifically, I wish to demonstrate that in shaping the catastrophe of *Samson Agonistes* Milton taps into the tradition of the Senecan revenger, tyrant, and atheist to fashion one perspective on Samson while simultaneously exploiting the resources of the Elizabethan (i.e., Christian) dramatic genres to fashion another. Thereafter, I will argue that in order to emphasize the play's ambiguous central theme, which may be phrased (ambiguously) as the gradual recovery of Samson's "heroic virtue," Milton exploits the figure of Seneca's hubristic conqueror largely from Garnier and English closet drama, the figure of the herculean hero largely from the Elizabethan popular stage (but based substantially on Seneca's Hercules plays), and the thematic crux common to both conqueror and herculean heroic traditions: the conflict between fortune and virtue.

I. Senecan and Christian Versions of Revenge

According to the Renaissance commonplace, the world is a stage, man is a player, and—depending on how one wishes to shade the relationship between divine determination and human volition—God's Providence is alternatively playwright, director, actor, or audience. Not surprisingly, in his epic assertion of eternal Providence and justification of God's ways to man, Milton twice invokes this metaphor as prefatory context, first generally to introduce Adam and Eve's life in Eden, then specifically to introduce the action of the Fall. The first theatrical metaphor likening paradise to a "Silvan Scene" and "woody Theatre" (IV.140–41) is familiar enough, but its reiteration in the proem to Book IX, with its generic identification and its assignment of two major parts, is not often given its full force as a theatrical metaphor:

> I now must change
> Those Notes to Tragic; foul distrust, and breach
> Disloyal on the part of Man, revolt,
> And disobedience: on the part of Heav'n
> Now alienated, distance and distaste,
> Anger and just rebuke, and judgment giv'n,
> That brought into this World a world of woe,
> Sin and her shadow Death, and Misery
> Death's Harbinger.
>
> (IX.5–13)

God, who would seem initially to be a celestial spectator of the "woody Theatre," allowing Adam and Eve to exercise their free will, is here identified as an actor in a tragic theater punishing Adam and Eve's sin. The procession of tragic scenes and choric commentary in Book XI confirms God's role as punitive agent in the fallen world and so reaffirms Milton's conception of tragedy as distinctly unclassical and distinctly (Protestant) Christian.

Sidney and Greville, two important figures in the English Senecan tradition, draw the distinction between classical Senecan tragedy and Renaissance tragedy sharply. It is "high and excellent Tragedy," states Sidney,

> that openeth the greatest wounds, and sheweth forth the Vlcers that are couered with Tissue; that maketh Kinges fear to be Tyrants, and Tyrants manifest their

> tirannicall humors; that, with sturring the affects of admiration and commiseration, teacheth the vncertainety of this world, and vpon how weake foundations guilden roofes are builded; that maketh vs know,
>
> *Qui sceptra duro imperio regit,*
> *Timet timentes, metus in auctores redit.*[22]

While numerous tyrant plays in the native dramatic tradition (among them *Damon and Pythias*, *Appius and Virginia*, and *Cambises* are extant and exemplary) invite Sidney to relate this kind of drama to the workings of divine retribution, his definition of the tyrant play and of tragedy in general is notable for the absence of Providence and an explicitly Christian coloring. Instead, Fortune is revealed to be the principal antagonist of the tragic hero. The quotation from Seneca's *Oedipus* pinpoints the source of this classical conception of tragedy.

Greville, even more clearly than Sidney, distinguishes classical from Renaissance conceptions of tragedy in the course of defining his own three Senecan closet dramas, principally political in import, as different from both:

> Now to return to the Tragedies remaining, my purpose in them was, not (with the Ancient) to exemplifie the disastrous miseries of mans life, where Order, Lawes, Doctrine, and Authority are unable to protect Innocency from the exorbitant wickednesse of power, and so out of that melancholike Vision, stir horrour, or murmur against Divine Providence: nor yet (with the Moderne) to point out Gods revenging aspect upon every particular sin, to the despaire, or confusion of mortality. . . .[23]

In *Samson Agonistes*, I will argue, Milton draws the same telling distinction between ancient tragedy and "Moderne" tragedy or, in the specific context of this essay, between classical Senecan tragedy and the Christian Senecan tradition of the Renaissance.

Milton's conception of providential Christian tragedy, which posits God's just but mysterious governance of human affairs and upon which hinges the poet's justification of God's ways to man, differs sharply from the passion, irrationality, wickedness and misery of the godless Senecan tragic world ruled by Fortune. And yet, *Samson Agonistes* contains both these tragic conceptions. The reader comes to recognize that while Manoa, the earthly father, is chiefly associated with a Senecan tragic perspective in the play, it might also be argued that the heavenly father, playwright of the world stage, has been authoring a tragedy in the tradition of Christian Senecanism. This double perspective Milton makes manifest by borrowing a set of familiar Renaissance Senecan conventions from his dramatic heritage.

Milton's evocation of a crucial dramatic tradition, that of Senecan revenge and Elizabethan revenge tragedy, is limited precisely to the catastrophe of *Samson Agonistes*. Had Milton's purpose been to effect a wholesale "transformation of the genre," presumably along the lines of *The Atheist's Tragedy*, which preaches in its subtitle that "patience is the honest man's revenge," he might easily have introduced revenge tragedy as context and Samson as revenger early in the play. But he does not do so.[24] In fact, the first association of Samson with the revenger and of the catastrophe with a revenge action is not invited until line 1591 when, after the fact, Manoa remarks in an apostrophe to Samson: "A dreadful way thou took'st to thy revenge." Two more evocations of revenge occur after the messenger's conventional *narratio*: one spoken by the chorus, "O dearly bought revenge, yet glorious" (line 1660) and the other again by Manoa: "*Samson* hath quit himself / Like *Samson*. . . on his Enemies / Fully reveng'd hath left them years of mourning" (lines 1709–12). The emphasis on Samson's individual triumph and personal revenge, together with the choral stress on the bloody, long-lasting, wholesale destruction visited upon his enemies, encourage the association of Samson with the conventional revenger. Indeed, those nebulous "rousing motions" (line 1382) that lead him to the revenge site seem readily understood as conventionally angry passions. So, too, his final taunt of the Philistines, accenting his physical strength (line 1640), is of a piece with Seneca's bloody revenger. Finally, the chorus in its role as interlocutor with Manoa, in its discussion of Samson as "self-killed" characterizes the event as a pagan tragedy of fate: "tangl'd in the fold / Of dire necessity, whose law in death conjoin'd / Thee with thy slaughter'd foes" (lines 1664–67).

Also in place at the catastrophe of *Samson Agonistes*, however, is the countervailing conception of tragedy as a revelation of God's justice and the Christian Senecan variation of the play-within-the play signifying God's control over the world stage. As Mary Ann Radzinowicz has amply documented, the catastrophe recounted by the messenger in *Samson* constitutes a virtual play-within-the-play:

> [The Messenger] gives to Manoa and the Chorus an account of a "horrid spectacle" (1542) which he still seems to "behold" in "dire imagination" (1544), a spectacle Manoa says "no preface needs" (1554). The Messenger presents the entrance of Samson costumed in "state Livery" (1615), accompanied by "pipes and timbrels" (1616-17), paraded in the midst of a military guard. He relates Samson's feats as a first act followed by an "intermission" (1629). The thoughtful silence of the actor is described, and then his words are given in direct discourse. Those words continue the metaphor of the stage: Samson, having offered his audience "wonder and delight" (1642) will now present a second act which "with amaze shall strike all who behold" (1645).[25]

What Radzinowicz does not suggest, however, is that the specific convention of the play-within-the-play is characteristic of the Elizabethan tragedy of revenge, and that it evokes for the catastrophe a Christian Senecan context distinguishable from the pagan context remarked earlier. From this perspective, the catastrophe may be isolated as a moment of divine "playing," as a providential inset in an expansive human drama, a moment when a just God asserts control over the world stage. In this providential scenario, Samson's role is to act as the agent of divine vengeance.

We perhaps are accustomed to thinking of the play-within-the-play as a device to carry out the act of revenge, as with Hieronimo's "tragedy" in *The Spanish Tragedy*, or at the least to advance the revenger's plot, as with Hamlet's "mousetrap." But in many revenge tragedies Providence itself actively participates in or presides over the meting out of vengeance, as is God's prerogative (Deut. 32:35). Sometimes Providence administers divine justice directly, perhaps best exemplified by the parodic ending of *The Atheist's Tragedy*, where the villain D'Amville, in lifting up the ax to execute Charlemont, accidentally brains himself, or by the ending of Massinger's *Unnatural Combat*, where the villain Malefort is struck by lightning. At other times, however, in a climactic segment of action given the force of a dramatic inset by an emphatic change of scene and metadramatic references, the hand of heaven is clearly discerned directing events on the world stage, ostensibly sanctioning the revenger as a minister of heaven and the revenge itself as a divinely appointed mission.

One thinks, for example, of Marston's *Antonio's Revenge*. The ghost of Andrugio announces the impending catastrophe:

> Now looks down providence
> T'attend the last act of my son's revenge.
> Be gracious, Observation, to our scene.
>
> (5.1.10–12)[26]

In *Hamlet*, after the revenger has invoked the "special providence" watching over him and there has been an emphatic change of scene in preparation for Claudius's "play" (5.2.219–20, 224 s.d.), there is enacted before those who are "mutes or audience to this act" (5.2.335)[27] an extraordinary catastrophe, a series of seemingly random accidents divinely shaped to a just end. The obverse of the Christian deus ex machina, a device typically associated with heaven's miraculous intervention to reward virtue, this providential play-within-the-play manifests God's vengeance working in mysterious and fearfully ironic ways to punish sin.

As we know, a salient characteristic of the convention is that villains are usually hoisted with their own petards, as are Claudius and Laertes in *Hamlet* or Hippolyta, say, in Ford's *'Tis Pity She's a Whore*. Significantly, one can say the same for the Philistines in *Samson Agonistes*. As we have seen, the Philistine lords had commanded Samson to "play" before their god (line 1340; see also lines 1448, 1639), but the God of the Hebrews will not be mocked. God transforms the Philistines' "play" into a scene manifesting divine justice, that is, into a providential play-within-the-play replete with conventional irony.

Milton's treatment of the Philistines' ill-fated, mad inspiration to convene the assembly at the temple and to call for Samson to play before it reinforces one's sense of divine retribution at the catastrophe. In some Senecan tragedies and Elizabethan plays in the Senecan tradition, the notion of an avenging fury inflicting madness is embodied by the figure of the ghost. Unlike the more familiar Senecan ghost that croaks for revenge, this kind of Senecan ghost often simply presides over the tragic action as if an infectious plague (as in Seneca's *Agamemnon*, for example, or Hughes's *Misfortunes of Arthur*) or serves as an external manifestation of the destructive rage within the protagonist (as in Seneca's *Thyestes*). At other times the ghost might serve as an active agent of confusion, leading to madness, despair, and suicide, which is precisely what Horatio fears in *Hamlet*:

> What if it tempt you toward the flood, my lord, . . .
> And there assume some other horrible form
> Which might deprive your sovereignty of reason,
> And draw you into madness?
>
> (1.4.60–74)

In *Locrine* the ghost of Albanact seems a virtual embodiment of nemesis, a fury whose function is not to incite others to avenge his death on Humber but to curse Humber himself: the ghost drives the tormented man to throw himself into the river that bears his name.

For the Christian dramatist, of course, nemesis was thought to be the "Sword-bearer of th'eternal Providence,"[28] and such avenging spirits were conceived of as instruments of divine retribution. The notion that God uses devils, furies, or malevolent spirits to punish the sinner is an Elizabethan commonplace that enters the Senecan tradition early on. In one of two tragedies by Shakespeare that show extensive Senecan influence, *Richard III*, the ghosts instill despair and confusion in the tragic tyrant at the play's catastrophe. In the other mature tyrant play influenced by Seneca, *Macbeth*, one encounters an Elizabethan avenging spirit in the ghost of Banquo, a figure that symbolizes the psychological torment visited upon the sinner's conscience. The clearest example of the fury's function to inspire confusion is presented by the ghost of Montferrers in *The Atheist's Tragedy*. Just before the providential catastrophe in which D'Amville is hoisted with his own petard, the ghost attends the sleeping villain, predicting, as if determining, the confusion that will overwhelm him:

> D'Amville, with all thy wisdom th'art a fool:
> Not like those fools that we term innocents,
> But a most wretched, miserable fool,
> Which instantly, to the confusion of
> Thy projects, with despair thou shalt behold.
>
> (5.1.28–32)

As if infected by the malignant influence of the vengeful spirit, D'Amville awakens and proceeds on exactly the mad course of action that leads to his tragic demise. Thus, it can be said, "the power of that eternal providence . . . overthrew his projects in their pride" (5.2.264–65).[29]

Despair, sleeplessness, confusion, madness, and psychological hell, naturalized in the pagan Senecan tradition, are conventionally understood in the Christian Senecan tradition as symptomatic of God's curse on the overweening tragic sinner. In his preface to his translation of Seneca's *Oedipus*, Alexander Neville gives a spectacular example of how classical tragedy in general and Senecan tragedy in particular were domesticated (read Christianized) in the English Renaissance. Neville attributes Oedipus's confusion leading to the matricide and self-blinding to a "fretting Fury common enemy and tormentor to corrupted consciences pricking him forward, all inflamed with Phrensie and boyling in inward heate of vile infected mind."[30] Indeed, he goes on to summarize the play's tragic lesson as a "dreadfull Example of Gods horrible vengeaunce for sinne":

> the Body plagued, the mynde and Conscience in midst of deepe devouring daungers most terribly assaulted . . . by meare misfortune (nay rather by the deepe hidden secret Judgements of God) piteously plunged in the most extreame miseries . . . [until] hee rooteth out his wretched eyes unnaturally, bereaveth his Mother her life . . . beastly, and in the ende in most basest kind of slavery, banisht, dieth miserably.[31]

Milton chose not to use the sensational, indecorous figure of the Elizabethan ghost in his dramatic poem. And yet, for the purposes of stressing divine retribution against the Philistines, he does invoke the Christian concept of psychological torment, what Neville refers to as "fretting Fury":

> Among them hee a spirit of frenzy sent,
> Who hurt thir minds,
> And urg'd them on with mad desire
> To call in haste for thir destroyer;
> They only set on sport and play
> Unwittingly importun'd
> Thir own destruction to come speedy upon them.
> (lines 1675–81)

Like those of so many sinners in the theater of God's judgments, the Philistines' projects redound against them. God visits a "spirit of frenzy" on them, a Christian Senecan version of an avenging fury that speeds them "with mad desire" toward their ironic demise at the hands of his appointed avenger.[32]

To summarize, Milton chose to complicate his tragedy by introducing into its catastrophe perspectives sponsoring two mutually exclusive readings. He did so with great care and deliberation, balancing the perspectives through a subtle but demonstrable program of generic allusion. And he did so wholly in accord with the spirit of humanist rhetorical tragedy in general and biblical tragedy in particular. While the critic might be free to establish the precise relationship between the two perspectives and, indeed, between *Samson Agonistes* and its companion poem, *Paradise Regained*, it would seem that to privilege one perspective and reading to the exclusion of the other would be unnecessarily reductive.

The second, Christian perspective on the catastrophe of *Samson Agonistes* confirms the conception of tragedy in Book IX of *Paradise Lost*: the fallen world is a tragic theater in which sin "on the part of Man" (i.e., the Philistines) will meet "on the part of Heav'n . . . Anger and just rebuke, and judgment giv'n." Paradoxically, however, Milton goes on to state in the proem to Book IX that his tragic argument is "Not less but more Heroic" than those of the classical epics (IX.13–19). It is so because in this fallen world the sinner's only "heroic" stance is patiently to accept God's justice, submitting voluntarily to the punishment that is the sinner's due. Essential to this patient disposition is the belief that God's punishment is purposeful, that it is, as Milton states in *The Reason of Church Government*, a "saving med'cin ordain'd of God both for the publik and privat good of man" (1:835).

When Adam and Eve awaken from their night of "unrest" following the fatal deed that was to have opened their eyes and expanded their minds, they discover the ironic punishment God has imposed upon them:

> up they rose
> As from unrest, and each the other viewing,
> Soon found thir Eyes how op'n'd, and thir minds
> How dark'n'd; innocence, that as a veil
> Had shadow'd them from knowing ill, was gone,
> Just confidence, and native righteousness,
> And honor from about them, naked left
> To guilty shame: hee cover'd, but his Robe
> Uncover'd more. So rose the *Danite* strong
> *Herculean Samson* from the Harlot-lap
> Of *Philistean Dalilah*, and wak'd
> Shorn of his strength.
>
> (IX.1051–62)

Although Milton does not moralize Samson's sad awakening here, distinguishing only his loss of strength from Adam and Eve's loss of virtue, the analogy drawn between Samson's awakening and the moment when Adam and Eve must first cope with punishment for their sin precisely anticipates the beginning of Samson's spiritual agon in the drama. Samson must recognize that the misery of which he complains, the physical and psychological torment, is God's just punishment for his sin. If from the pagan perspective the "sense of Heav'n's desertion" (line 632) and Samson's present misery and torment lead him and the chorus to complaints more typical of Seneca's godless tragic world, from a second perspective one might identify Samson's misery as God's ironic punishment for sin. In *Of Christian Doctrine* Milton describes the sinner's spiritual death metaphorically: the intellect is "blinded" and the will "enchained"; also, there occurs a "darkening of . . . right reason" and a "slavish subjection to sin" (6:321, 395). In the case of Samson's punishment, God seems not only to have reified these psychological effects of spiritual death but also to have made the blinding, servility, and imprisonment respond exactly to Samson's specific sin of slavish, irrational uxoriousness. Samson must confirm the abiding presence of God in his life, and more than this, he must understand that such divine punishment, if accepted patiently, is in fact the "saving med'cin" necessary for his spiritual health.

If the chorus and Manoa are bad physicians for Samson, the former attempting to apply "Salve" to his "Sores" and "balm" his "fester'd wounds" (lines 185–86) by attenuating the gravity of the sin and the latter by advising him to avoid God's punishment, the desperate Samson himself initially errs in his assumption that "death's benumbing Opium" is the "only cure" for the "maladies innumerable / In heart, head, breast, and reins," the "ferment and rage," the "wounds immedicable" that "Rankle, and fester, and gangrene," and the tormenting thoughts "arm'd with deadly stings" (lines 606–32). The point is that the maladies themselves, typical of the Elizabethan Christian tragic tradition from the most ridiculous appropriation (Neville's attempt to pull Seneca's *Oedipus* into the fold) to the most sublime enactment (Shakespeare's *Macbeth*), are a fitting punishment for Samson and a necessary cure.

Although it is not my purpose here to trace the well-trodden path of Samson's recovery, it is necessary to remark that Samson, like Adam and Eve and unlike Dalila,[33] completes an exemplary journey of *heroic* regeneration. Again, two perspectives on Samson's heroism coexist. On the one hand, Samson's heroism has a physical dimension, the return of heroic strength. Samson lifts himself out of the slough of despair, reaffirms his staunch classical moral virtue in the display of self-governance in the Dalila episode, asserts an awesome heroic self-confidence in the confrontation with Harapha, and proceeds on his journey to the awesome display of physical heroism at the end. Manoa serves as chief cheerleader during this process and principal celebrator of a heroic life crowned at the end with glory. On the other hand, the return of heroic strength also signals an inner, spiritual, "more Heroic" dimension of Samson's recovery: the reawakening of faith, the forgiveness of sin, and the rekindling of divine grace in God's champion. It will be the burden of the second part of this essay to demonstrate how Milton establishes contexts for these two perspectives on heroism by evoking classical epic and amoral Senecan tragedy for one and by evoking Christian Renaissance variations on classical norms and conventions for the other.

II. The Cultivation of Heroic Virtue

As remarked above, Manoa speaks for the pagan perspective on the return of heroic virtue. For him, Samson has achieved a personal revenge (as we saw earlier) and a personal heroic triumph:

> *Samson* hath quit himself
> Like *Samson*, and heroicly hath finish'd
> A life Heroic, on his Enemies
> Fully reveng'd hath left them years of mourning.
> (lines 1709–11)

Manoa's epitaph suggests that Samson's final act crowns a lifetime of similar heroic acts, great feats of strength and courage. He will take Samson "Home to his Father's house" (line 1733), build him a monument, memorialize his heroism with a trophy room; visitors will come, as to a shrine, bearing flowers and singing *epinicia*. From the beginning of the play, Milton is at pains to establish the basis for Manoa's perspective.

Before Samson's disastrous capitulation to Dalila, he had been renowned for his strength and invincibility. Milton presses the point by turning the chorus's initial recollection of Samson's heroic feats into a full-blown epic *aristeia*:

> Can this be hee,
> That Heroic, that Renown'd,
> Irresistible *Samson*? whom unarm'd
> No strength of man, or fiercest wild beast could withstand;
> Who tore the Lion, as the Lion tears the Kid,
> Ran on embattled Armies clad in Iron,
> And weaponless himself,
> Made Arms ridiculous, useless the forgery
> Of brazen shield and spear. . . .
> The bold *Ascalonite*
> Fled from his Lion ramp, old Warriors turn'd
> Thir plated backs under his heel;
> Or grov'ling soil'd thir crested helmets in the dust.
> Then with what trivial weapon came to hand,
> The jaw of a dead Ass, his sword of bone,
> A thousand foreskins fell, the flower of *Palestine*,
> In *Ramath-lechi* famous to this day:
> Then by main force pull'd up, and on his shoulders bore
> The Gates of *Azza*. . . .
> (lines 124–50)

So, too, when first seeing Samson, Manoa remarks the fall of a seemingly insuperable hero:

> is this the man,
> That invincible *Samson*, far renown'd,
> The dread of *Israel's* foes, who with a strength
> Equivalent to Angels walk'd thir streets,
> None offering fight?
>
> (lines 340–44)

Strength, martial valor, and renown are the hallmarks of pagan heroic *virtus*, an extraordinary quality associated preeminently with famous world conquerors such as Hercules and Bacchus in myth, and Alexander and Caesar in history. The epic portrayal of Samson places him squarely in this heroic tradition.

The heroic ideal embodied by Samson before his fall is a throwback to the Homeric age or the age of heroes, as described by Michael in Book XI of *Paradise Lost*:

> Such were these Giants, men of high renown;
> For in those days Might only shall be admir'd,
> And Valor and Heroic Virtue call'd;
> To overcome in Battle, and subdue
> Nations, and bring home spoils with infinite
> Man'slaughter, shall be held the highest pitch
> Of human Glory, and for Glory done
> Of triumph, to be styl'd great Conquerors,
> Patrons of Mankind, Gods, and Sons of Gods,
> Destroyers rightlier call'd and Plagues of men.
>
> (XI.688–97)

Samson's "Valor and Heroic Virtue" have brought him to this same high pitch of glory, and for the chorus as interlocutor (obviously lacking the ken of Michael, who decries the brutal heroic code with moral decisiveness), Samson's attainment of this state of excellence and renown, before the turn of fortune's wheel, is what makes the heroic conqueror's fall so rare, lamentable, *and classical*:

> O mirror of our fickle state,
> Since man on earth unparallel'd!
> The rarer thy example stands,
> By how much from the top of wondrous glory,
> Strongest of mortal men,
> To the lowest pitch of abject fortune thou art fall'n.
> For him I reckon not in high estate
> Whom long descent of birth
> Or the sphere of fortune raises;
> But thee whose strength, while virtue was her mate,

Might have subdu'd the Earth,
Universally crown'd with highest praises.

(lines 164–75)

I quote at length from *Paradise Lost* and from this typical classical complaint in *Samson* in order to make an important point: Samson's is a special kind of tragic example, not a mirror for magistrates but a mirror for heroes and conquerors who ascend to the top of wondrous glory on the wings of heroic *virtus* only to be toppled by heroic virtue's traditional adversary, fortune.

Milton labors to establish the heroic theme of fortune versus virtue. No sooner does the chorus introduce it than Samson himself expands upon it, discarding the chorus's primary metaphor of virtue's fall from fortune's wheel in favor of the submetaphor of heroic virtue's voyage on fortune's sea ("while virtue was her mate"):

How could I once look up, or heave the head,
Who like a foolish Pilot have shipwreck't
My Vessel trusted to me from above,
Gloriously rigg'd.

(lines 197–200)

This metaphor is preferable to the fall from fortune's wheel, of course, because it allows for a greater stress on personal failure as a cause of one's own downfall. Samson distinguishes his perspective from that of Manoa and the chorus as interlocutor when he acknowledges his own complicity in his fall.

The opposition between fortune and virtue, which is central to the Hercules myth and memorably formulated in Plutarch's *On the Fortune or Virtue of Alexander*, became standard fare for the Renaissance emblematists and was a familiar thematic staple in Elizabethan conqueror plays and closet drama. Marlowe's *Tamburlaine, Part I* and Greene's *Selimus* work the theme in a provocative way when their heroes, projecting amoral *virtus* and brazen *virtu*, conquer all in fortune's domain. Sir William Alexander's *Croesus*, *Darius*, and *The Alexandrian Tragedy*, on the other hand, preach the inevitability of fortune's victory and the need, therefore, to cultivate Stoic moral virtue. And several plays focused on the Roman conqueror, Julius Caesar—including Shakespeare's *Julius Caesar*, the anonymous play entitled *Caesar's Revenge*, Alexander's *Julius Caesar*, and Chapman's *Caesar and Pompey*—deliberately treat the fortune or virtue of Caesar as an unresolved *questio*. Of specific relevance to the nautical formulation of the theme, one recalls that the martial hero of Daniel's *Philotas* "must sayle [fortune's sea] by the Compasse of [his] minde" (line 169);[34] that Chapman's titanic Byron issues a call to the free spirit "that on this life's rough sea / Loves t'have his sails fill'd with a lusty wind" (3.3.135–36);[35] that in the mock-heroic context of Shakespeare's *Troilus and Cressida*, Nestor follows up on Agamemnon's insistence that virtue will survive fortune's buffets by distinguishing the "strong-ribb'd bark" from the "saucy boat" on fortune's sea (1.3.17–47); and that, in a bold twist of the metaphor, the epic messenger announces that heroic Macbeth, "Valor's minion," the man of epic *virtus* soon to degenerate into Senecan *scelus*, disdains fortune in winning his victory in a sea of blood (1.2.8–20).

Milton brings to this conventional theme of Elizabethan heroic drama three emphases that provide a second perspective on Samson's recovery of heroic virtue. First, we are made to understand that Samson's career has not ended with the "shipwreck"; rather, Samson's disaster inaugurates a new sequence of events on fortune's sea. And so, Dalila *sails into* Samson's spiritual agon at precisely the right moment (lines 720–24); a fortuitous wind blows Harapha toward Samson (lines 1070–75); Manoa, with "Locks white as down" (line 327) approaches Samson, and the chorus "steers" (line 111) their feet; and thus, indeed, the Chorus seems to sight a ship when it "descries" the Philistine officer tending toward Samson (lines 1301–2). Milton's iterative imagery insists that these are events on fortune's sea. Whereas their salutary, recuperative effect may suggest to some a happy return to fortune's favor at the end a heroic life, to others the uncanny sequencing of events leading Samson to his recovery of spiritual virtue insists that they are designed by God to advance Samson toward his divinely appointed mission. From this second perspective *Samson Agonistes* thus exemplifies what Milton states in *The Art of Logic*, that "fortune surely is to be placed in heaven, but its name should be changed and it should be called 'divine providence'" (7:14).

The second Milton variation on "heroic virtue" as spiritual strength in defiance of fortune needs elaboration. Samson's experience with Dalila has taught him the practical vulnerabilities as well as the ethical liabilities of mere strength, and early in the play Milton presents the hero in the process of reevaluating his reliance on classical *virtus*:

> But what is strength without a double share
> Of wisdom? Vast, unwieldy, burdensome,
> Proudly secure, yet liable to fall
> Of weakest subtleties, not made to rule,
> But to subserve where wisdom bears command.
>
> (lines 53–57)

The metaphor of rule and subservience psychologizes the attributes of wisdom and strength, associating them with reason and passion respectively. One perhaps ought to think here of the heroic ideal in Tasso's *Gerusalemme Liberata*, with Godfrey (regal understanding) in command of Rinaldo (ireful virtue),[36] or perhaps, alternatively, of Chapman's version of the Homeric ideal:

> [T]he first word of his *Iliads* is *menin*, wrath; the first word of his *Odysses*, *andra*, Man—contracting in either word each worke's Proposition. In one, Predominant Perturbation; in the other, over-ruling Wisedome; in one, the Bodie's fervour and fashion of outward Fortitude to all possible height of Heroicall Action; in the other, the Mind's inward, constant and unconquerd Empire, unbroken, unalterd with any most insolent and tyrannous infliction.[37]

Both Tasso and Chapman stress that although the attributes of *fortitudo et sapientia* are hierarchical, with wisdom overruling, they are finally complementary; strength needs wisdom to guide it, and wisdom needs strength to be effective.[38] Samson recognizes that his "Immeasurable strength" (line 206) and insufficient wisdom—"These two proportion'd ill" (line 209)—led to his "shipwreck." He now strives to achieve a balance between his disproportionate strength and wisdom to ensure that all displays of outward fortitude will proceed from and manifest a just, rational purpose. Heroic *virtus* must be redeployed as moral energy, redefined as moral virtue.

The English Renaissance Senecan tradition provides instructive dramatic parallels to Samson's cultivation of moral virtue. In Alexander's *Tragedy of Croesus*, Solon advises Croesus, child of fortune and slave to fortune, that reason must be monarch and that only moral virtue is immune to the ravages of time. The tyrant comes to appreciate Solon's counsel, but too late. In *The Tragedy of Darius*, Darius also learns too late about the insubstantiality of fortune's gifts and the danger of haughty, immoral behavior: "some higher power . . . can controull, / The monarchs of the Earth, and censure all" (lines 2219–20).[39] The emphasis is slightly different in *The Alexandrian Tragedy*. Alexander, who conquered the entire world, acknowledges that he could not conquer himself, could not control, that is, his own ambitious, tyrannical passions.

A more thoroughgoing "domestication" of classical *virtus* in the English Renaissance Christian culture is found in *Bussy D'Ambois,* a Chapman tragedy that is highly indebted in theme to the Senecan tradition, character, and structural doubleness. The opposition between unbridled *virtus* and moral virtue and self-governance is central to Chapman's tragedy. At the beginning, in a statement remarkably applicable to Milton's *Samson*, the hero issues a warning that he himself fails to heed:

> So when we wander furthest through the waves
> Of glassy Glory and the gulfs of State,
> Topp'd with all titles, spreading all our reaches,
> As if each private arm would sphere the world;
> We must to Virtue for her guide resort,
> Or we shall shipwrack in our safest Port.
>
> (I.i.28–33)[40]

Context defines "Virtue" as Senecan moral virtue, but in fact Bussy sets out on the sea of fortune trusting in his unbridled *virtus* and forgetful that moral virtue should be his "guide."[41] Like herculean Samson, moreover, herculean Bussy is brought low by a woman, an amatory entanglement that does not recommend his wisdom, morality, or self-governance. Arguably, in the two-part death scene, his initial heroic stance in outfacing death with heroic *virtus* is overruled by wisdom; he forgives his murderers and acknowledges his failure and thus returns to moral virtue at the end. But one might also argue that such a reading privileges closure in a kind of drama more consistent with the humanist tradition of dramatized debate, and that the claims of pagan and Christian versions of heroic virtue remain contested to the end.

From the Christian perspective on the play, the Dalila episode marks for Samson a moment of self-mastery and a turn toward moral virtue similar to those claimed for Bussy at the end of his tragedy. By laying a heavy, repeated metaphorical stress on the fact that Dalila had previously laid siege to and conquered Samson, Milton invites the reader to interpret the present confrontation as something like a return engagement. God gives herculean Samson the opportunity to correct the disastrous episode with Omphale-Dalila, and Samson does so by asserting wisdom, by overcoming the rational blindness and moral slackness associated with his former reliance on physical strength, which had made him "Proudly secure" ("Suffices that to mee strength is my bane" [line 63]). Indeed, Dalila's final temptation to sensuality ("Let me approach at least, and touch thy hand") (line 951), together with her voluptuous apparel, suggests that the choice of Hercules may stand behind Milton's Dalila episode. This time, Samson chooses Virtue/Wisdom over Voluptas/Vice, displaying herculean moral virtue.

Having conquered the woman who earlier had brought him down and having conquered himself, wisdom now ruling where strength had earlier usurped command, Samson would seem back on the course of moral virtue. There follows the Harapha episode, and Milton's third salient adaptation of the heroic theme of fortune versus virtue. Heroic *virtus* of the kind Samson had prized earlier in his career is inseparable from bold individualism and immense pride. Michael reminds us that those primitive heroes desired "to be styl'd great Conquerors, / Patrons of Mankind, Gods, and Sons of Gods" (*Paradise Lost* XI.695–96), and the idea was nowhere more prevalent than in Elizabethan dramatic portrayals of the conquerors.[42] In *Caesar's Revenge* pride leads Caesar to believe that he is like Jove, and the same point is implicit in Cassius's imagery (and elsewhere) in Shakespeare's *Julius Caesar*. In *The Tragedy of Darius* Alexander the Great speaks of attaining a "state like Ioves" and remarks how all "adore" him;[43] precisely this pretension to deity is implicit in Menenius's description of Coriolanus: "He sits in his state, as a thing made for Alexander.

. . . He wants nothing of a god but eternity and a heaven to throne in" (5.4.21). Samson makes a similar proud claim: "Fearless of danger, like a petty God / I walk'd about admir'd of all and dreaded" (lines 529–30). Although he can suggest, with Byron and Coriolanus, that he "Us'd no ambition to commend [his] deeds, / The deeds themselves spoke loud the doer" (lines 247–48), this lack of political ambition is only partly commendable since, as with Byron and Coriolanus, it is itself indicative of a proud, antisocial individualism. Like Coriolanus, Samson is self-fulfilled and "rewards his deeds with doing them" (2.2.127). A measure of Samson's gigantic pride, incidentally, is found in those paroxysms of shame triggered by thoughts of his "ridiculous," "foolish" debased state as slave and prisoner (see lines 34, 70, 196, 446–47, 457, 499, 563, etc.). From one perspective Samson would seem to rediscover his immense personal pride in his heroic *virtus* when he outfaces Harapha, but the sufficiency of that perspective is thrown into question by a competing Christian conception.

The ἀρετή that fires Homer's heroes is a special gift distinguishing them from mere mortals. It is a kind of divine afflatus, and its divine origins are made clear by those many moments when the Olympians actively assist their favorite warriors, kindling their strength and courage with heavenly fire.[44] Something more than mere choler, this is the heroic spirit that, accompanied by traditional fire imagery, is used to characterize extraordinary martial heroes on the Elizabethan stage—Tamburlaine, Bussy D'Ambois, Byron, and Coriolanus, among others. Samson's strength also derives from a heavenly source: he is "full of divine instinct" (line 526); he bursts the cords binding his hands and flies upon the Philistines when "toucht with the flame" (line 262); the "Spirit" of the Lord fires him "In the camp of *Dan*" (line 1435). Displaying the hubris of many pagan heroes, however, Samson had become "Proudly secure" in his strength, forgetful not only that strength must be governed by wisdom but that it was a "high gift . . . committed" (line 47) to him by God. Samson is punished for his selfish claims to strength by being deprived of it; in Milton's drama, significantly, this deprivation is symbolized not so much by the loss of hair as by the loss of sight. According to the play's imagistic pattern, blindness disarms Samson, not merely by making him incapable of effective heroic activity but by removing the light that is "almost life itself" (line 91) and, for the epic warrior, the divine afflatus that fires his heroic deeds. "Exil'd from light" (line 98), with the fire of heroic spirit quenched, Samson becomes what he later will expose Harapha to be, "bulk without spirit vast" (line 1238).

Arguably, the Christian perspective Milton encourages in the Harapha episode is a familiar one (because recurrent in the last poems): just as Samson's pride in his epic strength has been his bane, his humiliation and self-acknowledged weakness will be the source of his *heroic* recovery. The vast bulk, incapable of effective, self-generated heroic activity, now professes that his strength proceeds wholly from God: "My trust is in the living God who gave me / At my Nativity this strength" (lines 1140–41). Confident once again that God's power will now work through him, Samson goes on to challenge Harapha. In the Harapha episode, then, what initially may seem from one perspective as extraordinary bravado on the part of Samson and a return of self-confidence testifies, arguably, to an entirely different mode of heroism, patient acceptance of his humiliation; he places his confidence wholly in God, no longer in his own epic strength and prowess. This reading of Samson's change in attitude is driven home by the fact that blindness, which seemed an overwhelming liability to the self-sufficient hero earlier in the play, now seems utterly irrelevant to this new kind of hero who regards himself as an instrument of God's power.

According to this reading from the play's Christian perspective, Samson is now fit to become God's active "deliverer" and minister of God's revenge:

Hee all thir Ammunition
And feats of War defeats
With plain Heroic magnitude of mind
And celestial vigor arm'd,
Thir Armories and Magazines contemns,
Renders them useless, while
With winged expedition
Swift as the lightning glance he executes
His errand on the wicked, who surpris'd
Lose thir defense, distracted and amaz'd.

(lines 1277–86)

Implicit in the "plain Heroic magnitude of mind" is the reconciliation of strength and wisdom in the form of moral energy, as demonstrated in the Dalila episode, as well as the selfless faith in God's power evident in the Harapha episode. Into this humble, virtuous servant, God infuses "celestial vigor," the fiery heroic spirit that enables the Christian epic hero to rain down divine retribution and "amaze" the reprobate as a minister of God's justice.

The "rousing motions" that inspire Samson to the final display of heroic strength in the Philistine assembly might also be understood as gracious motions that culminate Samson's spiritual agon by signaling God's forgiveness. Indeed, from the Christian perspective the motions might be inseparable: it would appear that the heroic context of *Samson Agonistes* insists upon a physical manifestation of God's grace.[45] Like the Homeric deities infusing a heroic spirit in their champions, God inspires Samson with a divine grace that is manifested as the Christian version of heroic *virtus*:

But hee though blind of sight,
Despis'd and thought extinguish't quite,

With inward eyes illuminated
His fiery virtue rous'd
From under ashes into sudden flame.

(lines 1687–91)

To conclude this line of argument, Samson has been transformed from "reprobate scourge" to God's "inspired minister" acting in accord with moral virtue and with God's just providential purpose.[46]

III. Dragon, Eagle, and Phoenix

I have attempted in the first part of this essay to demonstrate how Milton simultaneously evoked the classical Seneca tradition of revenge and the Elizabethan Seneca tradition of revenge to foster two contradictory readings of the play's catastrophe. In the second part of the essay, I have attempted to demonstrate how Milton, by juxtaposing the pagan Seneca tradition of the heroic, amoral conqueror in Fortune's world with the Elizabethan homiletic tradition preaching Christian heroism in a providential world, seems consciously to authorize two readings of Samson's recovery of heroic virtue that advance the reader toward the ambiguous catastrophe. From the pagan, classical Seneca perspective, the return of physical strength and fiery inspiration to the epic hero and conqueror leads seamlessly to the bloody, passionate act of revenge at the catastrophe—all of which Manoa celebrates and plans to memorialize. From the Christian Renaissance perspective, the return of moral virtue and the erasure of overweening individuality have led Samson in his final heroic role as God's instrument and agent of divine vengeance. This double perspective, moreover, is wholly consistent with the Senecan rhetorical tradition in the Renaissance, which prized a drama of ideas, an explorative drama of open-ended inquiry, and employed dramatized questions, double perspectives, and structural doubleness to that end.

I will conclude by revisiting Milton's famous triple simile, which for many critics has served as a touchstone for their interpretive readings of the play:

And as an ev'ning Dragon came,
Assailant on the perched roosts,
And nests in order rang'd
Of tame villatic Fowl; but as an Eagle
His cloudless thunder bolted on thir heads.
So virtue giv'n for lost,
Deprest, and overthrown, as seem'd,
Like that self-begotten bird
In the *Arabian* woods embost,
That no second knows or third,

And lay erewhile a Holocaust,
From out her ashy womb now teem'd,
Revives, reflourishes, then vigorous most
When most inactive deem'd,
And though her body die, her fame survives,
A secular bird ages of lives.

(lines 1692–1707)

With much skill and alacrity, we Miltonists have attempted to reconcile the contradictory implications in this passage with whatever reading we were privileging at the time (or perhaps I should speak only for myself). In my latest engagement with the text, the contradictions are compelling: the awesome predator may be related to the brute strength and heroic wrath of the epic hero and world conqueror, but how could the dragon's brutality be translated into a fully sanitized Christian heroism? Or, if Milton were intent on describing Samson as minister of God's retributive justice, why did he choose the overtly pagan allusion to the eagle (Jove's bird) and force upon us a Christian allegorization of the pagan figure?[47] And finally, while the Son of God may be miraculously self-begotten and self-resurrected, how does one relate the "self-begotten" phoenix to the spiritual regeneration of Samson that has been guided by Providence and at the end fueled by divine grace? It is a far better and fuller response to the play, I now understand, to allow these contradictory implications to lie side by side, incompatible and unassimilated. Milton has posed the question in *Samson Agonistes*, not answered it.

Notes

1. *The Complete Prose Works of John Milton*, ed. Don M. Wolfe et al., 8 vols. (New Haven: Yale University Press, 1953–81); here and elsewhere in this essay, citations to this edition are given parenthetically within the text.

2. *John Milton: The Complete Poems and Major Prose*, ed. Merritt Y. Hughes (New York: Odyssey Press, 1957), 550. Subsequent citations to this volume (Hughes) are given parenthetically within the text.

3. See, among others, Wilmon Brewer, "Two Athenian Models for *Samson Agonistes*," *PMLA* 42 (September 1927): 910–20; P. W. Timberlake, "Milton and Euripides," in *The Parrott Presentation Volume*, ed. Hardin Craig (Princeton: Princeton University Press, 1935); William Riley Parker, *Milton's Debt to Greek Tragedy in Samson Agonistes* (Baltimore: Johns Hopkins University Press, 1937); C.A. Patrides, "The Comic Dimension of Greek Tragedy and *Samson Agonistes*," *Milton Studies* 10 (1977): 3–21.

4. Gretchen L. Finney, "Chorus in *Samson Agonistes*," *PMLA* 58 (September 1943): 649–64; E. T. Prince, *The Italian Element in Milton's Verse* (Oxford: Clarendon Press, 1962), 145–68; and Hughes's introduction to the play (Hughes, *John Milton*, 537–39).

5. See esp. Paul R. Sellin, "Sources of Milton's Catharsis: A Reconsideration," *Journal of English and Germanic Philology* 60 (October 1961): 712–30; Martin E. Mueller,

"*Pathos* and *Katharsis* in *Samson Agonistes*," *ELH* 31 (June 1964): 156–74; John M. Steadman, "'Passions Well Imitated': Rhetoric and Poetics in the Preface to *Samson Agonistes*," in *Calm of Mind: Tercentenary Essays on Paradise Regained and Samson Agonistes*, ed. Joseph A. Wittreich Jr. (Cleveland, Ohio: Case Western Reserve University Press, 1971), 175–207; Raymond B. Waddington, "Melancholy Against Melancholy: *Samson Agonistes* as Renaissance Tragedy," in Wittreich, *Calm of Mind*, 259–87; and, recently, Derek N. C. Wood, "Catharsis and 'Passion Spent': *Samson Agonistes* and Some Problems with Aristotle," *Milton Quarterly* 26 (March 1992): 1–9.

6. Barbara K. Lewalski, "*Samson Agonistes* and the 'Tragedy' of the Apocalypse," *PMLA* 85 (October 1970): 1050–62; but see also Joseph A. Wittreich Jr., *Visionary Poetics: Milton's Tradition and His Legacy* (San Marino, Calif.: Huntington Library, 1979), 193–207, which argues that *Samson* parodies the Book of Revelation. Also, see Wittreich's book-length study, *Interpreting Samson Agonistes* (Princeton: Princeton University Press, 1986).

7. On the Book of Job and the Psalms, see, for example, Ann Grossman, "Samson, Job, and the 'Exercise of Saints,'" *English Studies* 45 (1964): 212–14; John N. Wall Jr., "'The Contrarious Hand of God': *Samson Agonistes* and the Biblical Lament," *Milton Studies* 12 (1978): 117–39; Mary Ann Radzinowicz, *Toward Samson Agonistes: The Growth of Milton's Mind* (Princeton: Princeton University Press, 1978), esp. chap 11 on Job and appendix B on the Psalms. On the Book of Amos, see John C. Ulreich Jr., "'Beyond the Fifth Act': *Samson Agonistes* as Prophecy," in *Composite Orders: The Genres of Milton's Last Poems*, ed. Richard S. Ide and Joseph A. Wittreich (= *Milton Studies* 17 [1983]: 281–318). And on Samson and David, see Miriam Mushkin, "'Wisdom by Adversity': Davidic Traits in Milton's Samson," *Milton Studies* 14 (1980): 233–55.

8. The full essays of Thomas B. Stroup, "'All Comes Clear at Last,' but 'the Readiness is All,'" *Comparative Drama* 10 (Spring 1976): 61–77, and John F. Andrews, "'Dearly Bought Revenge': *Samson Agonistes*, *Hamlet*, and Elizabethan Revenge Tragedy," *Milton Studies* 13 (1979): 81–107, are notable exceptions.

9. On this point, see Patrides, "Comic Dimension," 4; also Steadman's related caveat on the danger of trying to deduce a "complete and coherent dramatic theory" from the fragmentary remarks of Milton's preface (Wittreich, *Calm of Mind*, 200).

10. Joel B. Altman, *The Tudor Play of Mind: Rhetorical Inquiry and the Development of Elizabethan Drama* (Berkeley: University of California Press, 1978); Gordon Braden, *Anger's Privilege: Renaissance Tragedy and the Senecan Tradition* (New Haven: Yale University Press, 1985); Bruce R. Smith, *Ancient Scripts and Modern Experience on the English Stage, 1500–1700* (Princeton: Princeton University Press, 1988), chap. 5; Robert S. Miola, *Shakespeare and Classical Tragedy: The Influence of Seneca* (Oxford: Clarendon Press, 1992).

11. My argument in this essay for the double perspective of *Samson Agonistes* most closely complements that of Stanley Fish, "Question and Answer in 'Samson Agonistes'," *Critical Quarterly* 11 (Autumn 1969): 237–64 and, even more pointedly, "Spectacle and Evidence in *Samson Agonistes*," *Critical Inquiry* 15 (Spring 1989): 556–86.

12. Altman, *Tudor Play of Mind*, 248.

13. *The Subtext of Form in the Renaissance: Proportion Poetical* (University Park: Pennsylvania State University, 1994), 31.

14. Altman, *Tudor Play of Mind*, 258, 270–71. See also Altman's discussion of *Gismond of Salerne* and *The Misfortunes of Arthur*, esp. 259–67.

15. Donald Stone Jr., *French Humanist Tragedy: A Reassessment* (Edinburgh: Manchester University Press, 1974), esp. 84–110.

16. See Dame Frances Yates's classic essay, "Some New Light on 'L'Ecossaise' de Antoine de Montchretien," *Modern Language Review* 22 (July 1927): 290.

17. Citations for *The Baptist* are to George Buchanan, *The Baptist, or Calumny*, trans. Archibald Brown (Paisley: Alexander Gardner, 1906).

18. Citations by act and page number are to George Buchanan, *Jephtha*, trans. A. Gordon Mitchell (Paisley: Alexander Gardner, 1903).

19. *Jephtha* V.104.

20. Richards Griffiths, *Garnier: Les Juifves* (London: Grant & Cutler, 1986), 78.

21. O. B. Hardison, "*In Media Res* in *Paradise Lost*," in Ide and Wittreich, *Composite Orders*, 32–33.

22. *An Apology for Poetry*, quoted from *Elizabethan Critical Essays*, ed. G. Gregory Smith, 2 vols. (London: Oxford University Press, 1904), 1:177.

23. *Life of Sir Philip Sidney* (1652; reprint, Oxford: Oxford University Press, 1907), 221.

24. Andrews, "Dearly Bought Revenge," 83. I part company here with Andrews, who educes a host of speculative parallels between Samson and Hamlet from early in *Samson Agonistes* even though Milton does not evoke revenge tragedy as an interpretive context until line 1591.

25. "The Distinctive Tragedy of *Samson Agonistes*," in Ide and Wittreich, *Composite Orders*, 268.

26. Citations are to *Antonio's Revenge*, ed. W. Reavley Gair, The Revels Plays (Baltimore: Johns Hopkins University Press, 1978).

27. All citations for Shakespeare are to *The Riverside Shakespeare*, ed. G. Blakemore Evans et al. (Boston: Houghton Mifflin, 1974).

28. Samuel Daniel, *The Civil Wars* (1595), VI.28.

29. Citations are to *The Plays of Cyril Tourneur*, ed. George Parfitt (Cambridge: Cambridge University Press, 1978).

30. *Seneca: His Tenne Tragedies* (1581), reprinted with introduction by T. S. Eliot (1927; reprint, Bloomington: Indiana University Press, 1966), 189, hereafter *Tenne Tragedies*.

31. Ibid., 190, 189.

32. Parker, *Milton's Debt*, 219–20, associates this "spirit of frenzy" with the Nemesis of Greek tragedy, but it also may be understood as a Christian adaptation of nemesis. My reading of the catastrophe of *Samson Agonistes* as a revelation of divine judgment from the drama's Christian perspective is compatible with Lewalski's important interpretation of the poem ("Apocalypse"). According to Lewalski, Samson, as a type of the elect Christian, is able to attain only "spiritual triumphs of patience and faith" (1056) in this life, yet "endures and struggles in hope of the apocalyptic victory which, at the end of time, the Elect will share with Christ" (1062). As Milton's apocalyptic imagery suggests (see 1511–15, 1645–51), that final victory is foreshadowed at the catastrophe of *Samson*.

33. Dalila, conversely, is unable to advance toward spiritual recovery and in this respect serves Milton's drama as a foil to Samson. Much as the chorus and Manoa had erroneously advised Samson to do, Dalila seeks to attenuate her guilt and, though ostensibly repentant, to avoid punishment in that she will not reject the advantages in money and stature gained by sin. Lacking Samson's moral courage, Dalila embodies the false contrition and false repentance he is able to put behind him. Like the confrontation with Claudius's prayer scene in *Hamlet*, her confrontation with Samson marks a turning point missed in a tragedy of damnation, and presumably she suffers her ironic

fate at the Philistine feast for which she is so sumptuously attired. See also Anthony Low, *The Blaze of Noon: A Reading of Samson Agonistes* (New York: Columbia University Press, 1974), 147-49, and Mary Ann Radzinowicz, "Eve and Dalila: Renovation and the Hardening of the Heart," in *Reason and the Imagination*, ed. J. A. Mazzeo (New York: Columbia University Press, 1962), 155–81.

34. Citations are to Samuel Daniel, *The Tragedy of Philotas*, ed. Laurence Michel (New Haven: Yale University Press, 1949).

35. Citations are to *The Plays of George Chapman: The Tragedies*, ed. Thomas Marc Parrott, 2 vols. (1910; reprint, New York: Russell & Russell, 1961).

36. See Tasso's "Allegory" appended to the Fairfax translation of the *Jerusalem Delivered* (London, 1600).

37. Quoted from *Chapman's Homer: The Iliad, The Odyssey and the Lesser Homerica*, ed. Allardyce Nicoll, 2 vols. (Princeton: Princeton University Press, 1956), 1:4

38. For a discussion of *sapientia et fortitudo*, see A. B. Chambers, "Wisdom and Fortitude in *Samson Agonistes*," *PMLA* 78 (September 1963): 315–20.

39. Citations for *The Tragedy of Darius* are to *The Poetical Works of Sir William Alexander*, ed. L. E. Kastner and H. B. Charlton, vol. 1 (Manchester: Manchester University Press, 1921).

40. Citations are to *Bussy D'Ambois*, ed. Nicholas Brooke, The Revels Plays (Cambridge: Harvard University Press, 1964).

41. On Bussy's setting off on the sea of fortune, see Waddington, *The Mind's Empire: Myth and Form in George Chapman's Narrative Poems* (Baltimore: Johns Hopkins University Press, 1974), 20.

42. One thinks first of Garnier's hubristic tyrants and the titular heroes of *Tamburlaine* and *Selimas,* but the concept Michael articulates is pervasive in other Elizabethan dramatic portrayals.

43. *Tragedy of Darius*, lines 372ff.

44. On the association of heroic spirit with fire, see esp. Cedric H. Whitman *Homer and the Heroic Tradition* (Cambridge: Harvard University Press, 1958), chap. 7.

45. Edward W. Tayler, *Milton's Poetry: Its Development in Time* (Pittsburgh: Duquesne University Press, 1979), 121, makes the point about the "rousing motions" signifying both God's grace and heroic emotion. The main contention of Tayler's chapter on *Samson*—that the drama's proleptic form of anticipation and fulfillment (according to which all comes clear at the close) is providential—is of a piece with my reading from the play's Christian perspective.

46. "Reprobate scourge" and "inspired minister" are terms used by Andrews, "Dearly Bought Revenge," 95. The distinction relies on Fredson T. Bowers, "Hamlet as Scourge and Minister," *PMLA* 70 (September 1955): 740–49.

47. On the traditional symbolism of the eagle, see Jane Aptekar, *Icons of Justice: Iconography and Thematic Imagery in Book V of The Faerie Queene* (New York: Columbia University Press, 1969), chap. 1.

Part II

Imaging England: The Chorographical Glass

ARTHUR F. KINNEY

I.

THE renaissance was a period of rapid change," S. K. Heninger Jr. wrote in 1977, "and man grew increasingly uncertain about the forces that affect the human condition. He asked insistent questions about his environment and about his place in it."[1] Heninger followed these prefatory remarks to *The Cosmographical Glass: Renaissance Diagrams of the Universe* with a discussion of cosmographies concerned with creation, with the geocentric universe, and with macrocosms based on Copernicus and the Pythagorean and Platonic traditions, and on correspondences with the human body as microcosm. What Heninger concluded was that

> The macrocosm . . . could be disclosed in many different models based upon the several disciplines of the quadrivium. It could be an arithmetical variation of a single number, such as the tetrad, or an amplification of a single number into a network of correspondences, such as the table for the number 12. It could be a geometrical configuration, plane or solid, that interrelates a group of symbolic forms. It could be a visual depiction of ratios between numbers, a configuration that exhibits proportions and symmetries—what later ages, following the Greeks, called harmony.[2]

Attempts to map the cosmos, to stabilize it in the period of Tudor and Stuart England had, in fact, destabilized the cosmos, had unmapped it.

Yet more recently, in "The Land Speaks," Richard Helgerson has noticed especially the "cartographically and chorographically shaped consciousness" of Tudor and Stuart England.[3] Maps seem to have been cropping up everywhere in the years of Elizabeth I. Doubtless spurred on by the intense interest (and use) of them by William Cecil, Lord Burghley, Elizabeth's principal secretary, maps were used to decorate halls, parlors, chambers, galleries, studies, and libraries. As Helgerson notes, "[R]eproducing them in tapestries, book illustrations, paintings, and playing cards, alluding to them metaphorically in poems, even bringing them on stage, as Shakespeare does in *1 Henry IV* and *King Lear,* sixteenth-century Englishmen exposed themselves to the pervasive influence of an image scarcely less potent and considerably more durable than that of Elizabeth herself."[4] But often the land and the queen were associated, even made analogous. The first atlas of Tudor England—Christopher Saxton's collection of county maps published in 1579—introduced the country by way of a full portrait of its queen; on the title page of Michael Drayton's *Poly-Olbion* (1612), the queen is robed as Britannia, in a garment whose printed design clearly reproduces[5] Saxton's maps. Here the clothing is made inseparable from the overflowing cornucopia that represents England's wealth in the crops of her land, "the fruits of her bounteous womb in the position traditionally reserved for the Madonna's divine child," as Helgerson has it.[6] Britannia, with her scepter, is flanked by Brut, Caesar, the Saxon Hengist, and William the Conqueror—the dynasties of the past paying homage to the fruitful land of the present and to its reigning monarchical spirit. As such, there is both tribute and cooperation in aligning history (chronology) with geography (chorography). Both argue an integral relationship between counties and crops, land and ruler. This renewed and reconfigured understanding of the growth and utility of chorography, which in some ways parallels Heninger's study of the growth and use of cosmographies, is what I wish to recount and interpret here.

II.

We are always limited by the texts and perspectives we inherit. The first extant work of Tudor chorography is John Leland's *Itinerary*. In 1533 Henry VIII commissioned Leland to search the libraries of monasteries and colleges for works of ancient writers; excited by his findings, he spent six years traversing England and Wales to see for himself what he read of in the historiographical works he had gathered. As he traveled he made descriptive notes, "such a description," he writes to the king in 1546, "that it shaul be no mastery after for the graver or painter to make a like by a perfecte exemple."[7] His pride was justifiable. "Such an undertaking as the particular description of England, the features of town and country interspersed with historical notes, was unheard of," Lucy Toulmin Smith writes; "it was a thing of magnitude demanding learning, months of laborious travel, and much expense; it was a mark at once of the increasing desire for information and of the growing pride of Englishmen in their country—of what we should now call the 'imperial spirit,' literally expressed by Leland's words to his sovereign, intending a table map of 'your world and impery of England.'"[8] Although Leland outlived his king, he did not live long enough to see his work into print (he died, mentally incompetent, in 1552). But it may have served his friend John Bale as a source for his *Illustrium majoris Britanniae Scriptorum Summarium*, printed in quarto in Ipswich in 1548, and through Bale's advertising of Leland's work, many manuscripts of the *Itinerary*, in whole or part, seem to have circulated throughout the remaining years of the sixteenth century. Sir John Cheke inherited the manuscript at first, other papers went to Lord William Paget, Cecil, Humphrey Purefoy, and his son Thomas, among others. Stow would use Leland, and so would Harrison and Camden, Holinshed and Lambarde and Burton.

Leland's accounts are a unique and inviting blend of personal observation and scientific record, a verbal mapping of Henrician England. Of Cornwall he writes in part:

> There resortith a broke to Porthissek: and there is a pere and sum socour for fisschar botes.
>
> Porthguin a fisschar village lyith a 2. miles lower on the shore, and there is the issue of a broke and a pere.
>
> And a 3. miles lower is the mouth of Padestow haven.
>
> From Dindagelle to S. Esse village a 4 miles
>
> Meately good ground about S. Esses selfe.
>
> From S. Esse to Trelille village 2. miles.
>
> From Trelille to [blank] wher master Carniovies alias Carnsey hath a praty house, fair ground, and praty wood about it.
>
> Thens 3 miles by good corne grounde but no wood to Wadebridge.
>
> Wher as now Wadebridge is ther was a fery a 80. yeres syns, and menne sumtyme passing over by horse stoode often in great jeopardie.
>
> Then one Lovebone, vicar of Wadebridge, movid with pitie began the bridge, and with great paine and studie, good people putting their help therto, finishid it with xvij. fair and great uniforme arches of stone.
>
> One told me that the fundation of certein of tharches was first sette on so quik sandy ground that Lovebone almost despairid to performe the bridg ontyl such tyme as he layed pakkes of wolle for fundation.[9]

As factual as it is, Leland's *Itinerary* is sufficiently personal to be always appealing; and in both subject and presentation it served as the fundamental model for William Lambarde's *Perambulation of Kent* (1576).

In July 1568, along with William, earl of Pembroke, and William, Lord Cobham, Lambarde was appointed to a Commission of Sewers from Lombards Wall to Gravesend Bridge in Kent. They were to oversee repairs of seawalls; the cleansing of rivers, public streams, and ditches; and the draining of low ground and marshes. Like Leland, Lambarde visited Kent and studied at first hand its climate, people, and customs, the crops of the land and the traffic of the rivers, the history of the county and the tenures of the land. In his *Perambulation* he organized his material not by a single traversal of the land as Leland did, but by two distinct walks, centered on the two dioceses, Canterbury and Rochester. The two journeys were preceded by seventy pages of introduction, including a section on Anglo-Saxon Kent, administrative lists, and a map of beacons. It was, in fact, Lambarde who first combined verbal and pictorial chorography. While the original appears to have been lost,[10] Lambarde drew another for the 1596 edition of his book, arguing that he meant to serve the public by showing them where a governmental system of warning signals were, so that inhabitants might effectively defend their homes in the event of attack. Conscious that such exposure of a defense system might be criticized, he added that such information, while not especially helpful to invaders, was essential for the people of Kent, especially in the light of Spanish threats of invasion.

Both Leland's *Itinerary* and Lambarde's *Perambulation* are dwarfed by the far more ambitious, and far more popular, work of William Harrison, whose *Description of England* was written to accompany the 1577 and 1587 editions of Holinshed's *Chronicles*. Harrison brought to the art of Tudor chronography a thoroughness of detail, comprehensiveness of scope, and factual objectivity that far surpassed any of his predecessors. But his purpose was not to establish a record or aid defense of the land; it was to write a tribute out of national pride. Perhaps inspired by Holinshed's comprehensive history with its own built-in panegyric, Harrison made a grand case for his land and its customs, such as we find in his account of a visit to Bath:

> The Common Bath, or as some call it, the Hot Bath, is two hundred foot or thereabout from the Cross Bath, less in compass within the wall than the other, and with only seven arches wrought out of the main enclosure. It is worthily called the Hot Bath, for at the first coming into it men think that it would scald their flesh and loose it from the bone; but after a season and that the bodies of the comers thereto be warmed thoroughly in the same, it is more tolerable and easy to be borne. Both these baths be in the middle of a little street and join to St. Thomas' Hospital, so that it may be thought that Reginald, Bishop of Bath, made his house near unto these common baths only to succor such poor people as should resort unto them.
>
> The King's Bath is very fair and large, standing almost in the middle of the town, at the west end of the cathedral church. It is compassed about with a very high stone wall, and the brims thereof arc mured round about, wherein be two-and-thirty arches for men and women to stand in separately, who, being of the gentry for the most part, do resort thither indifferently but not in such lascivious sort as unto other baths and hothouses of the main.[11]

For Harrison, townscapes were as central to chorography as landscapes.

Between the two editions of Holinshed came the first edition (in Latin) of William Camden's *Britannia*. The chorographical description of Britain in the first edition of 1586 emphasized antiquity, especially Roman Britain, and Camden arranged his material first by Roman provinces and only following that by county, city, and river. In the five subsequent editions published during

Camden's lifetime, he continually added more history, the 1607 edition being twice the length of the first. Finally, in 1610, Philemon Holland translated the work into English. Throughout, Camden shares an impulse for the antiquarian that links him with Leland, yet the opening of his *Remains Concerning Britain* (1614 ed.) is more resonant of Harrison:

> [T]he ayre [of Britain] is most temperate and wholesome, sited in the middest of the temperate Zone, subject to no stormes and tempests as the more Southerne and Northerne are; but stored with infinite delicate fowle. For water, it is walled and garded with the Ocean most commodious for trafficke to all parts of the world, and watered with pleasant fishfull and navigable rivers, which yeelde safe havens and roads, and furnished with shipping and Saylers, that it may rightly be termed the *Lady of the sea*. That I may say nothing of healthfull Bathes, and of Meares stored both with fish and fowle; The earth fertile of all kinde of graine, manured with good husbandrie, rich in minerall of coles, tinne, lead, copper, not without gold and silver, aboundant in pasture, replenished with cattell both tame and wilde, (for it hath more parkes than all *Europe* besides), plentifully wooded, provided with all complete provisions of Warre, beautified with many populous Citties, faire Borroughs, good Townes, and well-built Villages,strong Munitions, magnificent Pallaces of the Prince, stately houses of the Nobilitie, frequent Hospitals, beautiful Churches, faire Colleges, as well in other places, as in the two Universities, which are comparable to all the rest in Christendome.[12]

The same sense of patriotism informs the *Remains* that we find in the *Britannia*, but in this later compilation of notes and essays Camden deconstructs both history and chorography into smaller essays on language, names, money, impreses, apparel, artillery, and speeches.

The rapid growth of chorography in mid-sixteenth-century Europe incorporated townscapes almost from the start. While the first known map of London, a twenty-sheet plan engraved in copper between 1547 and 1559 and possibly prepared for Elizabeth's coronation in 1558, is now lost, its derivative one-sheet plan is now the most famous one of the Tudor period. It inaugurates the first of six volumes of the *Civitates orbis terrarum* of Georg Braun, a cleric from Cologne, and Frans Hogenberg, a refugee from Antwerp, published between 1572 and 1617. Printed in Cologne, this collection is almost certainly the counterpart of Abraham Ortelius's *Theatrum orbis terrarum* (1570) and would in time add other English cities such as Bristol (1581), Cambridge (1575), and Oxford and Windsor (1575), each drawing made from a bird's-eye perspective and noted for its scene of comparative tranquility.[13] In England Richard Lyne's map of Cambridge in 1574 (possibly a source for Braun and Hogenberg) was followed a decade later by one of Oxford as well as Ralph Agas's highly detailed map of London, "the earliest reliable survey of the extent and architectural features of London, Westminster, and Southwark."[14] It was first drawn around 1591 and is extant from a third edition of 1603. Agas has left a remarkable account of his methodology (see appendix), and John

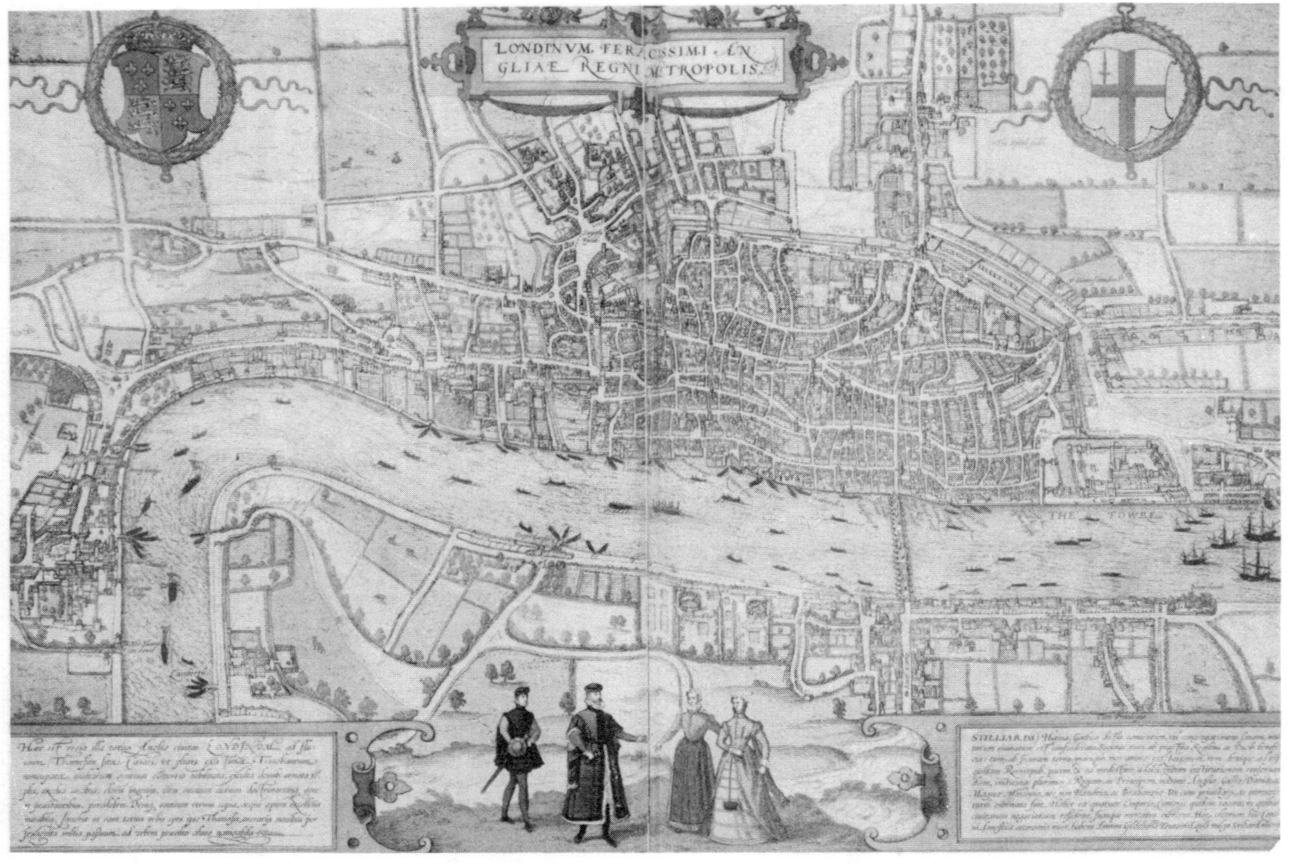

The Map of London in *Civitatis orbis terrarum* by Georg Braun and Frans Hogenberg (1572).

John Norden, Map of London (1593)

Norden created another map of London in 1593. The maps of Agas and Norden, along with the perambulations of Lambarde, doubtless inspired John Stow, whose *Survey of London*, first published in 1598 when Stow was in his seventies, displays all that we have seen so far: a love for antiquity, a desire to record authentic detail, and a tendency toward personal perspective and reminiscence. While the opening sections of the *Survey* are concerned with London's history, town walls, buildings, and customs, the greatest emphasis is on Stow's observations, by foot, of each of the city's wards. Cheape Ward is typical:

> Next adjoining is Cheape ward, and taketh name of the market there kept, called West Cheping. This ward also beginneth in the east, on the course of Walbrooke in Buckles bury, and runneth up on both the sides to the great conduit in Cheape. Also on the south side of Buckles bury, a lane turning up by St. Sithes church, and by St. Pancrates church, through Needler's lane, on the north side thereof, and then through a piece of Sopar's lane, on both sides up to Cheape, be all of Cheape ward.[15]

Stow continues enumerating the other streets before recounting the antiquities in the ward; the businesses there; those who are buried there; the history of Grocers Hall and of executions performed at the standard; the cross in West Cheape, site of coronations; historical joustings; famous residents past and present; Mercers Hall; the Guildhall and town government; and monuments of the past. All of this is done with the warmth and admiration of one whose devotion seems to be his highest, perhaps his only, motive.

Yet how pervasively and how deeply a sense of chorography swept through Tudor England, inciting patriotism and directed by it, is also evident in a voyage pamphlet and a portrait of the period. Mary B. Campbell has written that the "widespread imposition of Old World architectural forms on visual representations of the New World was a curious fact of contemporary iconography" in which Tudor works of chorography, as well as their Continental counterparts, directed even a writer like Walter Ralegh.[16] Thus in his propagandistic *Discoverie of the Large, Rich, and Bewtifvl Empyre of Guiana* (1596), Ralegh's descriptions seem not so much strange to the Tudor experience as strangely familiar:

> On both sides of this riuer, we passed the most beautifull countrie that euer mine eies beheld; and whereas all that we had seen before was nothing but woods, prickles, bushes, and thornes, heere we beheld plaines of twenty miles in length, the grasse short and greene, and in divers parts groves of trees by themselves, as if they had been by all the art and labour in the world so made of purpose: and stil as we rowed, the Deere came downe feeding by the waters side, as if they had been vsed to a keepers call.[17]

"All the beauty of the river country is English beauty," Campbell comments, "and the more so the closer he gets to Guiana itself."[18]

The portrait is the "celebrated Ditchley Portrait"[19] of Elizabeth I painted by Marcus Gheeraerts the Younger; it was commissioned by Sir Henry Lea, master of the queen's ordnance and her champion, to commemorate the Accession Day Tilt of 1590 and was named for Lea's country house where the portrait was eventually hung. Especially notable is the jeweled armillary sphere hanging close to the queen's left ear; the armillary sphere provides a model of the cosmos that Heninger describes in *The Cosmographical Glass*.[20] "She stands as an empress on the globe of the world," Sir Roy Strong writes,

> her feet planted on her realm of England, reflecting in paint George Peele's opening lines describing the retirement tournament:
> *Elizabeth, great empress of the world,*
> *Britannia's Atlas, star of England's globe,*
> *That sways the mighty sceptre of her land,*
> *And holds the royal reigns of Albion . . .*
> The clouds part to the left to reveal the dawn of a new age.[21]

The map over which she reigns—indivisible, this nation and this ruler—shows her standing firmly on Oxfordshire, in honor of Lea and Ditchley, and it is no ordinary map. It is quite precisely a redrawing of Saxton's map of 1579; and this portrait is an inversion of the title-page portrait where she introduces his work. The Ditchley portrait thus brings together the cosmos and the nation, joined by the monarch herself, but the references differ. The globe is a generalized curve; the nation, by contrast, is lovingly recreated from her master of maps. The portrait honoring Elizabeth I also honors Christopher Saxton.

III.

Such pictorial art suggests an implicit poetics in maps as in portraits. In his invaluable discussion entitled "Poet as Maker" in *Touches of Sweet Harmony: Pythagorean Cosmology and Renaissance Poetics* (1974), Heninger notes that

> Inspired by Plato's *divinus furor*, the poet surveys the plenitude of God's creation, from heaven to earth and back again. Excited by this experience, his imagination "*bodies forth* / The forms of things unknown"—makes particular, and therefore palpable, the Platonic ideas, which otherwise would remain for us ineffable and unknowable. The poet's pen turns abstract forms into concrete shapes; by means of characters, actions, and settings, he "gives to airy nothing / A local habitation and a name." In our terms, the poet physically extends his fore-conceit into our time-space continuum.[22]

This must have been something like the process Christopher Saxton underwent, too: visualizing in his mind's eye, before the sights of his fieldwork, the possibility of placing real geography on printed sheets, and in ways that would bring imaginatively before the viewer of his maps various shapes, elevations, distances, and relational perspectives. The analogy seems closer when Heninger goes on to remark that "To understand a poem, . . . a reader must survey the narrative as though it were a groundplat bodied forth by the poet's imagination"—the poet himself now virtually a mapmaker. It is Sidney's *Defence of Poesie* that Heninger is following here, and as Sidney merges Plato with Aristotle so does Heninger, both in a kind of creative tension: "In contrast, Aristotle . . . placed ultimate reality in the objects of physical nature, and by induction a poet might construct a universal statement from the facts of our environment." But for Heninger, the final stage implied here is crucial: we must finally see things whole, and not in parts.[23]

Such a poetics seems to have governed a chronographer like Christopher Saxton. The geographer J. B. Harley points out that "With regard to English county maps, for example, Saxton's surveys provided in the late sixteenth century a series of 'archetype' maps and 'archetypal meanings.'" At the same time, Saxton's maps rely on countless specific places and place-names, mimetically recreating the land on paper and in words. Such maps "present an intractable problem of duality," Harley continues. "In several respects—such as those of written language and graphic image, of mimetic and abstract sign, of art and science, and of reality and deliberate idealisation—the map image is a hybrid,"[24] much as Sidney would create a hybrid in a fore-conceit that imitates the ideal. The difference is one not of means but of ends. Where poetry, according to Sidney, aims to teach moral behavior (and inspire men to it), the end for the chorographer is more immediate and specific. He served his time and place: men needed to conceptualize space for traveling to war or to work; they needed to visualize their properties and scattered holdings; they needed to "see" the country to which they belonged when bargaining over territory and conquest, the resources and strength of their rivals at home and abroad.[25] It is clear why maps became so popular in late Tudor England and why men attempted to acquire them—"for defence, administration and wayfinding," as Harley puts it. He goes on:

> Thus to many Elizabethans the word "map" denoted a type of graphic tool to be used in their everyday business and which had taught them to think spatially. That they themselves did perceive this meaning is well documented. So John Dee, who had contacts with nearly everyone of importance in the age and can be regarded as the "leader of the Elizabethan Renaissance," and who recognised cartography to be a contemporary source of *objets d'art* [it is his remark of 1570 that Helgerson cites on the ubiquity of maps], also envisaged that men would collect and use maps to further their understanding of real places, as in the study of "things past, as battles fought, earthquakes, heavenly firings, and such occurrences . . . some other, presently to view the large dominion of the Turk: the wide Empire of the Muscovite: and the little morcel of ground where Christiandom

(by profession) is certainly known . . . some other for their own journeys directing into far lands, or to understand other men's travels."[26]

An explicit note in the upper-right corner of Lyne's 1574 townscape of Cambridge says that "Cambridge, a very famous city . . . immortalising the name and memory of the Founder, preserves a University dignity which is even more illustrious than that of old."[27] Key words here—*famous*, *immortal*, *dignity*, *illustrious*, *old*—suggest that the map is meant to be more than a matter of record and reference; it is a tribute infused with a pride that allows the buildings to serve as images as well as metaphors for the antiquity and achievement of England. For such ideal ends to the more pragmatic purposes of estate plans that allowed men to assess their worth, to buy and sell, to plan towns, to promote national consciousness, or to conquer a new overseas empire, all sorts of maps followed Saxton's atlas of 1579, both as works of art and as tools for particular purposes.[28]

But no matter what the use, much of the Tudor interest in maps began with the 1579 atlas that makes its later appearance in the Ditchley portrait of 1590. Saxton, the "father of English cartography,"[29] described himself in 1596 as "of Dunningley in the parish of Westardesleye in the Countye of Yorke, Gent., of the age of fyftye twoo yeares or thereabouts."[30] If he was by then unsure of his age, he could not have been unsure of his contribution to Elizabethan culture and knowledge. Although Humphrey Lluyd of Denbigh had contributed a map of England to Ortelius's atlas of 1573, it was Saxton's atlas of 1579, comprising a general map of England and thirty-four county maps, that constituted the first uniform national atlas ever produced. Its effect, as Helgerson claims, "was enormous. For over two hundred years—until the Ordinance Survey of 1794—nearly every printed map of England and Wales derived from Saxton."[31] Indeed, "Saxton deserves a place beside Shakespeare," Edward Lynam wrote in 1944, "as an interpreter of the national consciousness, unity and pride . . . of Elizabethan England."[32]

Saxton was employed by Thomas Seckford, as revealed by a privy council pass of 11 March 1576: "A placard to Saxton, servant to Master Seckford, master of the Requests, to be assisted in all places where he shall come for the view of meet places to describe certain counties in cartes."[33] Behind Seckford was Cecil himself, "the most cartographically minded statesman of his time";[34] Cecil used maps to decorate his walls, but he also used them in exercising national policy. In the early parts of Elizabeth's reign he collected maps of the Scottish Marches and of Berwick as well as of Ireland, places where he felt rebels were gathering. In the 1580s, fearing the threat of the Spanish Armada, he collected at Hatfield miscellaneous maps of the English Channel, some forty or fifty of them, as well as detailed maps of castles, plans of harbors and fortifications, and townscapes of Plymouth, Portsmouth, and Dover. Into his copy of Saxton's atlas Cecil interleaved some eighteen other maps, including one of Scotland made for Bishop John Leslie, confessor to Mary Queen of Scots, in the 1580s. He also annotated them. He wrote out for each county lists of justices of the peace, and for the counties along the south coast he noted possible sites for landing boats, stores of ordnance, post roads, and the names of gentry on whom he could call for aid as well as those he could not trust. The notes along the right margin of the map of Devon has, in Cecil's hand, "A Breef Note of ye places of Descent . . . yt are most daungerous and require greatest regard and assistaunce" and "A Note what powder and match was appointed to be kept in store in every corporate towne."[35]

Cecil relied on Saxton because his atlas "was unprecedented in its astonishing accuracy," according to Nigel Nicholson. "It contains only one major error—the Land's End peninsula points west instead of southwest—and minor misplacings, for instance of some coastal villages in Norfolk which are shown slightly inland."[36] As he completed drawing each sheet, Saxton sent it to London to be engraved by Flemish refugees in preparation for his atlas. The engraved frontispiece, attributed to Hogenberg, shows Elizabeth I enthroned under her canopy between two men she patronizes: Geography, on the right, with compasses and globe, and Astronomy on the left, holding an armillary sphere. In a medallion above the queen Righteousness and Peace kiss; below her feet are two surveyors, a topographic surveyor drawing a map and a geodetic surveyor shooting the stars to fix his spherical position. The cartouche between them has a verse of six Latin lines praising Elizabeth for her peaceful reign. In addition, the Index of Maps, in the most common setting, setting D, has a column of counties in alphabetical order, a column of counties in the order they appear in the atlas, and a table of judges' circuits and assizes. Most copies of D are also accompanied by a double-page spread giving eighty-four coats of arms as well as the numbers of cities, bishoprics, market towns, castles, parish churches, rivers, bridges, chases, forests, and parks. Saxton not only surveyed them; he compiled statistics. At another level of conceptualization, there appear on Saxton's general map the royal arms, Neptune, the fruits of sea and land, birds and flowers, galleons and merchant ships, all helping to articulate—in concrete images as well as idealized ones—a "myth of national pride and unity," making it an "ethnocentric figure of a map."[37]

Just how Saxton was able to map with such accuracy the whole of England in the brief years between 1573 and 1578 has long been a matter of debate. The early method of traversing, executed by a connected series of polar coordinates or angle and linear measurements (what the Elizabethans called "perticall dimensuration") was difficult and time-consuming; and it is therefore likelier that Saxton practiced triangulation, an advanced method probably brought to England by John Dee, who had left the country in 1547 to study with Gemma Frisius, professor of mathematics at the University of Louvain, and his pupil

Gerhard Mercator. In *The cosmographical glasse* (1559), William Cuningham explains triangulation and the "Geographical plaine Sphere" that was used: "It is made muche like the back parte of an Astrolabe conteininge in the circuite 360 degrees, and hath a ruler with twoo sightes. But it differeth from an Astrolabe in that it hath a Diall with a Needle fixed in it."[38] In *A Geometrical Treatise Named Panometria* (1571), Leonard Digges also discusses and describes triangulation, with its necessary angles and compass bearings, describing an instrument called the "theodolitus."[39] His practice of triangulation is supported by a letter from the Privy Council on 10 July 1576 that suggests he climbed church towers and hills to fix his distance and direction. Addressed to "justices and other royal municipal officers," it requires that they see Saxton "conducted vnto any towre Castle highe place or hill to view that countrey, and that he may be acompanied wi ij or iij honest men such as do best know the cuntrey for the better accomplishment of that service. and that at his departure from any towne or place . . . the said towne do set forth a horseman that can speke both welshe and englishe to safe conduct him to the next market Towne. etc."[40]

But Saxton did not only create works of scientific record and accuracy; he was also creating, simultaneously, "beautiful works of art. Ships and dolphins patrol the seas, cartouches and coats-of-arms (always including those of Queen Elizabeth and his immediate patron, Thomas Seckford) ornament the borders," Nicholson observes, "and where he had room, he had the county names engraved in lovely swash-calligraphy, minisculed to the easily legible names of smaller places."[41] "On so many of the county maps it is the elaborate decoration which may at first concentrate one's gaze," Ravenhill adds, "or, as some may claim, distract one's attention from the maps themselves. Neptune with his trident embracing a maiden off the coast of Anglesey symbolising the union of land and sea, galleons sailing or engaged in combat, fishing vessels, grotesque sea monsters disturbing the surface waters [illustrating strangeness and danger] enliven the sea voids offshore the maritime counties, all these give pleasure to the eye and make these maps such attractive works of fact and fancy"[42]—chorographic poems.

Indeed, Saxton's maps, like poems, work with images functioning as symbols. Hills and uplands, for instance, are indicated by "molehills" or "sugarloaves," rounded figures shaded at one side, such as those so prominent in his map of Cornwall. They are not always drawn to scale, and it has been theorized that he drew as largest those hills he actually climbed in the course of his surveying, while he selected to picture other hills because they were sites of windmills or beacons or the sources of streams and rivers. As for the rivers themselves, they are usually exaggerated in width and marked with conventional dots to show their movement. Tree symbols, shaded like the hills on the east side, point to extensive tracts of wood and forest.

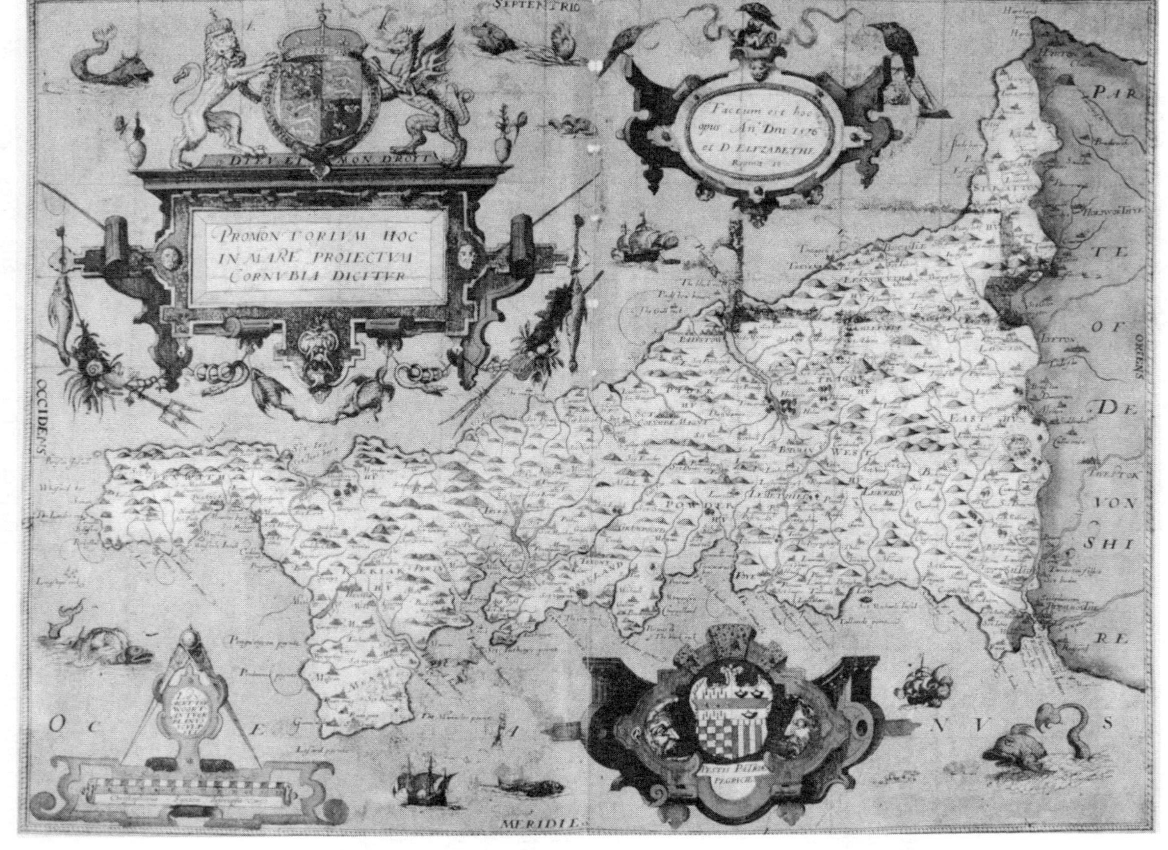

Christopher Saxton, Map of Cornwall from his [*Atlas*] (1579)

In addition to his topographical symbology, Saxton used his own sixfold classification of conventional signs for areas of heavy population. Although he provides no legend, like his European colleagues, he clearly felt no need to do so, for the images were striking and clear enough. Clusters of churches for Saxton indicate a city, small groups of buildings and roman lettering indicate market towns, cathedrals are indicated by a large cross; towns by three-spired churches; parish churches by single-spired churches; chapelries or hamlets by gabled houses; castles by buildings with two flanking towers; and parks by marking off the boundaries with a ring of palings. Bridges are also shown, and in the case of five counties—Cornwall, Essex, Hertford, Suffolk, and Norfolk—Saxton also indicated the boundaries of hundreds. The coloring, or "washing," of the maps added another symbolic means. Blue is used to denote rivers, lakes, and other water; green is used for woods; brown and green are used for wooded parts of hills; and red marks for settled or populated areas. A separate color is used to outline the boundaries of each county. By thus locating the special features of each of his landscapes, Saxton also helped his readers and viewers to locate themselves: together they came to *possess* the land and pay it allegiance.

Saxton's works were also a fountainhead for later Tudor and early Stuart culture. In 1591, John Norden completed a manuscript description and map of Northamptonshire where he was surveying former monastic estates that the queen had recently granted Sir Thomas Heneage, her vice-chancellor of the household; he sent them to Cecil, whose family had come from near Stamford in that county. These were the first realization of Norden's plans for a *Speculum Britanniae* that would combine the history of Camden and the chorography of Saxton; his *Historicall and Chorographical Discription of Middlesex* followed in 1593. Then, around 1604, he presented to King James his *Specvli Britanniae Pars A Topographicall & historicall description of Cornwall*, based on his own perambulations from 1577 and preserved today in Harleian MS 6252. By using radial lines as a test, William Ravenhill has demonstrated that Norden's Cornwall "is consistently a 15 per cent reduction of Saxton's map,"[43] which he copies even to the point of Saxton's errors. Norden's map adds sixty-four names of headlands, coves, havens, and offshore rocks and he indicates 209 parishes out of the 212 known before 1800. He concentrated, however, on landowners and on noting the houses of those better off; "Others there are, whose howses of name I have obserued in the generall and perticuler mapps: But time, and charge, and my necessitie *(Right gratious Soueraigne)* preuented my more serious desired scrutation of their owners."[44] A miniature *Atlas of the British Isles*, made to put in the pocket while traveling, was published without title page by Pieter van den Keere around 1605; thirty-one maps of English and Welsh counties, out of forty-four in the collection, are taken from Saxton; van den Keere

John Norden, Map of Cornwall from Harleian MS 6252

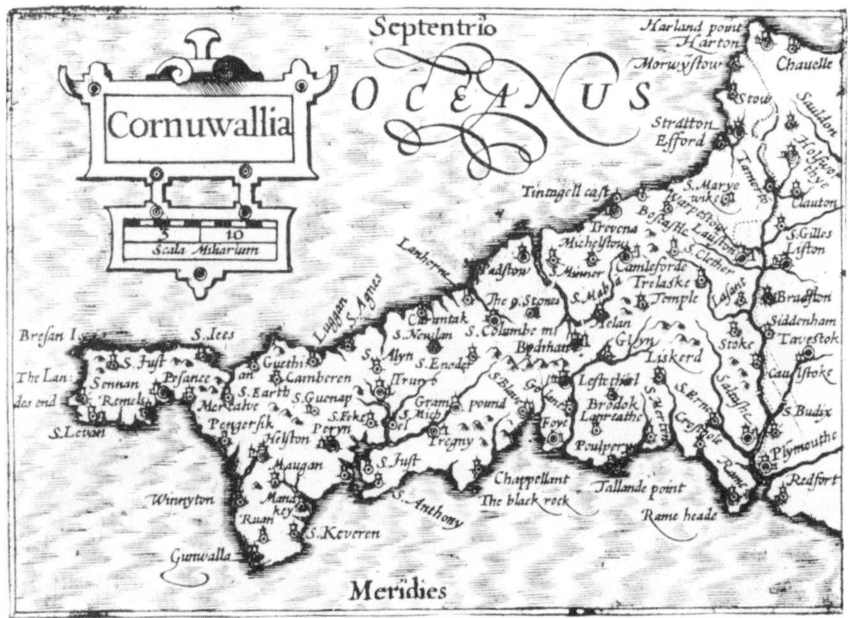

Map of Cornwall in Pieter van den Keere, untitled atlas of the British Isles (ca. 1605)

even employs Saxton's symbols. John Speed's *Theatre of the Empire of Great Britain* (1611) also followed Saxton but was heavily ideological; he tells us he was inspired by "the zeale of my countries glory," and his preface is an encomium for "the very Eden of Europe."[45] The title-page portraits show that "theirs was a country where Romans, Saxons, and Danes had fought over its space, while the landscape held a series of signposts to the destroyed monastic era[46] and in this way the cartographic images helped project a sense of time as well as of place into the landscape."[47] Speed's own map of Cornwallis absent of hills, showing a land especially bleak and infertile. By contrast, Drayton's map of Cornwall in *Poly-Olbion* (1612) is alive with personifications. "Drayton's Britain is 'peopled' by its natural and man-made landmarks," Helgerson remarks. "Its streams are nymphs; its hills, shepherds; its differing regions, rival choirs" (118). The ships offshore are outnumbered by mermaids and Neptunes, three of whom ride dolphins.

Following the premiere atlas of Saxton, then, numerous national and county maps were printed and reprinted, copied, reduced, and made into diagrams for almanacs, travelers' guides, and curiosities for wonder cabinets, and put on household tapestries and used as images on decks of playing cards. "Thus, in printed cartography at least, while the image of the nation and of its regions

John Speed's Map of Cornwall from his *Theatre of the Empire of Great Britaine* (1611)

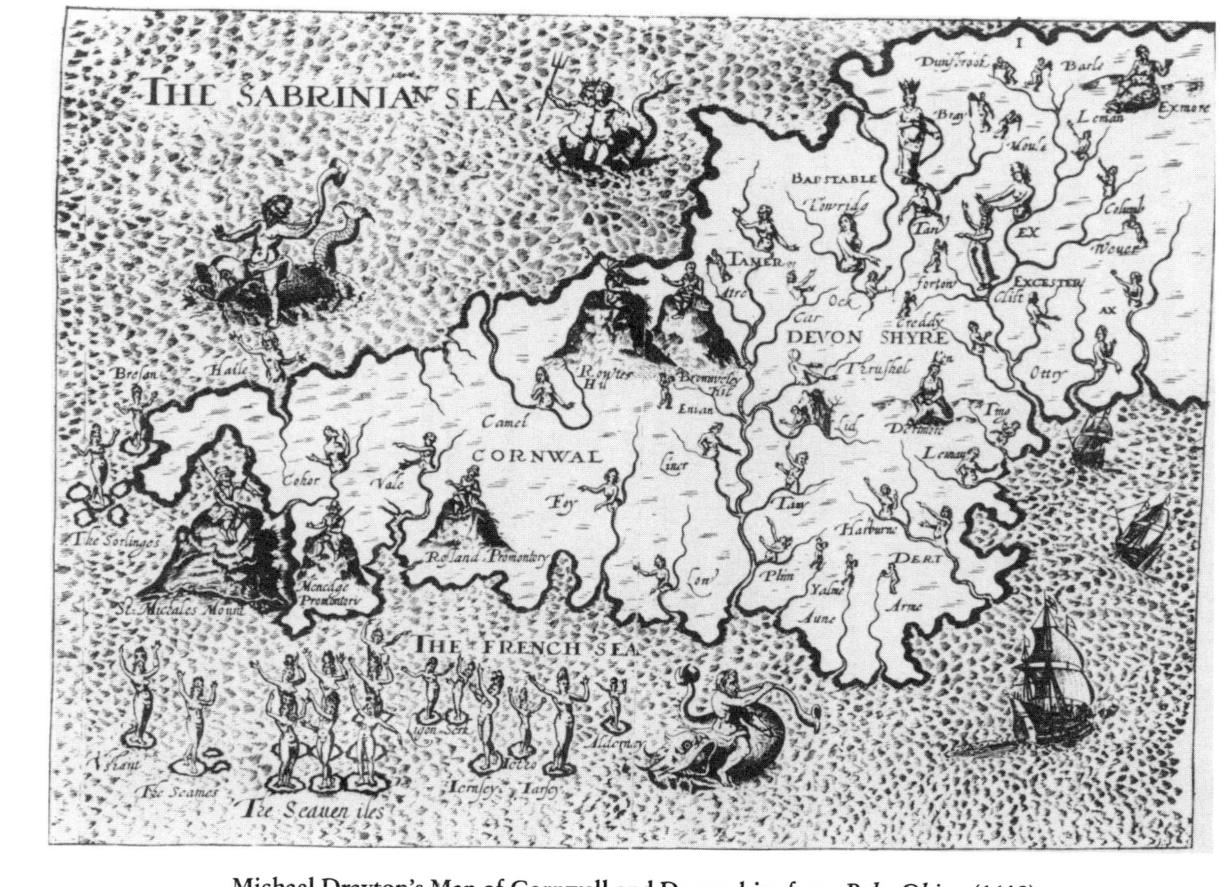

Michael Drayton's Map of Cornwall and Devonshire from *Poly-Obion* (1612)

was being gradually disseminated beyond the narrow circle of the Court and the gentry," J. B. Harley sums up, "the potential for divergent interpretations of the original image was greatly enhanced. The received meaning of maps was not always the meaning intended by the map-maker or by his patron."[48] Like the images of poems, the images of maps, from the sugarloaves of Saxton to the nymphs of Drayton, also began to float free from their landscapes and seascapes. They began to float into the realm of the imagination.

IV.

Tudor mapmakers can function like poets; Tudor poets make maps images. Shakespeare's King Lear displays his identity and legacy by bringing a map on stage, but his offer to divide the land among his daughters in response to their professions of love for him (and for the land he has imaged in his hand) is undermined when he announces before Cordelia can reply that he has already reserved for her an inheritance "A third more opulent than your sisters'" (1.1.86).[49] The scene repeats, almost exactly, the way in which Mortimer uses another map on stage to "divide our right" with Glendower and Hotspur in *1 Henry IV*. Mortimer claims authority from the Church:

> The Archdeacon hath divided it
> Into three limits very equally:
> England, from Trent and Severn hitherto,
> By south and east to my part assign'd;
> All westward, Wales beyond the Severn shore,
> And all the fertile land within that bound,
> To Owen Glendower; and, dear coz, to you
> The remnant northward lying off from Trent.
>
> (3.1.71–78)

But the division, like Lear's, is not made "very equally" at all: Mortimer has given himself England, returned Wales to Glendower, and left the Percies with the barren north and Scotland, as Hotspur is quick to note: "Me thinks my moi'ty, north from Burton here, / In quantity equals not one of yours" (95–96). In both instances, the map images the play's chief values; in each instance, valuing the map too much provokes tragedy, brings on slaughter.

Elsewhere Shakespeare lets the word alone do the work, without the actual map before us. For Solanio in *The Merchant of Venice*, "Piring [peering] in Maps for ports and piers and roads" (1.1.19), they are the single valued authority; Ulysses, in *Troilus and Cressida*, denigrates "bed-work, mapp'ry, closet war" (1.3.205) as the substitution of talk and tactics for actual fighting before the walls of Troy. But in each of Shakespeare's many uses, maps always point to something beyond themselves; they signify. They may do so with obvious farce, as in Maria's description of the duped Malvolio in *Twelfth Night*—"He does smile his face into more lines than is in the new map, with the augmentation of the Indies; you have not seen such a thing as 'tis" (3.2.78–81)—to an audience itself foreign to the discoveries of the New World. Or the use may be more deliberate and sinister, as when Osric misrepresents Laertes to Hamlet as "the card or calendar of gentry" (5.2.109–10). In each instance, the use of maps (or cards) is not factual, in the terms of Erwin Panofsky, but expressional. Such uses, he argues, only seem "natural" and "conventional"; actually, they are also "distinguished by an individual manner of viewing things and reacting to the world."[50] The map is a sign by its maker.

Victor Morgan goes farther, proposing "that to use maps as an image in literary works must depend on a prior familiarity with real maps and, to some degree, their practical uses, in order to make the cartographic image available. . . . it is in these literary allusions that we may hope to find any evidence for the degree to which in the contemporary mind maps were assimilated to other available visual images, and accommodated or undermined a pre-existent view of the ordering of the mental no less than the physical world."[51] Injected into the culture, maps then become the culture's sign. Sir Philip Sidney's employment of the image in *Astrophil and Stella* (1581–83; printed 1591) reconfigures and reinforces the Petrarchan lexicon that he has inherited for the amatory sonnet form:

> I can speake what I feele, and feele as much as they,
> But thinke that all the Map of my state I display,
> When trembling voice brings forth that I do *Stella* love.[52]

The poem as map—as direction, as foreign representation, as sign—gathers new cultural impetus, reconceiving the poet's role and reinventing the poet's form. The same cultural and poetic concerns are at work too in more sacred writing for Sidney, as in the "Voce Mea ad Dominum," the translation he made with his sister Mary of Psalm 142:

> My voice to thee it self extreamly strayning,
> Cries praying, Lord, againe it cryeng praieth:
> Before thy face the cause of my complayning,
> Before thy face my cases mapp it laieth
> Wherein my soule is painted
> In doubtfull way a stranger:
> But, Lord, thou art acquainted,
> And knowst each path, where stick the toiles of danger.[53]

The face as a map that indicates the painted (or washed) soul that in turn has made this pilgrim a stranger to God is nevertheless a guide to God on how his creature may have his soul washed clean; and it is partly with this recognition that the Psalmist cries out in the Sidneys' rendering.

This is the Sidney that S. K. Heninger Jr. describes in *Sidney and Spenser: The Poet as Maker* (1989): the poet who remakes language, who reconceives, who reinvents, who creates by recreating. Sidney is always the poet of the new, often the poet of the unexpected, mirroring a world attempting to stabilize. The opposite, Heninger argues, is true of Edmund Spenser, whose poetic delight comes in sharing the multilayered universe he inherits rather than making it over. In these terms, Spenser's imaging with maps in *The Faerie Queene* (1590) takes on its own deeper resonances. The most pointed usage comes when Britomart introduces herself to Redcrosse Knight:

> All my delight on deedes of armes is set,
> To hunt out perils and adventures hard,
> By sea, by land, where so they may be met,
> Onely for honour and for high regard,
> Without respect of richesse or reward
> For such intent into these parts I came,
> Withouten compasse, or withouten card,
> Far from my native soyle, that is by name
> The greater *Britaine*, here to seeke for prayse and fame.[54]

By setting herself apart from those voyagers away from Britain who make use of maps to discover the material riches of the New World, Britomart relies on hard adventures; her motives are honor for herself and high regard of herself and others. At a time when the bookstalls in St. Paul's Churchyard sold all sorts of books on voyaging—on the discovery of new lands and of the instruments of navigation employed to get there—Britomart's sheer dependence on fortune, on the goodness and stability of the world as she perceives it, is even more startling than Sidney's view. But that Britomart would rest on it the praise and fame not simply of herself but of her namesake Britain reveals Spenser's own deep belief in the order and goodness of God's world. By extension, he assigns such values to the other queen of Britain, Elizabeth I.

In the cases of Shakespeare, Sidney, and Spenser, then, maps used as images are signifiers that are bound up in and at the same time illuminate the texts they inhabit, the poets who create and employ them, and the audience to whom they are directed, all linked by cultural values that such images introduce and interrogate. They are imitative, representational, and rhetorical, making their plays and poems equally dramatic, since their meaning rests partially on the reception and understanding of the audience (or percipient). Heninger proposes this very dynamic in *Sidney and Spenser* when he writes that "any theory of art as imitation presupposes four isolable elements: an artifact, the artificer who made the artifact, an object which the artificer imitated in making the artifact, and a percipient who observes the artifact" and adds, "This list is exhaustive and exclusive. Nothing else enters into the system."[55] He illustrates this with his own method of triangulation.

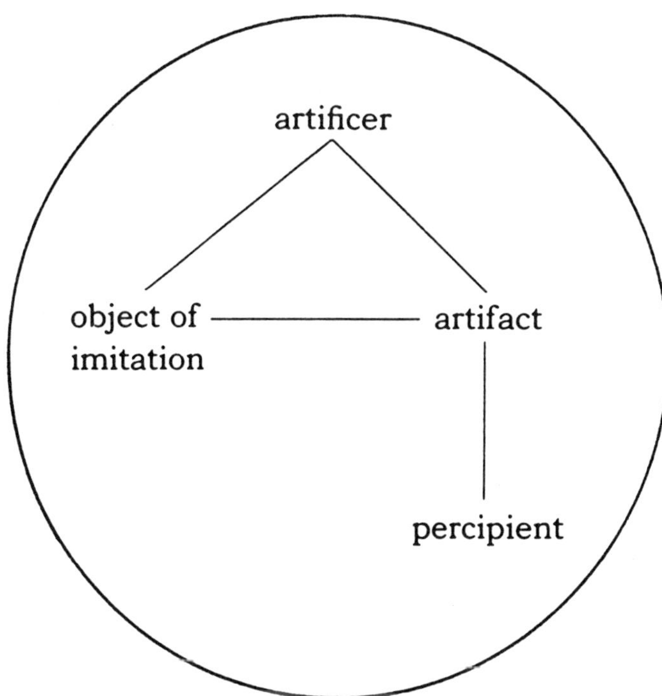

Drawing from S. K. Heninger Jr., *Sidney and Spenser: The Poet as Maker* (University Park: Pennsylvania State University Press, 1989), 21. Copyright © The Pennsylvania State University. By permission of the publisher.

This art of triangulation differs from that of the surveyor or mapmaker who measures distance and elevation by compass angles in which both measurements return to the site of the mapmaker (artificer) rather than, as in Heninger's chart, move away from him. The mapmaker, in his second step, transforming his observations in the field to a sheet or engraving (artifact), becomes the agent that moves physical objects (object of imitation) to the map by representation so that they may stand as signs and symbols to be acted on by the user of the map (the percipient).

Just how closely the poetics at the heart of *Sidney and Spenser* comes to the work of someone like Christopher Saxton may be seen at each step of Heninger's presentation. First, Heninger grounds art in the Aristotelian imitation of nature and finds testimony to this in the way the sixteenth century read Plutarch through the translation of Philemon Holland in 1603. There "Plutarch ascribes reality to the phenomena of physical nature, which the arts image as best they can," as with the molehills or sugarloaves of Saxton: "an empiricist aesthetic based upon sense perception of the phenomenal world."[56] Heninger then adds secondarily that the empiricist aesthetic might come from an empiricism of the mind, of ideal conceptualization, as it does with Plato, enlarging the field of possibilities and rejecting the absurdity of art as exact duplication (in which it would not be art, there being no active role by the artificer).

> Rather, the act of imitation involves a transposition from one level of existence to another. . . . He translates an idea across the line that marks off the world of becoming from the world of being, and embodies that formal essence in a physical object. This translation across the discontinuity between the two levels of existence is a "metaphor" in the literal sense.[57]

There is no way Saxton could hope to recreate a hill on a flat sheet to be impressed by a copper engraving; and he surely realized that sugarloaves were not exact replicas of the shapes of each hill he saw, since all his sugarloaves look alike and the hills were all in some way different from one another. His sugarloaves are metaphors, holding the concept and placement in his mind and transferring it to the mind of those who "read" his maps. Heninger's third and final step also follows the path of Sidney's *Defence of Poesie*, since it deals with the whole work of art after dealing with the method and images that create it. This whole work is organic for both Sidney and Heninger not because it necessarily carries a single meaning or even that it has a final organic form, but because it aims toward a single purpose or end, an idea Heninger also assigns to Scaliger: "'It imitates that it may teach.' Whatever the poet describes—councils of war, tempests, battles, various stratagems—all is for the purpose of instruction."[58] This stops short of Sidney, whose final end for poetry is to move his audience to virtuous action, but it is a usable poetic for maps as works of art. Saxton, after all, was assigned to draw maps that Cecil and even the queen could use to defend their realm from invasion—hence the setting out of beacons and the invention of a symbol for them—as well as for wayfaring generally. Saxton's maps were specially designed to instruct, and any artistic freedom had to be constrained by that overriding purpose if the maps were to function as he planned.

In Heninger's terms, then, Saxton follows a Spenserian aesthetic. His image might be multiple and imaginative—red could mean both cities and villages; a ring of palings could stand for a park that was unenclosed—yet they picture forth a consistent ordering that is within the grasp of any careful reader, even a largely untutored one, and so they guarantee instruction. This is the common "reading" of maps as J. B. Harley defines it, as "a mirror" or a precise representation "of some aspect of the real world. . . . The corollary is that when historians assess maps, their interpretation is molded by this idea of what maps are supposed to be. In our own Western culture, at least since the Enlightenment, cartography has been defined as a factual science. The premise is that a map should offer a transparent window on the world."[59] And yet that is not really the way we view Saxton's map of, say, Cornwall. Whether or not Land's End is correctly placed, the county is teeming with both sugarloaves and towns: they compete for attention in so evenly dispersed a way that we do not know whether to marvel at the fertility of the land or at the widespread civilization that has tamed it, while both, separately and together, argue for pride in Cornwall as a part of England and show it to be a worthy target for Spanish invasion. Rivers filter their way evenly across the county, and wholly imagined sea monsters, larger than the realistic galleons and merchant ships they accompany in the sea, keep their respectful distance from the heavily settled coasts as they do from the ships. Saxton communicates varied, and not necessarily always related, ideas to us through the medium of his map; while it is to a large degree scientifically accurate, we also, at the same time, construct and deconstruct that map through the ideas it invites and imposes. The map remains the map, but it is also something other and something more, and that something reopens meaning in the way Sidney's aesthetic is said to work.

This is precisely the position taken by two geographers, Denis Wood and John Fels, writing in 1992. The transparency of maps, they write,

> is, of course, an illusion: *there is nothing natural about a map.* It is a cultural artifact, a cumulation of choices made among choices every one of which reveals a value: not the world, but a slice of a piece of the world; not nature but a slant [for Saxton, a bird's-eye perspective] on it; not innocent, but loaded with intentions and purposes; not directly, but through a glass; not straight, but mediated by words and other signs; not, in a word, as it is, but in . . . *code*. . . . necessarily embody[ing] their authors' prejudices, biases and partialities.[60]

Wood and Fels argue that we should read maps as we might read poems—as opaque and transparent, as texts and through their texts. "It is not," they add, "that maps don't need to be *de*coded; but that they are by and large *en*coded in signs as readily interpreted by most map readers as the simple prose into which the marks are translated on the legends themselves."[61]

What is encoded is often cultural: there is no legend on Saxton's map of Cornwall, but there *are* legends that he has devised in just as formal if more individual a way. In the upper left corner of the map Saxton engraves the royal arms surmounting a rectangular cartouche that heralds the Tudor motto—"Diev et Mon Droyt"—giving him both permission and authority as well as providing authority for the map. As a counterweight, at the base of the right side of the map, Saxton engraves the coat of arms of Thomas Seckford, master of requests. The relationship along this axis is striking; it is both a partnership and a forced joining together of royalty and gentry, both tribute and blasphemy. On the other axis, forming an overall chiasmus, a similar relationship occurs: at the top right is the only place Elizabeth I's name appears, a nice touch in the dating; at the bottom left is the only place Christopher Saxton's name appears, under the compasses that are the means of his art and the claim for his work. That Saxton's map, then, needs no legend for its symbology is clear enough, even to the most inexperienced reader of maps, yet that meaning—Seckford's arms, for instance—is more immediate and more significant to Saxton's first Tudor audiences because they reflect and embody the culture of that time. Like all maps, Saxton's Cornwall reflects and reinterprets its culture, as Panofsky has said all art does:[62] conditioned by culture, maps in turn acculturate.

Maps look and read like texts because they function semiotically, as poems do. They are signs composed of signs; their function is to signify. But as Roland Barthes writes in *Mythologies* (1972), different signs operate simultaneously at different levels. Saxton's sugarloaves tell us one thing; the royal arms tell us another. The signs for hills are immediate; the royal arms are mediate; both function within cultural contexts. Barthes attempts to chart this complicated relationship in which sugarloaves function as language and the royal arms as myth.[63]

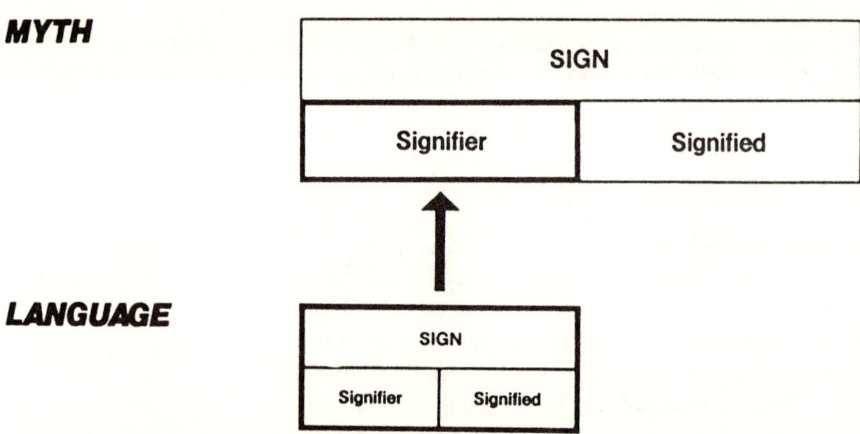

Drawing from *Mythologies*, by Roland Barthes, translated by Annette Lavers. Translation copyright © 1972 Jonathan Cape Ltd. By permission of Hill and Wang, a division of Farrar, Straus & Giroux, Inc.

As Wood and Fels remark, "Perched on top of a primary semiological system, myth resists transformation into symbols (which makes it hard to put into words, hence . . . *hard to talk about*). As a legend or a map or a photograph, it retains the fullness, the presence, of the primary semiological system to which it is endlessly capable of retreating. What viewed obliquely appears as an advertising slogan, confronted directly is the blandest of legends, so that the slogan, still ringing in one's ears, is apprehended as no more than the *natural* echo of the facts of the map."[64] The royal arms are prominently large on Saxton's map and, from the top, control what lies beneath—which is, after all, the whole of Cornwall and a bit of Dorset—and yet they seem to disappear from our field of vision as we continue to work with Saxton's map. We know they are there and we ignore them: they are there and they aren't there. It is what Barthes calls "the naturalization of the cultural." As Barthes puts it,

> This is why myth is experienced as innocent speech: not because its intentions are hidden—if they were hidden they could not be efficacious—but because they are naturalized. In fact, what allows the reader to consume myth innocently is that he does not see it as a semiological system but as an inductive one. Where there is only an equivalence, he sees a kind of causal process: the signifier and the signified have, in his eyes, a natural relationship. This confusion can be expressed otherwise: any semiological system is a system of values; now the myth consumer takes the signification for a system of facts: myth is read as a factual system, whereas it is but a semiological system.[65]

Saxton's map of Cornwall—all maps—is not seen as a semiological *system* because that would deny its primary claim of recording discrete *facts* without any intervening interpretation: the artifact seems to melt away so that the object of imitation and percipient come face to face. But we know, from Heninger's description and diagram, that this innocence is never the case; the artifact (map, poem) is in fact what "makes" statements, what makes Saxton a "maker." In part, this can be laid to Saxton's multiple audiences: he must honor the queen, please his patron, and inform the principal secretary, *all at once*. But the very combination here is what gives his map its own cast and character: what makes it Saxton's as well as theirs. He would not—and he could not—have it any other way. Nor, I think, would we. If there were no room for multiple signification, all texts would be one-dimensional: boring, with a short shelf life. What we *like* about texts is their endless retreat of meaning before us. We say it keeps the text living.

How this happens is not only a matter of the poet (or mapmaker) and his designs upon us, but of our willingness and ability to see the play within texts. This play—not restricted to one or two meanings but not so unrestricted as to admit anything and everything—has been addressed by Umberto Eco.

> A sign is always an element of an *expression plane* conventionally correlated to one (or several) elements of a *content plane*. Every time there is a correlation of this kind, recognized by a human society, there is a sign. Only in this sense is it possible to accept Saussure's definition according to which a sign is the correspondence between a signifier and a signified. This assumption entails some consequences: a *a sign is not a physical entity*, the physical entity being at most the concrete occurrence of the expressive pertinent element; b *a sign is not a fixed semiotic entity* but rather the meeting ground for independent elements (coming from two different systems of two different planes and meeting on the basis of a coding correlation).[66]

The frequency of Saxton's sugarloaves, that is, could signify (as elements of the content plane) a density of hilly country that is therefore undesirable; or, from a different expressive plane—Cecil's, for instance—there are good places to defend the land, since such hills can be used for lookouts and fortifications. But the content of the sugarloaves must meet the needs, predispositions, values, and understanding of some expressive plane for a sign to exist—and for meaning to occur. Otherwise, Saxton's Cornwall would be no more than a pretty picture. The beauty, then, of the semiotics of maps (as of poems) is that one meaning given to the content—one sensed sign—does not necessarily cancel out another, and that the possibility is always open for another expressive plane, or signification, to be found. It is just this destabilization of texts that Sidney also finds fascinating, and by the time of the *Arcadia* unavoidable. There role-playing, counterfeiting, and deceit, which measure the characters from Pyrocles and Musidorus to Cecropia and her son, allow a multiple play of meaning. Even the conclusion to the *Old Arcadia* (written around 1580) that was published with the *New Arcadia* near the turn of the century has Euarchus learning the value of equity over precedent, chancery over common law, in which the open possibility of exceptions to the rule may always override the rule. "We can only claim that a map actually resembles what it represents," Jonathan Culler tells us, "if we take for granted and pass over in silence numerous complicated conventions."[67]

Those sugarloaves characterizing Saxton's Cornwall take a significant part of their potential and actual meanings (significations) from their frequency, number, and density. Meaning is not just in their presence but in their relationships—to each other and to the rest of the map, where they seem to have little effect on preventing settlements. This is yet another way of reading Saxton's map, another way "into" it, as we might find various filiations of symbols in a poem, various networks of images. But as Wood and Fels recognize,

> Maps are about relationships. In even the least ambitious maps, simple presences are absorbed in multilayered relationships integrating and disintegrating sign functions, packaging and repackaging meanings. The map is a highly complex supersign, a sign composed of lesser signs, or, more accurately, a synthesis

> of signs; and these are supersigns in their own right, systems of signs of more specific or individual function. It's not that the map conveys meanings so much as *unfolds* them through *a cycle of interpretation* in which it is continually torn down and rebuilt; and, to be truthful, this is not really the map's work but that of its user, who creates a wealth of meaning by selecting and subdividing, combining and recombining its terms in an effort to comprehend and understand. But however elaborate, this is not an unbounded process. Inevitably, it has a lower bound, the most particular sign function that resists decomposition into constituent signs, and an upper bound, the integral supersign of the entire map that accesses the realm of extrasignification; and between these extremes it is stratified.[68]

This process in reading a map comes very close to Heninger's conclusion in *The Cosmographical Glass* about reading Renaissance diagrams of the universe. He found the continual investigation and speculation canceled any notion of fixed eternal truth: "This large assortment of diagrams fairly well destroys any notion that there was a prevailing image of the universe in the renaissance. Instead, there was a welter of differing images—many strongly appealing, none convincingly authoritative." He goes on, "As a corollary to this conclusion, we might conjecture that the artist, not bound by the constraint of cosmological dogma, felt free to engage in cosmological speculation of his own sort. He assumed a license to create his own universe. The worlds of Hieronymus Bosch, of Leon Battista Alberti, and of John Milton, to name a few notable examples, are the result. We might even go so far as to say that these artists would not have created as they did in a period of cosmological certainty."[69]

Just as Renaissance cosmographers, realizing no final view was now certain, tackled the problem of understanding the universe from a variety of positions, so we, more earthbound, can enter Saxton's map imaging England from any perspective, even from his bird's-eye view: so we can see Saxton's chorography of Cornwall as geographic, military, political, social, or economic. We can enter at a level of simple pleasure as well as at a level of abstract speculation: neither is prohibited; neither prohibits something else. That is the beauty of maps, which may rival even the Petrarchan poems of Sidney and the Platonic poems of Spenser as texts to be read. It is in endless dialogue with the viewer as reader, that map of Cornwall, with its constituent meanings, its range of significations and sign systems. Beyond the self-referentiality within the map—the chiasmus of meanings in its symbolic corners, for instance—there is referentiality to the culture that produces it, and to the reader who reads it. If it is this endless play that associates Saxton with Sidney, it is this endless dialogue, and this eternal potentiality of new meaning, that associates him with Spenser and with Shakespeare. Saxton's mapping of Cornwall shows us, once more, that there are multiple ways—surely more than three—to read the maps that Lear and Mortimer hold, again and again, as they stand on the stage before us.

Appendix

Lansdowne MS 73. Art. 29.

A Noate for the perfection of Lande Measure, and exact plattinge of Cities, Castels, Honors, Lordeshippes, Maners, and Landes of all sortes, by Rad. Agas.

The Measure of Landes (the grounde of our norishment) is necessarie for sale, demise, perfection in surveigh, tiltlie, &c.

The greate number of lande meaters at this presente, with the diversitie of device for measure are soe differinge amonge themselves, and from the truth of that action, as infinite errors are therein daielie committed, and the rare, and excellente skill in measure, almoste utterlie condempned.

Some useth the profitable stafe; some the square, &c., which instrumentes to the skillfull are full of perfection, wheare the subjecte is levell and even, but because landes are sildome soe founde and theire hedges, diches, and other limmittes, curved, and unstraight, sutch Instrumentes for lande measure are not to be used.

The bourde (as theie tearme it) which is commonly had for plattinge, and measure, is skilfully devised, but untrustie to sutch purpose. The stations are shorte, therefore manie, and one error multiplied, and in a platt continued, overthroweth the action. The lines drawen straight from angle to angle, resembleth not the limmittes, and boundes of the landes wett and stormie weather hindereth perfection, and blemisheth the woorke. It is combersom in carriage and troblesom to be attended uppon, espetially in a large and ample surveigh. It doeth not readily, and exactly, fitt percell to percell, neither doeth it descrie, and make perfecte, the unevenes of groundes, and therefore truely closeth not, as doeth the Theodolite made, and prepared thereunto.

Touching the measure to be applied to the instrumente, the poale whitch in time paste hath moste commonly benn used, is for the shortenes, and untrue cariage, not fittinge to the same.

All lines starched, seared, goomed, &c., through varietie of weather houlde not alwaies alike, and therefore uncertaine.

Because noe grounde maie truely be measured, without the forme of the same be firste exactly taken. The Theodolite of some 20 ynches in diameter, with a protracter of one foate at the leaste, I finde by longe experience, to be moste readie and perfect, for performaunce hereof. This truely fixte, with a sight prepared, for the readie triall of the unevenes of all groundes, with the difference thereof, by ascente and discente, in everie measure, concludeth with perfection, and performeth with speede even to the settinge out of the largeste maner, or greateste Citie, with everie member and percell of the same, in perfect measure, forme and proportion for th'accomplishment, and fulnes of Surveigh. It also setteth out anie quantitie of grounde in what shappe, or forme so ever as linely and proportionably, as anie artificer is able to performe in cloath, metall or other subject, which for parkes, buildings, fortificacions, &c., maie sometime faule in use with infinite other conclusions, as to the experienced maie better appeare.

The measure attendinge uppon this Instrument is of steele wier toe pole longe lincked foote by foote, excepte the halfe foot at either ende.

To the Righte Honorable the Lorde Highe Treasurer of Engelande. — Indorsed RAPHE AGAS, 22 February, 1592–3.

Notes

1. S. K. Heninger Jr., *The Cosmographical Glass: Renaissance Diagrams of the Universe* (San Marino, Calif.: Huntington Library, 1977), xv.
2. Ibid., 143.
3. Richard Helgerson, "The Land Speaks," in *Forms of Nationhood: The Elizabethan Writing of England* (Chicago: University of Chicago Press, 1992), 108.
4. Ibid., 114.
5. Ibid., 108.
6. Ibid., 122. I differ from Helgerson in my understanding of the ideology of Drayton's title page; he sees it as the pushing aside of royalty for an increased emphasis on the power of the land itself.
7. John Leland, "Newe Yeares Gyfte," in *The Itinerary of John Leland in or about the Years 1535–1543*, ed. Lucy Toulmin Smith (Carbondale: Southern Illinois University Press, 1965), 1:xli.
8. Lucy Toulmin Smith, introduction to Leland, *Itinerary*, 1:xiii.
9. Leland, *Itinerary*, 1:178.
10. Retha Warnicke, in *William Lambarde, Elizabeth Antiquary, 1536–1601* (London: Phillimore, 1973), 30.
11. William Harrison, *The Description of England*, ed. Georges Edelen (Ithaca: Cornell University Press, 1968), 290.
12. William Camden, *Remains Concerning Britain*, ed. R. D. Dunn (Toronto: University of Toronto Press, 1984), 5.
13. Sixty townscapes from Braun and Hogenberg have recently been published in their approximate coloring in *The City Maps of Europe*, ed. John Goss (London: Studio Editions, 1991). Two of the original twenty-sheet copperplates of London survive, covering the Finsburg and City areas immediately north of London Bridge. The map by Braun and Hogenberg must have been drawn between 1550, when Southwark was formed from three royal manors, and 1561, when the tall spire of St. Paul's that is shown was destroyed.
14. William Henry Overall, introduction to *Civitas Londinum: A Survey of the Cities of London and Westminster, the Borough of Southwark and Parts Adjacent*, by Ralph Agas, in facsimile (London: Adams and Francis, 1874), 1. Known copies of Agas's full map are six feet one-half inch long by two feet four and one-half inches wide (23).
15. John Stow, *The Survey of London*, ed. H. B. Wheatley (1912; London: Dent, 1987), 231–32.

16. Mary B. Campbell, *The Witness and the Other World: Exotic European Travel Writing, 400–1600* (Ithaca: Cornell University Press, 1988), 228.

17. Sig. G4v. My text is the facsimile published in the Bibliotheca Americana series (Cleveland: World, 1966).

18. Campbell, *Witness and the Other World,* 245.

19. Roy Strong, *The Cult of Elizabeth: Elizabethan Portraiture and Pageantry* (London: Thames and Hudson, 1977), 154.

20. Heninger, *Cosmographical Glass,* 26–27, 39, 41, 66–67, 178.

21. Strong, *The Cult of Elizabeth,* 154.

22. S. K. Heninger Jr., *Touches of Sweet Harmony: Pythagorean Cosmology and Renaissance Poetics* (San Marino, Calif.: Huntington Library, 1974), 294.

23. Ibid., 295, 316, 392–93.

24. J. B. Harley, "Meaning and Ambiguity in Tudor Cartography," in *English Map-Making 1500-1650: Historical Essays,* edited by Sarah Tyacke (London: British Library, 1983), 22–23.

25. These issues are discussed by J. R. Hale, *Renaissance Europe: Individual and Society, 1480–1520* (London: Faber and Faber, 1971), 52–53, as quoted by Harley in "Meaning and Ambiguity," 26.

26. Harley, "Meaning and Ambiguity," 26, 27.

27. Quoted by Harley in ibid., 30. "A map itself is a relative document. It is an approximate reality, neither objective nor absolute. When we look at a map, our own response is also relative. Our reading of a map depends on our need, experience, and memory. This flux of record and reflection reminds us that truth itself is relative. As our perception of truth changes, so maps change." So Lucy Fellowes, "Seeing Space: The Design of Maps," in the catalog for the Smithsonian Institution's exhibition, *The Power of Maps* (Washington, D.C.: Smithsonian, 1993), 10. I saw this exhibition in late January 1994 after completing this essay.

28. Harley provides a convenient chart of Tudor maps and their uses at "Meaning and Ambiguity," 31.

29. Quoted without source by J. B. Harley, "Christopher Saxton and the First Atlas of England and Wales, 1579–1979," *Map Collector* 8 (September 1979): 2.

30. Quoted without source by William Ravenhill in the introduction to *Christopher Saxton's Sixteenth-Century Maps* (Chatsworth, U.K.: Chatsworth Library, 1992), 9.

31. Helgerson, *Forms of Nationhood,* 107.

32. Edward Lynam, *British Maps and Map-makers* (London, 1944), 20; quoted by Harley, "Christopher Saxon," 2.

33. Quoted by Helgerson, *Forms of Nationhood,* 109.

34. J. H. Andrews, *Ireland in Maps* (Dublin: Georgraphical Society of Ireland, 1961), 5, as quoted J. B. Harley, "The Map Collection of William Cecil, First Baron Burghley, 1520–98," *Map Collector* 3 (June 1978): 12.

35. These instances are from Harley, "Map Collection of William Cecil," 19, 17.

36. Nigel Nicolson, introduction to *The Counties of Britain: A Tudor Atlas by John Speed* (New York: Thames and Hudson, 1989), 13. Gordon Manley has recorded several errors and omissions in Saxton's maps of the Pennines in "Saxton's Survey of Northern England," *Geographical Journal* 83 (March 1934): 308–16.

37. Harley, "Meaning and Ambiguity," 36–37.

38. William Cuningham, *The cosmographical glasse* (1559), fol. 131.

39. A surveying instrument found in Leonard Digges, *A Geometrical Treatise*

Named Panometria (1571). The circle of the radius, one foot or more, engraved on a metal plate, is graduated into 360 parts or degrees, providing an index and sights.

40. R. A. Skelton, *Saxton's Survey of England and Wales*, Imago Mundi Supplement 6 (Amsterdam, 1974), 16, prints a transcription by Alison Quinn of the document in the Privy Council Register. See Harley, "Christopher Saxon," 6. Actually, "every projection must sacrifice accuracy and tolerate distortion of one kind or another": even Mercator's projection. So Lloyd A. Brown, *The Story of Maps* (Boston: Little, Brown, 1949), 138–39. Brown discusses astrolabes (180–81) and triangulation (182ff.; see illustration, 214).

41. Nicolson, *Counties of Britain*, 14–15.

42. Ravenhill, *Saxton's . . . Maps*, 19.

43. William Ravenhill, "The Making of the Maps," chapter 4 of his introduction to *John Norden's Manuscript Maps of Cornwall and Its Nine Hundreds* (Exeter, U.K.: University of Exeter, 1972), 26.

44. Quoted by Ravenhill, "The Description of Maps," chapter 5 of his introduction to *Norden's . . . Cornwall*, 41.

45. Quoted by Harley, "Meaning and Ambiguity," 37.

46. M. Aston, "English Ruins and English History: The Dissolution and the Sense of the Past," *Journal of the Warburg and Courtauld Institutes* 36 (1973): 231-35.

47. Harley, "Meaning and Ambiguity," 37.

48. Ibid., 39.

49. All citations are to *The Riverside Shakespeare*, ed. G. Blakemore Evans et al. (Boston: Houghton Mifflin, 1974).

50. Erwin Panofsky, *Studies in Iconology: Humanistic Themes In the Art of the Renaissance* (New York: Harper and Row, 1962), 3.

51. Victor Morgan, "The Literary Image of Globes and Maps in Early Modern England," in Tyacke, *English Map-Making*, 46. Cf. Denis Wood and John Fels, *The Power of Maps* (New York: Guilford, 1992), 142.

52. Philip Sidney, "Astrophil and Stella," sonnet 6, lines 12–14, in *The Poems*, ed. William A. Ringler (Oxford: Clarendon Press, 1962), 168.

53. *The Psalms of Sir Philip Sidney and The Countess of Pembroke*, ed. J. C. A. Rathmell (Garden City, N.Y.: Doubleday Anchor, 1963), 326.

54. Edmund Spenser, *The Faerie Queene* 3.2.7, ed. Thomas P. Roche Jr. assisted by C. Patrick O'Donnell Jr. (London: Penguin, 1978), 403.

55. S. K. Heninger Jr., *Sidney and Spenser: The Poet as Maker* (University Park: Pennsylvania State University Press, 1989), 20.

56. Ibid., 107.

57. Ibid., 144.

58. Ibid., 58.

59. J. B. Harley, "Text and Contexts in the Interpretation of Early Maps," in *From Sea Charts to Satellite Images: Interpreting North American History Through Maps*, ed. David Buisseret (Chicago: University of Chicago Press, 1990), 3–4.

60. Wood and Fels, *Power of Maps*, 108.

61. Ibid., 98.

62. Panofsky, *Studies in Iconology*, 7–8.

63. Roland Barthes, *Mythologies*, trans. Annette Lavers (New York: Hill and Wang, 1972), 115.

64. Wood and Fels, *Power of Maps*, 104–5.

65. Barthes, *Mythologies,* 131.

66. Umberto Eco, *A Theory of Semiotics* (Bloomington: Indiana University Press, 1976), 48–49.

67. Jonathan Culler, *The Pursuit of Signs: Semiotics, Literature, Deconstruction* (Ithaca: Cornell University Press, 1981), 24.

68. Wood and Fels, *Power of Maps,* 132–33.

69. Heninger, *Cosmographical Glass,* xvi–xvii.

Housing Chessmen and Bagging Bishops: Space and Desire in Colonna, "Rabelais," and Middleton's *Game at Chess*

ANNE LAKE PRESCOTT

COMPARED to time travel, space travel looks easy. But each move we make is pressured, if only in our understanding, by how we and our culture conceive—or, as we say nowadays, construct—that space. Cultural pawns much of the time, we move on a board (space-time or Einstein's projected "unified field") divided and defined—if not by straight lines into squares, then by laws, assumptions, and metaphors—into often overlapping personal and social places; how we think, feel, and talk models and remodels our sense of the three-dimensional world. In this essay, moving spatially from Catholic Italy to Protestant England and temporally from the late quattrocento to 1624, I will examine three chess games and how they eroticize or politicize the space in which the pieces move and the game is played.[1]

The first is a dance performed to the intense pleasure of Polifilo, lover of Polia and dreaming protagonist of Francesco Colonna's *Hypnerotomachia Polifili*, written in the 1460s and published by Aldus at Venice in 1499. Polifilo's dream takes him through a landscape in which ancient and enigmatic buildings, monuments, and gardens appear with Vitruvian clarity and mathematical specificity against a spatially indistinct background. Not much happens in the dream's narrative; rather, psychological struggles take place within Polifilo in what one critic aptly calls "the frozen space of ekphrasis."[2] Some such visually activating space asks with particular urgency to be read, covered as its architecture often is with hieroglyphs and partially erased—but hence all the more emotionally compelling—inscriptions. Polifilo obliges by studying the structures carefully, deducing from them evidence of lost architectural wisdom and on one occasion adding his own voice to what they might mean—entered into a recumbent colossus, he makes the ancient statue resound again by breathing forth a love complaint for his Polia. Never, though, does he write graffiti or responses on the building's esoteric but not quite incomprehensible walls. Mostly he looks and longs.

Eventually Polifilo comes to the palace of Queen Eleuterilida ("Free Choice," or "Free Will"), where after examining the architecture, gardens, and nymphs, and after a good feast complete with an ingenious portable hand-washing machine, he watches enraptured as thirty-two costumed damsels dance out a fast-moving chess game on the banquet room's coral- and red-flecked green checkered floor. The gold and silver "kings" direct the action, ordering their pieces here and there to the music's Greek modes. The flower-crowned and loose-tressed dancers make "high Capers and Turnes, without affectation of straying, as it should seeme with facilitie and careles ease at pleasure and sweet jestures" (I quote the 1592 English translation by Robert Dallington).[3] Even those taken "did presently kiss their Conqueror, and voyded the place." Nor do the kings play with chivalric prowess alone, for Polifilo reports that as the dance proceeded, "the lesser number that there was, the more pleasure it was to perceive the pollicies [Colonna has "deceptione"] of either sides to overcome the other." The game is loving, but like most games—especially chess and love—it inscribes a power struggle requiring strategy. Silver wins this game and the next, but the third victory goes to the gold. Presumably on some other occasion, at some other happy feast, the silver will have another chance.

To say that Colonna's work at times shows a remarkable and luxurious sensuality thanks to its loving gaze at arches, obelisks, and fountains may sound bizarre, but this extraordinarily beautiful book embellished with a multitude of strikingly lovely woodcuts is uncommonly stirring in its languid and leisurely way, even before we and Polifilo finally meet Polia. In a recent article, Donald Hedrick has explored this "erotics of Renaissance urban design," as he puts it.[4] The new interest in perspective and the techniques required to create its illusion, he suggests, accompanied a newly focused "visual mastery," perhaps because "When perspective space is applied to the body . . . it invites novel and therefore erotic points of view, depersonalizing the subject as it personalizes the viewer, whose active participation and judgement are required in the viewing of difficult foreshortenings."[5] This is, as he says, the dynamic at work in a disgracefully clever building by Bracelli that imitates a supine woman spreading her legs and a witty illustration in Dürer's *Painter's Manual* showing a man sketching on squared paper as he responds to his female model with an interest indicated by the stiffly vertical perspective rod in front of him. As an example of this "relationship between erotic obsessiveness and visual perspective," Hedrick cites the *Polifilo* and the embrace of the lovers "on the expanse of an empty architectural grid."

Hedrick does not mention Colonna's chess game, but the picture he reprints from the *Polifilo* may explain the effect of the dance on the dreaming lover. The floor is eight squares wide; perhaps (we cannot quite tell) it is also

Colonna's lovers shown against a checkered floor. *Hypnerotomachia Poliphili.* A Facsimile Edition. London: Methuen, 1904. Sig. C5v.

eight squares long.[6] My suggestion is that Colonna was encouraged to imagine his chess dance, unillustrated in his book, by the similarity of chessboards to the checkered floors that Renaissance artists like to depict precisely because, I assume, their squares diminish so neatly along the lines of perspective, giving an illusion of an exactly perceived spatial depth and guiding the viewer's eye into that depth, those penetralia. A chessboard, in fact, is not unlike the Albertian "window" that S. K. Heninger has associated with the development of secular and autonomous narrative.[7] Like the implied lines of vision in a strictly calculated Renaissance painting, the board's demarcations are necessarily fixed. But even more than Alberti's pictorial and perspectival "window," a chess window's play space (its fenestral frame, so to speak) gives onto—visually contains—human activity: the figures we see through or in the window actually move, and their movements tell a story of advance, retreat, feint, victory, and loss. The parallel is not be exact, to be sure, for in a chess game each player has his or her own point of view on the squares and along the lines of play. Looking at or through *this* window, observers can be participants.

As Polifilo watches the chessladies dance, his mind does not go to politics and war, despite the invigorating Doric and Phrygian modes to which the pieces move and despite the twists and developments of a performance mimicking a battle. Perhaps the female gender and waving hair of the dancers has something to do with what happens next, or perhaps the experience of perspective, of a sharpened spatial sense and focus, has given him even more practice in gazing, in the forward motion of sight and imagination. For soon Eleuterilida sends him, guided by her nymphs Reason (Logistica) and Will (Thelemia), to the land of Queen Telosia, in whose misty kingdom he may choose his telos, his aim and end, among the several offered him. To Reason's disgust but Will's delight, Polifilo prefers the way of sexuality, love, and pleasure. Soon he will see Polia, the love he has freely sought and for whose sight an energetic but spatially contained chess dance in a closely observed and mathematically proportioned Vitruvian palace has in part prepared him. He will eventually marry her, although whether a ceremony performed by Venus counts as obedience to family values is doubtful.

Colonna's chess dance drew the appreciative attention of the person or persons unknown who wrote the fifth book of *Gargantua et Pantagruel* (1564). For want of a better name I will call the author "Rabelais." This "Rabelais" could even include François Rabelais himself, who enjoyed Colonna.[8] Whoever "Rabelais" was, he knew how to play chess, and not any chess but the early modern kind. To understand his reworking of Colonna's dance it helps to recall what had been happening to the game.

The most significant change—established certainly in the late fifteenth century and probably in Italy—was to allow the bishop to sidle on his own color as far as he could along uninhabited squares and to allow the queen to move in any straight line with the same restriction.[9] This shift in the rules meant that play could proceed sooner to what had been the endgame, making games shorter and also requiring, for good play, a faster and cannier eye on the opponent's strategy. Bishops and queens no longer needed to take their time in working out their tactics while sauntering thoughtfully at the back of the field; they could now rush forward and penetrate deep into enemy territory, killing as they went, perhaps, but also taking new risks. Long a game of the elite, chess became more than ever a game of the brainy, the cunning, and the aggressive.

There is a gender issue here, too, or so thought those bemused by the new chess. Some even called it and its newly empowered queen "rabiosa," or "echés de la dame enragée": crazy-queen chess.[10] Arthur Saul, author of a useful *Famous game of chesse-play* (1614), fusses a bit, not very seriously, over how the new rules for chess do not parallel those customs rightly governing the sexes. In a preliminary poem describing the various pieces, he reassures us:

> Through all the houses of the field,
> the Queene may take her pleasure,

And use her power to helpe her King,
still in a modest measure.
If in her march shee prove severe,
and taketh all she may,
Tis for the safegard of the King,
that shee makes cleare the way.
For this she may not blamed be,
that seekes her King to save,
It is her glory for to strive[,]
her King in peace to have.[11]

But, in his often translated mock-epic chess poem, *Scacchia ludus*, the humanist Vida calls the queen an Amazon, a potentially troubling epithet that "Rabelais" and Saul adopt.[12] In Vida's Olympian chess game blood flows fast, partly thanks to the new rules, and the kings who direct the action are accomplished at trickery and deception. True, Vida retains chess's ancient connection to the erotic as well as to military discourse, for he tells how Mercury is much taken by a lovely nymph, Scacchis, whom he has observed feeding her swans; to repay her for her lost virginity, the god gives her a chessboard, pieces, and directions for play.[13]

Added at the last minute (they are missing from the manuscript), chapters 23 and 24 of "Rabelais's" *Cinquième livre* describe a chess ballet derived in large part from Colonna (with a touch of Vida) but expanded and revised so as to conform to the new game, the one with the crazy queen.[14] The scene has been little commented upon, perhaps because it is so derivative and because its function in this sharply satirical and seemingly anti-Catholic (or at least anticlerical) text is hard to determine.[15] It will be recalled that Pantagruel and crew are en route to the Oracle of the Bottle to see if Panurge should marry despite the probability (or even certainty) that he will be beaten, robbed, and cuckolded. In Colonna's terms, he must finally decide what his Thelemia, if not his Logistica, tells him should be his telos. The voyagers, island-hopping their way to the oracle, have landed in the kingdom of Entelechie, whose very name, indicating the realized will, seems to point to some combination of Eleuterilida and Telosia. At the very end of the book we return, in a sense, to the kingdoms of those two queens, for the Oracle of the Bottle lives in a cave owing (as has been noted) a great deal of its architecture and décor to Colonna, not least the inscription "TOUTES CHOSES CE MEUVENT A LEUR FIN." Nor is this universal movement wholly deterministic, despite another inscription that says the destinies move the willing and drag the reluctant. As David Quint has argued, the Oracle's wine tastes different to each drinker so as to suggest the role of choice, of freedom, of individual *teloi* in life, in faith, in hearing or reading the Word.[16]

How does a chess game fit a movement toward a willed choice that is also in some sense destined? If it prepares Panurge for his final ecstatic decision to marry, it does not do so directly, for there will be other islands and more anticlerical and antilawyer satire before the ship reaches the Oracle. Nor does the whole scene's implied criticism of frenzied ingenuity and novel inventiveness, although entertaining, seem crucial for this particular trickster to grasp. The dance itself does come, however, in the exact center of the book if one goes by chapters, and the entire chess section is central if one counts the book's prologue (it is typical of Renaissance texts to have at least two ways of centering or shaping a pattern). Indeed, the chief activity of the island—abstracting the fifth essence—seems pertinent both to a fifth book and to conceptions of space and its relation to the four elements. The structural centrality of the scene and the heavy indebtedness of the *Cinquième livre*'s concluding chapters to Colonna's architectural passages indicate not mere "borrowing" but full intertextual incorporation and recollection. Is there also a touch of friendly parody, such as may shimmer about the abbey of Thélème, a structure much affected by Polifilo's dream? Perhaps. Much of the language is from Colonna: "Rabelais" retains the dancers' politesse as they remove each other from play, the ancient modes to which the three games are danced, the admirable speed and grace of the "mille ruses, mille assaulx, mille desmarches," and the granting to each side a victory or two. The humor, though, depends chiefly on delight and hyperbole; outright satire is reserved for the island's officials hard at work manipulating space and matter so as, for example, to make something out of nothing, toss houses out their own windows, catch wind in nets, and rejuvenate hags.

Small but telling changes in the chess dance, however, show thought about how to encourage Panurge onward to his own kingdom of Telosia. Because "Rabelais" modernizes Colonna's game, his gold queen, together with her knight and archer (bishop), can scour the board like the Amazon Penthesilea; yet she is soon ambushed by the silver archer and "knight errant," and the narrator remarks (as a matter of immediate strategy, or is there also a social point to be made?) that she would be better advised to stay closer to her husband and venture forth, if she must do so, otherwise accompanied. If Panurge is paying attention he might have further cause to worry about wives. Some changes seem less relevant to his dilemma, such as the substitution of a portable cloth board for the checkered floor, although it would be typical of François Rabelais himself, so given to evasion and ambiguity, to replace a permanent and stable parquet with movable and supple fabric. Nor in these chapters is there such an explicit focus on classicized architecture and perspective as one finds in the *Polifilo* and its illustrations. True, regendering the game by making only the queen and pawns clearly female allows a different sort of sexual electricity, especially as the text retains Colonna's stress on the pleasure of the watchers' gaze.

Most significant for the spatiality of desire, I think, and for Panurge's quest to locate his personal Thelemia, is a change in the source of the dancers' wills. The matter of how and why we will is of course central to Reformation arguments, for much if not all Protestant thought presupposes severe limits on the will, specifically the individual will to do good except when it flows along with and is carried by the divine will. As an Erasmian and Evangelical Christian (for so I believe him to have been), the "real" François Rabelais does not in this regard follow Luther or Calvin all the way to the bound will or predestination; but despite scenes like that in which the baby Pantagruel smashes his confining cradle, neither does he suggest a full-fledged imperial self whose will is law. Although the *Cinquième livre* has struck some readers as more narrowly polemical, perhaps because less richly indecisive, than the first four books, the Oracle of the Bottle's ambiguities seem to me to express a quasi-Erasmian and indeed traditional desire to avoid extremes—although Luther might second the proclamation that our wills are free when they are God's (or what the inscription calls destiny's) and bound when they are not.

In this regard chess is a provocative game to think about when it is turned into a dance, allegory, or even a little girl's looking-glass dream. Who plays Alice's chess? Who plays Colonna's? We are not told. But then, who plays us, for that matter? If God plays, does he play only one side? And does he allow his pieces any will of their own? In the *Polifilo*, pieces move through the space of the board at the command of the gold and silver kings and who or what moves the kings remains mysterious—buried in the *arcana imperii*, perhaps, where many said royal secrets belong. But "Rabelais's" dancers seem to have two wills, as though they had already read the Oracle's inscription. On the one hand the narrator ascribes feelings and aims to them: they scheme, dissimulate, seek revenge, desire, and, like the reckless queen, blunder. At the same time he is clear that the dancers receive direction from the music. That is, they do not merely move *to* the sounds but are instructed *by* the sounds. Polifilo had been reminded by the chess musicians' changing modes of the old story that Timotheus had governed the spirit of Alexander through changing his music's harmonic proportions. "Rabelais" retains this touch, although confusing the musician's name; but by giving his chessmen more intentionality, depriving the kings of their command, and locating the directing wills off the checkered cloth yet still arguably in the larger play space, he establishes a paradoxical dynamic of will and destiny exactly suiting what Panurge will find at the Oracle.

It also suits, I would argue, the book's delicate balance between religious claims. Who in turn tells the musicians what to play is not, to be sure, specified, but there may be a vague implication of cosmic and possibly providential harmonies at work. In any case, the dance reminds the narrator of a spatial paradox, for he finds some dancers, whirling on their squares, moving so fast that they are like the tops whipped by small boys: they seem not to move, and yet if you put a spot of color on one, that bright point will become a continuous circular line as the top spins, just as, he says, Cusanus describes God. Evidently the theological possibilities of chess were not lost on "Rabelais." The members of Pantagruel's crew, in fact, not only laugh (which, as the narrator reminds us, is the peculiarity of humankind) but feel elevated to Olympus, drawn outside themselves by this "plus qu'humain" spectacle, and (in another paradox) are both moved and stunned. Especially since their hostess has by now disappeared, they are free to sail on.

Several generations later, in England, the Protestant playwright Thomas Middleton dramatized a very different game in his *Game at Chess*, an enormous succès de scandale in 1624. It too involves marriage, sexuality, the will, and space. A few years ago Paul Yachnin plausibly argued that Middleton's allegorical comedy was in part inspired by the living chess ballet in "Rabelais's" *Cinquième livre*; more recently the evidence for this has thinned out as the extent of Middleton's use of the 1618 chess guide by Saul and Barbier has become clearer.[17] The entire play and its purported triumph of truth, however, is presented—as though in a dramatized Liar's Paradox—as the story of Error's dream, and as a dream it sooner recalls Colonna. In any case, a link remains between Middleton and the *Cinquième livre* because Saul and Barbier appear themselves to have been reading "Rabelais" as well as Damiano and Vida. In a section he added, Barbier says the French call bishops "archers" and derive "rook" from "custode de la roche," which certainly sounds like "Rabelais." As for Saul, his opening poem on the various pieces seems to echo the similar list in the *Cinquième livre*, although some overlap in chess vocabulary is to be expected.

Middleton would have been struck by other passages in the *Famous game*. Chess, we read, is a civilized game involving no chance; allegorically "like unto a well composed Common wealth," it contains "many morall mysteries." The promotion of pawns can hearten us all, but the queens' warlike fashion suits women in some ancient "Utopian countrey"—that is, Amazons are fictitious. Some call rooks "dukes" (Middleton adopts this notion), but perhaps the *queen* should be a duke, in view of the piece's power to go "abroad to and fro, with that unlimited commaund" and lead "men to Battell."[18] In other words, dukes get around; queens should know their space and, in the terminology of the time, not stray far from their "houses," as Saul calls squares. Middleton will follow this thought by victimizing and virtually immobilizing his white queen and by advancing his dukes, a strategy that makes for poor chess but more plausible early modern English politics, at least now that Elizabeth—hardly "enragée" but certainly dangerous—was dead.

A Game at Chess, performed to huge and appreciative audiences for nine days in August of 1624, allegorizes Catholic attempts to undermine or convert the Church of England and, more precisely—if also more allusively—a surprise 1623 trip to Spain by Prince Charles and the duke of Buckingham, an adventure in which, not wholly unlike Panurge, the prince was at least ostensibly in search of a wife (and a treaty). Despite King James's desire for the match, a marriage he thought would serve his policy of détente with Madrid, the projected marriage to the Spanish king's young sister was unpopular in Protestant England, so when Charles returned home, wifeless and by now happy to be so, he was met with rejoicing. Like many other Englishmen, Middleton affected to see what was in fact a shabbily dishonest affair not as a matter of changed Spanish and English wills (the infanta did not want to marry a heretic, while Charles and the duke came home angry and bellicose) but of stout English wits at work in foiling the diabolical plots of a sly Catholic enemy implacably bent on world conquest by any means.

Buckingham seems to have gone along with this fiction. His protection (or that of some other anti-Spanish magnate), together with the public's enthusiasm and Middleton's flattery of a king who could not afford to notice the accompanying hints that he was easily duped, shielded those involved from the worst of the government's dismay and the Spanish embassy's outrage.[19] Chess had long allegorized war and politics as well as love: one medieval Hebrew chess poem has Edomites battling Ethiopians, and in the eighteenth century some chess pieces were carved to represent the "struggle between the East India Company and the native states."[20] Middleton's play, though, may be the first work in which chess laughingly evokes a man's escape from wedlock.

In Saul's nomenclature a square is a "house," thus making the board a town with sixty-four dwellings, but in Middleton's play both the Spanish and English sides are "houses" in a more dynastic sense: black and white, morally speaking, have long genealogies. In this chess game, pieces venture forth from "houses" that in the implied allegory are spatially distinct but capable of mutual intrusion. The threat, so legitimate in chess yet so terrifying in geopolitics and—perhaps—religion, is that the black side will further infiltrate, debauch, and deceive the white house, pervert white visitors to the black house, and eventually rule the whole board through trickery, intelligence gathering, and seduction. The world as it seemed to many in 1624 London, that is, had two sides and one was diabolical. Chess had often been read as a metaphor for human conflict, but the stakes were now higher and the entire world—earthly space—felt divided, segmented, into black and white: them and us, Catholic and Protestant, Spain and England. One side, in this view, wanted all space for itself, permanently, as witness its behavior around the globe. (That many Protestants wanted the same would not have seemed illogical, not when the alternative was the triumph of an evil empire and the limitation of God's word.) If all the world's a stage, then all the world can be a chess game—even the lines that Mercator and other cartographers projected across the globe might seem to make the whole earth a sort of chessboard, as though Alberti's window had been curved into a three-dimensional perspectival space ready for geopolitical narratives.[21]

The play opens with the recently canonized Ignatius Loyola back on Earth and looking around him for his followers: "I thought theyde spread over the World by this time / Coverd the Earths face and made darke the Land."[22] Angry, he awakens Error, who has been dreaming of "a game of Chesse / Betwixt our side and the Whitehouse, the men sett / In theire just order, readie to goe to it" (ll. 43–45). After a brief chat about chess (Error has been reading the 1618 Saul), the pair settles back to watch what Error says should be seen as his dream or vision. To the sound of music, the two sides assemble. In fact, Loyola says, he would "rule my selfe, not observe rule," for he "would doo anye thing to rule alone, / Tis rare to have the world reignd in by one," but he agrees to "see 'em anon, and marke 'em in theire playe, / Observe, as in a dance, they glide awaye" (ll. 56–81).

The play proper begins, expectedly enough, with moves by the pawns, from whom we hear how the Jesuits are at work around the world laboring for "Universall Monarchie." As the plot proceeds, involving notably the black side's attempted seduction and slander of the white queen's pawn, it is clear that the white house's space is too permeable, subject not only to the intrusions expected in chess but to what one might call "extraludic" maneuvering, treachery, and espionage. Some pieces may seem white (with names like Blanche and Bridget), but from their "Sanctuarie" in "the Whitefriers" and "the bowells of Bloomsburie" (2.1.233–36) they operate as black moles and black informants. In the first scene the arrogantly witty black knight (representing Count Gondomar, recently ambassador from Spain), had spelled it out: "The Busines of the Universall Monarchie / Goes forward well now," aided by "all Intelligences [i.e., reports from spies] possible / Thorough the Christian kingdomes" (1.1.264–68). One source of his "intelligence" is, shockingly, a seemingly white pawn; not that the black side is grateful, for the black knight secretly scorns this "Poore Jesuite ridden Soule" for being "foolde" out of his "Alleagance" with no safe place on the board: "Wch path so ere thou tak'st thou'rt a lost Pawne" (1.1.358–60).

Less pathetic and much more comic is the book-scribbling Fat Bishop, representing the portly and prolific bishop of Spalatro—once black, now passing as white, but inwardly blackhearted in his gluttony for food, money, drabs by the "Holesale," and ecclesiastical preferments: his bulk expands in space as the integrity of this "greasie turnecoate Gurmundizing Prelate" shrivels (2.2.44, 57). The black knight, whose contemptuous description this is, imagines the Fat Bishop as a sort of miniglobe, the "mund" in "Gurmundizing," maybe:

> Ile make him the Baloom [*sic*] Ball of the churches
> And both the sides shall tosse him, hee lookes like one,
> A thing sweld up with mingled drinck and Urine
> And will bound well from one side to another![23]

The black knight in fact has globes almost literally on the brain. Aiming at planetary empire and thinking of the Fat Bishop as a balloon, he imagines his own brain as a mapped sphere. If the Fat Bishop pens "Fat and fulsome Volumes" (2.2.59), the black knight rewrites the world. In a frank conversation with his pawn he explains. The pawn has just told him that a plot of his has been discovered, to which he has merely replied, "Wch of the twentie thousand and nine hundred / Fourescore and five, canst tell?" The pawn is understandably impressed, if confused, noting that mere peasants have "but one plott / To Keepe a Cowe on." To make him understand, the knight asks him to remember the globe in his study. Oh yes, replies the pawn, "A thing Sir full of Cuntryes, and hard words." Well, says his master, "Just such a thing (if ere my Skull bee opend) / Will my Braynes looke like, . . . and some M[aster]-Politician / That has sharpe State Eyes will goe neere to pick out / The plotts, and everie Clymate where they fastened." Readers of his cerebral globe will "neede use Spectacles" to read the plots inscribed on it, he boasts, but in fact the "white Knights policie" has just uncovered one of the black knight's treacherous letters. This Machiavel is more legible than he thinks.

The following scenes see the black knight planning to "entrap" the white knight in the "black house" (a political allusion, of course, to marriage with the infanta and a treaty emancipating English Catholics) and the black side's continued efforts to seduce the white queen's pawn. Even white pieces, though, however reluctantly—"What a payne it is / For Truth to fayne a litle" (4.4.17–18), says the white king sadly to the white duke—must look about them and indulge in "policy." As the struggle intensifies, the white queen, who may represent the Church of England, is nearly "taken" by the Fat Bishop. Luckily, the white bishop (George Abbot, some say) rescues her and thus prevents a "Master check." In real chess, queens are fearsome protectors of the king; here, with a compliment to James I as head of the church, the white king tells the still trembling queen that "The doves house is not safer in the Rock / Then thou in my firme bosome" (4.4.85–86)—a loving sentiment, even if Saul might object that this nesting of bodies breaks the rule of one piece to a square. Foiled and himself taken, the Fat Bishop is put into the off-board bag, the repository of captured pieces sometimes moralized in the Middle Ages and Renaissance as the equalizing realm of death but here a seriocomic version of the older morality plays' Hell-mouth.

Toward the play's end, the white duke and knight are made welcome by the major black pieces and treated to some remarkably open admissions of black voracity for empire, a hunger expressed through metaphors of consumption at "the large Feast of our Vast Ambition" (5.3.92). Getting the black side fully to acknowledge its evil, the white duke and knight perform a checkmate "by discovery," a punning reference to a maneuver in which one piece moves so that another of the same color will thereby, without moving, automatically exert a checkmate. Their king captured and with (suggests the buried pun) no black "mate" for the white side, the black pieces tumble squabbling into the bag that "like Hell opens / To take her due" (5.3.197–98). The white pieces rejoice with (I think) some common Protestant puns on "room" and "Rome," early modern pronunciation encouraging such bitter spatial jokes on Roman expansion; then, thanking Heaven, the white knight orders the bag closed: "the fittest Wombe / For trecherie pride and malice" (5.3.238–39).[24] Despite defiant black threats, there is no indication either that it is ever to be reopened (Protestants, especially, argued that no one leaves Hell) or that any white pieces are in it. The black house has found its sphere, its room/Rome, for its paths of glory on the chessboard have, in its case, led but to an internal uterine but—so far as we know—infertile cul de sac (or *sac de cul*).

Middleton's play is indeed a game of chess, if a disheveled one,[25] yet its political wish is something no chess game could survive—that the black and white houses remain apart, not penetrate each other through espionage, corruption, or even sex and marriage. Unlike the *Cinquième livre,* this is implicitly—if only implicitly, for there were limits to Middleton's daring—a drama about *not* getting married, about staying put so as to avoid ideological exogamy. It is the black side that is just as sex-obsessed and penetration-oriented as many English Protestants supposed Catholics to be: the black urge to expand, to tumesce into full spherical imperium, is both expressed and disguised by its discourse of love and desire. For in truth the black house offers not a wife but the great Whore herself; in Panurge's terms, the white knight escapes an entanglement that would get his whole house, particularly its church, beaten, robbed, and cuckolded.

In this regard two other spatial issues are pertinent. First, whereas Pantagruel's crew leaves the mainland to island-hop toward the Oracle of the Bottle, the fear in Middleton's play (and in Middleton's England) is that the island kingdom will be absorbed by the Continent, swallowed by the nation and religion so often, in the Renaissance, symbolized by cannibal giants and in this play by geophagous gourmands.[26] England, that is, perceived its geographical marginality as providential protection against being beguiled and ingested by Madrid and Rome. The island is not the *Cinquième livre*'s Lucianic and fantasy "other"; the island is a besieged home.

Second, although I hesitate to make too much of this, is the function in some theological disputes of disagreements over the nature of space itself, including how space relates to bodies and eating. Jerzy Limon has made an especially compelling case that *A Game at Chess* thinks about the cosmos, not just about the Spanish marriage, and that it represents larger religious struggles.[27] Even he, though, defines the ideological questions largely in terms of power, of what many Protestants took to be a diabolical Catholic desire for empire under one tyrannical will. Several specifically doctrinal disagreements, however, also involved spatial (and linguistic) issues. For example, can two bodies inhabit the same space and can one body be simultaneously in two places? Modern common sense and Newtonian physics find such questions merely risible. Post-Heisenberg physics is at least a little less sure.[28]. The issues are not frivolous. Is the risen Christ's body wholly present on each altar during the mass, and, if so, can he be simultaneously in Heaven? Protestants who deny this simultaneous location, says the Catholic William Rainolds (for example), argue like pagans from mere Euclidian or Aristotelian assumptions about space.[29] Not that all Protestants adopted an Aristotelian view of bodies; Adam Hill, for instance, devotes much effort to showing how on Easter Saturday Christ could be wholly in the grave and wholly in Hell.[30] For the most part, though, it was Catholics who had more stake in what were soon to seem like unscientific conceptions of bodies in space, for if space is quite homogeneous and if bodies are finally distinct, even when apparently merged like water mixed with wine, then certain doctrines become harder—although many would say not impossible—to maintain.

Chess, I hope it is not too trivial to say, is in this regard an unambiguously Aristotelian game. One piece, one space, and no fair having two pieces on one or one piece on two; newcomers to a space must therefore expel the old, while vacators of a space open it to a new occupant. In Eucharistic terms, I suppose, *con*substantiation is quite impossible, whereas *trans*substantiation breaks the rules by having one body in two locations. True, the procedures for checks and checkmates imply that *energy* is less spatially confined by borders. My point may seem impertinent in every sense, but the fact is that chess haunts the mind more than most games and one reason, I suspect, is how it treats space. Middleton's play wisely ignores overtly theological arguments, but those arguments rendered even more acute the concern it registers about replacement and removal—and even consumption, for Protestant attacks on the mass were often expressed through worried or contemptuous sneers at Catholic "cannibalism."[31]

It is this dread of, and relief at so far escaping, hostile takeover and ingestion that energizes *A Game at Chess.* The takeover would mean the physical removal or blackification of white pieces and the rewriting of the planet's surface (to say nothing of Rome's continued scribbles atop God's Word), for the play geopoliticizes the flat chessboard into a sphere at risk of becoming a universal empire of evil. Chess slips outdoors, out of Polifilo's and "Rabelais's" perspectival and festive architecture of desire, and into the cold shadow war against the hungry "Other's" inflated will. Far from being inspired to marry by a focused and delighted perspective on an indoors chess dance, the white knight plays in an outdoors game so cleverly, with such suspicious "wit-wondrous strength, / And *circum*spective Prudency"[32] that he avoids losing his virtue and protects his friends from capture.

Is his cleverness his own? He and the other pieces self-consciously play themselves, in a sense; one frontispiece shows them doing so. Unlike Colonna's

Middleton's chessmen play the great game. Title page from Thomas Middleton, *A Game at Chess* (1625). By permission of the Beineke Library, Yale University.

chessmen, however, they receive scant instruction from their kings, and although there is music the pieces do not seem directed by it. Has the Protestant Middleton discovered free will—liberated his knight's Thelemia if not given it a marital telos? Not entirely, for while the black house appears voluntarily to serve a satanic overlord, the play also hints that Providence plays all the pieces, perhaps inspiring the willing and dragging along the recalcitrant by some inaudible off-board music of its own. Unlike Polifilo's and "Rabelais's" chess dances, however, this comedy rejoices not in festive, implicitly erotic, and lighthearted games to be replayed with different music and different outcomes, but in a single conflict played just once and for keeps. In real chess, luckily, we can take turns being white or black and challenge our victors to a rematch. But in real history, as it turned out, Protestantism's white knight escaped the infanta only to marry Henrietta Maria, a daughter of the now Catholic and Stuart-friendly house of Bourbon. On the real globe, after all, there are more than two sets of players—and more than two colors.[33]

Notes

1. This essay began as a paper read at the 1992 Sixteenth-Century Conference and the MLA in sessions organized by my colleague, Catherine Randall; the topic was Protestant constructions of space. I thank Skiles Howard, who read this essay while finishing a dissertation at Columbia on dance and space, for her challenging queries: when, for example, is space an unbound void (to the extent that Renaissance thinking allowed for a void) and when is it imagined as some sort of matter? Can a void be segmented? Does segmenting it make it more nearly material and hence more subject to power and erotic charge?

2. On the edifice's enigmatic quality and alternation with undefined space, see Gilles Polizzi, "L'Esthétique de l'énigme: le spectacle et le sens dans le *Songe de Poliphile*," *Rivista di letterature moderne e comparate* 41 (1988): 209–33; "l'espace pétrifié de l'*ekphrasis*" is on p. 211. See also his "Le Songe de Poliphile: Renovation ou metamorphoses du genre littéraire," in *Le Songe à la Renaissance*, ed. Françoise Charpentier (n.p., 1989), 85–97. There is some question about which Francesco Colonna wrote the *Polifilo*. Since the acrostic formed by the chapter headings includes "Frater," I prefer the traditional ascription to the Venetian monk—and, as A. Kent Hieatt (who read this essay with astute attention) reminds me, internal evidence shows that the author must have lived near Venice for a long time.

3. R[obert] D[allington], *The strife of love in a dreame*, ed. Lucy Gent (Delmar, N.Y.: Scholars' Facsimiles & Reprints, 1973), 137. The translation is sometimes called loose; it is indeed partial, but often (as here) closer to Colonna than Jean Martin's 1546 French translation. Some of Dallington's wording, such as calling his pawns "nymphs" and the specifying of Alexander as the monarch affected by his musician, seem to recollect *Gargantua et Pantagruel*, 5.23–24. Dallington knew Rabelais well, quoting him several times in his *View of Fraunce* (1604); like Rabelais, he uses a version of chess introduced after Colonna wrote (see below, 230 n. 8) and thus modernizes the dance somewhat.

4. Donald Keith Hedrick, "The Ideology of Ornament: Alberti and the Erotics

of Renaissance Urban Design," *Word & Image* 3 (January 1987): 111–37. I am less persuaded that the lines of sight he traces are "masculinist" (118) in their ideology and not merely masculine in their erotic perspective.

5. Ibid., 118–19.

6. There are two inverted scallop shells in the arches near the lovers; this was (and is) a common motif in architectural decoration, but it is appropriate here: mythographers called this shell a sign of Venus because she rose from the sea and because "concha" was Roman slang for vulva.

7. S. K. Heninger Jr., *The Subtext of Form in the English Renaissance: Proportion Poetical* (University Park: Pennsylvania State University Press, 1994), chap. 5 ("Alberti's Window: The Rhetoric of Perspective"). Like those of many other scholars, my own perspectives on space, form, and story in early modern England are much indebted to Heninger's work on Renaissance cosmology, literary structure, and spatiality.

8. On Rabelais and Colonna, see A. Kent Hieatt and Anne Lake Prescott, "Contemporizing Antiquity: The *Hypnerotomachia* and Its Afterlife in France," *Word & Image* 8 (spring 1992): 291–321; the article cites earlier work I omit here. Robert J. Clements, "The Chess Ballet: A Faraway Vision of Pantagruel and Polifilo," in *Connaissance de l'étranger: Mélanges offerts à la mémoire* de Jean-Marie Carré (Paris: Didier, 1964), 224–39, tries to calculate the degree of borrowing (he may exaggerate) and to sort out the more elaborate game that "Rabelais" invents; Clements seems unaware that the rules of chess had changed. It is usually said that Rabelais used the Italian original, not Martin's 1546 translation, although the opening of chapter 23 ("Le soupper parfait, fut en présence de la dame fait un bal") seems to me closer to the start of Martin's chapter ("Le banquet prodigue achevé, la royne . . . ordonna . . . un bal") than to Colonna, who has no parallel introductory phrase and starts the chess game further along in the chapter. Perhaps, then, the author(s) of the *Cinquième livre* had consulted Martin.

9. Henry J. R. Murray, *A History of Chess* (Oxford: Clarendon Press, 1913) gives a detailed history of the game's nomenclature, rules, and social status. For a convenient bibliography, see Karl-Ludwig Selig, "*Don Quixote* and the Game of Chess," in *The Verbal and the Visual: Essays in Honor of William Sebastian Heckscher* (New York: Italica Press, 1990), 203–11.

10. Murray, *History of Chess*, 777. Originally the "queen" had been the shah's male adviser—his "farzin"; European players soon regendered the piece, although long retaining the now mystifying name "fers."

11. Arthur Saul, *Famous game of chesse-play* (1614), sig. A8v.

12. *The Game of Chess: Marco Girolamo Vida's Scacchia Ludus*, ed. Mario A. Di Cesare (Nieuwkoop: De Graaf, 1975). So, too, Odemira da Damiano in *Ludus Scacchiae: A game, both pleasant, wittie, and politicke* (I give the 1597 title of the English translation; this edition includes "G. B.'s" fragmentary English version of Vida), sig. A2v, describing modern chess. An anonymous imitation of Vida in *Musarum Deliciae* (1655) calls the queen "Amazonian," specifically likening her to "our sixt Henryes Margaret"; see the facsimile edition with an introduction by Tim Raylor (Delmar, N.Y.: Scholars' Facsimiles and Reprints, 1985), sig. D6.

13. Murray, *History of Chess*, 183–85, notes that since in their language "rukh"—the origin of our "rook"—is a homonym for "cheek," Arabic love poets liked to pun by telling, for example, of a shah captured by two smooth and rosy (female) rooks.

14. The touch of Vida shows in calling the queen an Amazon and the bishops archers (in the *Polifilo* they are "secretaries" or "counsel-keepers").

15. But see Florence Weinberg, "Chess as a Literary Idea in Colonna's *Hypnerotomachia* and in Rabelais' *Cinquiesme Livre*," *Romanic Review* 70 (summer 1979): 321–35. This thought-provoking article reads both texts as tracing a Platonic movement from sense to reason (represented by the rationality of chess) to love (Polifilo's choice of a venereal telos and Panurge's Bacchic joy in the oracle's cave); she also thinks the triumph of gold represents a solar masculine perfection overcoming a more sluggish feminine lunar mutability. The presence of Bacchic Christian ecstasy in these texts' eventual celebrations of love is very likely, yet I suspect that Colonna, especially, is willing to affirm the continuing value of eros in and of itself, notably in a loyal and noble lover. In other words, progress there may be, but as Polifilo scales Plato's ladder he takes the lower rungs with him.

16. David Quint, *Origin and Originality in Renaissance Literature: Versions of the Source* (New Haven: Yale University Press, 1983), 192–206. Quint thinks the *Cinquième livre* by Rabelais; the complexity and insight, not just the extent, of the intertextual gestures toward Colonna do show a subtle imagination at work.

17. Paul Yachnin, "*A Game at Chess* and Chess Allegory," *SEL* 22 (spring 1982): 317–30, cites the prologue's discussion of chess pieces, a stress on the knight's "ability to plan ahead," and indeed the whole black side's capacity for dissimulation, the role of music, a tripartite structure to the procedure of play (three games in "Rabelais," two advances for black and a victory for white in Middleton), an allusion to children picking kernels from dung that resembles an earlier passage in Rabelais, and the prologue's comparison of Middleton's play to a dance. N. W. Bawcutt, "New Light on Middleton's Knowledge of Chess," *NQ* 232 (1987): 301–2, shows that the prologue's passage on nomenclature and the use of "duke" for "rook" (facilitating the allegory, for the white duke represents the duke of Buckingham) more probably derive from Barbier's additions to Saul.

18. Saul, *Famous game of chesse-play*, sigs. C3^{v}–C4.

19. There has been debate as to who protected Middleton, whether he needed protection (few that summer were pro-Spanish, and it may be that what disturbed James was the impudence of representing him on the public stage), whether the last-minute topical allusions distract us from more basic allegory about good and evil, whether the white side escapes Middleton's irony. On such issues I have found particularly useful: T. H. Howard-Hill, "The Origins of Middleton's *A Game at Chess*," *Research Opportunities in Renaissance Drama* 28 (1985): 3–14; Paul Yachnin, "*A Game at Chess:* Thomas Middleton's 'Praise of Folly,'" *MLQ* 48 (June 1987): 107–23, who also suggests that Middleton plays an older moralistic allegory against up-to-date diction; and Neil Taylor and Bryan Loughrey, "Middleton's Chess Strategies in *Women Beware Women*," *SEL* 24 (spring 1984): 341–54, who comment on the usefulness of chess to allegory. Richard Davies and Alan Young, "'Strange Cunning' in Thomas Middleton's *A Game at Chess*" *UTQ* 14 (spring 1976): 236–45, hear an irony in the treatment of the white side inaudible to some other critics; Margot Heinemann, *Puritanism and Theatre: Thomas Middleton and Opposition Drama under the Early Stuarts* (Cambridge: Cambridge University Press, 1980), may exaggerate the playwright's "Puritanism," but makes a good case that strongly Protestant writers were not always antitheatrical. For the political and cultural energies at work behind and in the play, see in particular Jerzy Limon, *Dangerous Matter: English Drama and Politics in 1623/24* (Cambridge: Cambridge University Press, 1986).

20. Murray, *History of Chess*, 526–28, 183–85.

21. Once a world is the play space, furthermore, players lose the rationality and safety of a frame. The Spanish "house" in Middleton's play is terrifying in part because its game is literally without limit. On Alberti's window, story, and projections beyond the frame, see Heninger, *Subtext,* esp. 167.

22. I quote the edition by R. C. Bald (Cambridge: Cambridge University Press, 1929), induction, lines 6–7; here and elsewhere, I normalize *i* and *j, u* and *v.*

23. 2.2.78–81. The bishop, greedy and ambitious though he was, and angry though he made all sides, seems in some regards to have been what later Christians would call "ecumenical"; nowadays the Vatican and Lambeth might ask him to head an interfaith committee.

24. Uncomfortable in the crowded bag, the Fat Bishop objects that "The Bishop must have Roome, hee will have roome, / And roome to lye [another pun?] at pleasure," to which the play's "Jesting pawn" replies, "All the bagg I thinke / Is roome too scant for youre Spoletta-Paunce" (5.3.211–14).

25. Middleton's knowledge of chess is unclear; for a defense and analysis, see John R. Moore, "Middleton's 'Game at Chesse,'" *PMLA* 50 (June 1935): 761–68.

26. For a psychologically relevant configuration of islands near mainland giants, see a map in André Thevet's *Grand insulaire* (c. 1586) of what is now southern Chile, reproduced in *Art et légendes d'espaces: figures du voyage et rhétoriques du monde,* ed. Christian Jacob and Frank Lestringant (Paris: Presses de l'école normale supérieure, 1981), 10.

27. *Dangerous Matter,* 98–129. Limon is particularly helpful on English dread of Spain's global ambitions and Jesuit trickery; arguing that the real players of the game are, finally, God and the devil, he too notes the frequency with which the black house thinks in the sexual terms that Protestants often associated with Catholic clergy and the Antichrist.

28. See Richard Sorabji, *Matter, Space, and Motion: Theories in Antiquity and Their Sequel* (Ithaca: Cornell University Press, 1988). On late-twentieth-century views see, although I am not expert enough to judge its accuracy, Paul Davies and John Gribbin, *The Matter Myth* (New York: Simon and Schuster, 1992), particularly chap. 7, "Quantum Weirdness." Space—at least very small and very large space—is once more nonhomogeneous and unpredictable, with somewhat more room for non-Euclidean geometry and non-Aristotelian logic.

29. *A refutation of sundry reprehensions, cavils, and false sleightes . . .* (Paris, 1583), sigs. M1–M2, which attacks his Protestant opponent for basing arguments against the real presence on Aristotle, Euclid, and rules of nature known even to mere "prentises and artisans in their shops." Rainolds is reacting to complaints such as that by William Fulke in *D. Heskins, D. Sanders and M. Rastell overthrowne* (1579), sig. L2v, that Catholic belief "that one bodie may be in another, and two bodies in one place" is "against naturall Philosophie and reason."

30. *The defence of the article: Christ descended into hell* (1592).

31. See Frank Lestringant, "Catholiques et cannibales: Le thème du cannibalisme dans le discours protestant au temps des guerres de religion," in *Pratiques et discours alimentaires à la renaissance,* ed. J.-C. Margolin and Robert Sauzet (Paris: Maisonneuve et Larose, 1982), 233–35. (It may be no accident that the future's understanding of space-time is neatly represented on the TV series *Star Trek* by the crew's fondness for three-dimensional chess, while Heninger's Alberti might have been amused to know that someday people would play chess in the virtual and mathematical space of "Windows.")

32. P. 47; my emphasis.

33. In turning gold and silver to white and black, is Middleton's play implicitly racist? The Spanish, although not the Hapsburg family itself, were darker than the English, but I think Middleton takes advantage of an old, and not just European, moral division.

Donne's Recreative Misogyny: The Critic as Spoilsport

STANLEY STEWART

> Don't take it as a matter of course, but as a remarkable fact, that pictures and fictitious narratives give us pleasure, occupy our minds.
>
> ("Don't take it as a matter of course" means: find it surprising, as you do some things which disturb you. Then the puzzling aspect of the latter will disappear, by your accepting this fact as you do the other.)
>
> ((The transition from patent nonsense to something which is disguised nonsense.))
>
> —Wittgenstein, *Philosophical Investigations*

I.

FRIEDRICH Nietzsche once remarked on the philosopher's idiosyncratic lack "of historical sense." Since critical theorists today are often, if unwittingly, "practicing philosophers,"[1] his observation relates to the situation of current literary studies, where criticism is moving on from theory to metatheory. Critics are becoming so overwhelmed by contemporary interests that self-concern replaces forthright interest in the past, and "abuse" replaces "use" of "history for life."[2] When history and the literary forms that are a part of history fail to comport with preferred explanations and beliefs, critics advancing those explanations and beliefs object to historical figures, their works, and often to "historicized" characterizations of those works. Then, since it is not achievement but character that counts, history devolves into psychohistory.

Nowhere is this tendency more evident than in recent Donne criticism, where we hear from some quarters that John Donne was a poet of the most disagreeable sort, that there is a "pitiless element in Donne's nature,"[3] that he was self-absorbed, adolescent, selfish, domineering, and by turns "homophobic,"[4] "homosexual" with sex,[5] and "homosexual" without sex (Halley, "Textual Intercourse," 197). More ominously, John Donne had "contempt for large segments of the human race" (Carey, *John Donne,* 96, 100, 106, 107)—women, for instance. He took advantage of the illiteracy of Anne, his wife, perhaps preventing her from becoming literate, and he made Anne have too many babies. Closer to home, Donne employed devices of domination and enforced "forms of oppression" for "homophobic purposes." He talked and wrote too much; he was "bulimic,"[6] and the more he talked and wrote the more he frustrated Anne's literary aspirations. At last, Donne drove his wife into protracted silence, which expressed itself in the absence of her voice from an array of genres and a variety of topics in which she might have been interested: "Amid the great torrent of words that her husband let loose, Anne Donne is silent" (Halley, "Textual Intercourse," 188). But Donne did more than dominate the conversation. He showed himself to be a coward, a turncoat, a careerist, a poseur, an abuser of language, and above all a terrible misogynist: "There is in many of the *Elegies* a persistent misogyny, indeed a revulsion at the female body. . . ."[7]

We cannot investigate all of these charges at once, so let us begin modestly. Assuming for the moment that all of these characterizations of Donne are fair, what are we to make of critics who admire his elegies and off-color lyrics? Assumptions underlying much of this misogyny-talk about Donne tend to picture the poet as a literary transgressor and by extension to see his admirers as vicariously transgressing through him. In this analysis, the concept of transgression concerns the imagined enjoyment of poet and critic; that is, transgression is the *mode* of literary enjoyment. This argument seems to require that the critics making the observation place themselves in a position to judge transgressive enjoyments by refraining from them, which assumption leads to this question: Why are these Donne critics not enjoying themselves? Obviously, critics of rectitude could say that they do not, should not, and cannot enjoy what is patently offensive. Certainly it does appear that gynocentric critics in particular seem to expect only "acrid rewards" (Halley, "Textual Intercourse," 203) from their efforts to extract from Donne's writings—from his letters as well as from his poetry—an accurate portrait of Anne Donne as the repressed victim of the poet's "masculinist ideology."

It seems to me that something is wrong with these contradictory characterizations of Donne, and I suspect that (as is often the case) the critical talk—rather than the poetry talked about—is the source of confusion. Perhaps we should expect confusion in what is a manifestly thriving Donne industry. For the hostility toward Donne that has been registered does not indicate flagging interest in his work. On the contrary, John R. Roberts has shown that, notwithstanding the obituaries for Donne's reputation published earlier in the century, articles and books on Donne run into the thousands of items;[8] and the Donne *Variorum* now underway may be the most successful collaborative venture in Renaissance studies of the century. Nevertheless a dissonant note in a usually harmonic chorus of critical voices arises from one inherently subjectivist bent in criticism, which deprecates and often reviles the recreative functions of Donne's more irreverent poems, especially the elegies. Where Donne makes fun, these critics make serious.

While attacking Donne's recreatively irreverent poetry, this hieratic order of critics, who sometimes refer to themselves as "radical feminists" or "cultural materialists," will claim that theirs is "not an *ethical* criticism."[9] This claim deserves close scrutiny, partly because it suggests that these critics would evade the stigma of normative statements, for if theirs *were* "an *ethical* criticism," its persuasive value would be diminished. Hence, the function of the disclaimer. But analysis shows that, in the oppositional rhetoric of such discussions, even the guise of "transgressive criminal or critical thoughts" purports to gain from this species of utterance the social values of "sincerity" and "nonhypocritical" prestige that, presumably, accompanies subversive, antibourgeois thought. We see, for instance, that Thomas Docherty arrogates an honorific status to his claim of having pronounced "the first critical, even criminal word on Donne" (*John Donne, Undone*, 9). Given this claim, we might ask: How, if critical remarks about Donne can be praised for their "criminal" and "transgressive" features, can we depreciate Donne's poetic achievement on the grounds that his poetry possesses repugnant, asocial characteristics? In pursuing an answer to that question, I suggest that we investigate the assumption that Donne critics err in enjoying Donne's recreational misogyny and in taking delight in the "image of Donne as a rakish young cad" (62). I question the minatory challenge to the "harmlesse follie of [Donne's] time," and I do so because some of Donne's best poems succeed, not in spite of, but *because* of their rakish, insouciant, male-to-the-marrow speakers. I should therefore like to inquire into the propriety of characterizing Donne's poetry as "misogynist" and a cruel calumny against women. This inquiry leads to the ethical question of how critics decide that, because these poems are "sick" (Fish, "Masculine Persuasive Force," 223), "adolescent," "selfish," "pitiless" (Carey, *John Donne,* 269, 100, 95), "phallocentric",[10] and full of "contempt for . . . women,"[11] they are as a result unworthy subjects of criticism and/or unsuited to the classroom.

II.

Let us take a close look at one picture of Donne-as-misogynist. Stanley Fish says his distaste for arch-rhetorician Donne stems from the fact that his "act of writing is gendered in ways that have been made familiar to us by recent feminist criticism" ("Masculine Persuasive Force," 228). Here, a well-known critic confesses that his reluctance to teach Donne derives from—is an effect of—his reading of "feminist criticism." That is, feminist criticism as he construes it is in some way responsible for the picture Fish has of Donne, in whose works, "The male author, like God, stands erect before the blank page of a female passivity" (228), exercising the creative power of language to manipulate audiences. The alternative to such masculine power is "the *feminine* principle"—egoless passivity—which is the logical opposite of "*self*-assertion." "The *feminine* principle" entails passivity; one lays oneself open to be acted upon. Now, one surrenders. In contrast, Donne is always domineering; he is, like God, "a self-aggrandizing bully" (241). Although more often than not Donne directs his aggression "against women" (229), still—and this is where the assumptions of the rhetorician intrude (assumptions which impute "depth" to language)[12]—Fish thinks that Donne is actually worried about his own identity in relation to this "*feminine* principle." The controversial nature of this characterization is evident if we recall that one critic finds in Donne "very tender feelings for several of his male friends" (Klawitter, "Verse Letters to T.W.," 86)—so tender in fact that it approximated "an obsession" (95) with Thomas Woodward and showed itself in "highly charged homoeroticism" (100). So the "masculine power" of Donne's voice is not at all self-evident.

Indeed, such divergent views of the "same" Donne's sexual temperament suggest the lengths to which the game of "reading as" may be taken. The same Donne canon provides for a composite portrait of a virtual Proteus of conflicting sexual impulses. The good news is that this is a game any critic can play; the bad news—which explains why the game is so popular—is that it is also a game no one can lose (because no one can win). Some players, apparently less fond of the "gender" game, advance political explanations, implying that interest in Donne's "misogynistic" poems is not entirely misplaced: "Donne's Ovidian elegies reflect some of the social and economic struggles of Inns-of-Court gentlemen who were involved not only in their immediate urban surroundings but in the larger society as well."[13] Again, Donne might be thinking of Queen Elizabeth as "a threat to patriarchy": "The *Elegies* suggest that Donne was deeply disturbed that the old hierarchical order was threatened by a blurring of gender and sex distinctions" (Guibbory, "Oh, Let Mee Not Serve So," 829). But for "gender feminists,"[14] the game is nothing if not serious, so serious, in fact, that they are inclined, after traducing Donne, to turn on his "(male) critics": "Most (male) critics seem to have condoned an image of Donne as a rakish young cad" (Docherty, *John Done, Undone*, 62).

In this context, "condone" implies more than overlooking or pardoning Donne. Offending critics appear immune to disapprobation; they even enjoy Donne. Clearly, Docherty does not condone Donne's critics' condoning of "Donne as a rakish young cad," but since his disclaimer imputes a negative value to any supposed ethical dimension of critical analysis, let us set that issue aside for the moment to consider the question of the "gender feminist's" condemnation of particular "(male) critics." The point here is that, for "gender critics," gender is important. By placing the word "male" in parentheses, Docherty draws attention to the demographics of the critical landscape. At the same time, the critic (presumably "male" [*Thomas* Docherty]) implies that in his case the issue of gender is beside the point because he either never had the capacity to enjoy Donne's persona as "rakish young cad," or if he ever could and did enjoy it, he rid himself of both the pleasure and the capacity to experience it before undertaking the critical task. Like Fish's registering of attitudes learned from feminist critics, Docherty's awareness of the faults of "(male) critics" results from his reading of the "gender feminists." What worries me here is the question of credulity: Has Docherty (and Fish's) reading of the "gender feminists" been informed by a proper skepticism? Docherty's proclaimed awareness, which is consistent with his purported "transgressive" style of criticism, pits him against an imagined hegemonic "(male)" Donnean. But what is the criterion for the application of this label, "hegemonic"? Why is enjoyment of the typical speaker of typical Donne elegies a gender issue for Docherty, Fish, and other (though by no means all) feminist critics?

Docherty and Fish are not alone in their misogyny talk: "A number of Donne's poems," Michael Schoenfeldt asserts, "are incorrigibly implicated in the most repressive forms of Renaissance patriarchy."[15] "Repression" and "patriarchy" are at their best not much sought after, but in this analysis, Donne was "implicated" in both, and "incorrigibly" so. We might ask: Why is this? For even if we set aside the epistemological implications of what a proof of an "incorrigibly implicated" assertion would look like, we would still be left with the odd assumption that there is a difference between "corrigibly" and "incorrigibly" implicated proponents of patriarchal repression—an oddity within an oddity. Are there poets who, although implicated to some comparatively lesser degree, are *not* "incorrigibly implicated in the most repressive forms of Renaissance patriarchy"? If so, how do we teach critics who don't perceive that difference to perceive it? But if not, what work, if any, is the word "incorrigibly" doing here?

The shared assumption of these critics seems to be that enjoyment of "incorrigibly implicated" texts results from "masculinist ideology," which is not only limited in its outlook but defensive as well: "This sexist approach to the poetry is in some degree anti-critical, even anti-intellectual, for it refuses to discover anything which is genuinely troublesome or problematic for the masculinist ideology within which it is written" (Docherty, *John Donne, Undone,* 62). In a telling appeal to a mental state as the relevant criterion of judgment, Schoenfeldt argues that the alternative to this line of thought would be "our aesthetic or ideological discomfort" ("Patriarchal Assumptions," 25). If I understand correctly, what such criticism regards as a gender lapse on the part "of most [Donne] critics"—namely, the failure to experience "discomfort," and, in fact, to take pleasure in "masculinist ideology"—is responsible for the erroneous production in "masculinist ideology" in Donne texts of the "ignorance of woman."

The logic of this line of thought is hard to see. It seems to require that a sexual utopia exist prior to any legitimate enjoyment of Donne's poetry. And the idea of a "hierarchized" system of critical reactions seems to be likewise confused, for it presupposes the availability of an alternative, non-"hierarchized"—or horizontal, "egalitarian"—system. Don't we justify vindictiveness by positing an element of choice? Unless we are talking about a fictive sexual utopia, we must be talking about a comparative system of judgment in which dimorphism cannot appear. I am aware that Janel Mueller tries to justify "Donne's thematics" (Mueller, "Lesbian Erotics," 116) on the grounds that "Sapho and Philaenis" represents a "fully utopian moment of human possibility" (125), but this hyperbolic defense of Donne makes too much of a rather strained joke and wrongly assumes that only certain kinds of political rhetoric justify critical interest in Donne: "Donne's thematics call into larger question the conventions of heterosexuality that ruled love poetry, erotic behavior, and social arrangements in his day" (116). The picture we get of Donne in such representations, whether they praise or malign the poet, depends on debatable assumptions about social history such as the belief that such categories as "patriarchy," "masculinist," "utopian," and "ideology" designate recognizable and "defined" sets, and that these in tandem function as an agency of the fictional responses of Donne's protagonists, some of whom may behave as if women they know are "ignorant." But can't we imagine experience—common sense—informing them of the same thing, without the help of ideology? I mean, just because some critics admit that the criticism of "gender feminists" shaped their reactions to Donne does not proscribe our imagining other causes of male attitudes and reactions to them in literature. Indeed, even the claim that Stanley Fish's attitudes derive at least in part from feminist criticism is only a claim that skeptical critics might consider, as they say in law, "subject to proof." Even more confusing is the assumption that a critic's perception of another critic's "discomfort" is a reliable basis for assessing what that critic might say about Donne. We can easily imagine a critic being comfortably or uncomfortably aligned with any ideology, "masculinist" or whatever, which suggests that comfort or discomfort cannot serve as reliable indications of judgment in criticism.

III.

One could infer from the title of my remarks that, like Philip Gallagher, who argued that "Milton is the first great feminist in Western culture,"[16] I want to defend Donne against the charge of misogyny, and to some extent this is true. But my less ambitious argument is that the very Donne texts most often cited as "misogynist"—the elegies—are not in fact misogynist, at least not misogynist in the sense that they are any more misogynist than they are misandrist. I do not insist on the strong but counterintuitive proposition that the protagonist in "The Perfume" does not treat his mistress badly, but on the more modest one that he treats everybody so, men and women alike—the mother of his mistress, yes, but her household's "grim eight-foot-high iron-bound serving-man" and her irksome brood of sibling informers, too. Self-centeredness, not contempt for women, is this lover's nature. He may hate his mistress, but only in the sense that he hates everybody and everything—even his squeaky shoes. And why is this? Because they are impediments to sexual liaison with his mistress, that's why. Hence, the tone of unrelenting harangue in the poem. Is this "misogyny" or only the resentment of a young man seriously beset by circumstances out of his control—wavering mistress, prying parents, nosy siblings? Why not take the initiative and, at least in the imagination, eliminate one enemy (by suggesting to his mistress that her mother has already lived too long)?

This (I think modest) perspective gains support even when we look at "The Anagram," which is the source of as much misogyny-mongering as any Donne poem. Surely the poem luxuriates in "woman-as-sex-object" feelings, so much so that one critic complains, "Donne strips woman of a stable identity," imposing, in effect, "anonymity" on women. This might seem like a point not worth quibbling about. What if Donne *had* imposed "anonymity" on women, so that woman in general becomes "stripped of stable identity, anonymous in fact" (Docherty, *John Donne, Undone,* 65)? The implication is that the poem accomplishes this end, and that it is pernicious. As Wittgenstein wryly remarks in response to the proclamation that one knows only one's own pain: "In one way this is wrong, and in another nonsense."[17] Flavia may be ugly; it could be said that even her name sounds faintly noxious or effluvial. But in fact that name does rescue her from the threat, if it ever existed, of "anonymity." The critic asks, "What's in a name?" And the answer in this case is, "Quite a lot"; for instance, there is in it the grammatical function of the genitive with all of its associated linguistic possibilities, among them being personal history (occupation: prostitute), venereal disease, unique distribution of body parts, and the like.

So we must recognize hyperbole in Donne's poem. Dildoes don't care what they touch. But cannot critics numb themselves to humor in order to muster a properly indignant response to Donne's representations? Under our system of government they have that right, but "must" implies, not that they are free to exercise it, but rather (for a reason or reasons not specified) that they are constrained to do so. In an effort to escape from misogyny, Docherty rushes into the clutches of misandry. For consider: In "The Anagram," the speaker proclaims his courage in touching Flavia, who, if she had her way, would have been more than merely touched by so many men that only the foolhardy lover will risk infection. Surely, in making this lover the imagined exception to the male norm, Donne advances the mischievous, misandrous suggestion that, unlike Flavia, who cannot help being ugly, the unsophisticated lover (and all men other than the speaker) inflicts suffering on himself.

"The woman in the last part of the poem," Docherty declares, "does not even seem to be the same person" described in the first. Suppose we assume for the moment the accuracy of this assertion. Wouldn't this concession entail the proposition that a change of Flavia's character constitutes a fault in either her or the poem? And isn't this faulty reasoning? Hamlet changes. In act 1, we do not know him to be a theater-goer, drama critic, playwright, stage director, swordsman and aspirant to the throne. Even if Flavia *were* to change, this would not necessarily besmirch her character, and certainly not that of womanhood in general. But in fact Flavia does not change. That is the more experienced lover's point. Other women change, she doesn't. Compared to "such as shee," they are fairer, but in being so, they are subject to the vicissitudes of flesh:

> Women are all like Angels; the faire be
> Like those which fell to worse; but such as shee,
> Like to good Angels, nothing can impaire:
> 'Tis lesse griefe to be foule, then to have beene faire.
>
> (lines 29–32)[18]

While "Women are all like Angels," they can be discriminated from one another on the basis of their moral qualities. Only Flavia and other ugly women are "Like to good Angels," because they do not give evidence of the Fall. Beauty fades into ugliness, but ugliness remains constant, and so, "good." Hence, Flavia's stability, which according to Docherty Donne undermines, is recaptured the moment it slips away. Docherty claims that the poem amuses by forcing a perspective in which "the normal opposition of fair and foul is disturbed." But what makes anything "disturbed"? "Normal opposition" is subsumed beneath the overarching standard of frustration; beauty exacerbates, ugliness attenuates, grief. Admittedly, one could insist that Docherty's claim of Flavia's not being the same person in the two halves of the poem is excusable hyperbole. But, hyperbolic or not, his assertion does not require Flavia's metamorphosis into a baneful "faire" mistress.

Rhetorically oriented critics should not overlook the venom directed toward men in "The Anagram." To whom, after all, is the speaker's exhortation to "Marry" addressed? Who is too blind to see that Flavia will make him the best wife? Who stands in need of the wisdom of the more experienced lover? Who, because of his inexperience with women, is on the verge of making the mistake most common to men? (I assume that the speaker is male, because, like the narrator of *The Story of* O, he seems to know what he is talking about.) Inclined to reject Flavia because of her appearance, this bachelor would be better off if he would reverse all of his values and expectations with respect to women, and repudiate his promiscuous appetite for female beauty. He should do so because beautiful women have a promiscuous appetite to cause men woe. And they succeed in their plunder because men are haplessly drawn to feminine color and texture in certain spatial arrangements. The problem is that, although Flavia has all the feminine qualities that young men desire, she possesses them in what seems in the here and now an unpleasant configuration. But this is where the novice makes a mistake. He is too quick to judge. Time will obliterate the disappointing aspects of the audience's expectations of beauty, and in so doing it will reveal that Flavia's anagrammatic charms, in the end, reward the understanding lover by removing all taint of disillusion from his relations with women. Thus, if he will but listen to and follow the speaker's advice, he will expect disappointment, and so, not be disappointed. Even now, if he behaves prudently in accord with his mentor's advice, the lover can spare himself the heartache of chasing after "beauties elements," with "all her parts in th'usuall place": "a good face," large eyes, small mouth, white teeth, smooth skin. And what of that imperceptible virtue, chastity? Flavia needs nothing from men to guarantee her unique state of chastity. Like "beauties," Flavia is available, but unlike them (for lack of opportunity), she is, in essence if not in fact, pure. At the same time, it would be pointless for the lover to think of lending his virginity to "Beauties." (What makes him think they need what none of them claim to miss?)

To the audience, it might seem that something important follows from the principle, "All love is wonder." Through the discipline of suffering, experience teaches that the "best land" is only that held without anxiety: love free from the torment of jealousy. But how, in a world of cruel mistresses, can the novice find and enjoy that blissful terrain? The answer is: only in the arms of Flavia. And why is this? Because, like the misguided novice, other men are too stupid to avail themselves of Flavia's anagrammatized value. They can't solve the puzzle of her availability. Paradoxically, her universal availability proves Flavia possessed of a rare chastity. Her anagrammatic charms could survive the greatest threats to chastity: life in a brothel, or a visit from the lover's best friend.

It is wrong, then, to construe "The Anagram" as a diatribe against either Flavia or women, much less against friendship or stews. The speaker's aim is in the other direction. Men are like this uninitiated lover: mindless sufferers of self-induced obsession to enjoy what all men desire. Each wishes to enjoy legions of beautiful women as if he were exceptional, that is, the only man for whom feminine charm was created and the only one on whom its blessings have been or could be legitimately bestowed. Since only Flavia has her virginity, only she can actually meet the condition that the young lover desires; but in order to have that condition met—copulation to his heart's content, and this without taint of jealousy—he must separate himself from what he shares with "th'usuall" male, namely, desire for unanagrammatized beauty. He can have what he wants if and only if he alters the spatial expectations of what he wants. The problem is that what he wants all men want; and, unfortunately for him, "things in fashion every man will weare."

The speaker's wisdom here is far from esoteric. According to one influential Frenchman, if a man "get himselfe a handsome wife[,] his neighbours commonly will have as much to doe with her, as himselfe."[19] They will do as he does—ignore Flavia, who longs to receive men promiscuously as her beautiful sisters do, to give men what they want. Pathologically, men prefer to suffer, just as he, the untutored lover, will suffer. Why? Well, at least partly because he willfully refuses to recognize that he only imagines "beauties" to be untouched. "Beauty and chastity," writes Jacques Ferrand, "seldome meet in one person. For beauty is as it were a kind of prey, that hath continually a thousand in chase of it" (*A Treatise,* 228). Since all men insist on importuning "beauties," understandably "beauties" are often importuned. For thanks, beautiful women teach men how to be jealous. In contrast, the mentor exhorts the novice to elude this self-inflicted pain and to enjoy the "best land" with no worry about proprietary rights. Once he marries Flavia, he need never fear betrayal. For if the tolerant bed staves refuse to touch her, why should he worry about sprouting horns? The social reality is this: He can without worry leave his wife with the men most likely to cuckold him, namely, his friends.

Here, Donne's mentor makes facetious use of an argument well known in feminist writing of the Renaissance. In *The Nobilitie and Excellencie of Womankynde* (1542), a popular work published and translated often[20] in the sixteenth and seventeenth centuries, Henry Agrippa argues that, since they were created by God with "one similitude and lykenes of the sowle,"[21] man and woman have "the same mynd . . . reason and speeche" (A2v). On the other hand, this "equall libertie of dignitie and worthynesse" is limited to the spiritual being that the two sexes share with angels: "But all other thinges, the which be in man, besydes the dyvyne substance of the soule, in those thynges the excellente and noble womanhed in a maner infynytely dothe excell the rude gross kynd of man . . ." (A2v–A3). Agrippa admits of many differences between the sexes, and invariably these indicate the superiority of woman. Holy Writ bears witness to the fact that even in their creation and name, woman, created last of all creatures—and fashioned from the part of man nearest the heart—was named for "life" (Eva) rather than earth (Adam). Furthermore, she is marked by signs other than name "of the very thynges, dueties, and merites" (A5v) declaring that "man is the worke of nature, and womanne the worke of God" (B2). She is in both sense and feeling more attractive, more amiable, than man: "In al the hole heape of creatures, there is noo thynge so wonderfull to see" (B4) as a woman. Not only is woman more beautiful than man, as can be seen in her serenity and pulchritude, but she is "endowed with a certain dignitie and worthines of honestie, which is not given to men" (B7), besides which she is, as her less pronounced genitalia indicates, "gyven more [to] shamfastnes than . . . man" (B7v). Woman is, as can be seen in man's weakness for her, more modest, less inclined to incontinency, and—for Renaissance criticism this is highly significant—not culpable for man's fallen condition. Contrary to vulgar opinion, Adam, not Eve, bore responsibility for the Fall, since it was he, not Eve, who was enjoined not to eat the fruit of the Tree of the Knowledge of Good and Evil (C5v). This important distinction can be seen in the significant role the Virgin Mary plays in man's redemption. For the Virgin Mary, whose female sex and modesty—virginity was the very sign and essence of chastity—became the vessel of divinely inspired parthenogenesis through which Adam's transgression was forgiven: "The man gave us deathe, not the woman. And all we synned in Adam, not in Eva" (C5v). To many such minds, even woman's faults must be understood in an exculpatory way, for, as Edward More proclaims in *Defence of Women* (1560), "It lyth not in them [i.e., women], these sayd thyng to correcte" (A4v). Written from the point of view of one who would be "a Champyan bold" (A4) of women, the *Defence of Women* protests that women cannot help being as they are formed by "Nature . . . accordyng . . . to gods wyll" (A4v). Thus, Adam had "strenght sufficient" ("sufficient to have stood, though free to fall"), while Eve did (and women do) not.

I think we should consider the hortatory form of "The Anagram" from the point of view of such expressions, not because they are apposite expressions of Renaissance feminism, but because they artfully exploit quite opposite notions of women without surrendering the comparative disdain toward men. After all, the most important rhetorical relationship exhibited in the poem is that between the enlightened instructor and his unsophisticated auditor: "Marry, and love the *Flavia* for shee / Hath all things." The speaker's tone implies that his pupil is in no mood to change his ways. If he were in a frame of mind to marry Flavia, the experienced lover wouldn't need to argue so strenuously. So why does the young man resist? Why can't he learn that the true virtue of women cannot be seen? That it is moral and spiritual? His erroneous thinking in the matter is the subject of the poem—the novice lover's false reasons for refusing to commit himself to Flavia. He does not accept that Flavia possesses everything that he desires, which is "all things" that womanhood can offer. Hence, the title. The anagram is a puzzle that, when solved, is clear and simple. The solution comes in knowing that the parts appear to be disordered only to the senses. But this is merely because the lover is blind to imaginative rearrangement. He needs to balance the usual organization of details with the "yet" of other possibilities:

Marry, and love thy *Flavia*, for, shee
Hath all things, whereby others beautious bee,
For, though her eyes be small, her mouth is great,
Though they be Ivory, yet her teeth are jeat,
Though they be dimme, yet she is light enough,
And though her harsh haire fall, her skinne is rough;
What though her cheeks be yellow, her haire is red,
Give her thine, and she hath a maydenhead.

(lines 1–8)

Now, we may smile perhaps because we, too, enjoy the difficulty of the rhetor's task here. Tactile enjoyment of large lips is possible, but difficult while one is distracted by a longing for small ones, and the same is true of the source of other sensations: "light"/"dimme," soft/"harsh," "yellow"/"red." It seems that the mentor cannot quite keep a straight face, for at the last he tells the young lover that he must part with what he does not have (except in the metaphoric sense of sexual inexperience) in order to enjoy what he really wants: the pleasure of a beautiful woman's love untrammeled by the woes that usually accompany this satisfaction. But of course the more the instructor argues the clearer it is that more argument will not work.

Such talk sounds like good fun, but it has, as Donne's poems often do, something of the "metaphysics" in it. For, notwithstanding his momentary lapse into common sense, the speaker does propound a corrective to the inexperienced lover's problem. If the novice will only entertain a different arrangement, adducing nonaesthetic but nonetheless perceptible value, he will see that all of the parts of the puzzle are already available: "These things are beauties elements, where these / Meet in one, that one must, as perfect, please" (9–10). That is, having had all of his demands of beauty met in discrete parts, the lover must not cavil about the spatial arrangement of those parts. To make his point more emphatic the mentor shifts attention from the visual to the olfactory sense. One experiences a fine perfume's lovely fragrance, not its source, which remains a tantalizing "wonder" or mystery, and by this shift in attention he tries to widen the scope of the lover's interest. He is in a position, then, to chastise the neophyte for his incapacity to see "unusually," that is, as most men do not see—with insight, as if all the pieces of the puzzle were not only present but in place.

IV.

One could brush aside this challenge to the misogynist description of Donne by saying that it is wrong to "objectify" women, even if one simultaneously "objectifies" men, because two wrongs don't make a right. But, as we shall see, this ethical aspect of the "gender feminist" attack is no more helpful than the mischaracterization of the poet as misogynist in the first place. Again, Docherty writes:

> Feared, as their Other, by the men who were in power, ideologically and factually, women are accorded only the status of "object" of study and thought; this demonstrates that the real source of this male fear is a worry about the subjectivity of the female, as a consciousness or mode of desire or will which could challenge male authority and domination or masculinist epistemology and ideology. (*John Donne, Undone,* 62)

In elaborating this now familiar line of thought, Docherty implies that "wholeness" and "stability" are a priori human values, which "Donne and his society" refused to extend to women, not only to "Flavia" in "The Anagram" but to women, generally. But although he is at pains to deny that this is "*ethical* criticism," surely this argument would impose on Donne critics—without warrant—an ethical norm for the humorous treatment of a young man in such a dilemma. Why is it wrong to strip "woman" of something she might never have had and might never need, especially if, in the process, the poet tenders opportunities for "enjoyment" to some, if not all, Donne critics? That is, even if the charge that "The Anagram " is "misogynist" were fair, it would not constitute serious grounds for disparagement of Donne's poem, nor would it say anything about the propriety of his moral outlook. The poem outrages Stanley Fish, for whom it represents a repulsive expression of a repulsive attitude. Donne looks down on women. He commodifies women. He turns them into objects. Valuing his poetry is therefore tantamount to physical oppression of women. For words are, as Donne uses them, fancied assaults. I want to say: What is wrong with that?

These critics assume that it is the job of criticism to expose licit and illicit critical enjoyments. But even if we accepted this assumption, the prior question would still be this: How do we discriminate between licit and illicit literary enjoyments? This is—Docherty's disclaimer notwithstanding—an ethical question. The designation need not dismay us, for it is amenable to analysis. When Wittgenstein asks, "What happens when we learn to *feel* the ending of a church mode as an ending?" (*PI,* §535), he implies that our recognition, if we have it, will concern hearing in a certain way in order to know or "*feel*" a sense of closure. Past experiences come into play. Although we can say that sound impressions are heard even by the tone deaf, we must concede that they might not recognize the crucial transition to the church mode. Even perfect pitch will not do the trick. To recognize the transition one must have heard others like it—one must have grown used to such musical developments. Wittgenstein continues:

> I say: "I can think of this face (which gives an impression of timidity) as courageous too." We do not mean by this that I can imagine someone with this face perhaps saving someone's life (that, of course, is imaginable in connexion with any face). I am speaking rather of an aspect of the face itself. Nor do I mean that I can imagine that this man's face might change so that, in the ordinary sense, it looked courageous; though I may very well mean that there is a quite definite way in which it can change into a courageous face. The reinterpretation of a facial expression can be compared to the reinterpretation of a chord in music, when we hear it as a modulation first into this, then into that key. (*PI*, §536)

It could be, as Fish and Docherty claim, that the men in the Donne poems under consideration think women are stupid, and that in so thinking they betray "male fear." But how do we justify saying so? Suppose that Donne critics are unable to perceive this aspect of the proposed picture of Donne? Suppose, too, that even though they try, well-meaning critics cannot perceive "male fear" of women's sexuality in a Donne elegy. Can we say that it is through some failure in the sensory process that these critics are unable to perceive this thematic interest in the text? I show you a picture, and then tell the story behind the portrait of the man who appears to you as timid. The portrait was painted just prior to a momentous battle, and the subject knew at the time of the sitting that he must lead his troops into battle against superior forces. And now, although the picture has not been changed by a brush stroke, the face that had seemed timid conveys a sense of firm resolve and courage. Wittgenstein writes that in such a circumstance, "Perhaps one says: 'Yes, now I understand: the face as it were shews indifference to the outer world'" (*PI*, §537).

Wittgenstein's point is that what goes before seeing and hearing will bear on seeing and hearing. So if I do not perceive the timorous aspect of the male protagonists in a particular Donne poem, and if, after hearing the narrative told by the critic who does perceive it, I am still unable to see it, what will constitute a criterion for deciding that this aspect is present in the text? ("Well," comes the objection, "somebody saw it!" So is this an answer to my question, or a statement of historical fact?) Recognitions of a shift to the church mode may involve quite diverse experiences in many keys and in many different circumstances; but they will share certain features—"family resemblances"—even though we might not be able to list or articulate them. This is what Wittgenstein calls "mastery of a technique" (*PI*, §150); it is like learning a language. In reading Donne poems with "rakish lovers" in them, we will want to know what notions fit. Are they customarily—or ever—like this? Are men in such poems afraid of women? Do they fear women's sexuality? Well, what counts as evidence here?

Now suppose that aspect—of timorousness—were suddenly manifest. Here is solid evidence that the speaker in "The Anagram" (or someone very like him) fears Flavia's (or some other woman's) sexuality. (The evidence might appear, say, from analogous contemporary situations in which a mentor explicitly expresses such apprehension to a less sophisticated lover.) The question now becomes: Where do we go from here? Are we then in a position to allay someone's fear—the lover's or Donne's? Or, failing that, are we doomed to watch helplessly as the bounder copes with what we know to be irrational fear of female sexuality? "Well, the speaker feels that men are losing their grip on women, and that is what they fear. The charge that women are ignorant only masks the speaker's anxiety, which is, in turn, a symptom of Donne's malady, namely, misogyny. The cynical lover in such poems as 'Communitie' and 'The Indifferent' and in certain of the elegies are afraid of women's sexuality, so they characterize women as stupid and amoral." I would like to disabuse anyone attracted to this belief by arguing that Donne's fictive indictment of women as moral idiots is actually an attack on the uneducable men who consort with them. Hence at the very least, a measure of misandry accompanies whatever expression of misogyny, if any, we find in these poems.

In making this assertion, we need not argue that misogyny and misandry have equal weight in every Donne poem. But even with the possible exceptions of a few poems like "Communitie" (in which men do not come off unscathed), I argue that we must complicate the picture of Donne's purported fear of or hostility toward women. Even when a Donne lover expresses fear of particular women—as in "Change" (Donne, *Elegies and The Songs and Sonnets,* 19–20), for instance—he soon reveals that it is neither that woman, nor women in general, that he fears, but men. Women cannot help being women, but neither can men help being men: "If I have caught a bird, and let him flie, / Another fouler using these meanes, as I, / May catch the same bird" (7–9). Nature made women "apter to endure than men" (14), but she also made a great multitude of men to compensate for the lack in individual stamina. Change—or its synonym, "incontinency"—is so much a part of nature that to rebel against it is pointless. True liberty is the product of movement and change, which means that the lover must adjust to the limitation on his endurance. Comfort comes in knowing that compensation for his insufficient sexual stamina is already available thanks to the ceaseless efforts of competing but likewise soon-tired males. He must only learn not to fear his—or their—incontinence, which is, to the mature initiate, "the nursery / Of musicke, joy, life, and eternity" (35–36).

Now where is the misogyny here? If anything, "Change" is misandrist, in the sense that, for many members of Donne's reading audience, incontinence probably implied a lack of moral rather than of physical stamina. One contemporary describes "Women" as "the second English Evill" (the first being drunkenness), for from them men are led into "*Incontinencie.*" Indeed, from the lips of beautiful women men will "sucke effeminate humours," and lose the capacity to take advantage of "advise from . . . freinds"[22] And what is the experienced lover in this and many other Donne elegies doing? Why, offering advice to a young lover that no man can be trusted, since they are all, like him, easily lured by incontinent women into incontinent ways. Is Donne's mature, well-meaning mentor in the way of the world a misogynist? Isn't he, instead, unduly pessimistic about men who seem never to learn how not to be manipulated by women?

On both descriptive and normative grounds, then, the charge of misogyny against a poem like "The Anagram" is overstated and, so, erroneous. Before we can rush to judgment about the dramatic and ethical characteristics of such poems, we need to know more about how such witty expressions were construed in Donne's time. Were men and women, alike, amused by Donne's self-centered young lovers? Or were men in particular offended by seeing male proclivities exposed and ridiculed? We can imagine a post-postmodern emergence of a critical school of masculism that would shun poems like "The Anagram" as a calumny on men, as de facto evidence of contempt for men. Suppose we as Donne critics were, under pressure of such a movement, forced to choose between a masculist understanding of this picture of "The Anagram" and enjoyment of the joke at men's expense. "Well," the masculist asserts, "our theoretical position requires determination in the here and now that we position ourselves as resolute opponents of such antimasculist propaganda. If we value poems like 'The Anagram,' how will we encourage young men to feel good about themselves?" Wittgenstein's aside might not answer this question, but it does suggest that critics need not respond to every joke as if it were a serious move in a universal propaganda war: "The real discovery is the one that makes me capable of stopping doing philosophy when I want to.—The one that gives philosophy peace, so that it is no longer tormented by questions which bring *itself* in question" (*PI,* §133).

Notes

1. *Twilight of the Idols*, "Reason in Philosophy 1," in *The Portable Nietzsche*, ed. and trans. Walter Kaufman (New York: Viking, 1983).

2. I am referring now to Nietzsche's *Thoughts of an Untimely Man*, the second essay of which is entitled "On the Advantages and Disadvantages of History for Life." It is unfortunate that the questionably canonical "On Truth and Lie in an Extramoral Sense" and other extracts from *The Will to Power* (Nachlass) are the most frequently cited "work" in discussions of Nietzsche's attitude toward historical truth. For a discussion of this matter, see Bernd Magnus, Stanley Stewart, and Jean-Pierre Mileur, *Nietzsche's Case: Philosophy as/and Literature* (New York: Routledge, 1993), 35–37.

3. John Carey, *John Donne: Life, Mind and Art* (New York: Oxford University Press, 1981), 95.

4. Janet E. Halley, "Textual Intercourse: Anne Donne, John Donne, and the Sexual

Politics of Sexual Exchange," in *Seeking the Woman in Late Medieval and Renaissance Writings*, ed. Sheila Fisher and Janet E. Halley (Knoxville: University of Tennessee Press, 1989), 1978.

5. George Klawitter, "Verse Letters to T. W. from John Donne: 'By You My Love Is Sent,'" in *Homosexuality in Renaissance and Enlightenment England: Literary Representations in Historical Context*, ed. Claude J. Summers (New York: Hawarth Press, 1992), 100.

6. Stanley Fish, "Masculine Persuasive Force: Donne and Verbal Power," in *Soliciting Interpretation: Literary Theory and Seventeenth-Century Poetry*, ed. Elisabeth D. Harvey and Katharine Eisaman Maus (Chicago: University of Chicago Press, 1990), 223.

7. Achsah Guibbory, "'Oh, Let Mee Not Serve So,'" *ELH* 57 (winter 1990): 812.

8. John R. Roberts, *John Donne: An Annotated Bibliography of Modern Criticism, 1968–1978* (Columbia: University of Missouri Press, 1982), 1.

9. Thomas Docherty, *John Donne, Undone* (London: Methuen, 19986), 7.

10. Janel Mueller, "Lesbian Erotics: The Utopian Trope of Donne's 'Sapho to Philaenis,'" in Summers, *Homosexuality in Renaissance and Enlightenment England,* 148.

11. Roma Gill, "*Musae Iocosa Mea*: Thoughts on the Elegies," in *John Donne: Essays in Celebration*, ed. A. J. Smith (London: Methuen, 1972), 55.

12. For a discussion of Stanley Fish's theory of rhetorical depth analysis, see my "Investigating Herbert Criticism," *Renascence* 45 (spring 1993): 131–58, esp. 147–53.

13. Arthur F. Marotti, *John Donne: Coterie Poet* (Madison: University of Wisconsin Press, 1986), 52.

14. For a discussion of the useful distinction between "equity" and "gender feminists," see Christina Hoff Sommers, *Who Stole Feminism: How Women Have Betrayed Women* (New York: Simon & Schuster, 1994), esp. 134–35; see also Richard Bernstein, *Dictatorship of Virtue: Multiculturalism and the Battle for America's Future* (New York: Alfred A. Knopf, 1994), 119–22. For a learned discussion of the notion that there is such a thing as a "feminist standpoint," see Paul R. Gross and Norman Levitt, *Higher Superstition: The Academic Left and its Quarrels with Science* (Baltimore: Johns Hopkins University Press, 1994), 135–36.

15. Michael Schoenfeldt, "Patriarchal Assumptions and Egalitarian Designs," *John Donne Journal* 9, no. 1 (1990): 25.

16. Philip J. Gallagher, *Milton, the Bible, and Misogyny*, ed. Eugene R. Cunnar and Gail L. Mortimer (Columbia: University of Missouri Press, 1990), 171.

17. Ludwig Wittgenstein, *Philosophical Investigations*, trans. G. E. M. Anscombe (Oxford: Basil Blackwell, 1958), §246; hereafter cited as *PI* in the text.

18. All citations from Donne in my text are from *The Elegies and The Songs and Sonnets*, ed. Helen Gardner (Oxford: Clarendon Press, 1965).

19. Jacques Ferrand, *A Treatise Discoursing of the Essence, Causes, Symptomes, Prognosticks, and Cure of Love, Or Erotique Melancholy* (Oxford, 1640), 227.

20. According to the British Museum Catalog, prior to 1700 Agrippa's *Nobilitie* was published separately no less than seven times; two English translations appeared in 1652 alone.

21. Henry Cornelius Agrippa, *The Nobilitie and Excellencie of Womankynde* (1542), A2.

22. Anthony Stafford, *The Guide of Honor* (1634), 33.

The First Individual

EDWARD W. TAYLER

THE problem of the "individual" has been a problem at least since Michelet, and disagreements about what constitutes this particular conception of selfhood—its origins, its nature, its very existence—become vociferous whenever we try to confront the mystery of human agents making human history. There have been, lately, all those well-intentioned efforts to avoid the problem by speaking of the "subject," the "decentered subject," and finally of "subject-positions," but this kind of evasive action, while it may appear to clarify for a moment a particular issue, obscures the semantic history of the problem.[1] And as the editors of *Reconstructing Individualism: Autonomy. Individuality. and the Self in Western Thought* point out: "[I]n all fields of humanistic study—from epistemology to the theory of moral development, from hermeneutics to sociology—the concept of individuality maintains both the centrality and the intractable complexity that have characterized its history."[2]

The Latin *individuum*, meaning indivisible, becomes naturalized by the end of the sixteenth century and can be used to refer to the (individual) member of a species, but it gradually loses out to "individual." Milton, as late as "On Time" (1633), can use "individual" in "individual kiss" to signify a latinized osculation that "long Eternity" bestows upon each one of us separately and that also remains with us indivisibly and forever. Whereas Donald Frame, the modern translator of Montaigne's "Of Glory," finds it easy enough to have "everyone seek it individually," Florio in 1603 writes: "[L]et every man in his particular seeke for it." It took awhile for people in the seventeenth century to extricate the word from its logical and metaphysical matrices and to become comfortable with the substantive "individual" as referring to a single human being distinct from family or society.[3] The semantic and cultural story of the human being notable for his singularity would certainly have been different if *individuum* had been allowed to retain its naturalized status until the rehabilitation of Epicurean and Democritean atomism: you and I would now be individuums, on our way to becoming subjects and subject-positions . . . or maybe not.

Had Socrates no individuality? Could not Augustine locate a selfhood in memory and confess its individual oddities? Dante? (Who, when chosen to lead the Florentine embassy to Rome, meditated the alternatives: If I stay, who then will go? but if I go, who then will stay?) Petrarch? Montaigne? John Donne? Is not the early Renaissance preeminently the age of individualism? In putting such questions we *could* conceivably be inquiring, among other and perhaps more obvious possibilities, whether the writers of the earlier stages of the Renaissance actually possessed a philosophical vocabulary that permitted them to refer to themselves as "individuals," or whether these writers could appeal to a theory or model of mind that would allow them to speak conveniently about the way one mind differs from another mind. If we specify the questions in this way, the unequivocal answer in each instance must be an unambiguous No.

In the Aristotelian-Christian tradition the individual—this particular man, horse, or apple—is a substance, mysteriously the union of form and matter. As Christopher Stead has demonstrated, the mystery will not go away.[4] Aristotle in the *Metaphysics* disarmingly asserts that "matter is obvious"; and "form," he says, neatly sidestepping what later became the issue, means "substance without matter." If that is the case, presumably one might try to imagine removing the "obvious" from Socrates until what remains is "form": one would, in this Aristotelian universe of discourse, mentally excise from Socrates all those endearing "accidents" or idiosyncrasies (his nose, his manner of questioning, his ability to hold his liquor), as well as bits of bone and pints of blood—until one finally comes upon form or essence (later the *verbum mentis*), which when put into words would be the definition of "man."

The meaning of "form" and "matter" in such contexts—not to mention their union in "substance"—may puzzle anyone who inquires too closely. And yet there is no pressing need—there *was* no pressing need until the seventeenth century—to fuss over such formulations unless one wants, for whatever reason, to assert one's *individuality*. For those Christians who found it convenient to make extensive use of Aristotle, the "soul" is the "form" of the "body," which means in Aristotelian logic that your "form" is that of Socrates or Callicles, and this in turn may be taken to mean that one individual of the species may be differentiated from other members of the species only on the basis of material or bodily conditions: ontologically the Christian soul is unique, logically it is the same in all—close to Averroism and far from what later came to be called "individuality." To speak strictly in this universe of discourse, matter is unintelligible, so that in asserting your individuality you might feel that you were saying—not that Aristotle had the least interest in saying it—that your individual identity is the identity of your matter and that in consequence your identity is as unintelligible to yourself as to others.

If you have been trained to think of yourself and others as *substances*, you will find it hard to conceive of yourself as an "individual." Aristotle assumed οὐσία as his basic category. It is usually translated by Seneca and Quintilian as *essentia*, meaning the nature of a thing, that which makes it whatever it is. Augustine uses *essentia* and *substantia* pretty much interchangeably; Boethius uses *substantia*, allowing *essentia* to be reserved for later inquiries into being and essence, existence and essence; in Thomas, *essence* is a *potentiality* on which *existence* is conferred by God, and the resulting *actuality* is a *substance*. During the earlier part of the seventeenth century thinkers tended to focus on two senses of substance: that which has independent existence, and that which functions as the subject of predicates and is not predicated of something else. In other words, there were two senses of substance, separate but not unrelated—substance as the substratum (*hypostasis*) of the attributes that exist only through the substance in which they inhere, and substance as subject of predications.

Nowadays we make fun of the notion, in all of its senses. Since Aristotle assumed that what required explaining was not so much how we recognize sensory particulars as how we manage the peculiarly human process of constructing abstractions, it did not bother him that this way of categorizing experience seemed to leave "matter" as the principle of individuation. He himself apparently felt no need, such as was felt by Thomas and others among the Scholastics, even to posit the principle as a principle. It is not, after all, entirely obvious that coherent thinking requires a "principle of individuation," and indeed there is no such principle in Aristotle's works as they have come down to us. Avicenna and Albert felt, for reasons too complicated to address in this context, that they needed the principle; Aquinas boldly, or desperately, accepts matter as the principle of individuation and draws out the consequences in the *Summa contra Gentiles* and *Summa Theologica*. All substances are what they are because of their union of form and matter, but it is matter, not form, that allows us to distinguish between individuals belonging to the same species. Although Thomas's formulation is in this, as in other instances, far more subtle than any generalizations I can devise, my crude summary may nevertheless suggest the difficulty as it was experienced, particularly by some of the Cambridge Platonists, in the seventeenth century.

Any account of how the thinkers of the seventeenth century sought to meet the difficulties posed by the category of substance would have to begin well before Hobbes and Locke. It would have to include the way the jurists of the twelfth through the fourteenth centuries showed the poets how to speak of their craft as creative as well as imitative.[5] It would also have to include the way that the rehabilitation of the atomism of Epicurus, Democritus, and Lucretius gave currency to a technical vocabulary that eventually permitted human beings to apply *individuum* (atom) or "individual" to themselves as well as to the fortuitous concourse of atoms or to entities in logic. Yet even if such histories had been written, we would find—in the absence of a Copernicus, a Darwin, a Freud—that we still lacked a definable moment of inception, a point of origin.

Nevertheless, we may, if we are attentive and lucky, come upon a writer—not a great thinker but, as it were, a case history—who announces his involvement, without full awareness of his involvement, in what must already have begun to assume the shape of a major revolution in the way people thought of themselves as selves. Suddenly, soundlessly at first, everything everywhere began, slowly, to move.

In 1631 Henry More entered Christ's College with what he later referred to as an "inordinate Desire after Knowledge of things." He immediately informed his tutor that he was there "That I may know"; and when his tutor asked him why, the young man replied, "That I may know." More hurled himself "over Head and Ears in the Study of Philosophy." "Aristotle therefore, Cardan, Julius Scaliger, and other Philosophers of the greatest Note, I very diligently peruse." Around 1635, perhaps just before becoming bachelor of arts, he suffered what would now probably be called an identity crisis and wrote in Greek an eight-line poem entitle 'Απορία, the "Perplexity of the Soul," in which he speaks of being torn by the "Claws of Greif." The first line, in his own translation for Lady Conway, reads: "Nor whence nor who I am . . . know I." In 1639, just after becoming master of arts, More wrote in Greek an eight-line poem entitled Εὐπορία, the "Extrication of the Soul," in which he exclaims that his "thoughts with joy oerflow." The first line, in the translation of his friend Edmund Elys and also sent to Lady Conway, reads: "Beame of aeternall light from Heaven I came."[6] The crisis had passed, but neither its cause nor its solution was solely religious, solely a question of "whence . . . I am" with its theological answer of "from Heaven I came."

The crisis included the question of "who I am," the question that, specifically, "Aristotle . . . , Cardan, Julius Scaliger, and other Philosophers of the greatest Note" could not help him answer. They were in fact part of the problem. The crisis may be traced to the personal anxieties aroused by, or expressed in, More's obsession with the Scholastic (more precisely the Thomistic) principle of individuation. Most of More's predecessors could not comfortably, without qualification or synonyms, refer to people as "individuals" in the modern sense, but in 1635 More, with consequences almost disastrous for his health, tried to confront directly the problem of what we would now call his "individuality." In the philosophers whom More had been reading the principle of individuation is neither soul nor mind but matter or body. Since the soul, the essential form of the human being, had been framed and furnished according to Aristotelian rules of architecture, there was no convenient way to distinguish, in the metaphysical terms of substance and accident then current, one rational soul from another. Quite the reverse. As Elyot puts it in *The Gover-*

nor, "And of that same . . . substance that his soul is of, be all other souls that now are, and have been, and ever shall be, without singularity or preeminence of nature."[7] Who am I? If you are looking for some means to distinguish yourself from others, you had better not put the question in these philosophical terms, for in this metaphysical economy you are distinguished only by material "accidents." With respect to your real self, your soul, you are of the "same . . . substance" as all others and "without singularity or preeminence of nature."

Henry More at first assumed that he could combine Cartesian atomism with his peculiar brand of Christian Platonism. Although *Democritus Platonissans* (Cambridge, 1646) appeared separately, More considered it to be a kind of fifth canto to the third book of *Psychathanasia* (1642). Indeed, in the edition of these Spenserian poetical tracts that came out in 1647 as *A Platonick Song of the Soul*, More had the later poem printed with the earlier ones in the same volume, though with different title pages and separate signatures. To subjoin a poetic treatise on atomism and the infinity of worlds to one proving the immortality of the soul may at first seem a trifle odd, but More (and Ralph Cudworth) had been reading Descartes, and from him, or so it might be supposed, there could be extracted a kind of spiritualized atomism. (Cudworth, in distinguishing it from the materialistic atomism of Democritus, traced it back to Pythagoras.)[8] More came eventually to reject Descartes, but in *Conjectura Cabbalistica* he professed to find in Cartesianism the learning of the Egyptians, of Moses, of Pythagoras, and of Democritus.[9]

Even as late as the *Collection of Several Philosophical Writings* of 1662 (2d ed.; corr. and enlarged) he could still in the Preface General defend himself "for interweaving *Platonism* and *Cartesianism* so frequently into his Writings" (vi): "It is therefore very evident to me that ancient *Pythagorick* or *Judaick Cabbala* did consist of what we now call *Platonisme* and *Cartesianisme*, the latter being as it were the Body, the other the *Soul* of that Philosophy" (xvii). Descartes's atomism, in More a Democritus Platonized, helped satisfy the need to show that "all souls are *not* one" (against Averroism) and that all souls are immortal, indivisible, *and* individual (*individua* or atoms). For Descartes the essence of the soul is pure thought, divorced from sensation; for More the essence of soul is self-activity, a "centreity" of motion and change often "occasioned" by sensation but never determined by it. This Platonizing atomism eventually provides a new language of the self, a new rationale for what constitutes the "individual" human being.

More's *Psychozoia, or A Christiano-Platonicall display of Life* (1642) was, according to the title-page, "Written in the beginning of the year of our Lord 1640." This particular "song of the soul" seems to have possessed some special—perhaps biographical—significance for More (he does not advertise the chronology of the other pieces). In "To the Reader" he explains that the poem has been designed for those who suffer

> A dayly Death, drad Agony,
> Privation, dry sterility:
> Who is well entred in those wayes
> Fitt'st man to read my lofty layes.
>
> (A2)

It seems possible that the poem played some part in More's own recovery from "dayly Death, drad Agony," or at least that it signaled the end of the period of "Privation, dry sterility." In it Psyche, the daughter of the Absolute, may be telling the tale of More's own regenerated soul. Next comes *Psychathanasia*, the first of many attempts to demonstrate the immortality of the soul. Finally, *Antipsychopannychia, or a Confutation of the sleep of the Soul after death* and *Antimonopsychia, or That all Souls are not one* (Averroism must be anathema to the "individual"). More published all four of these poetic tracts, done up as best he could in the manner of his admired Edmund Spenser, under the title *Psychodia Platonica* (Cambridge, 1642). They were to constitute, with the addition of *Democritus Platonissans*, his song of the soul—an "individual" song of an "individual" soul.

In *Democritus Platonissans* More imagines not only an infinity of worlds—denied by Plato in the *Timaeus*—but also a "Platonic" universe composed of an "immense field of Atoms" animated by "some living sprite": "these Atoms change their energies / Themselves unchanged into new Centreities" (stanza 14); these vital centers or "knots" in the "garment" of Psyche have special importance for More. As a boy he had on his own initiative denied the determinism of his Calvinist upbringing, and he maintained his position despite threats of severe punishment from his uncle. (Since life tends to imitate art, it may not be too much to suppose that his father's having read Spenser to him provided some of the impetus for his decision. Redcrosse and Guyon do not act on instructions from the Genevan pulpit.) Even as early as *Psychozoia* the "souls nature we may plainly see": a "beam it is of th'Intellectuall Sun," and that "free light hath given a free wonne / To this dependent ray" (II.22). The soul is free, vital, active—an individual center of light and energy. To enunciate this position More needed not only Democritus and the Neoplatonists but also Descartes, and not only the atomism of Descartes but also his optics. Chapter 19 of *Enchiridion Metaphysicum* and the letters to Descartes in *Collection of . . . Writings* (1662) reveal More's preoccupation with the *Dioptrics*, and in *Democritus Platonissans* More relies upon Cartesian optics in refuting the basic tenets of the Aristotelian-Christian view of the soul:

And as our soul's not superficially
Colourd by phantasms, nor doth them reflect
As doth a looking-glasse such imag'rie
As it to the beholder doth detect:
No more are these lightly or smear'd or deckt
With form or motion which in them we see,
But from their inmost Centre they project
Their vitall rayes, not merely passive be,
But by occasion wak'd rouze up themselves on high.

(stanza 15)

More's syntax is clumsy, his pronoun references careless, but his rejection of the epistemological tradition could not be more explicit. In the bizarre mix of Platonizing Christianity and Cartesian atomism called *Democritus Platonissans*, More goes out of his way to denounce the Aristotelian dictum that the mind is "colourd by phantasms," and he goes far out of his way to emphasize that the mind does not "them reflect / As doth a looking-glasse such imag'rie." These propositions must at the time have seemed provocative, even revolutionary; they would not, I think, have been countenanced at Oxford, still dominated by the "perspectivist" tradition. The soul of Henry More—"the image of her Maker"—is neither Aristotelian nor Aristotelian-Scholastic but Christian-Platonic, Christian-Platonic in a new register not dreamt of in the philosophy of Ficino.

Henry More, in his moment of crisis, had perceived the problem—and therefore refused to regard substance as the union of form and matter or to accept the Thomistic *principio individuationis*. Although he saw the problem and voiced the difficulty, he could not have been aware that he was merely part of a chorus otherwise mute:

> And after long searching and anxious enquiry into that most important question . . . in the works of the Thomists and Scotists concerning the Principio Individuationis (although it was dealt with by all), I could not discover any certain proof that I was an individual *[Individuum]*, or seize upon what I am when those qualities and attributes shared with the rest of the human race have been taken away. . . . With the result that I began to doubt whether I was a complete, separate Being *[Individuum distinctum & completum]* (a thought at which you may laugh) or but part of some enormous, or rather, enormously intelligent, Individual *[Individui intelliqentis]* (as the thumb is part of a man) to whom alone it is given clearly to understand what I am (as my thumb itself understands not at all its relationship to me).[10]

The immediate result for More had been aporia, the perplexity of the soul, but aporia was followed by euporia, the extrication of the soul; and this "euphoric" view of the human subject—as creative, individual, free—finds expression in the poems of the 1640s.[11] Henry More, himself Democritus Platonissans, had come to think of himself as a spiritual *individuum* or atom: the first individual.

Notes

1. Paul Smith, *Discerning the Subject* (Minneapolis: University of Minnesota Press, 1988), provides a useful, if awkwardly written and overly simple, survey of the current situation.

2. Thomas C. Heller, Morton Sosna, and David E. Wellbery, eds., *Reconstructing Individualism: Autonomy, Individuality, and the Self in Western Thought* (Stanford, Calif.: Stanford University Press, 1986), 13.

3. Raymond Williams, *Keywords,* rev. ed. (New York: Oxford University Press, 1976), neatly avoids the anachronistic, almost universal error of confusing logical and metaphysical with social meanings: "It was perhaps not till Locke . . . that the modern social sense emerged, but even then still as an adjective. . . . The decisive development of the singular noun was indeed not in social or political thought but in two special fields: logic, and, from C18, biology. . . . [And it] is not until 1C18 that a crucial shift in attitudes can be clearly seen . . ." (134–35). Properly if overly cautious: the crucial shift may be seen earlier if one knows where to look, though changes of this kind gain currency in the language at large only over a long period of time.

4. *Divine Substance* (Oxford: Clarendon Press, 1977).

5. See Ernst Kantorowicz, "The Sovereignty of the Artist: A Note on Legal Maxims and Renaissance Theories of Art," in *Essays in Honor of Erwin Panofsky*, ed. Millard Meiss (New York: New York University Press, 1961), pp. 261–79. For later developments, see also Allan H. Gilbert, *Literary Criticism: Plato to Dryden* (Detroit, Mich.: Wayne State University Press, 1962), 44, 413, 476, 500, 505–6; Ernst R. Curtius, *European Literature and the Latin Middle Ages*, trans. Willard R. Trask (New York: Pantheon Books, 1953), 443–45; Milton C. Nahm, "The Theological Background of the Theory of the Artist as Creator," *JHI* 8 (June 1947): 363–72; and the learned survey by S. K. Heninger Jr., "Poet as Maker," in *Touches of Sweet Harmony: Pythagorean Cosmology and Renaissance Poetics* (San Marino, Calif.: Huntington Library, 1974), 287–324.

6. The biographical details, culled mainly from Richard Ward, *Life of Dr H. More* (1710), ed. M. F. Howard (London: Theosophical Publishing Society, 1911), and from More's own utterances, may be found conveniently summarized in *Philosophical Poems of Henry More*, ed. with introduction and notes by Geoffrey Bullough (Manchester: Manchester University Press, 1931), and Aharon Lichtenstein, *Henry More: The Rational Theology of a Cambridge Platonist* (Cambridge: Harvard University Press, 1962). For More's translation of Εὐπορία or "Extrication," see pp. 299–300 of Marjorie Hope Nicolson's *Conway Letters* (New Haven: Yale University Press, 1930), a work of humane scholarship remarkable for its learning (when the learning had to be got the hard way) and its shrewdly sympathetic insights into the relationship of More and Lady Anne. So far as I am aware, no one has appreciated what was for More the crucial difficulty—that the *principio individuationis* failed him in his effort to "individuate."

7. Sir Thomas Elyot. *The Book Named the Governor*, ed. S. E. Lehmberg, Everyman's Library (1906; reprint, London: J. M. Dent, 1966), 165.

8. See Heninger, *Touches of Sweet Harmony*, 19 (and index).

9. Cf. ibid., 201–2 (and index).

10. An amusing account (particularly that thumb), as translated by Geoffrey Bullough from *Prefatio Generalissima*, *Opera Omnia* (1679), in his introduction, p. xvi, to *Philosophical Poems*; my additions in brackets are from the copy of *Opera Omnia* in The Huntington Library, 5 verso.

11. I use "Aporia" and "Euporia" only as clumsy markers ("Aporia" is derivative, as More himself admitted) to draw attention to a dramatic change in the way More thought about himself and his world: what is clear, or understandably unclear, is that somewhere in the period of 1635 to 1639 More suffered from some kind of spiritual angst, an intense spiritual deprivation, that resulted in (among other physical symptoms) an alarming loss of weight, and that by 1640, at the latest, he was once more in spiritual and physical health. In 1637 Benjamin Whichcote, an extraordinary teacher whose influence on More remains to be assessed, was appointed Sunday lecturer at Trinity Church, and apparently More told Richard Ward, his biographer, that in 1637 he found himself converted to a "new way" of "thinking."

"A More Safe Survey": Social-Property Relations, Hegemony, and the Rhetoric of Country Life

DON E. WAYNE

I. Ideology and Hegemony

WHEN, in his landmark study *The Country and the City* (1973), Raymond Williams treated seventeenth-century estate poems as allegorical descriptions of an emergent agrarian capitalism, a whole new way of thinking about topographical literature was inaugurated. Resistance to such thinking has persisted, especially in a literary field where the apparent conservative tenor and its correlative vehicle derived from classical models provide an easy mirror for neoconservative and what might be called neofugitive critical commentary. But the ideological nature of literary production no longer requires the spirited defense that Williams and others gave it in the 1970s and 1980s. If anything, today a hermeneutics of suspicion is nearly axiomatic in literary studies, though "ideology" is not always the rubric under which such interpretation is carried out. The terms "representation," "discursive formation," and "cultural construction" appear to have greater currency today, perhaps because "ideology" was for so long a term associated chiefly with Marxist criticism. The limitations of traditional Marxist ideological critique are acknowledged by Williams himself when he embraces Antonio Gramsci's notion of "hegemony":

> A lived hegemony is always a process. It is not, except analytically, a system or a structure. It is a realized complex of experiences, relationships, and activities, with specific and changing pressures and limits. . . . Moreover (and this is crucial, reminding us of the necessary thrust of the concept), it does not just passively exist as a form of dominance. It has continually to be renewed, recreated, defended, and modified. It is also continually resisted, limited, altered, challenged by pressures not at all its own. We have then to add to the concept of hegemony

the concepts of counter-hegemony and alternative hegemony, which are real and persistent elements of practice. (Williams, *Marxism and Literature,* 112–13)

One of the advantages of the concept of hegemony is that it allows us to reconnect in theory aspects of human practice that were ideologically separated in the Enlightenment. Kant's *Critique of Judgment* (1790), with its well-known distinction of the pleasure of the judgment of taste from the satisfaction derived from judgments of what is agreeable or good, is the most pertinent example of this separation in theory where the study of culture is concerned. Kant's aesthetic, which comes into the English literary critical tradition mainly through Coleridge's interpretation, was a relatively late, philosophical stage in the larger process of institutional separation between the state apparatus and civil society that was already under way in England by the end of the sixteenth century. From the standpoint of hegemony, aesthetic forms are not independent of economic and political practices; but neither are the former merely reflections or reflexes of the latter.

In the Marxist critical tradition, the primary category is that of *class*, though in contrast to sociological modes of interpretation, class is never merely a differential category but rather an oppositional one. Class struggle is then the principal form of counterhegemony that Marxists, including Williams, recognize. Marxist cultural criticism was at its worst when it reduced culture to economistic explanations. But even at its best, that is, at its most dialectical, the focus on class struggle as the driving force in history often entailed a subordination of other domains of oppression and opposition, those involving gender, race, ethnicity, sexual orientation. This perhaps accounts for the ease with which proponents of the most recent modes of cultural critique often dismiss Marxist theory as passé. One effect of this dismissal has been a shift of attention within materialist critical theory from the economic to the cultural, a shift that is currently being institutionalized under the rubric of "cultural studies." The problem with this dismissal is that it loses sight of a critical component of the Marxist project—the central importance of labor as the source of value and the exploitation of labor as the basis of wealth in all modes of production (specifically, of profit under capitalism).

Without contesting the validity of categories like "discourse" and "representation," which are central to recent scholarship in early modern studies, I would argue that such categories need to be reinscribed within a historical narrative that gives an account of the way social hegemony (as distinct from direct political control by the state) functions in a specific mode of production. Marx's version of such a narrative is usually thought of in terms of the base/superstructure metaphor, which has been subjected to considerable criticism within Marxist theory itself (Williams, *Marxism and Literature,* 75–82). But a more dialectical and interactive notion of what Marx sometimes calls "spiritual production" (what we would term "discourse" or "representation") and its relation to a particular mode of production is evident in the following:

> In order to examine the connection between spiritual production and material production it is above all necessary to grasp the latter itself not as a general category but in *definite historical* form. . . . If material production itself is not conceived in its *specific historical* form, it is impossible to understand what is specific in the spiritual production corresponding to it and the *reciprocal influence* of one on the other. (Marx, *Theories of Surplus Value,* 276)

The reciprocity of "influence" that Marx acknowledges here gives to "spiritual production" a certain active determinacy within the framework of a given mode of production, that is, within a specific historical form of the economic relationship between those who own the means of production and those whose labor they exploit by extracting a surplus. Discourse and representation are active cultural forces, but they are forces that mediate particular forms of hierarchical social relations at the level of material production.

As the form of such relationships began to change in the system of agrarian production on the estates of the gentry and aristocracy in early modern England, changes also occurred in the ordering of forms of literary expression within the elite culture. As Louis Montrose has shown, the flowering of literary pastoralism in the last quarter of the sixteenth century both registers the centrality of sheepherding in the English agrarian economy and displaces that historical reality into a "fictional time-space of countless eclogues" in which the shepherd's labor is magically transformed into a figure for aristocratic *otium* (Montrose, "Of Gentlemen and Shepherds," 427). Further intensification of agricultural production in the country, coupled with the growing institutionalization of a business ethic in the managerial apparatus of the state, is mediated by a different kind of poetic practice in the early seventeenth century. The topographical poem, composed in imitation of classical models, was perhaps better fitted than its courtly antecedents in pastoral, epic, and lyric poetry to serve as the cultural accompaniment to a developing agrarian capitalism.[1] The adaptation of this genre to English meters constitutes a stage in the emergence in England of a national culture closely identified with property in land, with value dependent on landed property and land tenure, and with the attendant values of good management, domesticity, and conjugality. It is also a genre that discloses a new politics based on contract in tension with the old status system, a politics in which aristocratic *otium* is no longer idealized, in which labor is valued and the distinction between intellectual and physical labor is employed to legitimate class divisions. Despite the fact that this kind of poetry is often connected with the institution of the country house, architectural description is rarely a concern of the poets. Instead, emphasis is on the abundant provision made by nature to the owners of these estates and their tenants. This abundance is mythicized in the tradition of the *locus amoenus* and functions, like the gardens attached to the actual houses, as an image of paradise regained (see Wayne, *Penshurst,* 105–8, 125–27).

But the land that produces so abundantly and easily is also real property, and the estate is celebrated as a sort of commonwealth in miniature to which the owner is entitled by virtue not only of his patrimony but because of his ability to govern.[2] Administrative skill and responsibility is an ideal in this poetry, an ideal rooted in Reformation theology and in humanist doctrine. But the ideal as celebrated in estate poems beginning around 1610 had its material ground in the necessary transformation of the English aristocracy's occupational status over the previous half century, when the function of administration displaced that of warriorship as the chief mark of honor among those of rank (Stone, *Crisis,* 239–40; James, *English Politics*). This shift in the occupation of the ruling class coincided with the reordering of the structure of social relations on landed estates from the relationship of overlord and vassal to that of landlord and tenant. The climactic period of this transformation is roughly between 1590 and 1640 when, as Lawrence Stone notes, rents on most estates doubled while agricultural prices rose by only about a third. Among the factors contributing to this development, Stone cites sixteenth-century population expansion, which led to an increased demand for holdings by prospective tenants and the concurrent need of many of the aristocracy for new sources of income. In addition, he suggests, "it is no coincidence that the first formal relaxation of anti-inclosure legislation occurred, admittedly temporarily, at just this moment" (Stone, *Crisis,* 329). The period was then one in which English landlords prospered by consolidating landholdings and, for the most part, leasing them out to tenants.

II. Topography

Within the culture of the ruling elite, the first expression of this change in social relations on the land occurs in architecture with the opening up of the fortified, closed courtyard design of the medieval manor house and its transformation, beginning around 1540, into a country house; set in a park with adjacent fields encompassing thousands of acres, the country house signaled the authority of those who dwelled within to the community of leaseholders and laborers over whom they presided (Mercer, "Houses of the Gentry," 13; Stone, *An Open Elite?,* 295–96). Subsequently, poets such as Ben Jonson, Thomas Carew, Robert Herrick, and Andrew Marvell produced a discourse that reasserted the authority of these houses and their owners, but tempered the display of power with an idealized representation of reciprocal relations between landlords and tenants, even extending the ideal of symbiotic class relationships to include mere laborers. By the second decade of the seventeenth century, when many of the aristocracy and the gentry were living near the court on incomes from their rented lands, such poetry probably began to serve a hortatory function as part of James I's protracted effort to order members of the landed elite back onto their estates (Marcus, *Politics of Mirth,* chap. 3). The poems develop the traditional theme of an ordered chain of being in nature as the rationale for an existing hierarchy in the social and political domain. They legitimate status on the basis of blood and assign obligation on the basis of status. In this respect, they are vehicles of a precapitalist ideology. But if kinship and status were the only operative ideology in these poems, they would be far less complex than they are and less effective in providing ideological mediation for the transition from feudal to capitalist social relations on the land they describe. Rather than displaying a univocal ideology, these poems embody a hegemonic strategy of negotiation among competing ideologies.

Before turning to the dominant tradition in such poetry, I want to look at a country house poem that recent editors suggest may antedate Jonson's "To Penshurst," conventionally thought of as the first of its kind (Greer et al., *Kissing the Rod,* 51). Aemilia Lanyer's "The Description of Cooke-ham," written prior to October 1610 and addressed to the countess of Cumberland, may be an earlier poem than Jonson's. It is certainly as powerfully evocative, though what it evokes is fundamentally different both in terms of the place and the speaker's response to it. That it did not become the model for later estate poems is itself significant, not only because its author's gender would have commanded less authority in a developing poetic tradition dominated by masculinist conventions, but because its mode of description and celebration is so different from that of Jonson's model. Both poems represent nature as animated by spiritual qualities and employ Christian and classical topoi toward that end. But Lanyer makes little reference to the estate as a site of production; nature at Cookham is described in terms of its aesthetic and recreational qualities rather than as a potential source of commodities, that is, as a form of capital. Social relations on the estate are barely alluded to, except, perhaps, in one crucial aspect involving the effect, on an economically dependent community, of the landlord's absence at court (or, in the case of Cookham, which was a royal property, the aristocratic leaseholder's absence).

> And you sweet Cooke-ham, whom these Ladies leave,
> I now must tell the griefe you did conceave
> At their departure; when they went away,
> How every thing retained a sad dismay:
> Nay long before, when once an inkeling came,
> Me thought each thing did unto sorrow frame:
> The trees that were so glorious in our view,
> Forsooke both flowers and fruit, when once they knew

Of your depart, their very leaves did wither,
Changing their colours as they grewe together.
But when they saw this had no powre to stay you,
They often wept, though speechlesse, could not pray you;
Letting their teares in your faire bosoms fall,
As if they said, Why will ye leave us all?

(lines 127–40)

The personification of nature barely conceals the sense of material loss to the local populace that comes with the departure of potential employers of rank. A few lines earlier, the speaker relates her personal sense of loss, proclaiming her love and devotion for Margaret Clifford, countess of Cumberland, while registering the pain of being no longer in the countess's immediate circle of favor:

And yet it grieves me that I cannot be
Neere unto her, whose virtues did agree
With those faire ornaments of outward beauty,
Which did enforce from all both love and dutie.
Unconstant Fortune, thou art most to blame,
Who casts us downe into so lowe a frame:
Where our great friends we cannot dayly see,
So great a difference is there in degree.
Many are placed in those Orbes of state,
Parters in honour, so ordain'd by Fate;
Neere in show, yet farther off in love,
In which, the lowest alwayes are above.

(lines 99–109)

Lanyer's rank was not much higher than Jonson's. Her father had been a musician at court and was of Italian Jewish descent; her husband, a lower-echelon civil servant, is mentioned favorably in a letter from Bishop Bancroft to Robert Cecil in 1604 (Greer et al., *Kissing the Rod,* 44, 51). Her intellectual qualities may have brought her into the Clifford circle, but as a woman there were no opportunities for her to develop a network of patrons or to have a career at court of the sort that Jonson did. "The Description of Cookham" carries resonances of Spenser's earlier pastoral poetry, but it is quite different from the sort of nature poem that became the standard in the seventeenth century. The difference is partly one of theme, as I've already suggested; but it is also one of tone. A striking feature of Lanyer's poem as compared to those of Jonson and his followers is the sense of interiority that is evoked here. The response to nature is more like that which would become a standard in the later eighteenth century under the rubric of "sensibility." That standard would supersede the Stoic rationalism of Jonson and his contemporaries, and would form the basis of modern bourgeois psychological conceptions of the alienated "self" and of romantic doctrines that sought recreation and restoration of the self through art.

Lanyer's position in the history of English poetry is therefore an ironic one. Excluded by her gender and her rank from the dominant culture in which poetry circulated, she wrote a poem that was in certain respects out of her time, a poem that anticipated another time when the evocation of a similar sense of interior depth would be aimed at in literature written primarily for and by women. As Nancy Armstrong argues, in the age of industrial capitalism, the cultivation of interior sensibility in both its idealized and its monstrous forms (the latter epitomized by the madwomen and prostitutes of Victorian fiction) "came to play a very powerful role in a discourse that redefined any form of political resistance as a form of individual pathology. To define political resistance in such psychological terms was to remove it from the snarl of competing social and economic interests in which every individual was entangled" (Armstrong, *Desire and Domestic Fiction,* 252). In Lanyer's time, the psychologizing of political alienation was not yet a developed practice. But already in the preceding generation, most notably in the career of Edmund Spenser, it is evident as part of the process whereby male poets of humble origin serving patrons of rank appropriated to themselves the status of "Author" (Montrose, "Spenser's Domestic Domain," 15–16). In the following generation, Jonson invoked the authority of an aristocratic poet, Philip Sidney, in appropriating the status of Author to himself, while at the same time registering the political inequity of his status in relation to other Sidneys whom he had to serve (see, e.g., Jonson's "Ode to Sir William Sidney," discussed at length in Wayne, "Jonson's Sidney," 235ff.). But in Jonson the psychologizing of political resistance takes the form of denial and projection: that is, in denying his own pain while pathologizing nearly everyone else in his society from the standpoint of the Author function that he institutionalizes with the publication of his *Works* in 1616. On the other hand, Lanyer, to whom such status is institutionally denied, manifests a more personal and affirmative sense of the psychological pain that results from social and political inequity. Her poem is an early instance in English of what Ruskin termed the "pathetic fallacy" and which he viewed as "morbid" precisely because it was unmanly. But by letting nature bear the burden of her own pain and grief, and by extension the pain of others in the community of Cookham, Lanyer achieved a more powerful sense of the *trauma* of social relations at a place like Cookham than do any of the subsequent estate poems.

Pain and grief as an effect of social inequity are hardly evident in these poems. Rather, by thematizing domestic values (marriage, family, household management), such poetry hints at an identification across class lines between the "stately homes" of the nobility and gentry and the more humble homes of those who work the land. This metaphorical relationship is grounded in the emerging notion of the family as a natural cellular unit of society and of the house as a *home* (Wayne, *Penshurst,* 114). The landlord of the estate is encouraged to think of himself as a paterfamilias for the estate as a whole and as a model for how his tenants and even their male laborers ought to comport themselves in their own households. Class distinctions are blurred in more ways than one, as the poetry strives to maintain a decorum of rank while representing the country as a place of common purpose and common-wealth. Real economic exchange, which is asymmetrical and exploitative, is magically transformed into a symmetrical economy of reciprocal obligation and mutual care. Tenants and laborers at Penshurst are depicted bearing gifts as expressions of their love for the lord and lady, rather than as paying rent in kind or in money:

> But all come in, the farmer and the clown,
> And no one empty-handed, to salute
> Thy lord and lady, though they have no suit.
>
> (lines 48–50)

Similarly, in the companion piece, "To Sir Robert Wroth," the scene in the hall at Durrance when the "rout of rural folk come thronging in" is a kind of virtuous country masque set in opposition to the extravagant masquing of the court (Orgel, *Jonsonian Masque*). In the presence of Comus and the Muses, the heroic hosts (Robert and Mary Wroth)

> Sit mixed with loss of state or reverence,
> Freedom doth with degree dispense.
>
> (lines 57–58)

The passage evokes the momentary freedom allowed the farm laborers during a time of festival. Citing this passage and others like it, James Turner points out that such occasions were rare; they functioned as "safety valves" and "set the seal of licence on the social order. Complete impropriation of the crop is legitimized by the harvest supper, the command to labor by occasional sports" (Turner, *Politics of Landscape,* 145–46). Herford and Simpson identify as a probable source for this part of Jonson's poem the account of an entertainment given to the people by the emperor Domitian during the Saturnalia in Statius's *Silvae* 1.6.43–45 (Jonson, *Works,* 11:36). They don't seem to notice, however, that what is most striking about the allusion is Jonson's deviation from his Roman source. Despite the mirth and cheer in the open hall at Durrance, the celebration there is depicted in far more sober terms and in a far more homely setting than the emperor's orgiastic festival in Statius's poem (see, especially, *Silvae* 1.6.51–97). Jonson's language testifies to the Wroths' responsible administration of their estate. Degree is hardly dispensed with here, despite the explicit assertion to the contrary, but is rather celebrated and validated as a natural order of rank in a natural community. Like other poems of its kind, "To Sir Robert Wroth" enunciates a doctrine of social order in which rank is legitimated by merit and contractual obligation rather than merely by patrimony and status.

Raymond Williams sees in these literary evocations of the country estate as a terrestrial paradise, the ideological suppression of a central facet of life on such estates, that is, the curse of labor. "Yet," he writes, "this magical extraction of the curse of labor is in fact achieved by a simple extraction of the existence of laborers" (Williams, *Country and the City,* 32). He cites one counterexample, Herrick's harvest poem "The Hock Cart," with its blatant acknowledgment of exploited labor:

> Come Sons of Summer, by whose toil
> We are the Lords of Wine and Oil. . . .

Williams remarks tellingly, "It is perhaps not surprising that 'The Hock Cart' is less often quoted, as an example of a natural and moral economy, than 'Penshurst' or 'To Saxham.' Yet all that is in question is the degree of consciousness of real processes. What Herrick embarrassingly intones is what Jonson and Carew mediate" (Williams, *Country and the City,* 34). Here, again, Williams's commentary marks a turning point in the critical tradition by discriminating which poems have served traditional interpretive schemes better and why. But the way Jonson and Carew mediate real conditions on the estates they address is perhaps not as unembarrassed as Williams suggests. Certainly in Jonson's case, the hyperawareness of his own intellectual labor makes the cancellation of another kind of mediation, i.e., the mediation of manual labor, somewhat ironic. In fact, in order to distinguish between these two kinds of production and mediation and to set them in a hierarchical order, Jonson must allow the curse of labor to reappear:

> . . . nor, standing by,
> A waiter, doth my gluttony envy:
> But gives me what I call, and lets me eat,
> He knows, below, he shall find plenty of meat.
> ("To Penshurst," lines 67–70)

While I agree for the most part with Williams's description of the magical extraction of labor in the poems by Jonson and Carew, it is also interesting to notice the strategic moments when such poems stumble on their way to achieving the mystified representation of unlimited production and easy consumption without labor. It is true that in some passages labor is extracted altogether. But in other places, labor is referred to while being represented as freely given and painless. In "To Penshurst" (lines 19–44) and in Carew's "To Saxham" (lines 21–28), the land is represented as giving up its bounty without the necessary mediation of labor. Here the miraculous extraction of the curse of labor is facilitated by the animate form of what is described: At Penshurst the "painted partridge" is "*willing* to be killed"; carps and pikes *run* into the net; and "bright eels that *emulate* them . . . *leap* on land / Before the fisher, or into his hand." At Saxham, "every beast did hither *bring / Himself*, to be an offering. / The scaly herd more pleasure *took*, / Bath'd in thy dish than in the brook" (my emphasis). But when the poems attempt to achieve the same magical or miraculous effect with respect to inanimate things, the question of human agency and mediation immediately presents itself. This is one reason why such a poem can barely allude to the architecture of the estate. When it does, the reference takes the form of negation and denial in marked contrast to the affirmative references to animate nature. The effect here is not that of magic or miracle but of alibi:

> And though thy walls be of the country stone,
> They are reared with no man's ruin, no man's groan;
> There's none that dwell about them wish them down;
> But all come in, the farmer and the clown . . .
> ("To Penshurst," lines 45–48)

> Thou hast no porter at the door
> T'examine or keep back the poor;
> Nor locks nor bolts: thy gates have been
> Made only to let strangers in;
> Untaught to shut, they do not fear
> To stand wide open all the year . . .
> ("To Saxham," lines 49–54)

> Safe stand thy walls, and thee, and so both will,
> Since neither's height was raised by the ill
> Of others; since no stud, no stone, no piece,
> Was reared up by the poor man's fleece.
> (Herrick, "A Panegyrick to Sir Lewis Pemberton," lines 115–18)

By a rather weak logic of association, the human agency required to rear up inanimate stones into walls or to open and close the great house's massive iron gates is assimilated to the animate nature that gives itself up so freely to the masters of the estate. Nature, then, in its animate forms provides the ideological basis for the effacement of labor in all areas of production, including not only hunting and gathering and farming, but building and by extension quarrying, mining, and manufacture as well. Indeed, what we may observe here is a sort of magical protonarrative of how ideology will primarily work under capitalism; that is, by naturalizing socially constructed conditions and categories of the real.

If such poetry simply provided legitimation for the extraction of a surplus in rent and labor, it would not be very interesting as literature. But the poetry also points to a split within dominant practices and ideologies, and in so doing acquires a measure of dramatic tension and irony. While "the country seat was a power centre, a showplace for the display of authority" (Stone, *An Open Elite?*, 299), the poems that celebrated such estates often based their claim for authority on a critique of conspicuous consumption and on an implicit rebuke of absentee landlordism—a claim epitomized early in this tradition by Jonson's apostrophe to Penshurst with its well-known conclusion: "[Others] may say their lords have built, but thy lord dwells." The compliment, here to Robert Sidney, idealizes an active courtier who is yet attentive to the land and the people he oversees. But even those who were less involved in politics at court than Sidney and who, therefore, spent longer periods of time in the country were increasingly reluctant to undertake the direct management of agriculture on their estates. Consequently, they either leased out much of their land or raised sheep and cattle on enclosed pastures (Stone, *Crisis,* 140). Perhaps, this is why poems celebrating prominent landlords do not, as a rule, represent their patrons as involved in the actual management of their estates.

An interesting exception to the rule is Herrick's poem to Endymion Porter, entitled "The Country Life." Porter is portrayed as taking personal responsibility for keeping accounts of profits and expenditures—

> . . . thy ambition's masterpiece
> Flies no thought higher than a fleece;
> Or how to pay thy hinds [farm laborers], and clear
> All scores, and so to end the year. . . .
>
> (lines 11–14)

—and as walking into the fields in order to oversee the plowing, knowing that "the best compost for the lands / Is the wise master's feet and hands" (lines 23–24). But, of course, the master does not labor with his hands; rather, as part of his role in the contractual community over which he presides, he provides the intellectual and administrative labor to which the material labor of farmers and servants is subordinated. He also provides ideological discipline, exhorting his laborers by "singing how / The kingdom's portion is the plow" (lines 27–28). The last quoted phrase—similar to Herrick's own exhortation in "The Hock Cart": "then to the plow, the commonwealth" (line 39)—is striking because it identifies the nation's wealth not only with land but specifically with agriculture. This raises the interesting question of what use of the land is in the best interest of the commonwealth as a whole, and what sort of estate management can best realize that usage. That the question is not so specifically addressed in Jonson's earlier poems may be because the consequences of aristocratic withdrawal from the land were not yet so clear. Stone traces a development from the reign of Elizabeth to the outbreak of civil war in which the landowning elite became less and less involved in demesne farming: "[N]ever agricultural entrepreneurs on a very large scale, noblemen contracted their activities in the early seventeenth century so that by 1640 the great majority were little more than rentiers, and often absentee rentiers at that" (*Crisis,* 143).

III. Social-Property Relations

The invocation of hospitality in early estate poems is motivated in part by an anxiety about the decline of precapitalist social structures in England. Hospitality is also invoked by Francis Bacon in a passage that is worth quoting at length here. Writing against the inflation of honors in his own time, Bacon looks back to the earliest years of the Tudor dynasty, which he represents in a nostalgic, idealized image of reciprocity between a limited number of noblemen and gentlemen and their respective attendants and villein or yeomen farmers. Comparing England to France, Bacon argues, too, that the latter "middle people of England make good soldiers, which the peasants of France do not":

> And herein the device of king Henry the Seventh. . .was profound and admirable, in making farms and houses of husbandry of a standard; that is, maintained with such a proportion of land unto them, as may breed a subject to live in convenient plenty and no servile condition; and to keep the plow in the hands of the owners, and not mere hirelings. And thus indeed you shall attain to Virgil's character which he gives to ancient Italy:
>
> > *Terra potens armis atque ubere glebae.*
> > [A land powerful in arms and in productiveness of soil.]
>
> Neither is that state (which, for any thing I know, is almost peculiar to England, and hardly to be found anywhere else, except it be perhaps in Poland) to be passed over; I mean the state of free servants and attendants upon noblemen and gentlemen, which are no ways inferior unto the yeomanry for arms. And therefore, out of all question, the splendor and magnificence and great retinues and hospitality of noblemen and gentlemen, received into custom, doth much conduce unto martial greatness. Whereas, contrariwise, the close and reserved living of noblemen and gentlemen causeth a penury of military forces. (Bacon, "Of the True Greatness of Kingdoms and Estates," 150)

Howsoever idealized, the class structure Bacon describes depends on attachment to the land and its community. According to one's status, such attachment is manifested through noblesse oblige or through service. The ideal espoused here by Bacon is fundamentally feudal; and the policy it implies when read in the context of Bacon's more general writings is that of a feudal reorganization that would accommodate entrepreneurial elements while maintaining political control over them. But by 1625 (the year in which the third edition of Bacon's *Essays* appeared), the social structure Bacon alludes to was being displaced by a different structure of class relations in England, that of landlord/capitalist and tenant/wage-laborer. Bacon's ideal—"to keep the plow in the hands of the owner, and not mere hirelings"—is thus anachronistic. It is precisely the opposite tendency in the organization of what Robert Brenner terms "social-property relations" that enabled an agricultural revolution that, "in turn, was the key to England's uniquely successful overall economic development" (Brenner, "Agrarian Class Structure," 49). Brenner points to a certain irony in the pre-history of English agricultural capitalism. Because the feudal English lords were more successful than their French counterparts in dispossessing peasants of the land, the extraction of rent was eventually insufficient by itself to sustain the development and profitability of land in England. Increasingly, landlords leased to tenants who operated large holdings as capitalist enterprises based on the extraction of a surplus from wage labor and on the intensification of agricultural development through capital investment and new technologies. Comparing such large entrepreneurial tenant holdings in England to the "rentier mentality" that prevailed in the management of similarly large farms in France, where capital improvement was limited and rent-squeezing was the principal means of extracting a profit, Brenner writes:

> In England, especially in the grain-growing regions, capitalist farmers controlled a highly capital-intensive husbandry, and the numbers of landholding peasants had declined drastically. In this situation, landlord incomes depended upon the tenants' ability to farm effectively on the basis of capital investment. Capitalist profits were, in short, a condition for landlord rents. To the degree that landlords attempted to squeeze tenants, preventing them from making a reasonable profit on their investment, the latter might cease to invest, and ultimately give up their leases, moving to another farm or perhaps even another field of production. On the other hand, there existed no mass of semi-proletarianized peasantry on the land—let alone one which could afford to pay a rent equivalent to that paid by the capitalist tenants. Economic success, in brief, depended on accumulation and innovation and, in this context, when the tenant was short of funds it was at times in the interest of the landlord to take over, to some degree, the function of capital investment (in which case the landlord would take part of his return in the form of profit). Thus . . . [a] sort of landlord/tenant symbiosis . . . had a good economic rationale and tended to condition a dynamic agricultural development. (Brenner, "Agrarian Roots," 314–15)

Bacon is also anachronistic in his focus on military service, which signals a feudal model of extra-economic compulsion and intra-lordly competition and conflict adapted to the emerging modern European system of competition among nation states. But in England, if not yet elsewhere in Europe, the social-property relations of agrarian capitalism required new forms of legitimation and control. Previously, the landlord's power was exercised "politically," that is through military force and laws governing rents and taxes. But by the seventeenth century "in England the landlord class, having uprooted the peasantry, could depend largely upon the operation of 'impersonal', 'economic' processes—the exploitation by capitalist tenants of free wage-laborers and, in turn, the operation of intracapitalist competition, especially among tenants in the agricultural sector, but also in the economy as a whole." In effect what occurred already in Bacon's time was "the emergence of an institutional separation between the state and civil society" (Brenner, "Agrarian Roots," 299). And Bacon's own writings in other respects contribute to this very separation, as for example in the essay "Of Empire," where in discriminating the various social classes he calls merchants the "*vena porta* [gate vein]; and if they flourish not, a kingdom may have good limbs, but will have empty veins, and nourish little" (Bacon, *Essays,* 119), and advocates that trade not be decreased by taxes and imposts; or in the essay, "Of Usury," where, once again, "merchandizing . . . is the *vena porta* of wealth in the state," the commodity nature of money is recognized, the "commodities of usury" are seen to outweigh its "discommodities," and state regulation of interest is limited to ways of freeing money for trade (183–86). Moreover, as a new literary genre, Bacon's *Essays*, like other forms of conduct literature in the period, exemplify the increasing importance of self-regulation as a component of the institutional separation of the public and private spheres.[3]

IV. Civil Society, Hegemony, and Domestic Economy

The literature of country life also contributed to the ideological process whereby this separation was historically legitimated. As part of the ideology produced in such poetry, an important complement of the theme of good estate management was that of domesticity coupled with discipline. This aspect of the tradition is epitomized in Marvell's "Upon Appleton House," where Mary, the daughter of Lord Fairfax and Ann Vere is said

> . . .to have been from the first
> In a *Domestic Heaven* nurst,
> Under the *Discipline* severe
> Of Fairfax, and the starry Vere.
>
> (stanza 91)

While genealogy is necessarily alluded to in poems addressed to those of rank, a primary vehicle of praise is the depiction of the patron and his wife as models of domestic and conjugal duty. In the owner of a country estate the roles of governor and father were conflated. This constituted an extension down through the social hierarchy of the monarch's role as it came to be defined in the sixteenth century. Max Weber describes the power of the court-centered state as deriving from "the authority of the master of the house within a domestic community." Legitimation of political power in monarchist ideology—that is, legitimation of "the rule of one master of the house over others who are not subject to his domestic authority" involved "the assimilation to domestic authority of power relationships differing from it in degree and content but not in structure" (quoted in Elias, *Court Society,* 41–42). In the patriarchal court state, the structural homology between domestic order and political rule required constant reminders of the father's authority in every household of the realm. In its role of legitimation with respect to patriarchy and the patrimonial state, the domestic theme is a fundamentally public one (Goldberg, *James I,* chap. 2).

But the repetition of the theme allowed for the emergence of a discourse extolling the virtues of conjugal affection and for the representation of home and family not only as a domain of public responsibility but as a haven of private retreat. Moreover, images of domesticity in royal and aristocratic households began to have wider application because they depended on the notion of a universal nature that could cut across class distinctions. As Jonathan Goldberg points out, the notion of the family as a retreat from the state is no less ideological than that which represents the family as the source of state power (88). Rather than conclude, as he does, however, that ideology is all-powerful in the service of a controlling state apparatus, I prefer to view this as an example of Gramsci's and Williams's notion of hegemony. The domestic theme, then, can be seen as both an instrument of hegemony (in its monarchist and aristocratic forms) and of counterhegemony (in its substitution of the marriage contract and conjugal duty for genealogy as the basis of authority). In Gramsci's conception, hegemony functions primarily in the institutions of civil society rather than in the more direct legal and coercive agencies of the state. Hegemony therefore involves interiorization by the subject of a certain fabric of values, beliefs, and behaviors, enabling what Gramsci terms "spontaneous consent" (Gramsci, *Selections,* 12). The notion is comparable to Louis Althusser's often cited conception of the subject as "interpellated" by ideology, with the difference that "hegemony" allows for the process of negotiation between dominant and subaltern groups, and even for modes of resistance by the latter. The organization of social hegemony in modern societies is, in Gramsci's view, the primary role of intellectuals: "The relationship between the intellectuals and the world of production is not as direct as it is with the fundamental social groups but is, in varying degrees, 'mediated' by the whole fabric of society and by the complex of superstructures, of which the intellectuals are, precisely, the 'functionaries'" (12). Literature and its dissemination through the new technology of the printed book provided an important vehicle for this mediating role of the intellectual in early modern culture.

To my knowledge, the first printed book in English on the subject of domestic architecture was written by Henry VIII's physician, Andrew Boorde.

Published around 1540, it bears the long and revealing title *The book for to learn a man to be wise in building of his house for the health of body, and to hold quietness for the health of his soul and body. The book for a good husband to learn.* A key word here is "quietness," with its suggestion of the comfort and well-being the husband ought to derive not only from the design of his house but from the relations that obtain within it—in other words, domestic tranquility. There is, I believe, an implication too that a householder and husband has a proprietary title to such "quietness." A hundred years later the idea is made explicit in Hobbes' *Leviathan,* where "conjugal affection" is a proprietary entitlement second only to a man's body itself: "Of all things held in propriety those that are dearest to a man are his own life, and limbs; and in the next degree, (in most men), those that concern conjugal affection; and after them riches and means of living (382–83). Domestic tranquility and conjugal affection are already important themes in Spenser's poetry, and domesticity is developed as part of the emergent discourse of colonialism in his *View of the Present State of Ireland* (Montrose, "Spenser's Domestic Domain"). But a more generalized shift away from the martial, erotic, and eroticized pastoral of the Elizabethan period can be seen in the topographical poetry of the seventeenth century, with its georgic resonances of good husbandry—even where Hesiod and Virgil are not direct sources of imitation—and with its idealization of estate management in the figure of the home.

This shift in genre helped to mediate the complex process whereby changes in social-property relations sought new political expression. As the English landed class grew to depend less on direct extra-economic means of extracting wealth, they required a new kind of state, one that would ensure order, protect property, and reinforce the new contractual basis of production at a relatively moderate cost. Although ultimately the means of securing this goal was to be the strengthening of parliament over royal prerogative, in the years leading up to civil war the domestic ideal was invoked on all sides of the political conflict. Emblematic of order on the domestic front was the motif and even the very phrase "country life." It appears in the title and opening line of Herrick's poem to Endymion Porter:

> Sweet country life, to such unknown,
> Whose lives are others', not their own!
> But, serving courts and cities, be
> Less happy, less enjoying thee.

Though set in opposition to court and city, the country here stands for a vision of domestic order throughout the realm.

The phrase appears in the title and text of another of Herrick's poems, this one written in a more intimate mode addressed to his younger brother Thomas. The scene is more humble than that of the estate poems quoted earlier. Thomas

Herrick had been apprenticed to a London merchant but appears to have left the city in 1610 to try farming a small holding in Leicestershire, apparently with little success (see ed. note in Herrick, *Poetical Works,* 504). Robert's poem "reports" Thomas's endurance of the hardships of daily toil, making a virtue of poverty and humility and of the limited fare provided by this less than glamorous setting:

> . . . Stand Center-like, unmoved;
> And be not only thought, but proved
> To be what I report thee; and inure
> Thy self, if want comes to endure. . . .
> Who keep'st no proud mouth for delicious cates:
> Hunger makes coarse meats, delicates.
> Can'st, and unurged, forsake that Larded fare,
> Which Art, not Nature, makes so rare;
> To taste boiled Nettles, Colworts, Beets, and eat
> These and sour herbs, as dainty meat?
> While soft Opinion makes thy Genius say,
> Content makes all Ambrosia.
> Nor is it, that thou keep'st this stricter size
> So much for want, as exercise:
> To numb the sense of Dearth, which should sin haste it,
> Thou might'st but only see't, not taste it.
> (Herrick, "A Country Life," lines 101–4, 109–20)

Herrick offers his brother not just the traditional consolation of philosophy, but the consolation of a *domestic* philosophy and of conjugal comfort, if not bliss:

> But that which most makes sweet thy country life,
> Is, the fruition of a wife. . .
> . . . [who] by chast intentions led,
> Gives thee each night a Maidenhead.
> (lines 31–32, 41–42)

The rhetoric is that of desire and pleasure contained by comfort and use. The imagery of immaculate coition in the controlled heterosexual safety zone of the marriage bed leads to a vision of untroubled sleep and of bucolic dreams in an Edenic landscape: "damaskt meadows," "purling springs, groves, birds, and well-weav'd Bowers, / With fields enameled with flowers. . . ." The sequence culminates in the image of a suckling lamb, which, by association, gives sensual presence and palpability to the qualities of safety, comfort, and fruition identified earlier with the wife and the marriage bed:

> Then dream, ye heare the Lamb by many a bleat
> Wooed to come suck the milky Teat:

While Faunus in the Vision comes to keep,
From rav'ning wolves, the fleecy sheep.
(lines 49–52)

After a brief interval in which the crowing of the cock brings back the reality of "work" and "sacrifice" (lines 56–62), the theme of domestic security is reinforced by setting it in comparison with the hazards of entrepreneurial ventures abroad undertaken by the "industrious Merchant," and with the extravagance and intrigue of the court. The phrase "but thou at home" is repeated twice (lines 69, 76), establishing the domestic scene as the viewpoint of a distant prospect, not of a grand estate, but of the dangerous world that lies beyond the compass of the householder's "Map" that provides "a more safe survey" (lines 72–73).

The last quoted phrase encapsulates the locutionary force of this poem, marking the household and the land attached to it as the limit of security. It is a centripetal force set against the outward movements of merchant capital in foreign trade and of courtly vices that may lead to entanglements with foreign "States . . . Countries, Courts, and Kings" (line 85). The rhetoric of country life is a rhetoric of containment; private property, the domestic economy, and the privacy of the conjugal scene are sanctified by the formula that substitutes comfort and use for desire and pleasure:

Thus let thy Rural Sanctuary be
Elizium to thy wife and thee;
There to disport your selves with golden measure:
For seldom use commends the pleasure. . . .
(lines 137–40)

While this rhetoric of security and containment is directed at the ordinary householder's self-image, it would eventually become one pole of the binary *home/foreign* in the centrifugal, expansionist rhetoric of trade and empire of British hegemony. The relationship is institutionalized in the names of the relevant secretariats of the British government: the Home Office and the Foreign Office.

V. Hardwick Hall: Domestic Economy and Female Authority

Poetry is not the only rhetorical vehicle for the idealization of domestic economy and of privacy that helped institutionalize the separation of civil society from the state. In domestic architecture and decor, there is already evidence in the Elizabethan period of a gradual privatization of space that further suggests a heightened sense of the importance of domestic and conjugal relations in the emerging social order. An early sign of this development is the decline of the entrance hall as a communal center of the great house. The newer houses of the elite included splendid rooms of state and often, for use on ceremonial occasions, an elaborate great chamber, usually located on an upper floor. At the same time, however, the growing tendency was for the lord and his family to dine in the relative privacy of smaller parlors and banquet rooms (Fumerton, *Cultural Aesthetics*, 113–31). An interesting synthesis of the function of hierarchical symbolism with a concern for some degree of privacy can be observed in the design of the new Hardwick Hall, begun by Bess of Hardwick, countess of Shrewsbury, in 1590. The house is built high on a hill and is well known for its impressive facade with huge windows, an exact symmetry, and the initials of its builder (ES for Elizabeth Shrewsbury) boldly displayed along the roofline. The interior is ordered hierarchically with lesser rooms including kitchen and servants quarters on the ground level, state apartments and the "High Great Chamber" on the second floor, and apartments used daily by the family in the middle. This three-tiered hierarchy is reflected on the exterior by the increasing height of the windows from level to level. As Girouard's isometric drawing shows (*Life in the English Country House*, 117), the design allowed for a degree of privacy unusual in Elizabethan houses by separating the family quarters from both the servants below and guests of state above.

The example of Hardwick Hall is all the more striking because it constitutes a variation on the conventional representation of masculine and patriarchal authority in the domestic scene. In addition to proclaiming her status by making the initials of her name prominent in the house's exterior design, Bess made conscientious use of classical and Christian topoi, and of allegorical figures in embroideries, tapestries, and carvings in wood and plaster to describe female authority in the household. The plan of the interior decoration is known from an inventory of 1601. Among the subjects depicted, a dominant motif is that of the virtuous wife. In a series of embroideries Penelope is flanked by figures depicting Patience and Perseverance; Lucretia is presented with the figures of Chastity and Liberality beside her; Zenobia with Magnanimity and Prudence; Artemisia with Pietas and Constancy. Though these are conventional figures, the references to Zenobia and Artemisia, both warrior queens in antiquity, are especially indicative of Bess's strategy of self-aggrandizement. Zenobia, a third-century queen of Palmyra (northeast of Damascus), ruled on the death of her husband and led her own armies in battle. In the Hardwick depiction she wears a helmet and carries a lance. Zenobia was celebrated not only for her military valor and political ability but for her learning and literary talent (she was the patroness of Longinus). In *The Masque of Queens* (1609), Jonson refers to Trebellius Pollio's praise of her: "Her chastity was such 'that she never even knew her own husband except in order to have children'"

Hardwick Hall, Derbyshire (1590—96). Entrance front. © National Trust Photographic Library/J. Whitaker.

Hardwick Hall, Derbyshire. Embroidered hanging depicting Penelope flanked by Patience and Perseverance, c. 1575. One of a set listed in the 1601 inventory. © National Trust Photographic Library.

(Jonson, *Works*, 7:311). There were two Artemisias in antiquity, both also celebrated as warrior queens. The first reigned over Halicarnassus in the fifth century B.C., and led her own ships in Xerxes' expedition against the Greeks. Jonson cites Herodotus's account of Xerxes' exclamation, after seeing her fight: "My men behaved like women, but my women like men." But in his notes to *The Masque of Queens*, Jonson confuses this Artemisia with a second who lived a century later (10:506). This second Artemisia succeeded her brother and husband as ruler of Caria (or Halicarnassus). It is she who is probably depicted in the Hardwick panel, where she appears holding a scepter in one hand and a cup in the other. She too was known as a warrior queen, having conquered Rhodes and neighboring islands.

Of more immediate significance for Bess of Hardwick was the second Artemisia's reputation as a builder. On the death of her husband, Mausolus, she erected a monument that was counted by the ancients as one of the seven wonders of the world and that gave the name *mausoleum* to later Roman sepulchers. On it was depicted an Amazonomachy "which was a celebration of the female warriors, spiritual sisters of Caria's two Artemisias" (DuBois, *Centaurs and Amazons,* 131). Among the multiple ironies of this topos is the fact that Bess was not building a monument to her husband, but one to herself. At the same time, the image of female power symbolized in these warrior queens is contained by the surrounding figures of feminine virtue. The figure for Piety beside Artemisia is particularly striking: it alludes to Valerius Maximus's account of Pero breast-feeding her father Cimon when he was condemned to starvation in prison. Pero is seen with her child at her side who points to a stork, an emblem of piety (Nevinson, "Stitched for Bess," 756). But to the extent that this figure of filial piety has the effect of containing the adjacent allusion to Amazonian power, it is a powerful image of female authority in the mode of nurturing.

The most important figure of the virtuous wife in Bess's iconographic plan is Penelope, who recurs in various depictions and is a central figure in the tapestries of the High Great Chamber. These were purchased in 1587, three years before construction began on the building itself. It is thought that the stateroom in which they hang was designed specifically to display them. If so, this would suggest the centrality of these wall hangings in Bess's allegorical as well as her decorative plan. Furthermore, the particular manner in which the Ulysses story is illustrated appears to be unusual, though commentary on the choice of subjects is limited by the absence of information concerning the original commission. Nevertheless, one striking feature of this set of Brussels tapestries is the depiction, very rare in the sixteenth century and not elaborated from literary sources, of Ulysses taking leave of his family and entrusting his wife to his father's care (Roethlisberger, "Ulysses Tapestries," 113, 115), as though to reinforce Penelope's importance in the narrative. The motif of feminine virtue

Hardwick Hall, Derbyshire. Pero breast-feeding her father Cimon. Detail from embroidered hanging of 1573. © Country Life Picture Library.

Hardwick Hall, Derbyshire. Ulysses taking leave of his family. One of a set of sixteenth-century Brussels tapestries in the High Great Chamber, listed in the 1601 inventory. © Victoria and Albert Museum.

is further elaborated in this room by a frieze depicting the court of Diana, presumably in tribute to Elizabeth I, whose authority on the basis of rank Bess of Hardwick was duty-bound to acknowledge, but whose authority on the basis of gender she could appropriate. Ulysses and Penelope are also central figures in a Flemish painting that hung in the company of portraits adorning the walls of the adjoining Withdrawing Chamber at the time of the 1601 inventory (Boynton, *Hardwick Hall Inventories*, 27) .

Girouard has remarked of Bess that "presumably she identified herself with [Penelope], as a virtuous and faithful wife addicted to spinning, or at least embroidery" (Girouard, *Hardwick Hall*, 93). This is borne out by the iconography throughout the house, which extols feminine virtue as epitomized in the good, industrious wife. Such virtue is identified not only with chastity but with the social value of feminine labor, which finds expression in both content (the image of Penelope's spinning) and form (embroidery, which Bess probably practiced herself and certainly supervised in her household). How much of the needlework was actually done by Bess and her gentlewomen is a matter of some speculation. There is little doubt that they were directly involved; but there is also evidence of the handiwork of wage laborers.[4] In any case, what is important here is the representation of such work as women's work in the tradition of Penelope, even if the representation was achieved with the labor of hirelings, some of whom were men.

In addition to the larger embroideries bearing a narrative content, such as those depicting famous and virtuous wives, there is a group of smaller pieces in the form of octagons embroidered with botanical subjects based on a Renaissance herbal book. Each octagon carries the picture of a plant with a surrounding inscription in what appears, at first glance, to be the manner of the emblem books popular in the period. The method of emblematic herbal literature is to provide an inscription that would conjoin a moral with some reference to the particular plant illustrated. "But at Hardwick," notes John Nevinson, "the embroideress seems to have had very little idea of choosing an aphorism or motto to fit her picture, except No. 9 where the laurel is to be regarded as a reward for virtue or bravery ('Virtutis praemium'). . . . Instead she turned to a school book, containing phrases to be memorized by the small boy learning Latin. This would almost certainly have been one of the numerous editions of the *Adages of Erasmus* which were extensively modified towards the end of the sixteenth century" ("An Elizabethan Herbarium," 66–67). The didactic function of the mottoes on the octagons appears to have been recognized in a mid-nineteenth century handbook on Hardwick, which concludes that "Dr White Kennet [who eulogized Bess of Hardwick in a funeral sermon] would have been right had he called them a lesson" (68). Nevinson's intriguing observations concerning Bess's divergence from the conventional emblem tradition and her use, instead, of mottoes to be memorized on the model of a humanist grammar-school book are especially interesting in light of Richard Halpern's recent discussion of Tudor pedagogy as a form of ideological training aimed at producing "civil" subjects.[5] These smaller embroideries can be seen as an integral part of the general iconographic pattern at Hardwick of asserting female authority in the domestic realm, here extended to authority over educational discipline.

The pattern was undoubtedly strategic on Bess' part. There is a certain irony to the implementation of this domestic and disciplinary theme by a woman of minor gentry parentage who amassed a fortune through successive marriages to four men of progressively higher rank and who was notorious for defying the authority of her fourth husband, the earl of Shrewsbury, during the last thirteen years of their marriage (Girouard, *Hardwick Hall,* 11–12). When he died in 1590, Bess was left one of the richest and most powerful women

Hardwick Hall, Derbyshire. Two of thirty octagonal embroideries with botanical subjects, each measuring about 14 inches by 14 inches. Moonwort and hazelnuts. © National Trust Photographic Library.

in England. She was free to build her house on land inherited from her own family and to build in a manner that laid claim to a status beyond her rank at birth and beyond that conventionally allowed to women other than the queen herself. Given these circumstances, the interior decoration at Hardwick suggests an attempt to link domestic imagery to the powerful symbolism of the house's exterior facade in an effort to rationalize and to normalize a shift in power involving relationships of both social rank and gender. The importance of the interior of the house to the final monumental effect is suggested by Bess's specific instructions in her last will and testament that the items in the 1601 inventory "remayne and Contynewe at my house or howses at Hardwick

according to the true entent and meaning thereof" (Boynton, *Hardwick Hall Inventories,* 23).

In spite of the fact that the narratives alluded to in the iconography of Hardwick Hall subordinate women to masculine authority, the monumental scale of the building in which this iconography is housed and the fact that it was built by a woman gave to the overall symbolic ensemble at Hardwick the potential counterhegemonic impact of a regendering of domestic authority. The effect in relation to aristocratic domestic architecture is not unlike that which Maureen Quilligan ascribes to Lady Mary Wroth's *Urania* poems, which, she argues, regender Petrarchan discourse—"to regender . . . is to effect 'a return to the origin,' as Foucault puts it, the possibility for such a return being one of the proofs that a discourse is, in fact, a discourse" ("Constant Subject," 329). The iconography at Hardwick in the context of Bess' monumental edifice similarly returns the discourse of feminine virtue under masculine authority to its origin as discourse, and in so doing appropriates a certain counterhegemonic power to itself. At the same time, however, I believe such an interpretation of the counterhegemonic discourse of female aristocratic authority at Hardwick calls for one further interpretive move; and that is to place that "discourse" within the emergent hegemony of "civil society" that ultimately would legitimate class domination under capitalism. In the eighteenth century, a central component of bourgeois hegemony would be the domestic woman whose authority over the domain of "private life," elaborated in conduct books and in novels addressed to women, establishes "sensibility" and "depth" as the basis of a more generalized psychological model of social relationships in the political world that is otherwise gendered as masculine (Armstrong, *Desire and Domestic Fiction,* 75). At Hardwick, already in the late sixteenth century, we can see the use of domestic arts to figure female authority in the private domain as a step in the direction of the eighteenth-century model.

VI. Intellectual and Manual Labor

While I said earlier that the Hardwick iconography and the media in which that iconography is presented have the effect of celebrating feminine labor, it is important to add the qualification that the kind of labor celebrated there is intellectual rather than manual. While Penelope's spinning is the principal figure for such labor, it is also more an allegorical figure rather than a literal one. Bess would not have confused her own status as an aristocratic woman with that of one of her hired embroiderers or embroideresses, nor even with that of one her gentlewomen in waiting. If the representational strategy at Hardwick was designed to legitimate feminine authority in the domestic sphere, then it was feminine authority to oversee that sphere that counted. It was not labor but management, not women's work in the domestic, privatized space of the home but feminine authority to manage that space.

The distinction between intellectual and manual labor is also a central motif of the poetry that celebrates the domestic ideals associated with "country life." This is true at the level of the subject who is thematized, usually a patron: Robert and Barbara Sidney's children "Read, in their virtuous parents' noble parts, / The mysteries of manners, arms and arts" (Jonson, "To Penshurst," lines 97–98); Herrick reminds Pemberton, "[Thou] know'st order, Ethicks, and ha's read / All Oeconomicks" (Herrick, "A Panegyrick to Sir Lewis Pemberton," lines 89–90); and, as we saw earlier, Endymion Porter's calling is to work, not with his hands but with his head. But the distinction occurs also at the level of enunciation, that is, in the subject who speaks (or writes) and in the very apparatus of writing itself. Discussing Elizabethan state servants and writers as "intellectuals," Alan Sinfield notes that "writing, even when it is purposefully in the service of an ideology, will very often manifest a slant towards the interests of the writer *as writer*" (*Faultlines*, 92). When Jonson addresses his patrons, it is always with a qualified deference that acknowledges the role of his own intellectual labor in legitimating their roles as managers of their private property and as public administrators in the broader state apparatus (Wayne, "Jonson's Sidney," 235–40). For the writer who is not an aristocrat, the standard of intellectual labor has the advantage of making quality dependent on merit. For the poet commoner it constitutes an implicit claim to entitlement, if not to equality with his aristocratic patron. At the same time, it is a standard that depends on the reassertion of a hierarchy in the distinction between intellectual and manual labor.

One source for the exaltation of intellectual labor and the subordination of manual labor by early modern humanist writers was the first book of Aristotle's *Politics*, in which it is argued that the distinction between master and slave is not just a matter of law but of character, and therefore of nature. Aristotle's case is based on the distinction between soul and body: "Where then there is such a difference as that between soul and body, or between men and animals (as in the case of those whose business is to use their body and who can do nothing better), the lower sort are by nature slaves, and it is better for them as for all inferiors that they should be under the rule of a master" (1.5.1254^{b}15). Aristotle also distinguishes between instruments of production (the shuttle) and instruments of action (the slave): "[L]ife is action and not production, and therefore the slave is the minister of action" (1.4.1254^{a}7).[6] But to what does "action" refer? It does not refer primarily to warfare, though that is the means of "justly acquiring" slaves. Rather, it refers to intellectual activity: "Hence those who are in a position which places them above toil have stewards who attend to their households while they occupy themselves with philosophy or with politics" (1.6.1255^{b}35). Similarly, the *Nicomachean Ethics*, where the foundational assumption is that all human activities aim at the *good*, begins with the designation of politics as the master of all arts and the highest of all forms of action (1.2.1094^{b}3).

In the late sixteenth century, as the English aristocracy began to represent its primary role in political rather than military terms, it opened up a space for the legitimation of quality on the basis of intellectual work. Into that space moved writers who were increasingly conscious of themselves *as writers*. When Raymond Williams says that Jonson and Carew "mediate" what Herrick "embarrassingly intones," because they possess a higher "consciousness of real processes," this only raises another question: what "real processes" are they conscious of? I suspect that it is not so much the reality of material labor, from which Jonson no less than Herrick, manages to dissociate himself. Rather, Jonson—to a much greater degree than either Herrick or Carew—is conscious of himself as an intellectual, conscious of the fact that it is his intellect activated in poetry that produces the magical extraction of the curse of material labor on the patron's country estate. Production, which depends in reality on the mediation of material labor, is thus mystified through the intellectual mediation of the poet. When Jonson addressed one of the most powerful politicians in the realm, Robert Cecil, earl of Salisbury, with the question: "What need hast thou of me? or of my Muse?" (*Works,* 43), he had already afforded a partial answer in the dedication to the earl of Pembroke, whom he gave "the honor of leading forth so many good, and great names (as my verses mention on the better part) to their remembrance with posterity." Poetry is itself a form of politics in that it gives historical legitimation to the acts of politicians. In another epigram celebrating Salisbury's accession to the post of lord treasurer (1608), Jonson refers to his own "labor" in making a poem that rehearses the virtues of its immediate subject and of the king who is commended for choosing his ministers wisely:

These (noblest Cecil) labour'd in my thought,
  Wherein what wonder see thy name hath wrought?
That whil'st I meant but thine to gratulate,
  I'have sung the greater fortune of our state.

(*Epigrammes,* 64)

Salisbury was an appropriate target of Jonson's self-conscious epideictic. He recognized the value to the state of the sort of learning Jonson claimed to embody. Writing in 1610, Salisbury remarked, "Most of our lawyers and judges, though learned in their profession, yet, not having other learning, they upon a question demanded, bluntly answer it, and go no further, having no vehiculum to carry it by discourse or insinuation to the understanding of others" (quoted in Jones, *Politics and the Bench,* 34). In a time when the English landowning elite was refashioning its state, when "what they needed, at least on the domestic front, was a cheap state, which would secure order and protect private property, thus assuring the normal operation of contractually based economic processes" (Brenner, "Agrarian Roots," 298), intellectual labor acquired status both for its practical value (in politics) and its value as an instrument of hegemony (in civil society). Poets who mystified real social-property relations by magically extracting the curse of labor from the production process did so as beneficiaries of an emergent doctrine that dignified intellectual labor while debasing manual labor or rendering it invisible.

Notes

1. Rosemary Kegl examines a related but quite different generic shift in an exemplary discussion of the complex of contradictory positions that are played out in Marvell's

mower poems. In "Damon the Mower," she writes, "Marvell participates in seventeenth-century class struggles by rejecting the conventional pastoral link between agricultural ease and poetic piping. . . . [The poem's] emphasis on labor distances Damon from the aristocratic shepherd who populates Elizabethan pastorals. It aligns him, instead, with the laboring plowman from an earlier sixteenth-century tradition [protesting enclosure] which the Elizabethan pastoral later suppressed" ("Joyning my Labour," 91–93). Kegl goes on to relate Marvell's appropriation of the voice of the wage laborer to the mower's own appropriation of "the position from which seventeenth-century women conventionally figured their oppression and issued demands for social change" (105).

2. Discussing representations of popular rebellions in Sidney's *Arcadia*, Spenser's *Faerie Queene*, and Shakespeare's *2 Henry VI*, Stephen Greenblatt offers a similar account of the generic shift from "heroic commemoration" to history play: "What is happening . . . is that status relations . . . are being transformed . . . into property relations, and the concern, as in Sidney and Spenser, for maintaining social and even cosmic boundaries is reconceived as a concern for maintaining freehold boundaries. Symbolic estate gives way to real estate" (Greenblatt, "Murdering Peasants," 25). The question remains, however, as to what constrains the one form of representation to "give way" to the other. For Greenblatt, Agnew, and most other recent commentators who do acknowledge the economic as a facet of early modern cultural development, the primary factors are the circulation and exchange of capital, real *and* symbolic. Indicative of this is the introductory chapter to Greenblatt's *Shakespearean Negotiations* with its revealing subtitle "The Circulation of Social Energy." In such models class relations are subordinated to the market, an institution in which the circulation of property and capital is regulated by contract rather than status, an institution which is seen as the material historical effect of a complex of cultural practices. While I share the view that such practices are fundamental and formative, I don't see them as self-explanatory. Cultural practices that produce interiorized notions of the self in terms of property and representation are themselves produced by structural changes in relations of production that, in England, occurred primarily on the land before the full development of a modern capitalist market economy (see the arguments and counterarguments of Robert Brenner in *The Brenner Debate*).

3. The ideological process whereby this separation was historically legitimated is too complex to summarize adequately here, but some key stages are worth mentioning. Reformed religion is, of course, a central component, as are the revivals of classical traditions of individual self-control, such as Stoicism; the distinction between *public* and *private* in Roman law as it was appropriated and resisted by disputants in the struggle over the respective authority of statute and the common law (Helgerson, *Forms of Nationhood,* 90); the publication of courtesy manuals for men of the upper classes (Whigham, *Ambition and Privilege*) and conduct books for women (Hull, *Chaste, Silent, and Obedient;* Jones, "Nets and Bridles"); the construction of interior subjectivity through literary discourse, first in aristocratic poetic genres, later in the more public media of the theater and print; the development in the related institutions of the market and the theater of a notion of the self as representation, and potential misrepresentation (Agnew, *Worlds Apart*); eventually, the elaboration of social and political theories based on notions of "human nature": possessive individualism (Macpherson, *Political Theory of Possessive Individualism*), the ethical/psychological "discourse of capacities" in classical political economy (Halpern, *Poetics of Primitive Accumulation,* 88–96); and a host of other theoretical and practical factors.

4. The Hardwick account books indicate that some of the embroidery was done

by professionals, including one "Webb the imbroderer," who was paid 18s.4d. a quarter, a wage that, according to Girouard, "put him lower on the scale than the porter, butler or blacksmith and higher than the laundress and glazier." Girouard also speculates that the quality of the work suggests the hand of another professional "of higher standing than the ill-paid Webb." But, he concludes, "it is likely that many of the smaller embroideries were the work of Bess herself and her gentlewomen, perhaps with the aid of a professional to set out the design" (*Hardwick Hall,* 24–27).

5. "Mimetic association was fundamental to all of humanist pedagogy. . . . The sovereign or juridical model of pedagogy, which operated on principles of punishment, inscription, and law, was thus transected by a 'civil' model based on the assimilation of styles derived from everyday life. These two models seem to project very different cultural regimes, one based on the forcible imposition of order from above and the other based on hegemony and self-regulation" (Halpern, *Poetics of Primitive Accumulation,* 34).

6. The relevant passage in Aristotle's *Politics* was recently brought to my attention in a fine, as yet unpublished paper by Benjamin Bertram of the University of California, San Diego. Bertram discusses the division of mental and manual labor as part of a more general mind/body problematic in *Hamlet* (Bertram, "Unmasking the Body," 1–2).

Works Cited

Agnew, Jean-Christophe. *Worlds Apart: The Market and the Theater in Anglo-American Thought, 1550–1750.* Cambridge: Cambridge University Press, 1986.

Aristotle. *Nicomachean Ethics.* In *The Basic Works of Aristotle*, edited by Richard McKeon. New York: Random House, 1941.

———. *Politics.* In *The Basic Works of Aristotle*, edited by Richard McKeon, 1113–1316. New York: Random House, 1941.

Armstrong, Nancy. *Desire and Domestic Fiction: A Political History of the Novel.* New York: Oxford University Press, 1987.

Bacon, Francis. *The Essays.* Edited by John Pitcher. Harmondsworth: Penguin Books, 1985.

Bertram, Benjamin. "Unmasking 'the Body': Skepticism and Materialism in *Hamlet* and Early Modern England." Unpublished paper. University of California, San Diego, 1994.

Boorde, Andrew. *The boke for to lerne a man to be wyse in buyldyng of his howse . . .* [ca. 1540]. Printed by Robert Wyer, n.d. (STC 3373).

Boynton, Lindsay, ed. *The Hardwick Hall Inventories of 1601.* London: The Furniture History Society, 1971

Brenner, Robert. "Agrarian Class Structure and Economic Development in Pre-Industrial Europe." In *The Brenner Debate*, edited by T. H. Aston and C. H. E. Philpin, 10–63. Cambridge: Cambridge University Press, 1985.

———. "The Agrarian Roots of European Capitalism." In *The Brenner Debate,* edited by T. H. Aston and C. H. E. Philpin, 213–327. Cambridge: Cambridge University Press.

DuBois, Page. *Centaurs and Amazons: Women and the Pre-history of the Great Chain of Being.* Ann Arbor: University of Michigan Press, 1982.

Elias, Norbert. *The Court Society*. Translated by Edmund Jephcott. New York: Pantheon Books, 1983.

Fumerton, Patricia. *Cultural Aesthetics: Renaissance Literature and the Practice of Social Ornament*. Chicago: University of Chicago Press, 1991.

Girouard, Mark. *Hardwick Hall, Derbyshire: A History and a Guide*. London: The National Trust, 1976

———. *Life in the English Country House: A Social and Architectural History*. New Haven: Yale University Press, 1978

Goldberg, Jonathan. *James I and the Politics of Literature: Jonson, Shakespeare, Donne, and Their Contemporaries*. Baltimore: The Johns Hopkins University Press, 1983.

Gramsci, Antonio. *Selections from the Prison Notebooks*. Edited by Quintin Hoare and Geoffrey Nowell Smith. New York: International Publishers, 1971.

Greenblatt, Stephen. "Murdering Peasants: Status, Genre, and the Representation of Rebellion." In *Representing the English Renaissance*, edited by Stephen Greenblatt, 1–29. Berkeley: University of California Press, 1988. Originally published in *Representations* 1 (spring 1983).

Greer, Germaine, et al., eds. *Kissing the Rod: An Anthology of Seventeenth-Century Women's Verse*. New York: The Noonday Press, 1989.

Halpern, Richard. *The Poetics of Primitive Accumulation: English Renaissance Culture and the Genealogy of Capital*. Ithaca: Cornell University Press, 1991.

Helgerson, Richard. *Forms of Nationhood: The Elizabethan Writing of England*. Chicago: University of Chicago Press, 1992.

Herrick, Robert. *The Poetical Works*. Edited by L. C. Martin. Oxford: Clarendon Press, 1956.

Hobbes, Thomas. *Leviathan*. Edited by C. B. Macpherson. Harmondsworth: Penguin Books, 1968.

Hull, Suzanne M. *Chaste, Silent and Obedient: English Books for Women 1475–1640*. San Marino, Calif.: Huntington Library, 1982.

James, Mervyn. *English Politics and the Concept of Honor, 1485–1642*. Past and Present Supplement 3. Oxford: Past and Present Society, 1978.

Jones, Ann R. "Nets and Bridles: Conduct Books for Women, 1416–1643." In *The Ideology of Conduct: Essays in Literature and the History of Sexuality*, edited by Nancy Armstrong and Leonard Tennenhouse. New York: Methuen, 1987.

Jones, W. J. *Politics and the Bench: The Judges and the Origins of the English Civil War*. London: George Allen and Unwin, 1971.

Jonson, Ben. *Works*. Edited by C. H. Herford, Percy Simpson, and Evelyn Simpson. 11 vols. Oxford: Clarendon Press, 1925–52.

Kegl, Rosemary. "'Joyning my Labour to my Pain': The Politics of Labor in Marvell's Mower Poems." In *Soliciting Interpretation: Literary Theory and Seventeenth-Century English Poetry*, edited by Elizabeth D. Harvey and Katherine Eisaman Maus, 89–118. Chicago: University of Chicago Press, 1990.

Lanyer, Aemilia. "The Description of Cooke-ham." In *Kissing the Rod: An Anthology of Seventeenth-Century Women's Verse*, edited by Germaine Greer et al., 44–53. New York: The Noonday Press, 1989.

Macpherson, C. B. *The Political Theory of Possessive Individualism: Hobbes to Locke*. Oxford: Oxford University Press, 1964.

Marcus, Leah S. *The Politics of Mirth: Jonson, Herrick, Milton, Marvell and the Defense of Old Holiday Pastimes*. Chicago: University of Chicago Press, 1986.

Marx, Karl. *Theories of Surplus Value*. Translated by Emile Burns. Part 1. Moscow: Foreign Languages Publishing House, [1956].

Mercer, Eric. "The Houses of the Gentry." *Past and Present* 5 (May 1954): 11–31.

Montrose, Louis Adrian. "Of Gentlemen and Shepherds: The Politics of Elizabethan Pastoral Form." *ELH* 50 (fall 1983): 415–59.

———. "Spenser's Domestic Domain: Poetry, Property, and the Early Modern Subject." In *Object and Subject: Reconstructing Renaissance Culture*, edited by Margreta De Grazia, Maureen Quilligan, and Peter Stallybrass. Cambridge: Cambridge University Press, forthcoming.

Nevinson, John. "An Elizabethan Herbarium: Embroideries by Bess of Hardwick after the Woodcuts of Mattioli." In *The National Trust Year Book*, 65–69. London: Europa Publications, 1975–76.

———. "Stitched for Bess of Hardwick: Embroideries at Hardwick Hall, Derbyshire." *Country Life*, 29 November 1973, 756–61.

Orgel, Stephen. *The Jonsonian Masque*. Cambridge: Harvard University Press, 1965.

Quilligan, Maureen. "The Constant Subject: Instability and Authority in Wroth's *Urania* Poems." In *Soliciting Interpretation: Literary Theory and Seventeenth-Century English Poetry*, edited by Elizabeth D. Harvey and Katherine Eisaman Maus, 303–35. Chicago: University of Chicago Press, 1990.

Roethlisberger, Marcel. "The Ulysses Tapestries at Hardwick Hall." *Gazette des Beaux-Arts*, 1972, 111–25.

Sinfield, Alan. *Faultlines: Cultural Materialism and the Politics of Dissident Reading*. Berkeley: University of California Press,1992.

Statius. *Silvae*. Translated by J. H. Mozley. London: Heinemann, 1928.

Stone, Lawrence. *The Crisis of the Aristocracy, 1558–1641*. Oxford: Clarendon Press, 1965.

Stone, Lawrence, and Jeanne C. Fawtier Stone. *An Open Elite? England, 1540–1880*. Oxford: Clarendon Press, 1984.

Turner, James. *The Politics of Landscape: Rural Scenery and Society in English Poetry, 1630–1660*. Cambridge: Harvard University Press, 1979.

Wayne, Don E. "Jonson's Sidney: Legacy and Legitimation in *The Forrest*." In *Sir Philip Sidney's Achievements*, edited by M. J. B. Allen et al., 227–50. New York: AMS Press, 1990.

———. *Penshurst: The Semiotics of Place and the Poetics of History*. Madison: University of Wisconsin Press; London: Methuen, 1984

Whigham, Frank. *Ambition and Privilege: The Social Tropes of Elizabethan Courtesy Theory*. Berkeley: University of California Press, 1984.

Williams, Raymond. *The Country and the City*. New York: Oxford University Press, 1973.

———. *Marxism and Literature*. Oxford: Oxford University Press, 1977.

"Under the Seal of Silence": Repressions, Receptions, and the Politics of *Paradise Lost*

JOSEPH WITTREICH

> The present paralysis in historiography affects . . . literary studies—not only by rendering suspect the writing of literary history, but also by questioning the possibility of assigning meaning to a text. . . . Both epochs and texts contain concealed, marginalized, subversive elements that prevent totalization and preclude a stable, definitive interpretation.
>
> —S. K. Heninger Jr.

> It is simply not enough to be an artist, unengaged. If you live in political times, if the lightning rod of history quivers with fire on your roof, then all art is political. And all art that is not *consciously* so partakes of the messiness of politics, if only to flee it.
>
> —Paul Monette

START with Jonathan Richardson who, in 1734, felt obliged to set the record straight concerning the reputation of *Paradise Lost*:

> It has been a Current Opinion that the late Lord *Sommers* first gave this Poem a Reputation. . . . *Paradise Lost* was known and Esteem'd Long before there was Such a Man as Lord *Sommers*. The Pompous Folio Edition of it with Cuts by Subscription in the Revolution-Year, is a Proof of what I Assert.[1]

John, Lord Somers is usually credited as the guiding force behind the 1688 edition illustrated by John Baptist Medina, Bernard Lens, and Henry Aldrich. Then "Current Opinion," apparently, was represented by those like John Dennis who lamented: "How long did *Milton* remain in Obscurity, while twenty paltry Authors, little and vile if compared to him, were talk'd of and admir'd?" And subsequently Dennis complained: "[T]he generality of the Readers of

Poetry, for twenty Years after it was published, knew no more of that exalted Poem, than if it had been writ in *Arabick*."[2]

Yet, when speaking within his correspondence "Of all the Commentators on the *Paradise Lost*," Dennis also allows for the existence of some critical attention of which his twentieth-century editor is dismissive:

> *Of all the Commentators on the Paradise Lost*. Strictly speaking, there had been only two up to the time when Dennis wrote this letter: Addison, and the slightly mysterious "P. H." . . . Only one edition had been printed to which the name of an editor had been attached: . . . Tickel . . . 1720. . . . The brief, and usually incidental, remarks of such men as Marvell, Dryden, Roscommon, Bysshe, and Coward scarcely entitle them to be called "commentators."[3]

Dennis's editor makes no mention of the fact that Tickel's edition of 1720 is the *eleventh* edition of *Paradise Lost*, and none of the fact that Milton's first editor is John Hughes, whose volume appeared (without crediting Hughes) the year before, in 1719.[4] Neither does Dennis's editor acknowledge female commentators or readers, nor does he seem to recognize that both translation and imitation are imaginative, and often subtle, forms of commentary; that illustration itself is interpretation; that, in the words of Jonathan Dollimore, at this point in history "appropriations were not a perversion of true literary reception, *they were its reception*."[5] All of the above are crucial to charting the unfolding of an understanding of *Paradise Lost*—a poem that, as it moves through history, evokes "the reader's horizon of expectations . . . only in order to destroy it step by step," as well as a poem that reveals "a process of directed perception."[6] That is, *Paradise Lost* reflects an early horizon of expectation that, over time, it alters. As contemporary report modulates into critical response, a finer understanding of the poem emerges, gradually, belatedly.

But back to Richardson, whose initial point was that sumptuous editions, illustrated books, attest to an *achieved* reputation, although this observation also contains (nearly in parentheses) the acknowledgment that *Paradise Lost* was republished in 1688, "the Revolution-Year"—the acknowledgment, it would seem, that whatever its own political content this poem was being made to serve others' political interests.[7] Moreover, this observation follows an earlier admission that Milton had no monument in Westminster Abbey: "[I]t was not permitted upon Account of his Political Principles," which, according to William Winstanley writing in 1687, had caused Milton's poetic fame to go out "like a Candle in a Snuff," ensuring that "his Memory will always stink."[8] These are the same political principles prompting Addison's lament of 1694 wherein the critic detects, and is deeply troubled by, a political subtext in a poem "whose clean Current, tho' serene and bright / Betrays a bottom odious to the sight."[9] Within Milton's lifetime, by the best of his critics, this poet was associated with political intrigue and motives, which doubtless occasioned some of Andrew

Marvell's brooding in his 1674 dedicatory poem to *Paradise Lost*, but which also prompted the occasional admission that Milton's failure to effect reform in the world of politics did not mean that the reforms he sought should not be effected.[10]

But back again to Richardson, who continued with his corrective to "Current Opinion" by way of explaining his query: "[I]s it not sufficient Reproach to our Country that *Paradise Lost* lay Neglected for Two or Three Years?"

> Sir *George Hungerford*, an Ancient Member of Parliament, told me, many Years ago, that Sir *John Denham* came into the House one Morning with a Sheet, Wet from the Press, in his Hand. What have you there, Sir *John*? Part of the Noblest Poem that ever was Wrote in Any Language, or in Any Age. This was *Paradise Lost.*

Denham died in 1669, a fact which, if this story is not apocryphal, helps to situate it in time, as does Richardson's further report: "['T]is Certain the Book was Unknown 'till about two Years after, when the Earl of *Dorset* produc't it."[11] Suffering from a mental disorder in 1666, Denham is known to have addressed Parliament "sanely" in 1667,[12] the probable date for Denham's reported reception and about the same time as another reported response, this one from the Quaker Thomas Ellwood, who allows that, once having read *Paradise Lost* in manuscript, he said to its author: "Thou hast said much here of *Paradise Lost*, but what hast thou to say of *Paradise Found*?"[13] It is well to remember that Ellwood had recently been incarcerated as a political prisoner just as Milton had been (however briefly) during the early years of the Restoration. It is also well to note the curious deflection from a poem Milton had written to one that, by Ellwood's account, he had yet to write.

Denham and Ellwood, then, represent two decidedly different receptions of *Paradise Lost*: one of expectations surpassed and the other, apparently, of expectations dashed. Within the history of Milton criticism, these two receptions might be accorded paradigmatic status. Yet Richardson has still other receptions and valuations to report (implicitly and explicitly) through a coffeehouse story told to him by Dr. Tancred Robinson but actually deriving from Fleet Sheppard, according to whom Milton's poem was available as "*Wast Paper*" at one booksellers: after a happy retrieval of the poem, he says, "My Lord took it Home, Read it, and sent it to *Dryden*, who in a short time return'd it: *This Man* (says *Dryden*) *Cuts us All Out, and the Ancients too.*"[14]

At least this is the version of the story available in most published accounts. Yet, as William Riley Parker has documented, this version is also corrected by Richardson: "Lord Dorset (not Sheppard . . .) 'told . . . [the story] to Dr. Robinson . . . at the Grecian Coffee House.'"[15] The manuscript life also helps make sense of Richardson's report already cited: "['T]is Certain that Book was Unknown 'till about two years later, when the Earl of *Dorset* produc't it." The supposed misprint (*two* for *twenty*) is probably not a misprint at all so long as we understand that, in this context, "produc't" refers not to the publication of the 1688 edition in which Dorset played a role, along with Lord Somers, Francis Atterbury, and Dryden, but to the act of producing *Paradise Lost* for Dryden, that is, of giving Dryden his own copy of the quarto edition of Milton's poem. The earl of Dorset, we know, bought *Paradise Lost* "for a trifle" (probably in 1667) and "read it many times over" and, when giving his copy to Dryden a couple of years later, learned that Dryden "had never seen it before."[16] Among poets, Milton's contemporary reputation commenced with Denham and Dryden,[17] not with S. B. or Andrew Marvell, each of whom, though, figures importantly in such a history and neither of whom was ever subject, as Dryden was, to Milton's rebuke. A rhymester, perhaps, but no poet, Milton allegedly said of Dryden, with whom he walked, along with Marvell, in Cromwell's funeral procession.

Moreover, Dryden's opinion of *Paradise Lost* had currency in Milton's own time in ways that earlier, private, often unpublished observation did not, though the existence of such opinion obliges us to examine commentary even before Dryden if we are ever going to set the historical record straight. It also requires us to observe that, whatever Dryden said early on, and later in an epigraph attributed to him and published under the frontispiece portrait to the 1688 edition,[18] elsewhere when Dryden commented on Milton, his approval was far more restrained. Other published comment curbs the seeming hyperbole registered in Dryden's epigraph, so much so that in 1685, unwilling to defend Milton's "antiquated words, and the perpetual harshness of their sound," Dryden would ask: "[A]m I . . . bound to maintain, that there are no Flats amongst his Elevations, when 'tis evident he creeps along sometimes, for above an Hundred Lines together," especially in those areas of the poem where he is following Scripture?[19] And he creeps along often enough that by 1697, as M. Manuel reports, Dryden did not even give Milton fourth place among the epic poets, in part because he made the devil rather than Adam his hero.[20] Apparently, Dryden's de-idealizing of Milton was a countermove against a tendency then taking hold in Milton criticism but may also be explained in terms of the critique of Milton that, having already taken shape in *The State of Innocence*, is implied by the different accents of that work's shifting title: *The Fall of Angels and Man in Innocence* in 1674, and in 1677 *The State of Innocence, and Fall of Man*.

Unlike Milton's, Dryden's fallen angels have no luster, deliberately. And if in Milton's poem the fallen Adam becomes blasphemous, his blasphemy is by Dryden shifted to Eve. Dennis once remarked that, in Book II of *Paradise Lost*, "Milton . . . makes the Devils . . . blaspheme in a most outragious Manner; and yet, as they speak agreeably to their Characters and the Occasion, no Man has ever been so weak or so unjust, as to accuse *Milton* for that Blasphemy."[21]

None may accuse Milton, but Dryden thus accuses Eve, and that accusation speaks volumes about each poet's supposed commitment to a feminist agenda. In Dryden's rendering, moreover, the last spoken words of the poem, no longer Eve's, are now Raphael's; and Eve's farewell speech near the end of Dryden's version imitates Satan's "Farewel happy Fields" speech in the first book of *Paradise Lost* (249–55).[22]

It is just a step from John Dryden to Samuel Slater who, in 1679, gendered wisdom male where Milton gendered it female and who, in response to Milton's identifying Eve as the mother of all things living, called her instead the mother of death, thereby reasserting woman's subordination and inferiority, first, by having God tell Adam (with Eve overhearing) that "thou art the Head, / It becomes thee to lead, her to be led." Thereupon Slater's imitation of Milton ends with Adam teaching Eve (once Michael has taught Adam) that woman should tend to the home and cease in her wanderings. Whereas Milton gives Eve the last spoken words in *Paradise Lost*, Slater, canceling every one of the poet's transgressive maneuvers, gives the last word to Adam.[23]

From such negative report, even from the seemingly positive gesture of Dryden's translating Milton's poem into a play, in the process changing its title from *Paradise Lost* and then dropping its already announced title, *The Fall of Angels and Man in Innocence*, in favor of *The State of Innocence, and Fall of Man*, we can infer that Milton's topic, the loss of paradise, was not for Dryden an altogether congenial choice, hence by some contemporaries it was judged unworthy of attention—whether for aesthetic or other reasons we are not always told. However, if Nathaniel Lee's comments are relevant, both aesthetics and ideology came into play—or, more exactly, supposed aesthetic faults were used to mask objections to ideology (Milton "rudely cast what you cou'd well dispose").[24] From positive report, on the other hand, we can gather that *Paradise Lost* sufficiently fired the enthusiasm of one reader that he passed it on to Dryden and, more, that *Paradise Lost* in the judgment of both Denham and Dryden, at least initially, surpassed any poem yet written—in any country or any age. Whether its *nobility* is a feature of its matter or manner (or both) we are left to speculate—and then this evidence is only hearsay.

If we do thus speculate, we are bound to wonder: what were the expectations of a contemporary readership concerning *this poet* (John Milton) and *this poem* (*Paradise Lost*)? How are expectations created, and by whom? Presumably by how any poet has come to be "known"—through representations by others and through self-representations. The dominant ideology, together with the ideologies competing with it, help to define an horizon of expectation for any poet, especially one who deploys the master myths of his culture. The method of deployment matters too: how is the material coded, both interpretively and generically, and how is it gendered? Does the poet stay within the margins of conventional discourse, the boundaries of received form, or transgress them; and what is the nature, the extent of his transgressions? That is, once expectations are formed, are they furthered or frustrated—and by whom: the poet or his readers? Or are expectations modified and, if so, again by whom and to what end? Jonathan Richardson has declared, and William Riley Parker and John Shawcross have provided documentary evidence, that we have dated the commencement of Milton's reputation as a poet rather too late. I would speculate that this has been so, in part, because we have failed to perceive (or perhaps have chosen to ignore) the extent to which the reputations of poet and polemicist were nearly always intertwined, hence interdependent and reciprocally illuminating, with Milton's political tracts contributing significantly to the formation of a horizon of expectation for his last poems.

More forcefully even than Parker, Shawcross annihilates the argument that "Real criticism of *Paradise Lost* begins only with the last decade of the century"[25]—an argument that carries no more historical authority than the similar one concerning *Lycidas*: "[T]his great poem seems to have passed unnoticed during Milton's lifetime. . . . No contemporary printed allusion to the poem has been so far discovered."[26] References to *Lycidas* in correspondence between Edmund Waller and St. Evremond,[27] exalting pastoral over epic, suggest otherwise, as do some lines (or just phrases) in Marvell's poems: the "gadding Vines" (610) and "heavy sedge" (642) in *Upon Appleton House*, "the last . . . brain" (28) in *Flecknoe*, the "beaked promontories" (358) in *The First Anniversary*, and "purple locks" (67) and "thou art gone . . . thou art gone" (299, 303) in *A Poem upon the Death of his Late Highness.*" All are plausibly reminiscences, or echoes, of *Lycidas*.[28] Then, too, there is the accumulation of phrases like "Flame in the forehead of the azure skie," or "Pansie streakt with shining Jet, / The tufted Crowtoe, glowing Violet / . . . the Faire Primrose (that forsaken dyes) / The Daffadillies with cups fill'd with teares, / All *Amaranth's* brood that Embroidery weares, / To strew her Lawreat Hearse" in the poetry of Richard Baron published in 1647.[29]

Otherwise, besides the possible echoes of *Lycidas* both in phrase ("Sicilian *Muse begin a loftier* Flight," "now Thou art gone") and repetition ("*Begin, my Muse, begin th'* Arcadian *Strains*," "no more . . . begin . . . begin . . . no more") in William Walsh's *Delia: A Pastoral Eclogue*,[30] there is also the striking parallelism between the first lines of "To the Excellent *Orinda*" (1667):

Let the male Poets their male *Phoebus* chuse,
Thee I invoke, *Orinda*, for my Muse;
He could but force a Branch, *Daphne* her Tree
More freely offers to her Sex and thee,
And says to Verse, so unconstrain'd as yours,
Her Laurel freely comes, your fame secures:
And men no longer shall with ravish'd Bays
Crown their forc'd Poems by as forc'd a praise. . . .[31]

and the opening of *Lycidas*:

> Yet once more, O ye Laurels, and once more
> Ye Myrtles brown, with Ivy never sere,
> I com to pluck your berries harsh and crude,
> And with forc't fingers rude
> Shatter your leaves before the mellowing year.
> Bitter constraint, and sad occasion dear
> Compells me to disturb your season due. . . .
>
> (lines 1–7)

The violent conceits of the one poem seem indebted to the other, and the radical feminism of the first contrasts with the latter where, however, not Phoebus Apollo but the "Sisters of the sacred well" (15) are the muses first invoked. If there is indebtedness here, the lines suggest what was initially at issue for Milton's female readership and what later criticism then chose to hide: namely, the sexual politics—or the politics generally—of Milton's last poems. In either case, the politics is complicated, enormously so; and if the "Orinda" poem does harbor an allusion to *Lycidas*, it allows us to say rather more precisely how Milton's sexual politics were construed in 1667 and thus to calculate what the horizon of expectation would have been for *Paradise Lost*, published in 1667/68.

In our own century, two positions separated by an interval of fifty years front one another. First, according to Parker, "Milton had tried to put politics out of his mind": by the time he turned to *Paradise Lost*, Milton the artist "emerged from the chrysalis of controversy."[32] For James Turner, who urges "the integration of poetry and prose, the literary and the political" in commentary on Milton, the situation is otherwise: "Political *engagement* may then have generated rather than aborted Milton's epic vision; in the words that Dryden applied to Charles II, 'crisis' may have '*authorized*' his skill."[33] Demotion of the prose writings, disconnecting them from the poetry, then depoliticizing the poetry—these impulses, as Turner perceives, have run through Milton criticism from the very beginning. But criticism should not be allowed to conceal the interfacing of religion and politics in Milton's poetry from the very beginning, nor the fact that the suppression of its political resonances has been the critic's way of undoing an early, supposed alliance between Milton's prose and poetry. These suppositions become all the more plausible if, in response to Jauss's urging, we follow the footprints of the immediate receptions of Milton's writings, and especially of *Paradise Lost*.[34]

The moment Milton's prose writings are brought in contact with, and allowed to afford an interpretive context for, Milton's last poems, different forms of the same questions arise concerning each of them. What are the points of intersection, of divergence? Are the poems replications of earlier postures, redactions or revisions of previous positions? How are scriptural sources and citations used in polemics and in poems? And with reference to the poems: what are their scriptural sources (acknowledged and hidden), and how do those sources relate to Milton's poems—as shadow texts or subtexts or cotexts? Indeed, how do Milton's poems relate to one another? Are the poems elaborations or exfoliations, simple mirrorings or significant modifications of one another's visions? Is their relationship one of concord or contention?

And what of their relationship to their scriptural counterparts: are the poems safe or risky elaborations of them? Are the biblical stories, along with the master myths they enshrine, a way of evading or encountering, of screening or searching, the history of Milton's own times? Do Milton's last poems authorize one hermeneutic—or accommodate several—that over time have become attached to each of their stories? How easy are the accommodations, if that is in fact Milton's tactic? Do these poems promulgate or prosecute received interpretation(s)? And to what extent do their religious/theological wrappings conceal a political agenda? How hidden are Milton's politics? Do these poems have a submerged, barely decipherable, political content—or rather a sheathed yet still sharp political edge? The irony tucked away in the inaugural phase of Milton criticism (to which we will momentarily return) is that expectations created for the poet by his prose writings—for a poet no less rebellious in his religion than in his politics—(however compatible those expectations may be with the poems Milton wrote) were resisted by different readers (as we shall see) for various reasons: in order to protect the poems themselves from the threat of censorship and Milton from the consequences thereof; or, sometimes, in order to allow for appropriations by those with contrary ideological commitments and a competing political agenda. As George Sensabaugh reports in this connection, Nathaniel Lee imagined Milton rising from the dead, filing off the rust, and another—"the right Party" choosing.[35]

Whatever the motive, the results were usually the same: Milton's poems, especially *Paradise Lost*, were wrested from the clutch of the prose works and represented as swerving from Milton's earlier subversions, religious as well as political—as swerving so completely that we are now only beginning to retrieve as a vital presence in criticism issues too long absent (but in the beginning never completely missing) from Milton commentary. If it was once fashionable to date the emergence of Milton's reputation as a major poet from 1688, the fashion constituted a convenient evasion of the conflicting signals, the ideological dis-ease, of early Milton criticism. The 1688 edition of *Paradise Lost* allowed for the mainstreaming of Milton as *the* reigning poet *in* the venerable tradition of epic (witness Dryden's now famous epigram), as a poet *in* step with the newly founded political liberalism and well *in*side the confines of religious orthodoxy (witness the conforming spirit of the illustrations by Medina and others).

This *appropriation* of Milton heralds others, but it also has its harbinger in an earlier stage of Milton criticism. Then critics valued Milton's poetry for the traditions, literary rather than intellectual, that it accommodates. Somewhat later, they would displace Milton's politics with a theology emptied of its subversions, thus privileging *Paradise Lost* over *Paradise Regained*, or would displace Milton's politics onto a poem like *Samson Agonistes*, which those politics, in their most extreme version, could marginalize and trivialize. This history in its abstract, philosophical form is inscribed in *Paradise Lost*. The same history, now concretized, is written during the first century of Milton criticism and bears retelling only because it keeps reproducing itself, with variations to be sure, right up to the present time and, so doing, becomes paradigmatic for repeated evasions and concealments. Shawcross is right: one of the byproducts of this history, of these critical attitudes—of conventionalizing *Paradise Lost* and radicalizing *Paradise Regained* and *Samson Agonistes*, of theologizing the former poem and politicizing the latter ones—is the "misreading" of all these poems.[36]

Not all but *too much* current criticism is preoccupied with erasure, the removal of political traces from poetry and of subversion (when political traces are allowed for) from the politics, even the theology that politics was made to subtend. Cancellations and appropriations are not the same thing, nor are containments and subversions. If containment is Shakespeare's metier, subversion is Milton's, his poetry challenging appropriations of it, subverting containments, as part of the war it wages against threatened cancellations. Not just politics but Milton's *sense* of politics gets short shrift in the deft subordinations of present-day academic discourses, even the most flashy of them, where increasingly the politics that matters is that of the academic profession. When political interpretations, because they defy containment, are moved against, then trivialized by ridicule, that ridicule becomes a frightening form of intellectual terrorism, masking as any number of isms.

If it can be said that Parker summarizes and Shawcross supplements the history of Milton criticism up to and through the time when *Paradise Lost* was published, it must also be acknowledged that Shawcross's supplementations have the effect of subverting Parker's conclusions concerning Milton's withdrawal from politics in the last poems. That is, the evidence assembled by Shawcross shows that, however submerged, politics is well within the horizon of expectation for this poet and his *Paradise Lost*, which, in Milton's lifetime, is always published as "A Poem," first in ten, later in twelve, books, with the signature on the title page, some of the time just "J. M.," in those instances relegating its author to near anonymity. *Why*, we may ask, even as one obvious answer comes tumbling back: to save the poem by saving *its* reputation from that of its author,[37] a reputation (at least in Milton's own time) founded chiefly upon the divorce tracts, where Milton was said to have scored his points at the expense of Scripture, twisting and turning, mutilating, then murdering, God's word, and upon the political pamphlets where, having murdered God's word, he now defends killing the king, God's vicar on earth.[38]

For his "sins," both religious and political, Milton was targeted for abuse: "wilde, mad, and frantick," he was to be "hiss'd at rather then confuted"—hooted from the stage of history as a forecaster and false prophet and as one whose opinions were "Anabaptisticall, Antinomian, Hereticall, Atheisticall."[39] At the Restoration, his books, in the 1640s recommended for burning, were finally burned (along with those of John Goodwin), a point Milton's early biographers and, for other reasons, some detractors never tired of making.[40] This divorcer and king-hater, sectarian and heretic, regicide and blasphemer, was like Sampson in his spiteful revenge, in his desire to pull down the pillars of both church and state, and was like Satan in his rebellion and subversion. With Goodwin, he was numbered among the "Rebellious Devils" and "Blinde Guides" of a now stumbling nation: speaking with the devil's mouth and sorted with the devil's party, this "Infamous," "Sacrilegious *Milton*" was called a "*Diabolical Rebel*"—"altogether a Devil" posing as a saint, a compendium of the most hated villains and their various villainies—and presumed metaphorically already to have "gone to hell."[41]

This is the reputation, these are the associations, of the author of *Paradise Lost*; and they are starkly foregrounded in the years from 1666 to 1668 by a single entry—"*Blinde Milton*"—in *Poor Robin . . . An Almanack*, an entry that reveals how profoundly early representations of Milton tainted the reception of *Paradise Lost*. The entry always appears in relation to the month of November, that month of plotting (even by poets), and, drawing upon Roger L'Estrange's portrayal of Milton as a practitioner and promoter of sedition in *No Blinde Guides* (1660), gathers its point from the logic of the various representations in what the subtitle to various of these volumes calls this "Almanack After a New Fashion." For every month there are two calendars, one white and the other black (so to speak) and two different chronologies, one of loyalists and another of fanatics; one cataloging heroes and saints, some mythological, some historical; the other computing, in analogy, the names of notorious villains and sinners—or "mock-Saints." Milton's name, in 1666, is paired with Saturn's, the mythological type of whom Milton, apparently, is the historical representative and perversion.[42] The implication is that Milton as well as "*Saturn* signifies . . . the devil and all"; the implied castigation is clearly directed against Milton's politics in this series of mock-calendars tabulating "the Roundheads, or Fanaticks: with their several Saints days" and with the names of "their chief Ring-leaders most eminent for Villany."[43]

Not just Milton, but John Bradshaw, Henry Ireton, James Nayler, and *St. Oliver*—all famous (now infamous) for their participation in the Revolutionary government—appear together in a sequence of mock-calendars; and all of these figures are aligned *as plotters* with "Guido Faux"; *as political leaders* with Nero; *as would-be prophets* with Tom-of Bedlam, Merlin, Mother Shipton, and Jane Shore; and *as artists* with Lucian and Rabelais. In subsequent editions of this almanac, moreover, Milton's name is moved to the head of the list for November, appearing opposite now All Souls' (1667, 1668) and now All Saints' Day (1669), with the suggestion that as an apostate Milton is a lost soul, as well as a limb of Antichrist, the prototypical figure for these plotters and mock-saints who, sometimes poets, are part of "that Rebellious force" which brought death to "Good *pious* Charles."[44] Blake may have thought that Milton was of the devil's party without knowing it, but certain of Milton's contemporaries (allowing for this affiliation) thought Milton knew full well whose side he was on and were not inclined ever to let him forget it. Before the publication of *Paradise Lost*, the time would come when "the Writings on which his Vast Reputation Stood were . . . Accounted Criminal, Every One of them, and Those Most which were the Main Pillars of his Fame."[45]

The indictment against Milton falls hard—is rendered without equivocation. The entry encoding it speaks through a shorthand, an epitome, referring to the reputation won by Milton the polemicist in which some would now try to wrap Milton the poet.[46] The notion of a seditious Milton is a reputation that sticks, for even after Milton's name disappears from *Poor Robin*, he continues to be dubbed "apostate bard" and, in images that recall the poet's not always pejorative association with Samson and Satan, is referred to as "a blind adder," "a Shimsi," "that serpent Milton."[47] The prologues to *Paradise Lost*, in their defensiveness, admit as much: Milton has fallen on evil days *and evil tongues* but, even in changed circumstances, remains steady in his principles; his blindness, no sign of dishonor, is the badge of his prophetic office and divine favor. *Blind* Milton may be, but he can nevertheless *see* and *tell* of things invisible to mortal sight. His song may be of loss but glimpses a recovered paradise at the end of time as well as the promise—a historical possibility still—of a paradise in history, with Milton figuring himself as a New Moses who will lead a New Chosen People into the still Promised Land. Representation is fronted by self-representation, Milton here challenging his detractors from the high ground, the expansive spaces, of *Paradise Lost*.

For a long time, it has been acknowledged that the multiple prologues to *Paradise Lost* are apologias, sites and centers of ethical proof from which Milton counters ad hominem arguments. In view of his reputation, what too often gets lost is Milton's audacity in beginning his epic in hell—with what has been for many an appealing portrait of Satan. That Milton could nevertheless win a favorable judgment from some of his readers, early ones, is attested to by the first documentable reception of *Paradise Lost*. Two letters by John Hobart, dating from early 1668, first assert, then reaffirm, an extraordinarily high evaluation of Milton's poem. These letters between cousins, one of whom has presented a copy of *Paradise Lost* to the other and eagerly awaits the cousin's own assessment of the poem, are interesting chiefly as evidence of Milton's power *as a poet* to refashion his reputation, to control through the power of his word (and the word of others) the reception of *Paradise Lost*.[48]

In each of the Hobarts' letters, there is some indication that the verse form, "not very com[m]on," was initially unsettling and, in its rhymelessness, may have seemed a disturbing, even disruptive, presence in the poem—a coded gesture of rebellion in a poem judged "more extraordinary for . . . matter, then verse" (Rosenheim, "Early Appreciation," 281). These letters also indicate that Hobart is aware of other writings by Milton, "severall pieces, good & bad," which "some moderne creticks will condemne," he says, regarding this author as "guilty" (because of his politics presumably) (282). But if so, such suspicions are allayed by, or perhaps just easily evaded in, a poem that, not only rivaling, surpasses the achievements of Milton's eminent precursors, ancient and modern. Not wishing to "injure" Milton with too extravagant, "too advantagious" praise (282)—or perhaps not wishing to "injure" the poet by getting too near the "matter" of his poem (281)—with a practiced restraint and in studied generalities Hobart claims that Milton occupies "soe high a place amounge our eminent Poets" because, like Homer and Virgil, he redeems language "from obscurity" and exercises it with an astonishing "liberty" (282).

So effective was Milton in embedding generic signatures that this poem, called simply "A Poem," was instantly recognized as an epic outdoing all others, those by Homer and Spenser especially:

> The subject [is] great, & it has this advantage, That ye Theme it treats off, is as much above Hyberbolyes; or Tropes, as others are usually below them: Some resemblance it has to Spencers way, but in ye opinion of ye impartiall learned, not only above all moderne attempts in verse, but equall to any of ye Ancie[nt] Poets. And his blinde fate dose not barely resemble Homers fate: but his raptures & fancy brings him uppon a nearer paralele: I must confess I have been strangely pleased in a deleberate & repeated reading of him, & more ye last tyme then ye first. . . . [M]y owne delight . . . has been soe excessive, That I can say truly I never read any thing more august, & withall more gratefull to my (too much limited) understanding. (281)

Given Hobart's praise of Milton's matter over his manner, his remarks are curiously elusive. We learn only that Milton's subject is great; that his theme (never stipulated) in manner surpasses all other such attempts; that Milton's prophetic raptures exceed Homer's and even Spenser's, with which, in any event, they find a nearer and neater parallel. On the face of things, subject, content, and theme—each is addressed without ever being identified or explored; each, if not voided, gets swallowed up in Hobart's aesthetic approval. But there is also a subtext to these observations, a commentary decipherable by inference.

In correspondence that is chiefly political, the author of these letters, Sir John, who once supported the Commonwealth and later, supporting the restoration of Charles II, took a pardon in June 1660, can himself be expected to speak guardedly of Milton. Hobart is sensitive to the unconventionality of Milton's verse and language, aligning *Paradise Lost* with a native literary tradition and crediting Milton with outdoing Spenser, his chief competition in that tradition. In his mention of the prose writings, which constitutes a veiled reference to Milton's politics, Hobart at least hints at the possibility, so astutely formulated by Terry Eagleton, that Milton's transgressive gestures in this poem suggest that *Paradise Lost* is "a radically political act"—an "assertive appropriation" of classical modes and models "for historically progressive ends."[49] Yet because of Hobart's curious deflections, his backing away from what he most admires in the poem, *its matter*, this kind of interpretive possibility remains submerged, though not completely silent, in a criticism with an aesthetic turn and focus. It would be hard to find a better illustration of the proposition that "reception mechanisms [for *Paradise Lost*] . . . at an early stage succeeded in aestheticizing potentially subversive material."[50]

Paradise Lost is obviously implanted with various interpretive codes; but in the early receptions, even where the prevailing concerns seem otherwise, it is the aesthetic code that predominates, and predominates so completely that the political code, when not fully silenced, is sealed within insinuations. Hobart's reception, in this sense, achieves paradigmatic status. It hardly matters whether those receptions reported by Richardson are apocryphal or not,[51] because their forms and terms, in a more restrained and pedestrian key, are authorized, if not authenticated, by Hobart's documentable reception: *Paradise Lost*—a poem for all times, epic in ambition and achievement, the noblest ever written—is authored by a poet who overgoes all his competition, both ancient and modern.

If there is a latent anxiety in Hobart's letters, it may replicate, in less extreme form, the more obvious discomfort of Ellwood, who blocks comment on the one poem (*Paradise Lost*) by wishing for another (*Paradise Regained*), and may be replicated, in turn, but now with a poetic rather than ideological emphasis, by Denham and Dryden in the awe they express at Milton's outdistancing all his eminent rivals. A predictable anxiety is registered at the margins of one poet's discourse concerning the unexampled and perhaps unmatchable successes of another—the sheer awe at Milton's achievement harboring the frustration of fellow poets who, in the face of another claiming so much imaginative ground for himself, are forced to clear new, perhaps less desirable and desired, poetic space for themselves.

The probable cause for fellow poets' frustrations is that Milton brought the highest form of poetry, the venerable epic, to perfection and has won for himself "The title of Most Excellent."[52] In the words of Edward Phillips, Milton had "lately published *Paradise Lost*, a poem which, whether we regard the sublimity of the subject, or the combined pleasantness and majesty of the style, or the sublimity of the invention, or the beauty of its images and descriptions of nature, will, if I mistake not, receive the name of truly Heroic, inasmuch as by the suffrages of many not unqualified to judge it is reputed to have reached the perfection of this kind of poetry."[53] Subsequent to Milton's death, when Ellwood needed no longer mince words, he celebrated Milton's triumph in poetry and prose equally, and equally the examples of epic as represented by *Paradise Lost* and *Paradise Regained,* where, "The common Road foresaking," Milton was "a new track making." [54] What Ellwood gives with one hand, Edmund Waller takes away with another: "The old blind school master hath published a tedious poem on the Fall of Man. . . . If its length be not considered as merit, it hath no other."[55] And what merit there may be in its length is eventually qualified by Dr. Johnson's "None ever wished it longer than it is."[56]

In different ways, for different reasons, the aesthetic code so governed the early reception of *Paradise Lost* that one must ask at the outset whether Milton himself was not partly responsible for the state of affairs of which nowadays some critics complain:

> Criticism has tended to contrast the aesthetic and the political. We think of genius and partisanship as at odds. . . . We evaluate the greatest writers as those least fettered by their age. Such appraisals have too often announced Shakespeare's detachment from Tudor politics; and they have too often presented Milton's poetry as a retreat from political concerns. The intention of Milton and Shakespeare to engage political arguments will remain a matter of interpretation. What is incontestable is that their languages were perforce political and necessarily conveyed political meanings. There is an important sense in which no seventeenth-century literature is not also political.[57]

How was it possible for such a poem as *Paradise Lost*, in part at least on the affairs of state, on the state of the nation, initially to go undetected? Milton, one supposes, never meant to announce political attachments, only to deflect attention from them by their artful concealment within the deep structure of his poem, deferring them until better (because less dangerous) times. Ellwood's forthright representation of Milton excelling, indeed triumphing, as both polemicist and poet, of Milton as a trailblazer, such representations coming only after Milton's death, open the possibility that Ellwood's earlier reported response, perhaps politically motivated, amounted to a deliberate jamming of Milton's message.

It is important to remember that if censorship forced Milton to camouflage his politics, it also forced politically sensitive and sympathetic readers of his poetry (Ellwood perhaps and Marvell almost certainly) to camouflage their political readings, which, more often than not, instead of making Milton into a champion of this or that cause, provided an occasion for examining the problematical moral and ethical issues that his politics raised: the relation of religion and politics, first of all, and the role of violence as a means to an end—apocalypse now or apocalypse deferred. As Milton learned to circumvent the bans of censorship by devising an art of crypsis through which he forces us to read between the lines, to wrest significance from silence, and wherein mere flickerings of unorthodoxy really matter, it becomes increasingly clear that the issue is not whether Milton withdraws from republicanism in the face of its betrayal but rather what sort of critique he can mount as he tries to account for political disappointments and revolutionary failures. The revolutionaries were in some ways wrong. Hence, they (and not the revolution) were Milton's target. Not his ideals but their implementation created a problem when, as Newlyn explains, "the leaders of the Revolution who initially had right on their side . . . allowed evil to become their good."[58] Milton embedded a critique easily ignored by his contemporaries yet readily accessible to future generations for whom Milton was no less seditious in his intentions but who simply came to value sedition differently.

The initial receptions of *Paradise Lost* bespeak Milton's success in this regard but also, in their statements as much as in their silences, anticipate expectations inscribed, receptions instated, during the 1670s, most notably by S. B. (often thought to be Dr. Samuel Barrow) and by Andrew Marvell, whose dedicatory poems form a headpiece to the second edition of *Paradise Lost*, which was published in 1674. Their poems deserve more attention than today they typically receive principally because, for a long time read as prologues to *Paradise Lost*, they had an astonishing impact, for better or worse, on the early reputation of both poet and poem, furnishing the commonplaces for Milton criticism in its formative stages: "Consummate Poet," "sublime poem," "mighty Milton" to whom all poets, whether ancient or modern, must now yield; "Poet blind, yet bold," "strong," "Mighty Poet" whom "Heav'n . . . / Rewards with Prophesie" and whose verse contains "a vast expence of mind" and in its "vast Design" and "Theme sublime" so fully compensates for artistic irregularities that it need "not Rhyme."[59] S. B. and Andrew Marvell thus generate the clichés of Milton criticism such as are still—some will say *still too much*—with us.

But more, their poems each align Milton with a different poetic tradition (the one classical and epic, the other scriptural and prophetic), thus pointing to the competing generic signals of *Paradise Lost*, the inward strife that is its hallmark. These dedicatory poems forge contrary perspectives on Milton's epic-prophecy, asking that it be read in very different ways: as a poem of new and perhaps unexpected revelations (S. B.), or, in the case of Marvell, as a poem not finally unsettling because it holds fast to the time-honored truths of Christianity, not ruining the scriptural tales, and holds fast also to the commonplaces of culture, received interpretation, thus not at all perplexing the usual explanations. If read as companion poems affording contending perspectives on *Paradise*

Lost, these pieces may be seen as establishing the different lines of critical inquiry, the conflicting attitudes toward Milton, that ever since have been at the heart of Milton criticism. Is *Paradise Lost* a poem of disclosure, revealing (in the words of S. B.) "whate'er lies hidden in all the world" (lines 5–8)? Or is it a poem written to allay all doubts—to put to rest a hermeneutic of suspicion—by promoting rather than prosecuting the old verities? The immediate effect of reading these poems together is to throw us into a quandary—is to bracket *Paradise Lost*, as well as our interpretive efforts, in question marks.

But let us remember, too, that what we are here bringing under review are *poems*; each may have troubled waters beneath its calm surface. Each poem seems to have the same subtext, as it were; each seems to be responding to the same horizon of expectation for *Paradise Lost*, but responding differently—S. B.'s through a curious focalization and Marvell's by a calculated contradiction. H. L. Benthem reminds us that Milton's closest friends, when they learned of the imminent publication of *Paradise Lost*, were filled with suspicions concerning the poet's intentions: would his poem be about the loss of paradise then—*or now*? From everything Theodore Haak confided to him and from his own reading of the poem, Benthem reports, "this very wily politician . . . concealed . . . exactly the sort of lament" his friends feared he would write and did so in a poem that would use scriptural myth to mask political commentary.[60] Within such a context, these dedicatory poems reveal their own complicity with Milton's disguised intentions as they may be inferred from a poem of "dark paths," with a "labyrinth perplex'd of heaven's decrees."[61]

The oddity of S. B.'s poem resides in the sharpness, the expansiveness of its focalization of the celestial battle in Book VI. If *Paradise Lost* is a poem of disclosure, inscribing a secret history, as S. B. implies and Milton's early editors speculate—if *Paradise Lost* is a poem that speaks through contradictions, tears on its surface—is S. B. then, through this unexpected yet extensive focalization, pointing to where the secret history is hidden? It is at the end of this narrative, we should remember, that Raphael confides: "I have reveal'd / What might have else to human Race bin hidden" (VI.895–96). Similarly gathered into focus by Wentworth Dillon, earl of Roscommon, the celestial battle in *Paradise Lost* is also a civil war, the one place in the poem where subsequent commentators have seen pointed political observation peaking out from under its mythic coverings.[62] The surface analogy between the rebellious Puritans and Satan, the king and God, hides the more immediately relevant analogy between the king and his men, who resemble the satanic rebels, though they attribute rebellion to others, and God whose allies are the Puritan saints, the quellers of such rebellion. However, the surface analogy here is not simply a subterfuge; for Milton's critique, here as in *Samson Agonistes*, cuts both ways—against the Royalists primarily, but also against the excesses and enthusiasms of Cromwell and his army. It is seldom noted that *Paradise Lost* begins and ends in prophecy with the intention, apparently, of putting prophecy itself under review.

This same sort of reading between the lines helps to unpack the significance of Marvell's still more curious poem, which has both a private and a public dimension, the former containing a gesture through which Marvell carves out poetic space for himself, staking claim to the middle ground of poetry as it were, and the latter containing a gesture on Milton's behalf through which Marvell would secure for this poet of paradise the ground he had claimed for himself. This latter project requires no small amount of subterfuge on Marvell's part, one signal of which is the apparent contradiction that is allowed to sit on the surface of his poem. Only after Marvell has emptied *Paradise Lost* of its potentially subversive content—that is, only after he has modified existing expectations—does he ally the poem with the most subversive of poetic traditions: "Just Heav'n . . . / Rewards with *Prophesie* thy loss of sight" (line 44; my italics). This claim has the effect of subverting the principal assertion of the poem so far; for prophecy, by the most restrained definition then common, refers to a new revelation, a new interpretation, that will displace the old (not preserve and confirm it) and that will advance understanding toward a higher truth than that already proclaimed. (This is why there were edicts against prophecy, especially political prophecy, during the Renaissance.)

The remainder of the poem, in its invocation of the rhyme controversy, in its endorsement of Milton's own asseverations on rhyme, moves in concert with, while also providing further testimony for, the subversion, which now belongs to both poets, Marvell as well as Milton, Marvell encoding within his poem, through its organization into verse paragraphs, the subversive signature of Milton's own. Rhyme was a matter not just of aesthetics but of politics, as Milton's early readers were quick to notice in their references to Milton's rhymelessness, allowing his poetry to tower in the sublime, to Milton's freeing poetry of this monkish, iron chain, rhyme being as much the emblem for stultifying theology as for repression in politics. Rhymeless verse, perhaps because it came to be associated with "verse unfallen, uncurst,"[63] was the expected flag of prophecy, an outward sign of its inward defiance, and, because of its studiously unpremeditated appearance, a sign, too, of its inspiration. An aspect of "Masculine Rhetorick," blank verse is opposed to the "*tinkling cimbal*" of rhyme, or feminized poetry, that, making "a pretty sound," would "rather inchant the mind then inform it."[64] This gesture of rebellion aligns Milton's poem with the revolutionary impulses of scriptural prophecy while encoding what has always been Milton's master theme: the recovery of ancient liberty from modern bondage.

This is but one of the many splicings that cause Marvell's poem to lock arms with Milton's. Moreover, it is such splicings that point to the "serious truth"[65] of his no less than S. B.'s verses: that they are a representation of the very strategies of subversion, of the multiple subterfuges, embedded in *Paradise Lost* and a representation, especially in the instance of Marvell's poem, of Milton's own self-representations. No blind guide, Milton was rather a poet who, if blind, could truly see. What must ultimately be said about both of these dedicatory poems is that they are entry codes into the very kind of readings that Marvell only *seems* to protest against; they are a reminder of the fact to which Stephen Greenblatt has alerted us: that literature, which is subject to censorship and which has passed through it, can be "relentlessly subversive," although the very form in which it is cast may have effected its evasion of censorship by seeming to provide containment for the kind of questioning that the poem, instead of restraining, actually provokes.[66]

If *Paradise Lost*'s identity as epic signals the containment of subversion, its alternative identity as prophecy suggests that it is such containment that is being subverted. *Paradise Lost* is a still more exaggerated example than Greenblatt's *King Lear* of a text that strains "the process of containment . . . to the breaking point"; in the words of Newlyn, it releases "the prophetic potential of *Paradise Lost* from the epic mode in which it is confined."[67] Each of Milton's poems is, as Peter Conrad observes, "an iconoclasm, shattering the models which have given it form, rebutting its own history," both aesthetically and intellectually.[68] Milton's poetry thus creates a poetics and spawns a whole tradition of revisionism; and there is no better illustration of this fact than that, from Boileau to Harold Bloom, the best critics have credited Milton (not always approvingly) with doing precisely what Marvell says the poet will not do: *ruin the sacred truths*. Thus Boileau speaks of those poets who in the representations of Satan and of Hell, "mingling falshoods with those Mysteries, / Would make our Sacred Truths appear like Lyes," thus filling their supposedly "Christian Poems" with "Fictions of Idolatry."[69] Apparently Boileau has Milton in mind.

But *Paradise Lost* is also a poem that turns the critique upon itself, upon its own generic identity, in such a way as to suggest the uses and abuses, the hopes for and hazards, of prophecy in a fallen world. *Paradise Lost* begins with Satan's remembering, then responding, to a prophecy concerning a new world. The attainment of a new world is always the objective of prophecy even when the new world is not envisioned therein; yet as Satan's response makes clear, the idealisms of prophecy are often subject to perversion. Even as Milton privileges prophecy he registers a certain distrust of it because, in a fallen world, this instrument for creation can become an agent in destruction, thus turning God's device for deliverance *from* into Satan's means of deliverance *into* thralldom and servitude. To be privy to God's prophecy (as Satan is) may result in man's freedom becoming his bondage. By deforming prophecy, Satan, ironically, devises just the sort of world that makes prophecy necessary, even if in that world prophecy remains a peril because, as Adam shows in Books XI and XII, prophecy is always subject to the misconstruals and confusions of fallen consciousness. This same critique of prophecy increasingly came to be wrapped around the Samson story once the Puritan Revolution had failed.

Of the two dedicatory poems, moreover, Marvell's has the unique feature of aligning *Paradise Lost*, through implied allusion, with *Samson Agonistes* and, in the same stroke, of disengaging Milton from the Samson analogy:

> . . . the Argument
> Held me a while misdoubting his Intent,
> That he would ruine (for I saw him strong)
> The sacred Truths to Fable and old Song
> (So *Sampson* groap'd the Temples Posts in spight)
> The World o'rewhelming to revenge his sight.
>
> (lines 5–10)

The Milton who goes out of the ring swinging, out of life raging, with one last revenge fantasy does not sort well with the Milton of the early biographers who reported that if, in old age, he exhibited any religious identity it was with the Quakers; nor does such a Milton sort well with what Marvell here says as he forces a contrast between Sampson who, spirited by the revenge motive, loses his life and Milton who, having relinguished such a motive, is providentially spared his through the intervention (we are probably meant to remember) of Marvell himself.

Marvell's poem especially focuses the contradictions that are at the heart of Milton's poetic vision and, in concert with the poem by S. B., the two poems relating to one another dialectically, pulling (at least on the surface) in opposite interpretive directions, emblematizes the dialectical nature of Milton's own poem. As Jonathan Richardson was later to observe, *Paradise Lost* is a poem of *contradictions* that does "More than Whisper."[70] Those contradictions, sometimes implanted within the fissures of the text, announce conflicts and confusions that, instead of being evaded, should be emphasized, although it is just this aspect of the poem that commentators as early as Theodore Haak,[71] even if unintentionally, obliterate from their imitations, translations, critiques, and illustrations. The very process of sanitizing the poem of those conflicts and contradictions enables the conventionalization of Milton's politics and theology.

But let us now return to Richardson with whom we began, this time turning to the annotations for *Paradise Lost,* credited to both father and son. Both apparently were acutely sensitive to the damaging consequences of Milton's political principles and to the extent to which Milton's poem, itself occasioned by political circumstances and secretly representing them, had also been aligned with political occasions, perhaps other than those Milton would have wished to sponsor or serve. Without in any way forcing the politics of *Paradise Lost* into the open, the Richardsons nevertheless acknowledge that there is a hidden politics to this poem; that it arises out of a political situation awkward, even dangerous, for Milton; and that in the prologue to Book VII, in its reference to "fall'n on evil dayes" (26), Milton hints at the "Secret History" inscribed by his poem.[72] The Richardsons, that is, hint at what Christopher Hill, Annabel Patterson, and, most recently, Nancy Armstrong and Leonard Tennenhouse have been telling us: that we "must deal with the fact that censorship returned with a new vigor in 1662. That is what killed off the political Milton, leaving us with the poet—or so a tradition of criticism," here under challenge, "has claimed."[73] Nor should it be forgotten that Milton's adversary Roger L'Estrange, obsessed with the political Milton, was the presiding official during this new phase of censorship and was still deriding "blind M[ilton]" as one of the "*Super-Reformists*" who speak "the *Language of the Beast*."[74]

Not just the Richardsons but also Francis Peck, in the eighteenth century, thought there was something curiously amiss in the current representation of Milton with reference not just to *Paradise Lost* but also to *Paradise Regained*: "I have often wondred in my self how the PARADISE REGAIN'D, under all this load of prejudice, hath nevertheless passed so many editions as I feel it hath."[75] The prejudices against that poem, owing to its transgressions of religious orthodoxy, reflect upon another kind of prejudice that was keeping *Paradise Lost* trapped within the interpretive codes of theology and aesthetics. By now it was a cliché of criticism that the *Aeneid* was the great political, *Paradise Lost* the great religious epic, and the function of that cliché was to hold these poems hostage to very different disciplines and contextualizations. What had become a divorce between politics and theology in the eighteenth century was in Milton's time still very much a marriage both sanctified and celebrated by *Paradise Lost*, yet also now violated by an interpretive tradition, then in its formative stages, that would neutralize by way of silencing the politics in Milton's poetry, in *Paradise Lost* no less than in *Samson Agonistes*; that would then snare both poems within the nets of orthodoxy.

Translation and adaptation, editorial emendation and excision, all of them the rage during the eighteenth century, though we see each of them as an aspect of Milton's burgeoning reputation, were also conspiratorial; each was a tactic, or could be so used, for suppressing the subversion. Witness, first, what happened to the last books of *Paradise Lost*, usually excluded from the translation mania of the eighteenth century. The most overtly political books in the whole of Milton's epic, they were censored by aesthetic condemnation: what could not be aestheticized had to be anesthetized. If these were the books in which politics were seen breaking through the surface of Milton's poem, they could be detoured, evaded on other grounds: as failures of poetic imagination in a poem already overlong; as mere excrescences in a poem that, by the end of its tenth book, had already accomplished its improvement of the epic tradition.

Even the tenth book showed signs of flagging genius; the epic vision now became personalized and privatized in autobiographical encroachments such as would envelop the whole of *Samson Agonistes*, where a bickering Adam and Eve, Samson and Dalila were none other than the squabbling John Milton and Mary Powell. If there was a politics in either poem, it was (in its positive aspect) a sexual politics, altogether conventional, in which Milton upheld the authority of the husband, even sanctioned despotic rule by him, and (in its negative aspect) a politics petty and churlish, surly and acrimonious. Milton hides in Book V, for example, when Satan goes off into the northern reaches of heaven—a fulmination over Royalist Scotland. He then hides in Book XI, in the account of the world destroyed by a flood, "To teach . . . that God attributes to place / No sanctity" (836–37), a jibe at Archbishop Laud over his manner of consecrating churches.[76] There were but these few traces of politics—of Milton the polemicist—in *Paradise Lost*; and if they were not easily detectable in the last books, those books could be scuttled as artistic disappointments or, as such, could even be salvaged by thematizations that, theologizing these books, could integrate them into a poem essentially religious, surely not political, in design and thrust.

For *Paradise Lost* to be political in the eighteenth century, if that meant an inscription of *Milton's* politics, was to risk trivialization and marginalization such as *Samson Agonistes* experienced at the very time that *Paradise Lost* was being institutionalized and canonized. It was hard for anyone, really, to deny Milton his politics, or to write politics out of his poetry generally: the tactic, pure and simple, was to evacuate politics from *Paradise Lost* and empty it into *Samson Agonistes*—was to save the one poem by sabotaging the other or, in the case of Milton's tragedy, by adapting what could not be adopted, converting this poem into operatic spectacle, translating it into typological, theological drama and substituting apocalyptic clamor for eschatological despair. The eighteenth century recognized in *Samson Agonistes*, perhaps mistakenly, the revenge tragedy (or fantasy) of Christopher Hill but, through adaptation and translation, transformed that poem into a drama of regeneration, the divine comedy, the very terms by which many read the poem, even today.

The theologizing of *Paradise Lost*, the politicizing of *Samson Agonistes*—the institutionalizing of both poems within these disparate categories—can be dated from Thomas Newton's variorum edition of 1749. By this time, when Newton's commentary on *Paradise Lost* was first published, earlier expectations concerning *Paradise Lost*, if not Milton himself, had become dislodged and, under the weight of Newton's commentary, were all but silenced, at least for a time. Newton is a particularly interesting interpreter because, for all his maneuverings in behalf of securing *Paradise Lost* as a purely theological poem, integrity prevents him from altogether scrapping the poem's political content, although from Newton's perspective that content seems to be confined to, contained by, the last, the inferior, books of the poem—the Nimrod passage in Book XII affording the notable example: "And from rebellion shall derive his name, / Though of rebellion others he accuse" (36–37). "This [passage] was added," Newton conjectures, "probably not without a view to his own time, when himself and those of his own party were stigmatiz'd as the worst of rebels."[77] Newton's integrity obliges him to acknowledge a strain in Milton commentary that he himself, at least with reference to *Paradise Lost*, does not wish to credit. In one way or another, each of his major predecessors had made such a gesture without usually acknowledging the extent to which Milton rewrote the Nimrod and other stories with a political valence in order to denounce not only the Royalists but just as often the treacherous Parliamentarians. Milton's political critiques, like his gender discourses, are double-voiced and display a dual consciousness. They reflect on history usually obliquely and always complexly.

By 1698, John Toland discerns a similar encoding of British history in the very first book of *Paradise Lost*:

> I must not forget that we had like to be eternally depriv'd of this Treasure by the Ignorance or Malice of the Licenser; who, among other frivilous Exceptions, would needs suppress the Whole Poem for imaginary Treason in the following lines.
>
> —As, when the Sun new risen
> Looks thro the Horizontal misty Air
> Shorn of his Beams, or from behind the Moon
> In dim Eclipse disastrous Twilight sheds
> On half the Nations, and with fear of change
> Perplexes Monarchs.
>
> (I.594–99)

But Toland is also quick to turn from the public and the political to the personal and autobiographical in a poem that "perpetuats the History of [Milton's] own Blindness";[78] and he is quick, also, to place the political under the aspect of personal history, as the Richardsons would do in their exfoliation of the secret inscribed in the prologue to Book VII and as Newton would later do in his annotation for the Nimrod passage in Book XII. Eventually, the politics implicit in Book VI, conceivably part of a critique of the Revolution, was reconceived by conservative apologists as Milton's recantation of the Revolution. Thus in 1763-64, a commentator in the *London Chronicle* would ask of this poet, usually supposed to be of the devil's party: "[H]ow could [Milton] better refute the good old cause he was such a partisan of and such an advocate for than by making the rebellion in the poem resemble it, and giving the same characteristics to the apostate angels as were applicable to his rebel brethern"?[79]

This strategy of letting politics underride autobiography in a poem that was thought to transcend both is particularly evident in the memoir by Francis

Peck where we are not allowed to forget Toland's comment about the censor with reference to the perplexed monarchs of Book I, but also where the political is said to be submerged within the autobiographical mode, as early as *Lycidas* and its reflections on the corruption of the contemporary church and as late as *Samson Agonistes*, where "the severe satyr on woman, in SAMPSON'S discourse with DALILA" is taken as conclusive evidence that Milton "still resented . . . MARY POWELL," as likewise is Adam's misogyny in *Paradise Lost* (X.940ff.). Both *Paradise Lost* (VII.23) and *Samson Agonistes* (695) are thought to register Milton's fears of being tried for his life by Charles II and his judges or of "being torn in pieces by the mob, just as ORPHEUS was." But it is again Books XI and XII where the traces of the political, however scant, are strongest: in the Nimrod passage reminiscent of *Lycidas* where yet once more the poet registers his aversion to the clergy in any guise.[80]

What is evident from the foregoing comments is that a political interpretation had already been affixed to *Paradise Lost* and *Samson Agonistes*, even if submerged within the autobiographical content of each poem. Newton's project of claiming *Paradise Lost* as a theological poem by marginalizing, even silencing, its politics had already been undertaken, this time with *Samson Agonistes* as the target, in Handel's *Samson: An Oratorio*. What is curious in light of these parallel efforts is that Newton should simply shift what was once thought to be the political content of *Paradise Lost* to *Samson Agonistes*, taking his initial lead from John Jortin's annotation for line 241, "That fault I take not on me":

> Milton certainly intended to reproach his countrymen indirectly, and as plainly as he dared, with the Restoration of Charles II, which he accounted the restoration of slavery, and with the execution of the Regicides. He pursues the same subject again [lines] 678–700. I wonder how the Licensers of those days let it pass.

Then Newton himself chimes in, saying of line 268, "But what more oft in nations grown corrupt," that here too Milton "very probably intended . . . a secret satire upon the English nation, which according to his republican politics had by restoring the King chosen *bondage with ease* rather than *strenuous liberty*." When Samson declares later, "So much I feel my genial spirits droop, / My hopes all flat" (594–95), Newton speculates that "Milton in the person of Samson describes exactly his own case, what he felt and what he thought in some of his melancholy hours." Alternatively, when the Chorus contemplates "th' unjust tribunals, under change of times" (695), doubtless Milton himself, in their voice, reflects upon "the trials and sufferings of his party after the Restoration" and probably has "in mind particularly the case of Sir Harry Vane"; and of course, Newton continues, "this was his own case; he escaped with life, but lived in poverty, and tho' he was always sober and temperate, yet he was much afflicted in the *gout* and other *painful diseases*."[81]

The excesses of Samson and the Israelites are not Milton's own, Newton seems to be saying, with both being merely counters through whom the poet can vent his own, and his party's frustrations, even in "bold expostulation," both "with Providence for the ill success of the *good old cause*" and with its leaders who managed to overthrow monarchy "without being able to raise their projected republic." They fell lower than they did rise because of "trespass" and "omission" by which Milton means, according to Newton, that the "Independent Republicans," quarreling among themselves, made no viable constitution, no "new modelling" of either the law or the national religion. By the end of *Samson Agonistes*, however, Milton's otherwise controlled critique gives way to "that inveterate spleen," focused on "Dagon and his priests" (1463), which Milton always unleashed against "public and establish'd religion."[82] If there was a politics to Milton's poetry, a poetry to his politics, both were emptied into *Samson Agonistes*, a poem that conspicuously harboring such content more easily than *Paradise Lost* could be marginalized and trivialized by it. Very simply, *Samson Agonistes* was an autobiographical poem tethered to Milton's own times, a poem written in analogy with classical tragedy but unworthy of comparison with it—the poem by Milton that ignorance has admired and bigotry applauded, a poem that the world could well afford to let die.

The abutment of *Paradise Lost* and *Samson Agonistes*, encouraged by Marvell's poem but also by the last books of *Paradise Lost*—in their allusion to deliverance "By Judges first, then under Kings" (XII.320)—makes a telling point: the tragedy enfolded in the one poem is exfoliated by the other with the paradise lost by Adam being but a metaphor for John Milton and his Englishmen who are unparadised by the failure of the Puritan Revolution, the Samson story mirroring that failure. Yet Samson's tragedy defeats, Milton's liberates—or should. The problem is that we are still in the vise of the tragedy from which Milton won release, at least for himself. "[W]e . . . no longer know what is tragic and what is not," writes Stanley Cavell, "so it is not surprising that tragedies are not written."[83] To which we might add: nor surprising that when they are written we do not understand them and in our misunderstandings, or refusals to understand, let tragedy repeat itself until it collapses into farce. Isn't it odd that our first critical inquiries about tragedy, the great tragedies, seem always to involve source study, which leads to other literary texts usually, to other artificial formations, and away from human life, actual *lived* history, political and religious history, which are the blood and guts, the body and bones, of tragedy? As Jonathan Dollimore reminds us, tragedy is "resolutely political" in the Renaissance,[84] powerfully so in Milton's usage, where it is at once re-creation of and resistance to tyranny. Not in literary tradition but in the history of Milton's own times, we find the earthly foundations for a new Jerusalem of the spirit that is, after all, the desire and soul of all great tragedy and the very heart of Milton's last poems.

Milton's idealisms were tempered, not defeated, by the failure of the Puritan Revolution. Milton was no poet sloughing off politics and surrendering faith in time of trouble but rather, like Virginia Woolf in our own century, he held on to the hope that a new republic (Milton would say a new paradise) could be brought into being by a poem. Milton's last poems—his epics, along with his tragedy—are reflections on how, *and how not*, to establish that new Jerusalem in history, and they are written by a poet who could say as resoundingly as Blake:

Bring me my Bow of burning gold:
Bring me my Arrows of desire:
Bring me my Spear: O clouds unfold!
Bring me my Chariot of fire!

I will not cease from Mental Fight
Nor shall my Sword sleep in my hand:
Till we have built Jerusalem,
In Englands green & pleasant Land.

After his death, in the very twilight of his own century, Milton would be used to illustrate the proposition that poets oppose all systems of enslavement, "that there is no where a greater Spirit of Liberty to be found, than in those who are Poets."[85] In poetry no less than in prose, Milton committed himself to rescuing his people from bondage, to reviving their liberty and restoring their freedom.

Notes

The research for this essay was completed with the generous support of The PSC-CUNY Research Foundation. The epigraphs are from S. K. Heninger Jr.'s *Subtext of Form in the English Renaissance: Proportion Poetical* (University Park: Pennsylvania State University Press, 1994), 3, and Paul Monette's *Last Watch of the Night* (New York and San Diego: Harcourt Brace, 1994), 117. All quotations of Milton's poetry are from John T. Shawcross, ed., *The Complete Poetry of John Milton*, rev. ed. (New York: Doubleday, 1971).

1. Jonathan Richardson, "The Life of the Author," in *Explanatory Notes and Remarks on Milton's "Paradise Lost"* (London, 1734), cxvii–cxviii. Francis Peck comments similarly: "I need not . . . remind the reader how long PARADISE LOST itself lay neglected . . . before it could obtain its due credit in the world"; see *New Memoirs of the Life and Poetical Works of Mr. John Milton* (London, 1740), 83.
2. See Dennis's letters to Thomas Sergeant (27 August 1717) and Steele and Booth (25 May 1719), in vol. 2 of *The Critical Works of John Dennis*, ed. Edward Niles Hooker (Baltimore: Johns Hopkins University Press, 1943), 401, 169. Although he provides

rich documentation for early receptions, John T. Shawcross comments similarly in *John Milton: The Self and the World* (Lexington: University Press of Kentucky, 1993), 275, 278.

3. For this note to Dennis's observation in "Letters on Milton and Wycherley" (1721–22), see Dennis, *Critical Works*, 2:223 (for Dennis's comment) and 2:493 (for Hooker's annotation).

4. For a publication history rich in detail and laden with statistics, see R. G. Moyles, *The Text of "Paradise Lost": A Study in Editorial Procedure* (Toronto and Buffalo: University of Toronto Press, 1985), 49–51.

5. Jonathan Dollimore, "Introduction: Shakespeare, Cultural Materialism and the New Historicism," in *Political Shakespeare: New Essays in Cultural Materialism*, ed. Jonathan Dollimore and Alan Sinfield (Ithaca: Cornell University Press, 1985), 9 (my italics).

6. Hans Robert Jauss provides the theoretical underpinnings for this essay in *Toward an Aesthetic of Reception*, trans. Timothy Bahti (Minneapolis: University of Minnesota Press, 1982), 23, 24.

7. George F. Sensabaugh contends that, during the Whig Revolution, Milton achieved "a stature commensurate with that for which he had struggled in the days of the Puritan Rebellion," even that some of Milton's positions "became fixed planks in the platform of the Whig party." He implies that the 1688 edition of *Paradise Lost* may be intended to further this new political agenda. See *That Grand Whig Milton* (Stanford, Calif.: Stanford University Press, 1952), 125, but see also 127, 134–42. Moyles is dubious; see *The Text of "Paradise Lost,"* 33. But see also John Walter Good on the Whig party and its espousal of Milton, in *Studies in the Milton Tradition* (Urbana: University of Illinois Press, 1915), 145–46, as well as the fine essay in which William Kolbrener contends that, historically, *Paradise Lost* has been a field of contention for various Whig positions, old and new: one extreme position fronts another with the Grand Whig Richard Bentley attacking the radical Whig John Toland. See Kolbrener's forthcoming essay, "Those Grand Whigs, Bentley and Fish."

8. See both Richardson, "Life of the Author," xcvi; and Winstanley, *The Lives Of the most Famous English Poets; or, The Honour of Parnassus* (London, 1687), 195. Space allotments are revealing: Milton gets a short paragraph in contrast to Roger L'Estrange's two and one-half pages, which are said to be "far short of his deservings" (221).

9. See Addison's "Account of the Greatest English Poets," in *Milton: The Critical Heritage*, ed. John T. Shawcross (London: Routledge and Kegan Paul, 1970), 105.

10. Marvell's dedicatory poem is discussed below. See also Charles Goodall, "A Propitiatory Sacrifice, To the Ghost of J—— M—— by way of Pastoral," in *Poems And Translations, Written Upon several Occasions, And To several Persons* (London, 1689), 115–16.

11. Richardson, "Life of the Author," cxvii, cxix.

12. See William Riley Parker, *Milton: A Biography*, 2 vols. (Oxford: Clarendon Press, 1968), 2:1115.

13. Ellwood, *The History of the Life of Thomas Ellwood*, 2d ed. (London, 1714), 246.

14. Richardson, "Life of the Author," cxix–cxx. Later, Dryden would describe *Paradise Lost* as "one of the greatest, most noble, and most sublime POEMS, which either Age or Nation has produc'd"; see *The State of Innocence, and Fall of Man: An Opera. Written in Heroick Verse; and Dedicated to Her Royal Highness The Duchess* (London, 1677), b2.

15. Parker (quoting from Richardson's manuscript "Life" housed in The London Library), in *Milton*, 2:1116.

16. See ibid. "Fleet Sheppard . . . often told the Story" that "My Lord was in *Little-Britain*, Beating about for Books to his Taste; There was *Paradise Lost*; He was Surpriz'd with Some Passages he struck upon Dipping Here and There, and Bought it; the Bookseller Begg'd him to speak in its Favour if he Lik'd it, for that they lay on his Hands as *Wast Paper*. Jesus!"; see Richardson, "Life of the Author," cxix; and see also David Masson, *The Life of John Milton: Narrated in Connexion with the Political, Ecclesiastical, and Literary History of His Time*, 7 vols. (London: Macmillan, 1880), 6:631–32.

17. Masson gives chief credit to Dryden: "Buckhurst [Charles Sackville Dorset, Lord Buckhurst], Roscommon, and other of the Restoration wits and critics, may have helped in the first appreciation of *Paradise Lost*; but Dryden was their leader" (*The Life of John Milton*, 6:635).

18. See John Milton, *Paradise Lost. A Poem in Twelve Books* (London, 1688): "Three Poets, in three distant Ages born, / Greece, Italy, and England did adorn. / The First in loftiness of thought Surpass'd, / The Next in Majesty; in both the Last. / The force of Nature could no farther goe: / To make a Third she joynd the former two."

19. Dryden, ed., *Sylvae: or, The Second Part of Poetical Miscellanies*, 3d ed. (London, 1702), a3v.

20. M. Manuel, *The Seventeenth-Century Critics and Biographers of Milton* (Trivandrum, India: University of Kerala, 1962), 86 (see also 84).

21. Dennis, "The Stage Defended," in *Critical Works*, 2:312.

22. See Dryden, *The State of Innocence*, 40–41, 44, 45. My own observations here challenge the conclusions of Jean Gagen: "Dryden has . . . presented an Eve who is a genuine intellectual and spiritual partner to Adam and who is much more capable of 'careful questioning' and 'sober reflection' than Milton's Eve"; see "Anomalies in Eden: Adam and Eve in Dryden's *The State of Innocence*," in *Milton's Legacy in the Arts*, ed. Albert C. Labriola and Edward Sichi Jr. (University Park: Pennsylvania State University Press, 1988), 147.

23. See Samuel Slater, "A Discourse Concerning The *Creation*, *Fall*, and *Recovery* of Man," in *Poems In Two Parts* (London, 1679), 8; but see also 3, 33, 52–56, 68–69.

24. See Nathaniel Lee, "To Mr. DRYDEN, on his Poem of Paradice" (1674?), in *The State of Innocence*, A4.

25. Manuel, *Seventeenth-Century Critics and Biographers of Milton*, 44. See also Parker, *Milton's Contemporary Reputation* (Columbus: Ohio State University Press, 1940); and John Shawcross, *Milton: A Bibliography For the Years 1624–1700* (Binghamton, N.Y.: Medieval and Renaissance Texts and Studies, 1984).

26. Manuel, *Seventeenth-Century Critics and Biographers of Milton*, 12, and Parker, *Milton's Contemporary Reputation*, who comments almost identically: "[T]here seems to have been not a single printed reference to the elegy in the whole period of Milton's life" (11).

27. For the Waller correspondence on *Lycidas*, see Good, *Studies in the Milton Tradition*, 141.

28. Christopher Hill observes: "Thirteen references to Milton's 1645 *Poems* have been noted by Marvell's editors, and many more to Milton's prose"; see "Milton and Marvell," in *Approaches to Marvell: The York Tercentenary Lectures*, ed. C. A. Patrides (London, Henley, and Boston: Routledge and Kegan Paul, 1978), 22.

29. Baron, *EPOTOIIAI NION Or the Cyprian Academy*, 2 vols. (London, 1647), 2:28, 44.

30. Walsh's "Delia" appears in *Poems on Several Occasions*, in *The Works of William Walsh, Esq; In Prose and Verse* (London, 1736), 68, 71, 81–82.

31. This pseudonymous poem, signed by "Philo-Philippa," is published in *Kissing the Rod: An Anthology of Seventeenth-Century Women's Verse*, ed. Germaine Greer et al. (London: Virago, 1988), 204.

32. Parker, *Milton's Contemporary Reputation*, 47–48.

33. James Turner, "The Poetics of Engagement," in *Politics, Poetics, and Hermeneutics in Milton's Prose*, ed. David Loewenstein and James Grantham Turner (Cambridge and New York: Cambridge University Press, 1990), 259, 266–67. See also Lucy Newlyn, *"Paradise Lost" and the Romantic Reader* (Oxford: Clarendon Press, 1993), 92–93; and Nancy Armstrong and Leonard Tennenhouse, *The Imaginary Puritan: Literature, Intellectual Labor, and the Origins of Personal Life* (Berkeley and Los Angeles: University of California Press, 1992), 9-10. Armstrong and Tennenhouse resist the tendency to translate contradictions in *Paradise Lost* into contradictions within the personality of the author when, from their point of view, the contradictions are actually an aspect of Milton's culture inscribed within his poetry.

34. That Jauss's theorizing eventually impacts upon *Paradise Lost* in a way that corroborates some of my own readings is evident in *Question and Answer: Forms of Dialogic Understanding*, trans. Michael Hays (Minneapolis: University of Minnesota Press, 1989), 101–5.

35. Sensabaugh, *That Grand Whig Milton*, 124.

36. Shawcross, *John Milton*, 93.

37. Noting that "Milton . . . was not a popular man," Moyles seconds David Masson's earlier suggestion, arguing that "many people, seeing the name JOHN MILTON on the title-page, would throw down the book with an exclamation of disgust": see *The Text of "Paradise Lost,"* 14.

38. See *An Answer to a Book, Intituled, The Doctrine and Discipline of Divorce* (London, 1644), 31; *The Censure of the Rota Upon Mr Miltons Book, Entituled, The Ready and Easie Way* (London, 1660), 6; and William Prynne, *A true and perfect Narrative Of What was done* (London, 1659), 50.

39. See *An Answer to a Book*, F2v; James Howell (1655), in Parker, *Milton's Contemporary Reputation*, 92; and William Prynne, *Twelve Considerable Serious Questions touching Church Government; Sadly Propounded* (London, 1644), 7.

40. Like most of his predecessors, Shawcross reports that *Eikonoklastes* and *Pro Populo Anglicano Defensio* were "burned publicly in France, again in England by order of King Charles II in 1660, and yet once more in Oxford on July 21, 1683"; see *John Milton*, 171.

41. See Roger L'Estrange, *No Blinde Guides* (London, 1660), A2; Thomas Long, *Dr. Walker's True, Modest and Faithful Account of the Author of Eikon basilike* (London, 1693), 2–3; Joseph Jane (1660), in Parker, *Milton's Contemporary Reputation*, 105; G. S., *Britains Triumph, for her Imparallel'd Deliverance* (London, 1660), 15; and *A Third Conference Between O. Cromwell and Hugh Peters in Saint James's Park* (London, 1660), 8. Diana Treviño Benet makes the same point: "[I]n early 1660, . . . willy-nilly he [Milton] became a member of the devil's party"; see "Hell, Satan, and the New Politician," in *Literary Milton: Text, Pretext, Context*, ed. Diana Treviño Benet and Michael Lieb (Pittsburgh: Duquesne University Press, 1994), 97. See also Sharon Achinstein, *Milton and the Revolutionary Reader* (Princeton: Princeton University Press, 1994), 195, 263.

42. *Poor Robin. 1666. An Almanack After a New Fashion* (London, 1666). In *Poor Robin, 1671*, on the verso of the title page, an author's name finally appears: William

Winstanley. The phrase "mock-Saints" appears in *Poor Robin, 1668* in "An Advertisement."

43. See both *Poor Robin. 1666*, "A Discourse of the Heavens," and *Poor Robin, 1669*, "The Contents of the Almanack."

44. See *Poor Robin, 1667*, A4. In *Poor Robin, 1676*, "Blind Milton" appears in connection with 10 November (in reference to Milton's possible death date?). After 1677, Milton's name disappears from *Poor Robin*, although he should probably be comprehended in the reference to "Smectymnus [*sic*]" on 8 November in *Poor Robin, 1688*.

45. Richardson, "Life of the Author," lxxxix.

46. What is at work in these early receptions is a process given astute explanation by Lucy Newlyn, for whom Milton "is constructed by the cultural needs of his readers, being invoked or named by them, frequently in a kind of symbolic shorthand for the concepts with which he comes to be associated"; see *"Paradise Lost" and the Romantic Reader*, 24. For this reason, the key terms from various phases of Milton criticism may speak volumes even as some of the terms, remaining constant, change their valuation.

47. For Thomas Yalden's verses on Milton (1698?), see Good, *Studies in the Milton Tradition*, 59. On Milton "*evidencing* that *Devils may indue Human Shapes*," see L'Estrange, *No Blinde Guides*, A2, and also Masson, *Life of John Milton*, 5:690. On Milton's contemporary reputation as a satanic figure, see ibid., 6:636.

48. The Hobart letters are reprinted by James M. Rosenheim, "An Early Appreciation of *Paradise Lost*," *Modern Philology* 75 (February 1978): 280–82. Original spellings (however eccentric) are retained throughout. Page references are given parenthetically within the text of the essay.

49. Terry Eagleton, *Criticism and Ideology: A Study in Marxist Literary Theory* (1976; reprint, London: Verso, 1978), 56.

50. See Newlyn, *"Paradise Lost" and the Romantic Reader*, 33.

51. Masson states the case exactly: for all the confusions and uncertainties surrounding the early reported receptions, they nevertheless allow us "a glimpse of the real facts"; see *Life of John Milton*, 6:631.

52. Ellwood, "Epitaph on Milton" (1675?), in Shawcross, *Milton: The Critical Heritage*, 87.

53. Masson (quoting Phillips), in *The Life of John Milton*, 5:635–36.

54. Ellwood, "Epitaph on Milton," in Shawcross, *Milton: The Critical Heritage*, 86.

55. Robert Graves (quoting Waller), in *Wife to Mr. Milton: The Story of Marie Powell* (1944; reprint, New York: Noonday, 1962), 364–65.

56. Johnson, "Milton," in *The Oxford Authors: Samuel Johnson*, ed. Donald Greene (Oxford and New York: Oxford University Press, 1984), 711.

57. Kevin Sharpe and Steven Zwicker, "Politics of Discourse: Introduction," in *Politics of Discourse: The Literature and History of Seventeenth-Century England*, ed. Kevin Sharpe and Steven Zwicker (Berkeley and Los Angles: University of California Press, 1987), 2–3.

58. Newlyn, *"Paradise Lost" and the Romantic Reader*, 103; and see also Benet, who argues that, in a sweeping critique, without ever "endangering himself or marring the integrity of his poem, Milton deflates and in some respects indicts seventeenth century politics and politicians"; see "Hell, Satan, and the New Politician," in Benet and Lieb, *Literary Milton*, 113.

59. See the title of the poem by S. B., plus lines 1–2 and 39; and see Marvell's poem, lines 1, 2, 7, 23, 42, 44, 53.

60. Dating from 1686-87, Benthem's comments are reported by Christopher Hill, *Milton and the English Revolution* (New York: Viking, 1978), 391-92.

61. F[rancis] C[raddock], "To Mr. John Milton, On His Poem Entitled Paradise Lost" (1680), in Shawcross, *Milton: The Critical Heritage*, 89.

62. For the earl of Roscommon's lines on Book VI of *Paradise Lost*, dating from 1685, see Shawcross, *Milton: The Critical Heritage*, 92–93.

63. Newlyn (quoting Edward Young), in "*Paradise Lost" and the Romantic Reader*, 193.

64. John Spencer, *A Discourse Concerning Vulgar Prophecies* (London, 1665), 2.

65. I borrow the phrase from Francis Peck, who is quoting Bishop Atterbury, in Peck, *New Memoirs*, 62.

66. Stephen Greenblatt, *Shakespearean Negotiations: The Circulation of Social Energy in Renaissance England* (Berkeley and Los Angeles: University of California Press, 1988), 65. For a discussion of how "Marvell seals off any subversive reading of the poem [*Paradise Lost*] for public discussion," see Sharon Achinstein, "Milton's Spectre in the Restoration: Marvell, Dryden, and Literary Enthusiasm," *Huntington Library Quarterly*, forthcoming, as well as *Milton and the Revolutionary Reader*, esp. 212–13.

67. See references in note 66, and Newlyn, "*Paradise Lost" and the Romantic Reader*, 261.

68. Peter Conrad, *The History of English Literature: One Indivisble, Unending Book* (Philadelphia: University of Pennsylvania Press, 1985), 244 (see also 280).

69. See Boileau, *The Art of Poetry*, trans. William Somers, altered by J. Dryden (London, 1683), 40–41; and cf. Bloom, *Ruin the Sacred Truths: Poetry and Belief from the Bible to the Present* (Cambridge: Harvard University Press, 1989), 91–113.

70. Richardson, "Life of the Author," cxxiv. The Richardsons are not the only—and certainly not the first—critics to notice contradictions in *Paradise Lost*; see Richardson, *Explanatory Notes and Remarks*, 20; and earlier see Dennis, who likewise remarks upon inconsistencies and contradictions deriving from the poem's Christian machinery, in "Letters on Milton and Wycherley (1721–22)," in Dennis, *Critical Works*, 2:228. In *Paradise Lost*, Milton develops a poetics of contradictions or, better perhaps, uses contradiction to develop a poetics of interrogation and disclosure. See again Kolbrener's forthcoming essay, "Those Grand Whigs" and its argument that *Paradise Lost* captures the chief contradictions (philosophical, political, and theological) of early modern, and modern, culture.

71. See Pamela R. Barnett, who argues that in Haak's translations no allowance is made "for the internally contradictory"; see *Theodore Haak, F.R.S. (1605–1690): The First German Translation of "Paradise Lost"* (The Hague: Mouton, 1962), 183.

72. Richardson, *Explanatory Notes and Remarks*, 291.

73. I am quoting from Armstrong and Tennenhouse, *Imaginary Puritan*, 115; but see also Annabel Patterson, *Censorship and Interpretation: The Conditions of Writing and Reading in Early Modern Europe* (Madison: University of Wisconsin Press, 1984), and Christopher Hill, "Censorship and English Literature," in *The Collected Essays of Christopher Hill,* volume 1: *Writing and Revolution in Seventeenth-Century England* (Amherst: University of Massachusetts Press, 1985), 32–71.

74. L'Estrange, *A Common-place-Book Out of the Rehearsal Transpros'd* (London, 1673), 36.

75. Peck, *New Memoirs*, 83–84.

76. Thomas Newton, ed. *Paradise Lost. A Poem, In Twelve Books*, 9th ed., 2 vols. (London, 1790), 1:406; 2:384.

77. Ibid., 2:397.

78. Toland, "The Life of John Milton (1698)," in *The Early Lives of Milton*, ed. Helen Darbishire (London: Constable, 1932), 180.

79. See Jackie DiSalvo (quoting the *London Chronicle*), in *War of Titans: Blake's Critique of Milton and the Politics of Religion* (Pittsburgh: University of Pittsburgh Press, 1983), 29; and Newlyn, *"Paradise Lost" and the Romantic Reader*, 93. Merritt Y. Hughes resists the "attribution of any topical political intention to Milton's epic plan"; see *Ten Perspectives on Milton* (New Haven: Yale University Press, 1965), 173. But for contrary opinions, see G. Wilson Knight, *Chariot of Wrath: The Message of John Milton to Democracy at War* (London: Faber and Faber, 1942), 137; and especially Sensabaugh, *That Grand Whig Milton*, 22–23, 173, 201.

80. For Peck's various comments, see *New Memoirs*, 59–60, 85, 89, 272–74, 276–78.

81. Newton, ed. *Paradise Regain'd . . . To which is added Samson Agonistes* (London, 1785), 227–28, 229, 249, 256.

82. Ibid., 256, 257, 302, 303.

83. Cavell, *Must We Mean What We Say? A Book of Essays* (New York: Charles Scribner's Sons, 1969), 350.

84. Jonathan Dollimore, introduction to Dollimore and Sinfield, *Political Shakespeare*, 9.

85. See "The Preface," in *Poems on Affairs of State: from the Time of Oliver Cromwell, to the Abdication of K. James the Second* (London, 1697), A4v.

List of Contributors

JUDITH H. ANDERSON is Professor of English at Indiana University. She is the author of *The Growth of a Personal Voice: Piers Plowman and The Faerie Queene* (1976), *Biographical Truth: The Representation of Historical Persons in Tudor-Stuart Writing* (1984), *Words That Matter: Linguistic Perception in Renaissance English* (1996); and coeditor of *Piers Plowman* (1990) and *Spenser's Life and the Subject of Biography* (1996).

JEAN R. BRINK is Professor of English at Arizona State University. She is the author of *Michael Drayton Revisited* (1990). She is currently at work on a documentary biography of Edmund Spenser.

STUART CURRAN is the Vartan Gregorian Professor of English and Director of Italian Studies at the University of Pennsylvania. His books include: *Poetic Form and British Romanticism* (1993), an edition of *The Poems of Charlotte Smith* (1993) and *The Cambridge Companion to British Romanticism* (1993).

RICHARD S. IDE is Professor of English and Vice-Provost for Undergraduate Education at the University of Southern California. He is the author of *Possessed with Greatness: The Heroic Tragedies of Chapman and Shakespeare* (1986).

ARTHUR F. KINNEY is the Thomas W. Copeland Professor of Literary History at the University of Massachusetts, Director of the Massachusetts Center for Renaissance Studies, and Adjunct Professor of New York University. He is editor of *English Literary Renaissance;* his books include *Humanist Politics: Thought, Rhetoric, and Fiction in Sixteenth-Century England* (1986); *John Skelton, Priest as Poet* (1987); and *Continental Humanist Poetics: Studies in Erasmus, Castiglione, Marguerite of Navarre, Rabelais, and Cervantes* (1989).

RICHARD C. MCCOY is Professor of English at the Graduate School and University Center of the City University of New York. He is the author of *Sir Philip Sidney: Rebellion in Arcadia* (1979) and *The Rites of Knighthood: The Literature and Politics of Elizabethan Chivalry* (1989).

PETER E. MEDINE is Professor of English at the University of Arizona. He is the author of *Thomas Wilson* (1986) and editor of *Thomas Wilson's Art of Rhetoric* (1994). He is currently at work on a critical edition of Roger Ascham's *Toxophilus.*

ANNE LAKE PRESCOTT is Professor of English at Barnard College, Columbia University. She is the author of *French Poets and the English Renaissance: Studies in Fame and Transformation* (1978) and coeditor of *Edmund Spenser's Poetry* (1993). Her study *Rabelais and the English Renaissance* is forthcoming.

STANLEY STEWART is Professor of English at the University of California, Riverside. He is coeditor of *The Ben Jonson Journal;* his books include: *George Herbert* (1986) and, with James A. Riddell, *Jonson's Spenser: Evidence and Historical Criticism* (1995). *"Renaissance" Talk: An Ordinary Language Approach to Critical Problems* is forthcoming.

EDWARD W. TAYLER is the Lionel Trilling Professor of English and Comparative Literature at Columbia University. His books include: *Milton's Poetry: Its Development in Time* (1979) and *Donne's Idea of Woman: Structure and Meaning in the* Anniversaries (1991).

DON E. WAYNE is Professor of Literature at the University of California, San Diego. He is the author of *Penshurst: The Semiotics of Place and the Poetics of History* (1984).

SUSANNE WOODS is Professor of English at Franklin and Marshall College. She is the author of *Natural Emphasis: English Versification from Chaucer to Dryden* (1985) and editor of *The Poems of Aemelia Lanyer: Salve Rex Judaeorum* (1993).

JOSEPH WITTREICH is Executive Officer of the Ph.D. Program and Distinguished Professor of English at the Graduate School and University Center of the City University of New York. His books include *"Image of That Horror": History, Prophecy, and Apocalypse in* King Lear (1984), *Interpreting* Samson Agonistes (1986), and *Feminist Milton* (1987).

Index